Secrets of Bali

Secrets of
BALI

Fresh Light on the Morning of the World

JONATHAN COPELAND
in consultation with
NI WAYAN MURNI

Orchid Press

SECRETS OF BALI: Fresh Light on the Morning of the World
Jonathan Copeland

Text copyright © Jonathan Copeland 2010
Overall design © Orchid Press 2010

Published by:
ORCHID PRESS
PO Box 1046,
Silom Post Office,
Bangkok 10504, Thailand

www.orchidbooks.com

ISBN: 978-974-524-118-3

For Geoffrey Woolf
who told me in 1986 that I should write a book on Bali

About Secrets of Bali

"In *Secrets of Bali* Jonathan Copeland and Ibu Murni present a wonderfully fast moving account of Bali—from the outside in and from the inside out. *Secrets of Bali* places Bali into the warp and weft of the rich tapestry of historical context and ever changing contemporary life. It generously offers us a feast of rare and passionate insights from a man who has so obviously fallen in love with Bali and from a woman who, in so many ways, is Bali."

Dr Rob Goodfellow
Author, journalist, researcher, academic
and Principal Consultant of Cultural Consulting

"Fortunately for the reader, the author of *Secrets of Bali* is not in the slightest bit secretive. The outcome is an accessible and wide ranging guide to the island's culture and history. The casual reader can dip into it to answer specific questions, whereas the enthusiast can read with equal pleasure from cover to cover."

Professor Michael Hitchcock
Deputy Dean (Research and External Relations),
Faculty of Business, Arts and Humanities
University of Chichester

"Eloquent, enthusiastic, and jargon-free."

Dr Angela Hobart
Visiting Reader at Goldsmiths College, University of London
and Honorary Research Fellow at University College London

———

"From Balinese Gods to Balinese gamelan, difficult subjects are simply explained in this beautifully written and illustrated work."

Bill Dalton
Author of *Bali Handbook*, USA

———

"I feel that *Secrets of Bali* will join the ranks of the definitive and authoritative volumes of reference books for lovers of Bali everywhere."

Andrew Charles
Writer and long-term resident of Bali

———

"In Bali they say… when the durians come down the sarongs go up."

Julia Suryakusuma
Author of *Sex, Power and Nation*

———

About The Authors

Jonathan Copeland was born and went to school in Belfast, Northern Ireland before going to London to study law at University College London. He practised law in two major law firms in the City of London for 25 years. Throughout that time he travelled to Southeast Asia on a yearly basis and developed a passion for Balinese culture and a strong desire to understand it.

After retiring from the law, and with some brain cells still intact, he was able to spend more time in Bali, researching and photographing all aspects of Balinese culture. The fruits of that research appear in this book.

Ni Wayan Murni, born in Penestanan, Bali, is a very well-known personality on the Bali scene and a pioneer of Balinese tourism. During her career she has lived in Sanur and Ubud and has travelled widely. In 1974 she opened Ubud's first real restaurant, *Murni's Warung*, overlooking the Campuan River. Since then thousands of people have enjoyed her food and hospitality. She is still very active in the restaurant.

Murni was also the first person in Ubud to have a proper gallery of antiques, textiles, costumes, old beads, tribal jewelry, stone carvings, masks and other ethnic pieces. Many of her pieces are museum quality. Her fine arts credentials are impeccable. She understands and participates in Balinese culture on a daily basis and plays in a women's gamelan group at important religious ceremonies.

Murni's architectural abilities are best appreciated in *Murni's Villas*, which are twenty minutes outside Ubud and a world away from life's cares and concerns. These three luxury accommodations are known as *Villa Kunang-Kunang*, named after the fireflies that sparkle above the surrounding rice terraces at night. Murni lives in one and offers the others to guests.

Jonathan Copeland created Murni's web site *www.murnis.com* which gives further details, includes an on-line shop, and is updated daily.

Prologue

The origins of this book go back to October 1984, when I went to Bali for the first time. I knew nothing but the name of the island and the only book I had was the first edition of the Lonely Planet *Guide for Bali & Lombok*, a travel survival kit. It had been published in February 1984 and was 200 pages. The 2009 edition is 400 pages.

Apart from a few days in Kuta, I spent three weeks in Ubud, which was a charming, sleepy village. Very few people spoke intelligible English, which was frustrating as this was clearly a fascinating place. I had many questions which were not covered by the Lonely Planet Guide. I was hungry to know the secrets of Bali.

Friends in London had recommended *Murni's Warung*, a famous romantic restaurant, perched on the river gorge in Campuan. I was extremely lucky to meet the eponymous owner, Murni, on my first visit. She speaks fluent English, is very active in the community and is a mine of information.

I have spent the following twenty and more years commuting between London and Bali, asking and reading as much as possible about this mysterious and complex island, and have tried to organise it into self-contained chapters that I wished had been available in 1984. Frequent sojourns in *Murni's Villas* helped the process.

I thank all my sources, especially Murni, without whom nothing would have been done. I also thank Roger Owen, who read the book in draft on a computer screen and made numerous helpful comments and observations. Richard Mann has been an enormous help. Over the years I have had the benefit of many stimulating conversations with Michael Hitchcock. I thank Roger Pipe who encouraged me to travel to the Far East in the first place. My thanks also go to I Made Ariasa for his wonderful illustrations which demonstrate the Balinese love of detail. I am very grateful to Andrew Charles, who meticulously corrected many infelicities of language, grammar and punctuation.

It goes without saying that I am deeply indebted to Christopher Frape, who, to my great surprise, within the first twenty minutes of meeting him, agreed to publish the book.

The reader should be aware that the sources often conflict and in such cases I have favoured the most authoritative source. There is also the problem that it is difficult for anyone from one culture to represent another accurately and meaningfully. We all have cultural baggage and use words that have connotations, such as god and witch and many more. Mistakes are my own, and the only reason I can give is the answer that Dr Johnson gave when he was asked why he wrote the wrong definition for the word 'pastern' in his Dictionary: 'Ignorance, madam, pure ignorance.'

I hope to rectify any ignorance, errors and omissions in future editions and welcome all comments by e-mail. I plan in the future to devote the *Secrets of Bali* website (*www.secretsofbali.com*) as a forum for supplementary materials, reactions, discussions, questions and answers.

Jonathan Copeland
Rye, East Sussex, UK
jonathan@secretsofbali.com

Contents

Preface

Bali is the world's best-known 'tourism brand'. It is not just an island but a phenomenon. Ironically, until recent times, most Americans, Europeans, Japanese and Australians knew something about Bali, but were largely unsure where Indonesia (of which Bali is a province) actually was; but more importantly, what Indonesia actually is. Yet, increasingly, Bali is the prism through which the world sees, or rather judges, Indonesia—geopolitically one of the most important countries on Earth.

If all is well in Bali, then, in the most part, and as far as the all-pervasive global media 'industry' is concerned, all is well in Indonesia. The world-wide media coverage of the 2002 and 2005 Bali bombings is evidence of what happens when the perception of this relative tranquility is disturbed. Suddenly, Indonesian home-grown terrorism was thrust on to the world's conceptual radar screen—where it has remained. This has come into sharper focus as 'The West' (wherever that is and whatever that means) has become increasing concerned about the advent of a pan-Southeast Asian Islamist movement—one that combines the mass base of Indonesia's 200 million Muslims, with the justified fury of the mistreated Southern Thai Muslims, with the organisational capacity and global connections of the Malaysian Muslims, with the oil wealth of the Muslims of Brunei and Aceh and the guerrilla warfare experience of the South Philippines Moros... and on the very outer geographical rim of this potential ideological 'ring of fire' is the extraordinary outpost of Hindu culture and religion we know of as the Island of Bali.

The Indian Prime Minister Jawaharlal Nehru once poetically and affectionately called Bali, 'The Morning of the World'. The island is in itself a glimpse of what Indonesia may have become had the Java-based Islamic Kingdom of Mataram not defeated Hindu Majapahit over five hundred years ago—irrevocably changing the character of the then 'East Indies', and in turn, modern Indonesia. For this reason Bali is sometimes referred to as 'a living museum of Hindu-Buddhist Java'. However, for many, the fascination with Bali is not about the past at all, but about right now—today.

Bali can teach us many lessons. One lesson is about the values and virtues of an ancient culture that has stood the test of time—and withstood the trial of fire that is the worst aspect of globalisation—cultural homogenisation. Above all, Bali represents the hope that human diversity can survive the 21st century. For reasons not completely understood by anthropologists, Balinese culture remains vibrant, complex and colourful—both in spite of mass tourism and because of it. Bali has not withered into a pale brochure-like parody of itself because of the spoiling onslaught of the shallow mores that accompany mass tourism, but rather has thrived and prospered by continually reinventing itself—in parallel with, and not in isolation from, other influences.

Human cultures are never static; they are always changing. They may be in decline like the tribal cultures of Africa, the Indian sub-continent, China, Russia and Australia, or they may be in the ascendancy, like American consumer 'Coca Cola culture', but they never stand still. And so Bali is changing, but in ways that often surprise and delight.

In *Secrets of Bali* Jonathan Copeland and Ibu Murni present a wonderfully fast moving account of Bali—from the outside in and from the inside out. *Secrets of Bali* places Bali into the warp and weft of the rich tapestry of historical context and ever changing contemporary life. It explains, clarifies and reveals. It generously offers us a feast of rare and passionate insights from a man who has so obviously fallen in love with Bali and from a woman who, in so many ways, is Bali.

Dr Rob Goodfellow
Wollongong, Australia

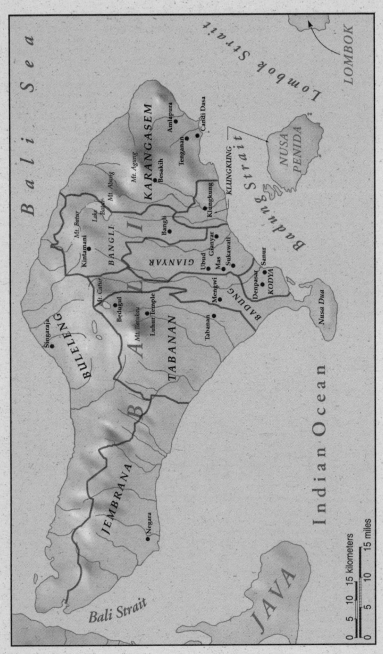

Map of Bali

Chapter 1

Bali: Vital Statistics

Bali, the Island

Bali is a small island with a big reputation. It is perhaps the most famous tropical island in the world. More or less in the middle of the Republic of Indonesia, it is the smallest province, becoming such on 11 August 1958. It is split into eight *kabupaten*, a territorial division based on the old pre-colonial kingdoms.

Bali is turtle-shaped (the Balinese think of it as a chicken and a couple of eggs) and measures about 90 miles (150 kilometres) east to west and about 50 miles (80 kilometres) north to south, and a little over 2,100 square miles (5,000 square kilometres) or 0.29% of the total area of Indonesia. You can drive around it in a day. Bali lies about 8° or 9° south of the Equator and between 114.6° and 115.5° longitude east.

The famous Wallace Line, which divides the lush flora and fauna of sub-tropical Asia from the arid landscape of Australia, runs along the very deep, narrow strait that separates Bali from Lombok, which is its neighbouring island to the east, 15 miles (24 kilometres) away. The large island of Java, about the size of California, 600 miles (966 kilometres) long and 100 miles (161 kilometres) wide, lies to the west.

Wild Life

The environment is humid and encourages rich tropical vegetation. There are gnarled and twisted trees, bamboo thickets, creepers and ferns. Numerous wild plants provide food and herbal medicines. Rivers provide a habitat for freshwater crabs and prawns, fish and eels. Ravines are home to many forest-dwelling land animals such as porcupines, pangolins, lizards, cockatoos, civet cats, bats, green snakes and pythons. There are about 300 species of birds which live in or visit Bali and there is one endemic species known as the Rothschild's Myna or the Bali Starling. Sacred monkey forests are popular with locals and tourists alike.

Until the 1920s or 1930s deer and wild pigs roamed the forests and wild monkeys were common until the 1950s. Today these animals are found primarily in the dry, western part of Bali and the once numerous small Balinese tiger is probably now extinct.

Bali is pretty much self-sufficient. Apart from rice, there is maize, sweet potato and red peppers. Tobacco is grown in north Bali. Cassava or taller trees such as sugar palms, banana trees, coconut trees are common and clove trees have been growing since the mid-1970s. There are vanilla vines.

Sacred monkey forests are popular with locals and tourists alike. The Monkey Forest, Padangtegal, just south of Ubud has been there for hundreds of years. The temple in the forest is at least 400 years old.

The Balinese

There are approximately 3 million people. The census of June 2000 indicated a population growth of 1.22% between 1990 and 2000, a success for its birth control programme, and a population density of 555 people per square kilometre, which is high. For rural Balinese, life expectancy is 64.6 years and for urban dwellers 61.1. The average white Australian male can expect to live to 77 according to research published in the *Medical Journal of Australia* in December 2002.

Raffles in his *History of Java* (1817) said,

> The natives of Bali, although of the same original stock with the Javans, exhibit several striking differences, not only in their manners and the degree of civilisation they have attained, but in their features and bodily appearance. They are above the middle size of the Asiatics, and exceed both in stature and muscular power, either the Javan or the Malayu.

What's in a Name?

Bali's name reflects its Indian heritage: it is Sanskrit, much older than the name Indonesia. It means 'offering' in Sanskrit. In High Balinese, Bali is called *Banten*, which also means offering, usually to the gods.

Bali may be named after the monkey called Bali or Subali in the Ramayana epic. Subali did a wicked thing: he stole Tara, the wife of his half-brother, Sugriwa. On discovering this, Sugriwa challenged Subali to a fight, which was seen by Rama, who killed Subali with an arrow in order to get Sugriwa's help. Subali was therefore an offering given by Rama to Sugriwa.

Village Life

The Balinese live in villages. In pre-colonial times, before the Dutch took control at the beginning of the 20th century, there was just one kind of village, called the *desa* which is now called the *desa adat*. *Desa* is a Sanskrit word. *Adat* is a Malay word of Arabic origin and means 'custom' or 'tradition'. It was not based on territory, but on a feudal system whereby the ruler could call on villagers' labour. Although the right to insist on labour has gone, *adat* villages still exist and there are about 1,500 of them.

The *adat* village organisations deal primarily with ritual and religious affairs, which are extensive in a society where religion permeates every daily activity. Religion is of critical importance, because the Balinese believe that the prosperity and safety of the world depend on harmony between people and the gods. The *adat* village is centred on three communal temples.

During the colonial period the Dutch reorganised village administration along territorial lines in order to control the inhabitants easily and created villages called *desa dinas*. They are responsible for civic matters and security. There are therefore two concurrent village organisations.

Republic of Indonesia

Bali is part of Indonesia, formerly the Dutch East Indies, and the fourth most populous country in the world with about 230 million people. In terms of population, it is only overtaken by the People's Republic of China, India and the United States.

It is the biggest Muslim nation in the world: about 90% of all Indonesians are Muslims, but not the Balinese, who follow Balinese Hinduism, a unique religion. A British naturalist, George W. Earl, coined the word 'Indonesia' in 1850 from the Greek words *indos* meaning 'Indian' and *nesoi* meaning 'islands'. It was first used by his colleague James R. Logan, but was not used by the locals as a political term until April 1917. Nationalists liked the word as it implied a single people and used it consistently in the 1920s. It caught on despite being banned by the Dutch.

There are more than 17,000 islands, but only about 6,000 or so are inhabited, and more than 250 ethnic groups. These diverse peoples, speaking about 550 languages, or approximately a tenth of all languages in the world, are united by a common language, very similar to Malay, called 'Bahasa Indonesia'. Malay is an Austronesian language, probably originating in East Kalimantan, which has been spoken throughout the archipelago for centuries by traders. It was a trading *lingua franca* also spoken in the Philippines, Japan, Sri Lanka and Madagascar. Unlike the British in India, the Dutch discouraged Indonesians, except civil servants and servants, from learning their language, and refused to allow them to speak Dutch. They communicated to them in

Malay. At Independence, after 350 years of Dutch rule, less than 2% of Indonesians spoke Dutch.

The greatest Dutch legacy was the idea of Indonesia as a national entity. It was by no means a foregone conclusion in such a diverse region. An important milestone was the Youth Congress of 1928 which proclaimed 'One Nation, One People, One Language'. The language was the local version of Malay, now called Indonesian. This famous 'Youth Pledge' is still repeated on its anniversary every year.

Unity in Diversity

The Indonesian motto 'Unity in Diversity' underlies most aspects of Balinese life. In the religious sphere, the diverse gods and spirits are a manifestation of the Supreme god, Sanghyang Widi Wasa. There are many examples of the desire to achieve unity. The high priest aims to achieve unity with God through his mantras. In village affairs individual interests are subordinated to the group through organisations like the *banjar* and *subak*.

The Balinese love uniforms, which identify individuals with the group, whether at school or the temple or the gamelan orchestra. For example, there is no star performer in the gamelan. The ensemble plays as a whole. Indeed it is a criticism if they lack unity or do not play in time with the dancers.

Chapter 2

The Big Bang

Creation, the Hindu View

The Hindu view is that the world began with Divine Oneness, but, refreshingly, there is no certainty about the matter. About 3,500 to 1,000 years ago, the poets of the *Rig-Veda*, the oldest religious text on the planet, wrote of their doubts in the *Hymn of Creation*:

> But, after all, who knows, and who can say
> Whence it all came, and how creation happened?
> The gods themselves are later than creation,
> So who knows truly whence it has arisen?
>
> Whence all creation had its origin,
> He, whether he fashioned it or whether he did not,
> He, who surveys it from highest heaven,
> He knows—or maybe even he does not know.

From the Divine Oneness, the supreme god, Sanghyang Widi Wasa, created the other gods, who in turn created the waters, earth, sky, sun, moon, stars, clouds, planets and wind. Then, at the direction of the Supreme god, Siwa created the world in the following order: mountains, rice, trees, people, rain, fire, fish, birds and animals. The order of creation, to some extent, indicates Balinese priorities.

Unlike the Big Bang and many other religious views, the Hindu view of creation is not bringing into being something from nothing, but rather a fragmentation of the original Oneness and unity of nature into countless forms. Hindus believe in a cycle of birth and death and rebirth and the purpose of life is to escape the cycle and merge into the original Oneness.

Saraswati, the Later Hindu View

A later Hindu view is that Saraswati, the goddess of poetry and wisdom, brought humans into existence by writing. Christianity, which post-dates Hinduism by perhaps 3,000 years, also saw creation through the medium of the Word. 'In the beginning was the Word, and the Word was with God, and the Word was God' (*John 1.1*). Christ is seen in terms of the Word: 'The Word became flesh and dwelt among us, and we beheld His glory…' (*John 1.14*).

How Old is Mother Earth?

After creating the waters, the gods created the Earth, both of which are fundamental to human existence, but how old is the Earth? It is about 4,500 million years old. We know this because the age of the Earth can be measured by radiometric clocks, which measure radioactive elements in rocks.

Year Zero

There are other plausible views, of course, like the Western scientific view, which is that in the beginning, there was nothing. So far, so good. It gets more difficult.

Edwin Hubble (1889-1953), an American lawyer, boxer and astronomer, made the discovery in 1929 that the universe is expanding. Just before that, in 1927, a Belgian astronomer and cosmologist, Georges Lemaître, realised that if galaxies are moving farther and farther outwards in time, it must follow that if you go back and back in time, you reach the point where everything collapses into a hot, small, dense sphere, which he called the 'primaeval atom'.

He thought that the universe began when this atom spontaneously exploded and matter and radiation were hurled forth into the, well, yes, the universe. Time and space also began at this point. A microsecond earlier, there had been absolutely nothing, not even a microsecond.

Sir Fred Hoyle, an astronomer from Yorkshire working at Cambridge University, was the theory's leading opponent and mockingly called it the 'Big Bang' in a radio broadcast in 1952 and the term stuck. If you know the speed of any galaxy, you can work out the age of the universe. It is 15 billion years, give or take a few years.

It is indeed curious that something can be created out of nothing, but obviously it can, because before the universe was created, there was nothing, and now we have a universe. It has been explained by quantum physics: in the quantum world particles pop into and out of existence and in the 1970s physicist Edward Tryon of New York City University suggested that the tiny atom from which the universe grew could have come into existence in that way.

The latest theory put forward in 2006 from Sir Roger Penrose is that before the Big Bang there could have been a series of Big Bangs.

How Old is Bali?

Bali was built by volcanic action. The subterranean shakings of tectonic plates heaved the continental rock under the sea above sea level perhaps only a couple of million years ago and Bali was born.

How Old are Humans?

Simple life, such as bacteria, appeared 3,500 million years ago and complex forms evolved during the last 600 million years. Many, many millions of years later, about 195,000 years ago, our species, *Homo sapiens*, appeared. We were the last to arrive at the Life on Earth party and we were party animals.

To get an idea of how recently we showed up imagine the history of the Earth as having taken place in a single year. If the Earth was formed on 1 January, apes appeared on 30 December, the first modern humans appeared in the last 20 minutes of New Year's Eve, and Christ was born at 15 seconds to midnight.

Chapter 3

Balinese African Origins: The First Wave

Out of Africa into Bali

Humans originated in Africa. We know this because the first two to three million years of fossilised humans are entirely in Africa, and the first appearance of fossilised humans outside Africa is much later. There is a debate as to whether early humans evolved in Africa and then moved to the rest of the world, the 'Out of Africa' theory, or whether they evolved separately in Africa, Europe and Asia, the Multiregional theory. There are many theories in between these two models.

The Lay of the Land

Continents drift slowly over millions of years. Sea levels depend on the amount of frozen water in the north and south poles. During ice ages, there is more water locked up in ice, and therefore more land over which animals and humans can travel.

Over 250 million years ago, there was only one giant landmass called Pangea. It split into two parts, separated by a mid-world ocean. Laurasia lay to the north and Gondwana to the south. Over time, India moved to the north, collided with Asia, and created the Himalayas, while Arabia and the Fertile Crescent moved east towards Asia.

There have been many ice ages. In an ice age, many of the islands of Southeast Asia become part of the Eurasian mainland and Australia forms a single landmass with New Guinea and Tasmania. This phenomenon made migration possible without a boat. About 14.5 million years ago, Africa ceased to be isolated from Europe for the last time and fossilised apes appeared in Europe for the first time. There was a land connection between Africa and the Middle East, and when sea levels were low, migration was possible.

Apes and Us

It is not possible to pinpoint when humans first evolved. Human characteristics appeared gradually in apes over millions of years. About 4 million years ago a new species of ape, called *Australopithecus* (Southern ape) *anamensis*, was walking upright in Kenya; we believe that this species was ancestral to our own genus, which is called *Homo*. Brain size more or less tripled over the last 3 million years, the greatest growth being between 1 and 2 million years ago. A large brain and a complex nervous system were initially required to enable bipedalism. Having been formed it was useful for other things, including eventually, about 50,000 years ago, language.

When creatures become sufficiently like humans, they are classified as *Homo*. The earliest is called *Homo habilis*, meaning 'handy man', because he seems to have been the first toolmaker, with a brain size of 500 cc. Chimpanzees have a brain size of between 300 and 500 cc and modern humans about 1200 cc.

Java Man

Java Man was *Homo erectus*, meaning 'erect man'. It is generally accepted that Homo erectus was indeed human, and many believe the first human. Java lies just across the shallow strait to the west of Bali, less than 2 miles (3 kilometres) away, and if the sea is low, is actually joined to Bali. There is no evidence that Java Man reached Bali, but equally no evidence that he did not.

Charles Darwin had postulated that Africa was Man's birthplace in *On the Origin of Species* (1859). Eugène Dubois, a young Dutch doctor, went to Java in 1889 to find proof that Asia was Man's ancestral homeland, and not Africa. Some scientists still think that this is or could be the case. Like the Scottish geologist Charles Lyell and British naturalist Alfred Russel Wallace, he believed that the home of the orangutan and gibbon was more likely to be the cradle of mankind than that of the African apes, the chimpanzee and the gorilla.

Within two years he discovered the skull cap of a very human-looking primitive. He found a strong thighbone the following year, which indicated that the creature could walk upright, hence he called the creature *Homo erectus*. He had discovered Java Man.

Dubois published his findings in 1894. The claim that human ancestors went back a million years threatened current scientific and religious teachings. The outcry became so intense that Dubois buried his discoveries under his house, where they remained for the next thirty years.

Later, in 1929, *Homo erectus* was also found at the village of Zhoukoudian on the outskirts of Beijing, and in that part of the world he is called 'Beijing Man'. The discovery was made in a limestone quarry. His (or her) braincase was larger than earlier creatures and about 75% of our brain size. The teeth were large, but already human. They were hunter-gatherers. Agriculture had not yet been invented; it started in various parts of the world shortly after the end of the last ice age around 10,000 years ago.

A number of other *Homo erectus* remains have been found in Java. The earliest are about 1.5 million years old and the youngest are about 100,000 years old. Over this time brain size increased slightly.

Dwarf Human

In 2003 a new human species, 3.2 feet (1 metre) tall with a grapefruit-sized brain (380 cc and overlapping with the size of a chimpanzee's brain), an unknown branch on the family tree, was discovered in the Liang Bua caves on the island of Flores, 350 miles (563 kilometres) east of Bali. The Manggarai people live in this part of Flores and the Manggarai name Liang Bua means 'Cool Cave'. The archaeological team found thirteen individuals and fossils of animals including a snake, frog, monkey, deer and pig. It is thought that *Homo erectus* made the journey to Flores about 840,000 years ago, part of which must have involved crossing by sea, became isolated for several hundred thousand years and evolved their small size. Having no predators they had no need to be big, requiring a large amount of food, a phenomenon known as island dwarfism. Despite their small brains they were smart and made use of fire and made stone tools, but created no art or adornments nor buried their dead, all characteristics of modern humans.

Eugène Dubois, a young Dutch doctor, discovered *Homo erectus*, Java Man, in 1891.

It is a momentous discovery because it is the only known case of dwarf humans. They have been given the name *Homo floresiensis*. The 'hobbits', as they are popularly called, existed until a mere 12,000 years ago. At that time a massive volcanic eruption probably wiped them out or possibly they were all killed by a wave of modern intruders from nearby Papua. It is a curious fact that local stories are told of a past time when small, hairy people with flat foreheads lived in Flores. That suggests that modern humans may have a folk memory of sharing the island with another human species.

The discovery is resulting in a major revision of theories of hominid evolution and dispersal in this part of the world. It could be that the first human may not be African at all but from the other side of the world. Did *Homo* evolve in Asia and move to Africa rather than the other way around? Maybe Eugène Dubois was correct that the ancestors of Man lie in the East. The explanation reported in the prestigious science journal *Nature* has, however, been questioned. An analysis, published in *Proceedings of the National Academy of Sciences* for August 2006, says the small head was probably a case of microcephalia, a developmental condition often inherited and that the bones do not represent a new species at all. It states that a far more likely explanation is that the bones belonged to a sick modern human being who suffered from microcephalia, a disease which causes small brain size, often associated with short stature. This conclusion has, needless to say, been roundly rejected by Professor Mike Morwood of the University of New England, Australia, the co-discoverer of the hobbit with Professor Raden Soejono of the Indonesian National Research Centre for Archaeology.

Peter Brown, one of the authors of the original University of New England paper, was quoted in the January 2006 edition of *Discover* magazine as saying that Robert Eckhardt, one of the authors of the *Proceedings of the National Academy of Sciences* was as 'thick as a plank' for trying to refute *Homo floresiensis*. Eckhardt, attending a scientific meeting, took off his shirt and had his wife measure his chest. He said, 'We were able to establish to the satisfaction of the audience of 300 people that I was in fact thicker than two short planks'.

Dean Falk, world-renowned paleoneurologist and chair of Florida State University's anthropology department, along with an international team of experts, compared computer-generated reconstructions of microcephalic human brains and normal human brains and concluded the hobbits' brains were properly classified with normal humans rather than microcephalic humans. The hobbit's brain is unique and nothing like a microcephalic's. It merely got rewired and reorganized and is consistent with its attribution to a new species. These findings were published in the 29 January 2007 issue of the journal, *Proceedings of the National Academy of Sciences*.

The debate goes on. In March 2008 Dr Peter Obendorf and Dr Ben Kefford, from RMIT's School of Applied Sciences, and Professor Charles Oxnard of the University of Western Australia, published their findings that the hobbits were dwarf cretins and human. Their small stature and distinctive features were the result of severe iodine deficiency in pregnancy in association with a number of other environmental factors. Iodine was absent from their diet. Its main source is in fish and seafood which would have been at least 14.9 miles (24 kilometres) away on the coast. Need I say that the claims are disputed by the team that found the hobbit?

Out of Africa 1

The origins of *Homo erectus* are uncertain, but most experts think they originated in Africa about 1.9 million years ago. Their departure from Africa has been called 'Out of Africa 1'. They probably left in search of food but maybe it was a case of the Everest syndrome, a desire to explore new lands simply because they were there. Their descendants, acclimatised to new climates, moved on bit by bit, until they reached Java and China.

Out of Africa and Multiregionalism

Homo erectus evolved into our species *Homo sapiens* ('wise man') between 400,000 and 130,000 years ago, most probably about 195,000 years ago. The debate at the two extremes is whether our species evolved only in Africa or also and separately in other parts of the world where *Homo erectus* has been found, such as Java and China. The Multiregional theory is very much a minority view, especially since the recent advent of genetic research. Most people now support the Out of Africa theory. The terminology is confusing, as even the Multiregionalists agree that *Homo erectus* was originally from Africa. We are just talking about the date that we, and the Balinese, came out of Africa and survived. It is thought that Java Man and Beijing Man became extinct, and all modern humans emerged from Africa in the second wave, the event being called 'Out of Africa 2'.

The Eve Gene

One tiny piece of our DNA ('deoxyribonucleic acid') is very stable and inherited only through the female line. It is mitochondrial DNA, popularly called the Eve gene, and mutates approximately once every 1,000 generations. By knowing all the different mutations around the world, we can reconstruct a gene family tree on the female side, right back to the shared mother of that gene. Because of the consistent rate of mutations, we can also calculate the time when mutations occurred and the age of the person we are testing.

Genetic evidence has added greatly to archaeological and fossil evidence and brought new theories and revisions to existing ones. From the late 1990s migrations of humans around the world have been traced and when they took place. We now know that there was a single common female ancestor for all non-Africans. She came out of Africa and has been called 'the African Eve'. The population of Africa, when *Homo sapiens* came into being around 195,000 years ago, may have been only between 2,000 and 10,000 people. We, and the Balinese, made it by the skin of our teeth.

Chapter 4

Balinese African Origins: The Second Wave

Out of Africa 2

The Out of Africa 2 theory postulates that about 85,000 years ago African *Homo sapiens* started to move out again. He reached Malaysia about 74,000 years ago, Australia about 65,000 years ago, Europe about 50,000 years ago and the Americas about 15,000 years ago. Genetic studies support this model.

Homo erectus persisted in Southeast Asia until about 30,000 years ago, so there could have been some overlap, but they were replaced by the new wave of *Homo sapiens*. Recent studies show that *Homo erectus* may have been living in Java 50,000 years ago at Ngandong and Sambungmacan on the banks of River Solo.

Some scientists think that interbreeding between Java Man's descendants and the new wave occurred, but there are no genetic traces of *Homo erectus* in living humans, so it is unlikely, or if it happened, they died out. Other scientists think that interbreeding occurred with local populations during the whole journey.

The Great Escape: Rare Window of Opportunity

For most of the last 2 million years, humans froze in Africa, but once every 100,000 years or so, there is a warm spell. There have been only two warm periods since we have existed as *Homo sapiens*. The last one was about 8,000 years ago and continues today, and the one before that was about 125,000 years ago, soon after humans came into being. During that time the Sahara became a grassland and allowed humans in the south to move north and at the next cold snap, when the sea levels fell, get out of Africa by crossing the Red Sea on the Eritrean coast to Yemen, a short distance of 7 miles (11 kilometres) away.

To Boldly Go Where No Man Has Gone Before

It looks like the first break out of Africa by *Homo sapiens* was about 120,000 years ago, but they died out, perhaps because they were stranded on the other side without any food during a cold spell. From the mitochondrial DNA we know that the next great escape was about 85,000 years ago and there was just one group, who all left at the same time, survived and gave rise to all non-Africans, and that includes all Balinese, living today.

Getting Cold Feet

They moved fast. Once over the Red Sea, it seems that they walked along the Indian Ocean coast from Aden to Bali and arrived within 10,000 years. Because the sea levels were low, they could have walked on dry land all the way. At its coldest, 65,000 years ago, the world's sea levels were 340 feet (104 metres) below today's levels. They probably ate seafood on the beaches as they went. After Bali, they island-hopped and reached Australia, probably crossing from Timor, the nearest island, about 65,000 years ago (long before Europe was colonised).

The Ice Age

According to the explanation so far, *Homo sapiens* arrived in Bali about 75,000 years ago. Ice ages, caused by a tilt in the Earth's axis and its closeness to the sun, are the norm with warm periods in between. Luckily, we are currently living in a warm interglacial stage. The last Ice Age started about 25,000 years ago. When it was at its height, about 18,000 years ago, the northern hemisphere was covered in ice and lost much of its habitable land.

On the other hand, as sea levels lowered, Southeast Asia saw a dramatic increase in its landholdings. It was much warmer in the south and became an attractive place to escape the winter. Australia and New Guinea joined to form the continent of Suhul. India and Sri Lanka also merged. The South China Sea, the Gulf of Bangkok and the Java Sea dried up and China, Malaysia, Borneo, Java and Bali became one landmass called Sundaland.

It began to thaw about 15,000 years ago and ended about 8,000 years ago. Many of those on coastal plains would have drowned or seen their livelihoods destroyed as the tides rushed back in and separated the islands. Flood myths permeate many mythologies and the end of the Ice Age may have given rise to these stories.

Slow Boat from China, 3000 BC

The south-to-north story that we have given so far is based on Stephen Oppenheimer's theories, which take into account oceanography and the latest genetic research. The earlier conventional theory of Balinese origins, propounded by Australian archaeologist Peter Bellwood, is based on relatively slim archaeological and fossil records, supplemented in part by linguistic analysis, and suggests the reverse route, namely north to south.

Peter Bellwood's archaeological reconstruction is that the first Mongoloid settlers were south Chinese, who sailed south from Taiwan to the Philippines and then to Indonesia arriving between 4,000 and 5,000 years ago, cultivating rice as they went. This theory assumes that China domesticated rice about 8,000 years ago, although that is now in doubt too. These people replaced the descendants of *Homo erectus*, and from Indonesia went as far west as Madagascar off the east coast of Africa and from the Philippines as far east as Hawaii and Easter Island in the Pacific.

The Neolithic rice farmers, who sailed from Taiwan, invented the double-outrigger sailing canoe, which was a huge advance as two logs, sitting parallel to the dugout canoe, prevent it from capsizing. Reconstruction of their language does show that they had a word for outrigger canoe, which proves that they existed. Monsoon winds would have helped them on their journey, and it is noteworthy that Balinese fishermen use similar outriggers today.

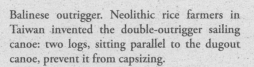

Balinese outrigger. Neolithic rice farmers in Taiwan invented the double-outrigger sailing canoe: two logs, sitting parallel to the dugout canoe, prevent it from capsizing.

Chapter 5

Appearances Can Be Deceptive

Why Do the Balinese Look, well, Balinese?

The Balinese have light brown skin, black hair and dark eyes and are Southern Mongoloid in physical appearance, which is not very African. Mongoloid types are divided into the Northern Mongoloid, and the Southern Mongoloid, which includes the southern Chinese. Variations in appearance are superficial and probably date back only 50,000 years, perhaps less, maybe only 10,000–20,000 years. The process of change, the most likely cause of which is adaption to environmental conditions, is still going on.

Skin Colour

Dark, highly pigmented, skin affords protection against harmful ultraviolet sun, which causes skin damage and cancer. It also radiates excess heat efficiently and protects the skin against destruction of folic acid, which is an essential vitamin. Evolution and natural selection would favour these advantages in tropical and subtropical lands.

Sunlight provides calcium and vitamin D. In North Asia and Europe, where there is less sun, dark skin would be a disadvantage. In those places, lack of sunlight causes a fatal bone disease called rickets. The main victims are children, who need calcium and vitamin D for bone growth and without it grow up with deformed skeletons. Dark skin filters sunlight. In colder climes evolution favours lighter skin to allow the limited sunshine through. African-Americans in North America absorb a third of the sunlight of white skin and suffered badly from rickets until the early 20th century when diet, including calcium and vitamin D, improved.

Those are the two extremes. Evolution grades skin colour according to latitude and the amount of ultraviolet light. The optimum for the Balinese appears to be light brown skin. The first Balinese would have been dark.

The Eyes Have It

Southern Mongoloid eyes have an extra so-called epicanthic fold protecting the upper eyelid. It is even more marked in the Northern Mongoloid and may have evolved to reduce heat loss. They also have more insulating fat around the eye on the cheeks, jaw and chin and a flatter face.

Voltaire's Dr Pangloss observed that 'the nose is formed for spectacles' and Richard Dawkins has added that nostrils are beautifully directed to keep out the rain. Balinese noses are smaller than Western ones, which may have increased in size to facilitate warming of inhaled cold air, an unnecessary attribute for the Balinese variety.

The African tooth shape has also changed. In terms of height the Balinese are shorter than Westerners. That may be due to their diet of eating rice without much animal protein.

Sexual Selection

It may even be that sex is the reason or part of the reason. Charles Darwin described the principles of sexual selection, which are just as important as his earlier theory of natural selection, in *The Descent of Man, and Selection in Relation to Sex* (1871). The theory states that females have to be choosier than males as they have a much more limited opportunity to produce offspring. Males therefore develop those appearances that appeal to picky females.

Balinese women may just prefer men with lighter skin or eyes with a fold and these appearances have been inherited by the population at large. It is easy to assert this proposition but much more difficult to justify it and explain why. This is especially the case when you consider other groups of people which have not chosen, say, lighter skins or eyes with a fold. Why the difference?

If it is correct, however, the result is that sexual selection, operating in tandem with natural selection, repeated over a number of generations, changes appearances.

The Truth of the Matter

There is a theory that skin colour may even be camouflage. The truth of the matter is that we do not know the reasons for all the physical differences or even when or where they first occurred. The earliest undisputed Mongoloid remains anywhere in the world are only 10,000 years old. We have not yet discovered genes governing body moulding.

The reason may even be genetic drift or founder effect or a combination of both. Genetic drift is just a random change, which is accentuated in a small population. Founder effect happens when a small group of isolated founders starts a colony and a characteristic is repeated many thousands of times until eventually everyone looks the same.

The Balinese have light brown skin, black hair and dark eyes and are Southern Mongoloid in physical appearance.

Chapter 6

Bali's Early Days

Sources

History begins with writing. Before that it is pre-history. Historical data in Bali is scant, scattered and battered. There have been some archaeological excavations. The main sources for the period from the 9th century to the end of the 14th century AD are old bronze inscriptions, mainly issued by rulers and kept in temples. In later centuries, manuscripts have survived—called *babad* texts—which tell the stories of the noble families, no doubt heavily biased.

The Dutch made the first serious attempt to record history. This was often biased in an attempt to justify Dutch occupation. The motivation was sometimes the need to understand the economy so that it could be taxed. Nevertheless there were excellent scholars, for example, V. E. Korn, a senior official in the colonial government, who published a 732 page ethnography of Bali in 1932.

Historical Periods

In Bali it is convenient to break the historical periods down as follows:
- Old Balinese kings
- The Majapahits
- The Spice Race
- The Dutch
- Japanese Occupation and National Revolution
- Independence

Archaeological Excavations, 350 BC-350 AD

It is not known when Bali was first inhabited, but there is evidence of habitation about 1,800 years ago at two sites in Bali, one in Gilimanuk on the northwest coast and the other in Sembiran in the north, a few kilometres east of Singaraja.

Gilimanuk

Gilimanuk was then a small island off the coast of Bali and close to Java. A ferry now shuttles the fifteen minute, 2 mile (3.2 kilometres) strait between Gilimanuk and Banjuwangi in Java. The ancient site indicates a population of fishermen, hunters and farmers. Glass and shell beads were discovered, which show that they may have been traders using beads as currency. The archaeologists also found evidence of chickens, horses, pigs, dogs, mice, rats and bats.

The graves contain gold, copper, bronze and iron objects, which, if they did not know how to make them, must have been imported. They indicate that the people had a religion and a sense of an afterlife. Some were buried with jewellery, weapons, fishhooks, ceramics and earthenware pots, and it is thought that those buried with metal objects were of high status.

In 1964 a grave was discovered of a man and his dog. The corpses face the Prapat Agung mountain to the north, where presumably their gods or spirits resided. There were also graves for pets. Museum Situs Purbakala in Gilimanuk contains displays of digs in the area.

Sembiran

The excavation at Sembiran, carried out by Balinese archaeologist I Wayan Ardika in the 1990s, revealed a 2,000 year old stone stamp, which would have been used in connection with the casting mould for a bronze drum, like the famous drum at Pejeng. Up to this point it was not known if these bronze drums could have been made in Bali or were imported. They are similar in style to the Dong Son drums, which required great skill to cast. The materials would have had to have been imported from afar, as there have never been any copper or tin mines in Bali, the raw materials for making bronze, but the stamp suggests that they were actually made in Bali.

Sembiran is thought to have been a trading station visited by Indian ships. Pottery from India was discovered. The pottery is of the type found at Arikamedu, a Roman trading station at Pondicherry in south India, which possibly indicates early trading with India, but it is not conclusive. There could have been middlemen.

If there was trading it is likely that it included silks and spices. Spices certainly appeared in Rome from somewhere. Roman writers of the 1st century AD mention cinnamon, sandalwood, nutmeg, cloves, and other tropical spices.

Pacung

Similar Indian pottery sherds have been found in the village of Pacung, which is about 656 feet (200 metres) east of Sembiran. The type of pottery is called Rouletted Ware and was made between 250 BC and 200 AD. The director of excavations at Arikamedu considers the Balinese finds indicative of contact between India and Southeast Asia in the 1st century BC, but it could be later. It was reported in the magazine *Antiquity* in an article entitled 'An Indian trader in ancient Bali?', published in 2004, that a tooth was found in 1999, which is believed through radiocarbon dating to be the same age as the pottery. Stable carbon isotopic analysis of the tooth suggests that the owner dined on terrestrial food rather than marine food, indicating a foreign (or possibly inland Balinese) rather than coastal owner of the tooth. Mitochondrial DNA analysis points to it as likely belonging to a person of northeast Indian origin.

What a difference a tooth makes! The important point about the tooth is that, if the dating and analysis are correct, it provides the earliest evidence for individual contact between ancient Bali and India. It predates earlier estimates and suggests that there was indeed direct contact between Bali and India. A follow-up article in *Antiquity* of March 2006 reports that there is a 88.6% probability that the dates are between 210 and 30 BC and a 6.8% probability that the dates are between 350 and 300 BC.

The Metal Age: The Pejeng Moon

The Pejeng Moon is the largest Dong Son style bronze drum ever found. It is housed in the temple Pura Panataran Sasih, Pejeng, not far from Ubud. Nobody knows how old it is, but on the evidence of the north Bali archaeological excavations, the Pejeng Moon could be 1,800 years old. Richly decorated gong-like drums were probably imported by Indian traders before the Balinese could make them themselves.

The drums are part of a rich tradition stretching from south China to eastern Indonesia. The Early Metal Age in south China probably started during the 7th or 8th century BC and came from Central Asia. It marks the beginning of a new era in the history of mankind. From south China it spread to the northern provinces of mainland Southeast Asia. The most famous centre was in northeast Vietnam, around the Dong Son area in the Red River Delta region, where there was a flourishing metalworking culture from about 500 BC to 300 BC. That seems to have come to an end in the 1st century AD but continued in Indonesia for longer.

The Dong Son smiths made their drums in one piece but the technique was very difficult. The drums manufactured in Bali and east Java differ in two respects: they were cast in two pieces and they have a protruding tympanum. The Pejeng Moon is the first of this kind to have been found.

The Pejeng Moon may be a ritual object, a massive kettledrum or just the ultimate status symbol for a ruler who has everything. The blind naturalist G.E. Rumphius, who was a German working for the Dutch East India Company, first mentioned the existence of the drum to the Western world in 1708 in *Ambonesche Curiositeiten Kamar* ('A Room of Ambonese Curiosities'), a collection of discoveries throughout Indonesia. Being blind, he had not seen it and was relying on hearsay reports from Dutch sea captains.

The Dutch artist W.O.J. Nieuwenkamp, on his second trip to Bali in 1906, wrote up the first accurate data on the drum. Before then there were no details, measurements, drawings or photographs. He made wonderful, haunting drawings of the faces on the sides, the large round eyes, tattoos and earrings. Nieuwenkamp also recorded the legends surrounding it. The Balinese believe that it is heavily charged with power. The intense pairs of staring faces, between the handles, are among the earliest representations of the human face in Indonesia.

There are many stories about its origin and all have to do with the moon. One story is that it is the chariot that takes the goddess of the Moon across the night sky. Another is that it was her earplug, which fell into a tree. A nocturnal thief, attracted by its brilliance, decided to dim the light by

The Pejeng Moon is the largest Dong Son style bronze drum ever found. It is housed in the temple Pura Panataran Sasih, Pejeng, not far from Ubud.

urinating on it. He died instantly and the Moon Drum lost its glow.

In the mid-1980s villagers dug up another Pejeng style drum in the village of Pacung.

Indians, 250 BC

Trade with India possibly began as early as 250 BC. Indian pottery of that period has been found in Bali. The Indians were apparently not interested in conquest or migration, just trade, and probably the numbers were small. Their vernacular vocabularies are not found in Indonesian languages, which suggests that they did not settle. It seems that Indian visitors came from different parts of India, the earliest contacts coming from the eastern part and later the south.

Silk, spices and gold were on their shopping list. India needed to go abroad for gold as their own deposits had been exhausted. There was gold in the centre of Borneo and northwest and central Sumatra.

They introduced their religions, Hinduism and Buddhism, to Indonesia. The kingdom of Srivijaya, around modern Palembang in Sumatra, became a major centre of Mahayana Buddhism, whose political influence was felt all the way up the Malayan peninsula as far as Thailand. Monks and priests travelled from Srivijaya to Bali. It was so cosmopolitan that it was said that even the parrots spoke four languages in Palembang.

In Java the great Sailendra dynasty built the largest Buddhist temple in the world some time between 780 and 830 AD—a great stepped, pyramid-shaped mandala, Borobudur, constructed of half a million blocks of stone on the outskirts of Yogyakarta in central Java. It proclaimed the Javanese rulers' privileged access to heaven and right to rule in a series of terraces leading up to the top of the symbolic mountain at the centre of the world. Reliefs depict stories from Buddhist scriptures.

There may have been other means by which Indonesia became acquainted with Indian culture. There could have been pilgrimages to India, visits by Indian scholars and monks to Indonesia, perusal of literary works, and appreciation of Indian art in Indonesia or India itself.

Chinese, 5th century AD

India was trading with Southeast Asia for centuries before China. Very few Chinese products dating to before the 4th century AD have been found. Except for Vietnam, Southeast Asian societies seemed to prefer to integrate parts of Indian culture and by the time the Chinese made contact it was probably too late for Chinese culture to make much headway.

Maritime trade between India and China developed between the 3rd and 5th centuries AD. The Chinese were trading with Indonesia by at least 400 AD. Ships sailed back and forth between India, Indonesia and China. The Chinese scholar Yi-Jing reported in 670 AD that he had visited a Buddhist country. It may have been Bali.

Chinese records mention 'Poli' and many think it is a transliteration of Bali, but it is difficult to be sure because it is a phonetic translation into Chinese characters and could be wrong. Anyway, whatever the entity called Poli was, it sent five embassies to China between 473 AD and 630 AD.

Chapter 7

Old Balinese Kings

Rsi Markandeya, 8th Century AD
The Markandeya legend accounts for the beginning of Hinduism in Bali. He was the son of a *brahmana* Hindu saint from India and—according to the legend—the first person to set foot on Bali. He and 8,000 followers left Mount Raung in east Java at the end of the 8th century to settle in Bali. At that time the land masses of the two islands were joined together.

The gods were unhappy, because Markandeya did not perform the correct rituals and they made him and his followers sick. They returned to Mount Raung. Some years later he returned with fewer people, 4,000 followers, from the village of Aga on Mount Raung. This time he performed the necessary rituals and buried the five

Rsi Markandeya was the son of a *brahmana* Hindu saint from India and the first person to set foot on Bali.

elements, gold, silver, iron, copper and bronze, and a precious stone, at a place called Basuki ('Besakih') on the slopes of Mount Agung. This makes Besakih the very first place where a Hindu ritual was performed.

The gods were happy and the newcomers settled in the areas around Campuan, Taro, Tegallalang and Payangan and the present temple area of Besakih. In these places Markandeya and the settlers from Mount Raung are still commemorated.

Markandeya resided at Taro, where the temple called Pura Gunung Raung is orientated west towards Java, as opposed to the more normal orientation towards Mount Agung. The Gunung Lebah temple in Campuan was also allegedly founded by him. He is credited with establishing the basic institutions of society, including the *subak* (the irrigation societies), the *desa* (the village), and the *banjar* (the civic organisations). A number of his followers remained behind in various villages. Hence the current name of Bali Aga for people who live in villages that pre-date the later Hindu invasions.

Kingship

The first Balinese kingdoms appear in the first millennium AD. We know this from the existence of seven bronze inscriptions from 882 -914 AD. They are in Old Balinese. In less than a hundred years Old Balinese was replaced by the language of the Javanese court, which is called Old Javanese. The edicts were the legal foundation for what the kings did and dealt with matters such as taxation.

On the question of taxation it is surprising that the early kings did not have a treasury or a centralised system of collecting taxes. Instead they gave people, such as ministers, artists and barbers, the right to collect taxes from the villages. This system is called tax farming; it was how the kings paid their bills. Taxes were collected in gold or silver coins, labour or food.

Early Balinese kings did not claim to be gods and did not build large palaces, but they encouraged the villages to build royal temples and reduced the villagers' taxes in return for help in building them. Balinese kings intervened directly in village affairs without an official administrative layer. The royal edicts came to an end in the 14th century at the time of the conquest of Bali by the Majapahit empire.

Kesari Warmadewa, 913 AD

The earliest ruler, whose name is known, is Kesari Warmadewa. Three of his inscriptions have been found. The first was found in Sanur and is dated 914 AD from which it appears that there was a kingdom in Pejeng. He ruled from around 913 AD and left a dynasty which continued to rule for several centuries. He is probably the same man as Sri Wira Dalem Kesari, who is said to have built the first great buildings at Besakih.

Feudalism

Bronze edicts from 915-942 AD show the kings using Indianised names. It was a feudal system, but not based on landholdings as in the Western model of feudalism. The king and nobles offered protection and mediated in village disputes. In return the villagers provided services, maintained temples, and carried out rituals and ceremonies. They paid taxes and on request provided the king and nobles with armed guards. There was no professional army. Communications between king and commoners went through a village council.

There are references to weavers, iron and goldsmiths, irrigation tunnel builders, carpenters, masons, shipbuilders, musicians, singers and dancers. Specialisations suggest a healthy surplus-producing economy, based on wet and dry rice cultivation. Vegetables, cotton and kapok were grown and horses, cattle, goats and pigs were bred.

Villagers' services were not necessarily all provided to one noble family. A villager may have worked the land for one noble house, provided armed protection to another and paid taxes to a third. Taxes were paid on land irrigated from a single watercourse. Split allegiances helped reduce the political power of any one faction.

Udayana, 989-1011 AD

The Balinese prince Udayana married an east Javanese princess, Gunapriya Dharmapatni, also known as Mahendradatta, who brought Javanisation to the Balinese court. Her name, coming before that of her husband in documents, suggests that she had higher status than him and may have been more powerful.

Old Javanese became the court language and after 989 AD royal decrees were written in Old Javanese. It is thought that she introduced Tantric rites and sorcery to Bali. Some historians say that she is the notorious widow Rangda in the Calonarang story. Belief in witches and witchcraft is still strong. Goa Gajah, the Elephant Cave, near Bedulu, not far from Ubud, was built around this time, as a rock hermitage for Saiwite priests.

The Queen probably died first. Their last joint edict was issued in 1001 AD. Udayana ceased to rule in 1011 AD and died sometime between then and 1022 AD. Their three sons were Airlangga, Marakata and Anak Wungsu. Airlangga is said to have been born in Bali.

Goa Gajah, the Elephant Cave, near Bedulu, not far from Ubud, was built around the 10th century as a rock hermitage for Saiwaite priests.

Airlangga, 1037-1042 AD

East Java fell into a state of anarchy and a group of nobles requested Airlangga to accept the crown. He ruled it from 1037 to 1042 AD, while his younger brother ruled Bali, perhaps in his name. Airlangga developed a deep interest in a mystical, inner religious life, renounced the throne and became a hermit. Tradition has it that he had the body of a king and the head of a Hindu mystic. He died in 1049 AD.

The nine massive, stupa-shaped royal tombs, hewn out of solid rock on either side of the river Pakerisan at Gunung Kawi, near Tampaksiring, Bali's 'Valley of the Queens', were completed around 1080 AD and are evidence of a royal funeral cult and strong Javanisation. There was probably one tomb for the king—thought to be for Anak Wungsu, who became the king of Bali—four for his principal wives, and the rest for his consorts. Several hermits' niches, 23 feet (7 metres) high, and monasteries were added. A tenth tomb farther away has also been found. They are reached by walking down 300 steps.

Contemporaries of Airlangga were two influential *brahmana* priests, Empu Kuturan and Empu Baradah. Empu Kuturan is credited with introducing *adat* and the village temple system. He also brought magico-medical manuscripts from east Java. Airlangga and Empu Kuturan entrusted the *Pasek* and the *Bandesa* clans with leadership. These clans remain powerful.

Massive stupa-shaped royal tombs, hewn out of solid rock on either side of the river Pakerisan at Gunung Kawi, near Tampaksiring, Bali's 'Valley of the Queens', were completed around 1080 AD.

Java Conquers Bali, 1284 AD

Bali was conquered for the first time in 1284 AD and became subject to foreign rule under the powerful east Javanese king Kertanegara, whose capital was in Singosari. He was brilliant and erudite but brutal and a drunkard. The king of Bali, Adidewalankana, was imprisoned and brought to Java, where he died. Religion was brought back to and centred in the court.

There were strong Tantric elements, black magic and sorcery. These ideas are still evident in today's trances, occult practices and beliefs in witches and evil spirits, which are especially dominant in the south and southwestern parts of Bali, where the court had the most influence.

Bali is Independent Again

Kertanegara was murdered in 1292 AD, probably during a Tantric ritual. Raden Vijaya, a Javanese prince, married all his daughters and founded a new dynasty called Majapahit, which means 'bitter gourd' from the name of the trees that grew in the fields where he lived. He built a small city as his capital and named it Trowulan. Bali was left alone and independent for another fifty years.

Bali was conquered for the first time in 1284 AD and became subject to foreign rule under the powerful east Javanese king Kertanegara, whose capital was in Singosari.

Chapter 8

The Majapahits

Majapahits Invade Bali, 1343 AD

For the Balinese, history begins in 1343, when, according to legend, the great Majapahit kingdom of east Java, at the height of its powers, sent Gajah Mada, the successful commander, to defeat the king of Bali.

What Gajah Mada, whose name means 'Mad Elephant', may not have realised before he set off was that the king was a supernatural monster with a pig's head, who lived in Bedulu near Pejeng. While this may not be historically quite true, it does seem that Bedulu was sacked and the Balinese king captured or killed by Gajah Mada's forces.

Following the conquest Gajah Mada, assisted by a number of Majapahit nobles, controlled most of Bali. There were some people in the mountainous areas who did not capitulate and were never fully integrated into Balinese society, and have still not been. After Gajah Mada returned to Java, the situation deteriorated and he asked Ida Dalem Ketut Kresna Kapakisan to go there and bring the Balinese into line.

Kapakisan, 1350 AD

Kapakisan, as ruler of Bali, under Majapahit suzerainty, established his court and palace at Samprangan, just east of Gianyar, around 1350. He founded a dynasty that would last until the 20th century. Born a *brahmana*, he changed his status to a *satria*, in order to rule. It is noteworthy that caste can be altered in this way. His royal descendants had the title *satria dalem*.

Kapakisan subdued most of Bali and ordered the construction of buildings at Besakih. The two leading Balinese clans, the *Pasek* and the *Bandesa*, who had helped Airlangga and Empu Kuturan, also collaborated with Kapakisan, and were given special tasks in respect of the temple system and the village.

When Dalem Ketut Kresna Kapakisan died, his eldest son, Dalem Samprangan, became the king, but he was weak and vain and was replaced by his younger brother, Dalem Ketut Ngulesir.

Court Moves to Gelgel, 1383 AD

In 1383 the court and capital were moved to Gelgel, near Klungkung on the southeast coast, where Dalem Ketut Ngulesir ruled until 1460, the first of the Gelgel rulers. He founded the Gelgel dynasty. Gelgel became an artistic centre and remained the capital until the end of the 17th century. Dalem Ketut Ngulesir died in 1460 and was succeeded by his son, Dalem Baturenggong.

The accuracy of the historical accounts is difficult to ascertain, as primary sources are rare, but the present day Balinese, especially the gentry, certainly see themselves as the descendants of the great Majapahits, with the exception of a few pockets of aboriginal Bali Aga people.

Indonesian nationalists claim that the Majapahit empire stretched over what is now modern Indonesia as well as the Malay peninsula, but the actual area was probably only Java and some nearby coastal regions, with a nominal tribute being paid by other coastal states.

Kapakisan, as ruler of Bali, under Majapahit suzerainty, established his court and palace at Samprangan, just east of Gianyar, around 1350. He founded a dynasty that would last until the 20th century.

Majapahit Exodus to Bali: Bali's Golden Age

Over in Java, in the late 15th century, disputes sparked off civil wars and the Majapahit empire declined. Islam entered through Sumatra in the 13th century and made headway along the coasts of Java at the beginning of the 16th century. They pressed inland and dealt the empire a fatal blow in 1527 when the last king of

Majapahit was defeated and died. The aristocracy, priests, jurists, artists, artisans and those unwilling to be Islamised moved to the easternmost parts of Java and Bali. The descendants of the former vassal Balinese kings stayed in power and eased the process.

Newcomers who were engaged in the same crafts lived together in certain villages. Their descendants still do today. Goldsmiths and silver-smiths lived in Celuk, painters in Kamasan, ironsmiths in Klungkung and Kusamba, coppersmiths in Budaga and gongsmiths in Tihingan.

Dalem Baturenggong succeeded in integrating the aristocracy and the people. The empire extended beyond Bali to include parts of east Java, Lombok and Sumbawa and there was peace and prosperity.

Nirartha, the Priest

Baturenggong's priestly teacher and poet, Nirartha, set about reforming government, religion and caste and travelled throughout Bali, Lombok and Sumbawa and established many temples. He concentrated on rituals, was responsible for the supremacy of the Siwa cult of the *brahmana* priests, and encouraged villagers to engage actively in the court arts. He also cured many people and purified areas which suffered from epidemics.

God-king worship changed. Although the king was still believed to be the incarnation of Wisnu, people no longer actually worshipped him as they had done. Nevertheless he was associated with the divine. The emphasis in religion was on complex classification systems and numerological and colour symbolism.

Arts Flourish

Baturenggong visited many parts of the island, kept close contact with ordinary people and mounted theatrical performances. Painting, literature, music and drama were promoted as propaganda for royal policy. During his reign, cremation, which was a privilege of the nobility, began to be practised by all strata of society. The *Pasek* and *Bandesa* clan members were entrusted with temple properties and leadership tasks.

The Boondocks: Bali Aga

The Bali Aga people were living in Bali before the Majapahits arrived from Java. They were subject to Buddhist and later Hindu influence. The Majapahits were not able to assert their authority on all parts of the island, because of limited resources. It was more profitable to concentrate on the rich, low-lying areas. The Bali Aga villages were, and are, in the mountains on the northern and eastern coasts, such as Trunyan, near Mount Batur, and Tenganan, near Candi Dasa, and the island of Penida in the south.

They comprise about 2% of the population and still display marked differences from the rest of Bali; for example, there is no caste system, they do not speak High Balinese, and do not cremate their dead. Their architecture dates from Austronesian times. They build longhouses similar to those found in other parts of Indonesia.

Decay sets in

With Baturenggong's death around 1558, the Golden Age went into rapid decline. There were tremendous rivalries, scheming and decay. This state of affairs continued for about a hundred years until eventually a new king, Dewa Agung Gusti Sideman, came to power.

Court moves to Klungkung, 1686 AD

As Gelgel seemed to have lost its power and to be polluted spiritually, the capital was moved to neighbouring Klungkung. At this time the Dutch were becoming solidly established in the rest of the East Indies.

Dewa Agung Gusti Sideman became the first king of Klungkung in 1686 and was known as Dewa Agung, a title inherited by all kings of Klungkung since that time. For the next 200 years the Dewa Agung was the nominal, supreme king of Bali.

A number of tiny autonomous states grew up, ruled by powerful aristocrats, who claimed to be descendants of the nobles who accompanied Kapakisan from Java. They ruled as kings or princes.

In the end Bali had nine small kingdoms: Karangasem, Badung, Mengwi, Gianyar, Tabanan, Buleleng, Bangli, Negara and Klungkung. They all regarded Klungkung as the highest royal authority. There was great rivalry among them, which manifested itself in a flourishing of the arts. The kingdoms still exist as distinct administrations.

Chapter 9

The Spice Race

Eastward Ho! Empire Building

Spices drove European explorers to Indonesia in the 16th century and launched the Age of Exploration and European capitalism. Competition for control of the spice trade led to the Far Eastern Portuguese, Spanish, Dutch and British Empires. It is a strange fact that horticulture in tiny islands on the other side of the world determined the rise and fall of European empires.

The Spices

Initially the Europeans craved three spices: nutmeg, cloves and pepper. Later cinnamon and mace were added. Spices had been used and treasured from ancient times—the Chinese and Romans used them. The reason: fragrance. Yes, but also because they cured both bad food and sickness.

When the Queen of Sheeba called on Solomon, she brought a gift of 'camels that bear spices'. She was the first Spice Girl. Cloves in an ordinary kitchen dating back to 1700 BC have been found in a Mesopotamian site in Syria. The Han Chinese in the 3rd century AD used nutmeg as a cure for bad breath and Roman priests used it as incense. For centuries it masked and disguised the smell of decomposing food in an age when there were no fridges. Nutmeg slowed down the rotting process. Spices increased the flavour of food and drink. It was added to beer. Nutmeg was also a perfume, an embalming ingredient, a relief for sore teeth and an aphrodisiac.

The Romans liked pepper in cooking and it was used as a preservative. It was imported to England in the 10th century. The Guild of Pepperers was one of the first city guilds to be established.

The price of nutmeg rocketed overnight in the 15th century when Elizabethan physicians claimed it cured the plague, which was sweeping

London's streets. This provided the economic impetus that made it worthwhile sailing into the unknown and risking lives, limbs and fortunes.

Cut Out the Middlemen

The problem was that nobody knew where the spices came from. Marco Polo (1254-1324), the Venetian, claimed he saw a nutmeg tree in China when he returned from his travels between 1271 and 1295 but that cannot have been true. He awakened Europe's interest in the East.

For centuries Arabs, Malays and Chinese had monopolised the spice trade. The supply to Europe started in the Moluccas, the fabled Spice Islands to the northeast of Bali, thence to the Persian Gulf, overland by camel to Alexandria on the Mediterranean coast, then to Constantinople, now Istanbul in present day Turkey, and finally by Venetian ships to Venice. Spices contributed greatly to the richness of Venice. Would we have had Titian's masterpieces without the spice trade? I doubt it. A conservative estimate is that spices rose in value 100% every time they changed hands, and they changed hands hundreds of times.

The Portuguese were first in line and wanted to go straight to the source and cut out the middlemen. Europeans in the Middle Ages believed that the Garden of Eden was a real place and that it was in Asia. This idea also inspired the explorers. Prince Henry the Navigator sponsored the first trip in the early 15th century.

The Perils

It was totally perilous. Ships had never sailed to the Indian Ocean and maps were non-existent. The Spice Islands could have been in Outer Space for all they knew. Unknown to Marco Polo and the new spice merchants, the nutmeg tree only grew in the Banda Islands, which are part of the Moluccas. It took over two years' dangerous sailing through pirate infested seas to get there and back, and if the pirates did not kill them, scurvy, typhoid or dysentery usually did. It took 200 years from Marco Polo's time before a European reached the Spice Islands.

Spices drove European explorers to Indonesia in the 16th century and launched the Age of Exploration and European capitalism.

The Spice Race

Portugal, Spain, England and later Holland were in the race to get to the source of spices. They were also in search of gems and silks. It is not surprising: the profit was immense. In the Banda Islands, 10 pounds (4.54 kilograms) of nutmeg cost less than one penny. In London it sold for more than £2.10s—a profit of 60,000%. It was like winning the lottery.

Portugal, 16th Century

In 1500 Portugal was the only serious maritime power in Europe. Vasco da Gama opened up the East by sailing around Africa in 1498, arriving at Calicut on the west coast of India, where calico comes from. He left Lisbon with three ships and a crew of 170 and returned two years later with only half the crew. The cargo paid for the expedition sixty times over. He noted, with excitement, that you could buy pepper for three ducats a hundredweight in India and sell it for eighty in Venice. His next trip to the Spice Islands gained his investors a return of 4,700%. After da Gama a large number of Portuguese sailed east and dominated the trade. Camels gave way to sailing ships in short order.

In 1511 Afonso de Albuquerque conquered Malacca on the west coast of Malaysia and became the first European to set foot on the Banda Islands. He brought back a full load of spices. Ferdinand Magellan was on board—his later expedition was the first to circumnavigate the globe in search of the Spice Islands and he was named the Great Navigator. The days of the Venetian spice trade monopoly were numbered. By 1520 it had passed to Lisbon, which became known as the 'Gateway to the Orient'.

The discovery of new lands and peoples was timely for the Catholic Church, which had become corrupt and lost its balance after the Reformation. Francis Xavier, an early Jesuit missionary priest from the

Basque country, sailed from Lisbon in 1541 and succeeded in converting many souls in Asia, including the Spice Islands. He died from a violent fever in China, aged 46, and became a saint seventy years later.

The Portuguese decided to build a fort in Malacca and sent a ship filled with supplies but the ship was wrecked on the reefs in the Bukit area in the south of Bali. Only five survivors made it ashore in 1580. They were treated well by the Dewa Agung, given houses and women and never returned.

England, 16th Century

In 1577 the English explorer, Sir Francis Drake, sailed west in the Golden Hind with a group of four other ships and eventually reached clove-perfumed Ternate in the Spice Islands. He was on a reconnoitering mission for the English crown. There are reports that he may have set foot on Bali in 1579 and, if he did, he would have been the first European to do so.

Holland, 17th Century

Over the ensuing period of one hundred years English and Dutch technology outpaced the Portuguese. Their shipbuilding skills were immense. They had the raw materials too: oak for hulls and linen for sails. Cannons assumed their classic form at the beginning of the 17th century and they had those as well. They were all set.

Nine merchants sponsored the first Dutch voyage of 249 men to the Spice Islands in 1595. Cornelis de Houtman commanded the operation and they set off in four ships. He had spent two years in Lisbon stealing Portuguese maps and charts—these were valuable commodities and guarded jealously.

It was an ill-fated journey. Within a few weeks many of the sailors contracted scurvy. By the time they reached Banten in Java in June 1597 only a hundred were alive. De Houtman insulted the Sultan of Banten, which was not a good idea, and he was ordered to leave. They sailed east, were attacked by pirates off Surabaya and twelve of the crew were killed.

Chilling Out in Bali

De Houtman landed in Bali and, like so many after him, chilled out in style. He was entertained by the King of Bali, who was 'a good-natured fat man who had 200 wives, drove a chariot pulled by two white buffalos and owned fifty dwarves'. The population was then about 600,000. He met one of the survivors of the Portuguese mission, who was now a father. Two of the Dutch sailors stayed put in Gelgel, Jacob Claaszoon from Delft and Emanuel Rodenburg from Amsterdam, which intrigued the Europeans back home, who attributed the desertion to the beauty of the Balinese women. De Houtman liked Bali so much that he wanted to call the island *Jonck Hollandt*—'Young Holland'. The King gave him a few pots of black peppercorns, which de Houtman brought back to Amsterdam to the delight of the sponsoring merchants.

De Houtman's reports and engravings captivated the public. The one that caught the popular imagination the most was of widow-burning, even though it turned out to be of Indian origin! The merchants were more interested in the pepper pots. They knew they could go east and get more.

Willem Lodewijcksz, a member of the expedition, drew the first map of Bali in his ship's log. It was an excellent attempt and was copied almost immediately and used well into the 18th century. Before the end of 1601 fourteen fleets, comprising sixty-five ships, travelled to the Indies. They had broken the stranglehold of the Portuguese and within fifty years Portugal only had Macao, Flores and Timor in the east. The burghers of Amsterdam were on their way to becoming extremely wealthy.

Dutch East India Company

In 1602 the Dutch East India Company (*Vereenigde Oost-indische Compagnie*), known as the 'VOC', was founded. It was at the cutting edge of European capitalism. The VOC was a joint stock company, which enabled merchants to own a share of the company's value. Its shares were listed on the Amsterdam Stock Exchange, which was the first stock market in the world. The Dutch government gave it a monopoly on all trading matters to the east of the Cape of Good Hope, rights to enter into treaties with local princes and even maintain its own army.

The Dutch East India Company ruled most of the East Indies, controlled the spice trade for two centuries and was the world's most important trade organisation of its time. Amsterdam became the richest city in Europe. Would we have had the Dutch masters without the spice trade? I doubt it. The VOC restricted production to meet demand and kept prices high. Strangely, it was not realised until the mid 18th century that it was possible to take trees and plants and grow them in places where they were not native.

Wars with Britain imposed huge financial burdens on the VOC. The demand for spices became less and it finally went bankrupt. The Company collapsed under mismanagement and corruption and the charter was not renewed in 1799. The Dutch government took charge of the East Indies as a mere colony. Over the 200 years of its existence the VOC paid an average yearly dividend of 18%. Not a bad return.

England, 17th Century

England was a slow starter. Queen Elizabeth was hesitant, anxious not to complicate peace talks with Spain, which united with Portugal in 1580, but by 1600 she could not stand by as Holland forged ahead. The English East India Company was formed on 31 December 1600. Captain James Lancaster commanded its first fleet and founded the very first English colony anywhere in the world in March 1603 on the tiny island of Run in the Banda group of islands of the South Moluccas. Run is 2 miles (3.2 kilometres) long and half a mile wide and covered with fragrant nutmeg trees. Later in 1603 Queen Elizabeth died and James of Scotland became 'King of England, Scotland, Ireland, France, Puloway [Pulau Ai] and Puloroon [Pulau Run]'.

Their colonisation attempts led to three wars with Holland between 1652 and 1674. The Dutch came out on top. After William of Orange from Holland became King of England in 1688, effectively a merger, a deal was done whereby the spice trade and Indonesia were left to the Dutch, and England would be free to develop the newer Indian textiles trade, which, in the event, turned out to be good for England as the market for textiles was soon greater than the market for spices.

The English gained another benefit. The treaty known as the Peace of Breda in 1667 required the English to surrender Run in exchange for a Dutch settlement in North America, which was founded in 1625 by Peter Stuyvesant at the mouth of the Hudson River. It was called New Amsterdam. The new island changed its name to New York and Americans would in the future speak English rather than Dutch.

Chapter 10

Going Dutch

HQ in Batavia

The Lords Seventeen, the seventeen directors of the Dutch East India Company, sitting in a Dutch interior in Amsterdam, decided that they needed a regional headquarters to administer their possessions, which comprised the East Indies and outposts in Japan, Taiwan, India, Burma, Laos, Thailand, Cambodia, Vietnam, Mauritius, Sri Lanka and Cape Colony in South Africa.

They appointed the 30 year old, dour and cruel Calvinist, Jan Pieterszoon Coen, in 1618 to be Governor-General of the Dutch East Indies. He founded the capital, Batavia, which was the old name for Holland, named after the Batavi tribe. Batavia was called 'Queen of the Eastern Seas' in Holland. Its previous name was Jayakarta, and since Independence, Jakarta.

The Dutch felt insecure and built walls around the city. At first the Javanese were not allowed to live inside, and for the first 150 years the Dutch were prohibited from employing Javanese slaves in case they rebelled against them. Balinese and Sulawesi slaves were the most popular.

Bali's Isolation

The Dutch did not pay much attention to Bali until the middle of the 19th century. One reason was that Bali had no good, natural, protected harbours and the coral reefs around the coasts caused shipwrecks. The seas were rough. Apart from slaves, Bali lacked useful resources.

Bali was isolated commercially. The British had long regarded Bali as a possible base, but did not pursue their designs for the same reasons as the Dutch.

Balinese Slaves

Bali's chief export at that time was slaves. Captives of the petty wars between Bali's kingdoms were a good source. One of the punishments of criminals and bankrupts was slavery. Slaves were employed in the fields locally in Bali by the aristocracy, but not on a huge scale. In the 17th century between about twenty and a hundred were exported to Batavia every month. Slaves were a luxury for those living in Batavia and those that could afford them had hundreds. The slaves must have had plenty of free time in such households.

The city's population was dominated by slaves. In 1673 there were 13,278 slaves out of a total population of 32,068 (about half of which were Balinese). By 1778 there were said to be 13,000 Balinese slaves in Batavia. In 1815 there were 14,249 slaves out of a total population of 47,217.

The slaves were often kidnapped or tricked by Balinese rajas and district heads. They gained the most, but it was usually a Chinese middleman who clinched the deal. The slaves endured horrendous conditions in cramped ships before arriving at Batavia to be sold at market. Those that could not be sold were auctioned.

Slaves were used for heavy labour. Batavia was being developed as the jewel in the crown of the Dutch empire. By the early 19th century, however, slaves were used mainly for domestic labour. Often they had specialised tasks, such as making the tea, preparing chilli condiments or ironing. Some were trained musicians and entertained visitors.

The mortality rate was high and women were often victims of sexual abuse. Punishments were severe—whipping and imprisonment were common. Wealthy homes had cells to incarcerate disobedient slaves and sometimes there were revolts. Some ran away outside the city walls and formed gangs and attacked people. The most famous was a Balinese called Untung Surapati, who was in the Dutch army, but he made a bad mistake: he had an affair with a white woman. He would have been executed if he had been discovered. He fled, turned against the Dutch and founded his own fiefdom in east Java in the late 17th century, and became a national hero.

There are stories of love affairs between European women and their male slaves. Dutch men also found local women attractive. A female slave was freed if she bore her master's child. When the master died, his slaves were sold, and if he willed it, the fortunate ones were freed. By the middle of the 19th century, as cheap labour became available, the need for slaves declined and the trade was abolished in 1859. At the end of the 19th century mixed marriages were legalised.

Opium

In 1617 there were a thousand opium dens in Jakarta and 100,000 registered users. The Dutch earned a large amount of revenue from opium, especially in the 19th century. They started by taxing it, but decided that it was more profitable to create a monopoly over all aspects of the trade. By 1895 they achieved a monopoly over the whole empire and had plantations in Java and Sumatra. The profits were immense. By the end of the century nearly every Balinese adult, male and female, was an opium addict.

The British Interregnum, 1811-16

The French Napoleonic wars led to a renewed British interest in Bali. Napoleon I occupied Holland and installed his brother Louis as King of Holland in 1806. The East Indies became part of his empire and for the next ten years Britain was at war. The Dutch government went into exile in London. The British, who had kept a fleet off Batavia since 1795, invaded and took control.

Thomas Stamford Raffles (1781-1826) was appointed Lieutenant Governor of Java and the East Indies by the British in 1811 and he loved it. He wanted to keep the East Indies as part of the British Empire. Raffles began his career in 1795 as a clerk in the British East India Company, was sent to Penang in Malaya in 1805 and learnt the Malay language and customs.

He had a great respect for the local people. A believer in free trade, he thought that the old feudal structure was an impediment to progress. He reorganised the administration, launched reforms in taxation, granted security of land tenure, introduced coffee and sugar to Sumatra and established schools. Raffles halted the slave trade in Indonesia, but when the Dutch returned in 1816, following Napoleon's defeat at Waterloo in 1815, the sale of slaves resumed and the lucrative business continued until 1859, and probably thereafter illegally.

He studied and admired Bali's civilisation and visited in 1815. In *History of Java* (1817), he wrote,

> On Java we find Hinduism only amid the ruins of temples, images and inscriptions; on Bali, in the laws, ideas, and worship of the people. On Java this singular and interesting system of religion is classed among the antiquities of the island. Here it is a living source of action, and a universal rule of conduct.

Raffles therefore saw Bali as 'a kind of commentary on the ancient condition ... of Java' and he believed it represented the lost achievements of Java. The image is of Bali as a living museum. Bali, however, is dynamic and the stress should be firmly on 'a kind of'.

The British needed Dutch support in Europe against the French and in 1816 they returned the East Indies to the Dutch government. The British had enough on their hands with India. Raffles was knighted in 1817. He stayed in the East and founded Singapore in 1819.

The Theatre State

Clifford Geertz (1926-2006), the anthropologist, has written a description of the pre-colonial 19th century Balinese kingdoms, which he refers to as 'theatre states'. He argues that the royal palaces maintained neither military nor economic control over the villagers. What control they did exercise was essentially based on moral authority through which the villagers joined in elaborate and dramatic state rituals derived from sacred texts, which were handed down by the Majapahits.

Borders define modern kingdoms and states. Traditional Southeast Asian kingdoms, however, were defined by their centre, similar in concept to a mandala. Move closer to the centre, and you move closer to power and influence.

The relationship between the rulers and villagers was one of mutual dependence. As an example, take the rajas of Ubud, who according to oral accounts owned large tracts of land, kept the harvest in the palace and dispensed it to the population. It is unclear when this practice ended, but presumably it played a part in the close relationship, still evident today, between palace and people.

The royal family of Ubud is still active in building a theatre state. It is winning hearts and minds through restoring temples, organising and contributing to ceremonies, sponsoring dance and gamelan groups, researching and interpreting *adat* and renovating *Barongs*. Income from tourism, flowing from and based upon Ubud's reputation as a centre of traditional culture, is maintaining its leading position in the fields of religion and cultural conservation.

Chapter 11

The Dutch Take Bali

Trade

After Raffles left and the Dutch resumed power in Indonesia, British trade with Bali increased rapidly in the 1820s and 1830s. England, Holland and France all came to see the strategic importance of Bali's location on one of the world's most important shipping routes. The Dutch were concerned that the British would annex Bali and convinced themselves that they had to make a pre-emptive strike and take the island.

North Bali

They started in the north. It took the Dutch three invasions before they could beat the Balinese and then it was only part of the island. The first expedition, the largest military expedition that had been launched in the East Indies, was in 1846, the pretext being that a stranded Dutch ship had been plundered; the second was in 1848; but it was the third in 1849, when 12,000 men were shipped over, that the Dutch were finally successful.

This gave them control over the kingdom of Buleleng in the north, although at a heavy cost. A contemporary account described the Balinese as the most formidable military opponents that the Dutch had met in the region. That was soon followed by the fall of the kingdom of Karangasem. The Dutch entered into a peace treaty with the ruler of Klungkung, which each side interpreted as a victory for itself.

The Balinese kings remained in power, but had to recognise Dutch sovereignty and promise not to enter into agreements with other 'white men'. Dutch control was perhaps more theoretical than real, and, in any case, only extended to the west and northern half of the island. It took another fifty years for the Dutch to control the whole island. As a result of longer Dutch occupation, the northern part of Bali was influenced more by foreign influence than the south. Today, with tourists more prevalent in the south, the reverse is the case.

Dutch weapons outgunned the Balinese. With the defeat of Klungkung in 1908 the Dutch completed their conquest of Bali and incorporated the island into the Dutch East Indies.

South Bali

In 1891 there was internal fighting among the rulers of Bali, which the Dutch were able to turn to their advantage. The kingdoms of Badung and Tabanan allied together and defeated the king of Mengwi. That reduced the number of kingdoms in Bali to eight.

The king of Gianyar turned to the Dutch in 1900 as a protective measure against his Balinese rivals. The king of Bangli did the same.

They both signed treaties acknowledging Dutch sovereignty. That left three kingdoms: Badung, Tabanan and Klungkung.

Badung, 1906

The Dutch had an opportunity to confront the king of Badung in 1906. A Chinese ship, the *Sri Kumala*, sailing under a Dutch flag, coming from Borneo, was wrecked on a reef near Sanur on the south coast. A dispute arose because the Balinese plundered the beached ship. The villagers were entitled to shipwrecked goods according to Balinese custom, but this was against Dutch law.

The Chinese owner demanded compensation from the Dutch government, which in turn passed the demand to the king of Badung, who repudiated any responsibility. It has subsequently been shown that the beaching was a deliberate attempt to claim fraudulent compensation. The Dutch sent six warships, armed with cannons, five packet boats, 4,000 troops and 1,500 porters, and dropped anchor at Sanur. The ship's artillery fired for days on Badung, today's Denpasar, which is about 4 miles (6 kilometres) from Sanur, and left it in ruins.

Then 3,000 troops, with cannons, marched into the capital on 20 September 1906. They were faced by men, women and children. The entire royal court, decked out in ceremonial dress, armed only with their ceremonial lances and *krises*, streamed out of the two palaces and hurled jewels in contempt at the Dutch soldiers a hundred paces away. The king ordered his palace to be burnt down so that the Dutch would gain nothing.

Loyal retainers carried the king in a palanquin at the head of the procession. At about 330 feet (100 metres) from the amazed Dutch, the procession stopped and the king gave a pre-arranged signal to a priest, who immediately stabbed him right through the heart with a *kris*. Immediately there was a frenzy of killing. The Dutch fired on the court ladies and their bodies, covered in blood, fell in piles. Others turned their daggers on themselves or upon one another. Dutch cannons, bayonets and guns mowed down the rest.

Dutch Courage

Although the official reports said 450 died, it has been estimated that 3,600 Balinese perished in the mass murder and suicide, called *puputan*.

Puputan means the 'ending' and was the traditional sign of the end of a kingdom. It was the duty of a Balinese king to display the necessary courage to die rather than be taken prisoner. Only a few wounded women survived. Dutch casualties are unknown, but would have been very slight. The Dutch artist W.O.J. Nieuwenkamp, who witnessed it, wrote that only four Dutch died. He saved a number of royal treasures and today they are among the prize possessions of the Balinese collection at the Leiden Ethnological Museum.

War correspondents from the major Dutch papers saw the whole thing and reported. The tragedy attracted worldwide attention. It was not well received and was regarded as shameful in Holland. The responsible cabinet minister promised an inquiry but it was never held.

Tabanan, 1906

A few weeks later the Dutch marched on Nerario Ngurah Rai Perang, the king of Tabanan in the west. It was one of the most cultured courts, founded about 1350 by Batara Hario Damar, one of the great semi-mythical field generals of the 14th century East Javanese kingdom of Majapahit. The ruling king was the eighteenth generation of unbroken succession. When he went to treat with the Dutch, he was taken prisoner. The Dutch demanded unconditional surrender. That night he cut his throat with a blunt knife. The crown prince, who was with him, took an overdose of opium. The Dutch sacked and burnt the palace and a 500 year dynasty was terminated. That only left the Dutch to have to deal with Klungkung.

Klungkung, 1908

On 28 April 1908 the Dutch blasted the oldest, largest and most sacred Balinese palace to rubble. That led to another *puputan*, the ritual mass suicide of the Dewa Agung of Klungkung and thousands of his followers, including women and children, who marched out of the palace in formal Balinese attire straight into the Dutch line of fire.

With the defeat of Klungkung in 1908 the Dutch completed their conquest of Bali and incorporated the island into the Dutch East Indies.

Chapter 12

Life Under The Dutch

Direct Colonial Rule

When Klungkung fell, five of Bali's kingdoms, Buleleng, Jembrana, Badung, Tabanan and Klungkung, came under direct Dutch control. They were the ones where there had been military resistance. Rajas had died in the process. Those of their families who were alive were exiled to Lombok, Java, Madura and Sumatra and their property was confiscated.

Indirect Colonial Rule

The other three kingdoms, Bangli, Gianyar and Karangasem, who had allied themselves to the Dutch, kept their kingdoms and wealth intact, and much of their royal status, and were governed indirectly by the Dutch. As time went on, however, even they lost almost all their governing functions. Bangli and Gianyar became directly governed in 1916 and Karangasem in 1922.

Patronage

The Balinese kings lost their ability to be patrons of the arts. In many ways that was the core of their existence. It tied lords and subjects together. The commoners helped with the massive preparations for huge ceremonies and also attended them. With the loss of royal power, the village temples became more important as protectors and patrons. People turned to the local gods for the security that previously the kings and nobles afforded. Government and tourists became the new patrons of the arts, as the Dutch pursued the idea of promoting Bali as a living museum.

Old Terms, New Meanings

The Dutch appointed members of the gentry, the *triwangsa*, to administer Bali. They used old terms for the new posts. The system was very hierarchical. The new village headman was called a *prabekel* and he administered the *desa*. Above him was a *punggawa*. Then there were two regency officials: the *regen* and the *residen*. The Dutch kept a low profile, even in the directly ruled territories. There were never more than a few hundred Dutch officials in Bali, so colonialism was practically invisible to most Balinese.

Ethical Policy

Following the exposé of Dutch oppression and brutality, not just in Bali but in other places, the Dutch in Holland suffered a nationwide crisis of conscience. On 17 September 1901, a new queen, Queen Wilhelmina, 20 years old and only two years on the throne, proclaimed a new policy known as the 'Ethical Policy'. She remained queen for fifty years. The policy did not last so long.

A number of the local Balinese élite were educated in new schools in Malay and the skills of government service. Hundreds of paramedics were trained. Hospitals were set up in urban districts, but rural areas were ignored. There were agricultural reforms, designed to help the people, but it was too little, too late.

Education introduced a significant number of Indonesians to Western political philosophy, anti-colonial and revolutionary literature. Ironically this led to Indonesia's first anti-colonial movement, and in 1928 youth groups swore an oath to uphold 'One Nation, One People, One Language'.

Benefits

There were some good things. Suttee, called *satya* in Balinese, the act of self-immolation of a Hindu widow burning herself alive on her husband's funeral pyre, was banned in 1895. It was the supreme act of marital fidelity and piety. The Dutch also abolished the princely right to confiscate widows and female children and their possessions on the death of the head of a family without male heirs. The feudal right to take property had made the rulers extremely rich. New criminal courts were established. Punishments, although more frequent, were less bloodthirsty than under the Balinese kings.

Hardships

The Dutch introduced a tax collecting system and a register of land ownership. Taxation was increased. Before the Balinese aristocrats collected tax, now they paid it. After opium, land tax was the largest single source of revenue for the Dutch, then rice. They extended the compulsory unpaid labour system, *corvée*, and made it a priority to build roads all over the island within ten years. They also built bridges and public buildings.

As an example of the hardship of unpaid labour, the royal palace in Bangli required unpaid labour of one day a month. The Dutch increased this to between thirty and fifty days a year and forced not just able heads of families but also children to work. The gentry were excused, as they were in pre-colonial days, and it sharpened the differences between the *triwangsa* (gentry) and *sudra* (commoners). At the beginning of the 20th century there were revolts against *corvée* in Bali which were put down with violence. Gradually the burden was reduced to twenty-five days a year in 1931 and twenty days in 1938.

Corvée

The way the unpaid labour and military support system worked in pre-colonial times was that a village would have a certain number of noble houses, maybe fifteen or so, and possibly a royal family, who were all related to each other. Each noble house had the right to call upon a certain number of commoner families, perhaps seven or eight, scattered throughout a few neighbouring villages. The royal family usually had a few subject families in every village in the kingdom. Political power was therefore personally, rather than territorially, based.

Feudalism under the Dutch

The personal right of a lord to call upon the services of a commoner was abolished by the Dutch and replaced by a territorial relationship, more in the Western style. Services were now performed by the lord's tenants. Since Independence, that aristocratic perk has been abolished.

It is a widespread mistake to portray the relationship of villagers and gentry as separate and opposed. This view derives from colonial ideology and was used to justify Western rule, so that they could say that they were freeing the masses from tyranny. The better view is that the gentry were an integral part of Balinese society and the two groups played complementary roles. Aristocrats and commoners were bound together politically, militarily, economically and ceremonially.

Caste System

The pre-colonial 'caste' system was fairly fluid, but under the Dutch it became rigid. Dutch policy had a strong high caste bias. They disproportionately appointed members of the higher castes to high political, judicial and religious offices. More *sudra* were in these positions before colonial rule than after it.

The privileges previously enjoyed by the *Bandesa*, *Pasek* and *Pande* clans were lost. These groups did not fit in well to the new rigid caste system. They were theoretically *sudra* but set apart from the other *sudra*.

In 1910 an official decision was taken to uphold the caste concept. The new rigidity was sanctioned by the state and caused resentment, especially among the educated *sudra*. Caste became a controversial matter. The Dutch sold certificates granting the right to use the title *Gusti*.

The Dutch classified the population according to caste and introduced laws against certain inter-caste marriages. The sanction was exile, either to Lombok or within Bali. One of the first actions of the Bali regional government after Independence was to rescind the ban on inter-caste marriages in 1951.

Education

The Dutch introduced Western education to provide high caste fodder for the civil service and encouraged attendance. Admission rules favoured the higher castes: higher castes did not require sponsors, lower castes did. In the 1920s and 1930s, royal children were often sent to Java, usually to Malang.

The first school in Bali was established in 1875. Schools were racially segregated. Each racial group, Chinese, Arab, European and local, had a different type of school. The Balinese gentry initially avoided them, as they were worried that the schools would be egalitarian in the use of language and seating arrangements would not place the higher castes in a high position in the purest direction. They believed that a violation of these traditional rules could cause a high caste to fall to a lower caste.

In 1920, in Bali and Lombok, 6.7% of boys and 0.25% of girls aged five to fifteen years were attending school. 8.01% of males over fifteen years and 0.35% of females were literate.

In 1926 there were ninety-eight schools in Bali; 70% of them provided just three years' education. By 1929 the number of primary schools, which was all there was, had increased to 128, attended by 14,372 students. Girls comprised 10.45%. Seventy-three Balinese students were attending secondary schools outside Bali, mainly in Java. It was not until the Japanese occupation that education was greatly improved.

Return to Royalty

The Dutch concluded that their decision to strip away the powers of the Balinese kings had been a mistake. There were strong stirrings of nationalism and communism in the 1930s and it was decided that a return to Balinese royalty would win the favour of the Balinese and they would then look more kindly on the Dutch. It was, however, a form of royalty that never actually existed. Perhaps they thought nobody would notice the cardboard thrones.

In 1938, on the Balinese holy day of *Galungan*, eight Balinese aristocrats were consecrated as rulers, *Zelf-Besturders* which means 'self-rulers', at the Mother Temple of Besakih. Above each of them was a Dutch civil servant called a *controleur*, whose task was to guide them on how to move Bali into the modern age.

The royal families' job was to facilitate the colonial administration. At the same time they were to defend customary *adat* law and be patrons of the arts, in other words to maintain Bali as a living museum. It was the official end of direct Dutch rule in Bali, and before long, of all Dutch rule in the East Indies. In four years time the Japanese would be knocking at the door, uninvited.

Chapter 13

Cultural Tourism

The First Tourist, 1902

In 1908, the year that the last Balinese kingdom fell, the Dutch opened a tourist bureau in Batavia to promote the Dutch East Indies as a tourist destination. It extended its scope to Bali in 1914. Bali was described as the 'Gem of the Lesser Sunda Isles' in official brochures.

The first tourist to visit Bali was a Dutch Member of Parliament, Herr H. Van Kol. He was a tourist because he was there purely for pleasure, not on official business. He had just been to Sumatra and Java, arrived in Bali on 4 July 1902 and visited Klungkung and Karangasem. When he returned to Holland he wrote *Uit Onze Kolonien* ('Out of Our Colonies'), which was published in Leiden in 1903. It had 826 pages, of which 123 were devoted to Bali. He gave advice to travellers, such as:

> If one wants to meet with the lords of the island when they
> are neither sleepy nor in a daze, it is best to visit just before
> noon or in the early evening. Otherwise the chances are that
> you will find them intoxicated with opium or preoccupied
> with their fighting cocks and other such regal activities.

With the introduction of a regular weekly KPM (*Koninklijke Paketvaart Maatschappij* or 'Royal Packet Navigation Company') steamship from Java to Bali in 1924, tourism took off. The first tourists were from the colonial administration. The schedule consisted of passenger disembarkation on Friday morning, a round trip of the island by KPM car and departure on Sunday. They slept on board ship or rest houses, which were originally built to accommodate Dutch officials on their periodic inspections of the island.

In 1928 the first hotel, the Bali Hotel, was opened by the KPM in Denpasar, built on the site of the massacre in 1906. It was the first building in south Bali to have glass windows and a tiled roof. The first hotel in Sanur, the Sindhu Beach Hotel, opened in 1956 and tourists started to stay in Sanur. KPM was nationalised in late 1957, along with all other Dutch assets, and the National Tourist Agency, Natour, took over all the KPM hotels. The Bali Hotel is still there, a government owned three star hotel. So is the Sindhu Beach Hotel.

Leisurely Travel

Europeans had gone through the First World War and were keen to forget the experience. The Netherlands was neutral. Those who could afford it started to travel. They looked to Bali to escape from the post-war world. All they wanted was sunshine, simplicity, tropical food, palm trees, no obligations, no work, bronze-bodied girls and bronze-bodied boys. The pursuit of leisure was leisurely: it took about six weeks to go to Bali by ship from America.

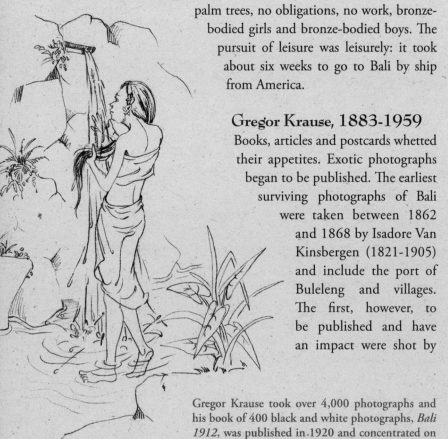

Gregor Krause, 1883-1959

Books, articles and postcards whetted their appetites. Exotic photographs began to be published. The earliest surviving photographs of Bali were taken between 1862 and 1868 by Isadore Van Kinsbergen (1821-1905) and include the port of Buleleng and villages. The first, however, to be published and have an impact were shot by

Gregor Krause took over 4,000 photographs and his book of 400 black and white photographs, *Bali 1912*, was published in 1920 and concentrated on Balinese bodies, especially female bathing bodies. His book had a huge influence in publicising Bali.

Gregor Krause, a German doctor, who was posted to Bali, lived in Bangli and worked in a Dutch hospital from 1912 to 1914. Bringing one of the world's earliest portable cameras, a 35 mm Leica, he was the first person to document the island thoroughly. On returning to Holland, he participated in a large exhibition of Balinese art in Amsterdam in 1917. He took over 4,000 photographs and his book of 400 black and white photographs, *Bali 1912*, was published in 1920 and concentrated on Balinese bodies, especially female bathing bodies. Krause enthused,

> The Balinese women are beautiful, as beautiful as one can imagine, with a physiologically simple and dignified beauty, full of Eastern nobility and natural chastity.

The book had a huge influence in publicising Bali and inspired the Mexican artist, Miguel Covarrubias, the Austrian novelist, Vicki Baum, and maybe even Walter Spies to travel to Bali. Bali became a metaphor for paradise. In the 1920s a few hundred tourists visited Bali every year.

Miguel Covarrubias, 1904-1957

Miguel and Rose Covarrubias went to Bali on their honeymoon in 1930 and were among the few thousand who were now visiting annually in the 1930s. Miguel was a Mexican artist and Rose was a dancer and choreographer on the Broadway stage. They were stressed and wanted to get away from it all. Apart from Gregor Krause's book of photographs they had read *Bali: The Last Paradise* by the journalist Hickman Powell, the first book on Bali in English, which was inspired by André Roosevelt's exploits in Bali in 1924 as a guide for Thomas Cook and American Express. He was a member of the American family of politicians. They had also seen the film *Goona Goona* ('love magic' in Balinese), which Roosevelt and Armand Denis made in 1929.

Covarrubias remarked, 'When I sailed with Rose for the remote island, no one seemed even to have heard of the place; we had to point it out on a map, a tiny dot in the swarm of islands east of Java.' On arriving in Bali they went immediately to see Walter Spies, who welcomed them and helped them enormously. They initially stayed with him in Campuan. Miguel had not studied anthropology or Asian art, but he was deeply interested in everything and his geniality endeared him to the Balinese, especially the elders and priests, who explained their rituals and daily life. He observed as an artist and participated.

Miguel made copious notes and drawings and Rose took more than 1,500 photographs. They took fifteen reels of film and shortly after they got back showed a documentary at the Brooklyn Museum in 1932. *Town & Country* magazine called them the 'most remarkable moving pictures of Bali'.

The first time they stayed six months, returning in 1931 by way of Paris, where Balinese dancers and musicians were the sensation of the Colonial Exhibition. In 1933 they returned for eleven months leaving in August 1934. Again they stayed with Walter Spies and carried out more research. On his return to New York Miguel wrote *Island of Bali* and published it in 1937. It is still one of the most authoritative books on Balinese culture, full of detailed observations of daily life. Miguel wrote,

> Undoubtedly Bali will soon enough be 'spoiled' for those fastidious travellers who abhor all that which they bring with them.

Ironically his book, which included his caricatures and some of his paintings and Rose's black and white photographs, was very influential in attracting tourists to Bali. Fortunately he was wrong: Bali was not spoiled. They also produced a film *La Isla de Bali* of footage they shot in 1930 and 1933 with an 8 mm camera. Miguel never returned to Bali and died in 1957 from septicaemia following surgery for an ulcer which did not heal. He was 53.

Walter Spies, 1895-1942
Walter Spies, Bali's most famous expat, who lived in Ubud from 1927 until his death in 1942, was a draw to the rich and famous, who visited and stayed with him.

Colonial Exhibition, Paris, 1931
Spies promoted Bali's image abroad at the Colonial Exhibition in Paris in 1931. It was a great success. The prince of Ubud was the leader of the first Balinese dance troupe ever to go to Paris and many members of the Ubud royal family went with him.

Legong, Dance of the Virgins, 1933

The French socialite Marquis Henry de la Falaise de la Coudray, a Hollywood dilettante then on his second celebrity wife, the actress Constance Bennett, being previously married to Gloria Swanson, filmed *Legong: Dance of the Virgins* entirely in Tampaksiring in Central Bali in 1933. Perhaps he had been inspired by the Colonial Exhibition. It was one of the last silent films to be released commercially and is a simple thwarted love story, well shot in beautiful two-strip Technicolor. The 55 minute film featured so many topless Balinese women, nearly all of whom were under 25 years, that more than half of it was cut by the censors and it was forgotten until Milestone discovered and released it in 2004.

Hindus and Hondas

By 1940 the number of tourists had increased to about 250 a month. The Bali Hotel in Denpasar then cost about US$7.50 a night. The Dutch were building new roads, using forced labour, to boost the economy and tourism. Until the beginning of the 20th century people walked and the rulers and important people travelled by horseback. In 1917 there were only about five cars on Bali: two or three in north Bali and two in south Bali. The king of Ubud had one and so did the king of Karangasem. The number of cars began to increase, but not much. The greatest number of vehicles in the early 1950s was in Denpasar. In January 1953 there were 1,497 motor vehicles; fifty years later Denpasar had a traffic problem. There has never been a railway in Bali.

President Sukarno's VIPs

Sukarno, Indonesia's first President, who was half Balinese, took an intense personal interest in Bali and toured the island in 1950 at least twice and spoke to large crowds. He built a palace in Tampaksiring and visited several times a year bringing many distinguished guests, including Jawaharlal Nehru, Ho Chi Minh, Tito and Khrushchev. It was on a visit in June 1950 that Nehru, the then Prime Minister of India, famously described Bali as 'the morning of the world'. He and his daughter Indira Gandhi were given a welcome lunch in Kintamani. Nehru liked Bali and also called it 'the last paradise' and 'the hope of the world'.

Hard Times

The Second World War, the struggle for Independence, political difficulties in the 1960s, the Gunung Agung volcanic eruption of 1963 and the bloody headhunt for 'communists' in 1965 and 1966 put tourism on hold. In 1964 there were 35,915 visitors. This dropped 18.23% to 29,367 in 1965. Not surprisingly, there was a further drop of 32.79% to 19,911 in 1966.

President Suharto took power in 1966 and instituted a new pro-Western régime. It coincided with a better world economy. Gradually tourism improved. In 1968, the numbers were still low at 10,997, but were set to increase.

Bali Beach Hotel, 1966

President Sukarno used Japanese war reparations to build the first five star hotel, which was opened in Sanur. It was the first building to have lifts and automatic doors. The general manager's wife took the pregnant Murni up in the lift and like most Balinese she felt queasy. In a strange coincidence the Bali Hotel in Denpasar had been built on the site of the Dutch *puputan*, the place of the ritual suicide of the Badung royal family in 1906, and the Bali Beach Hotel was built on the spot where the Dutch landed prior to that *puputan*, which was a cemetery.

Many Balinese felt uneasy about the cemetery and some employees had fits. They were convinced that they were disturbing the spirits of the dead. There was also the strange room number 327 in the hotel where furniture moved in the night and guests refused to sleep. It was believed to be the residence of the god Ann Meduwe Karang, the guardian deity of the cemetery. Finally the hotel stopped offering it to guests.

It turned out that most tourists found the place too international and modern and preferred to spend their time in thatched cottages. They imagined living accommodation in paradise ought to be under a grass roof. The hotel was also too tall and a law was passed that future buildings should not exceed 49.2 feet (15 metres) or the height of a coconut tree. Donald Friend (1915-1989), the Australian painter who lived in Sanur in the late 1960s, called it 'a big boring modern many-storeyed air-conditioned nightmare in the style of architecture often blamed on Corbusier'. Many were relieved that it burned down completely on 20 January 1993. Well, not completely—that strange room, which belonged to the god, was left intact, and many Balinese believed that the god did it.

Many thought this was the opportunity to rebuild the hotel in a more tasteful manner, but it was not to be. It was reconstructed exactly as it had been before and renamed the Grand Bali Beach. The law limiting the height of buildings is still on the statute books, but Governor Pastika suggested at the end of 2008 that it should be revised because of the shortage of land in Bali. It is unlikely, however, that Bali's Provincial Legislature will permit any variation.

Ngurah Rai International Airport, 1969

In 1938 an airport was built at Tuban, near Kuta, but it did not have much impact. Early flights were very expensive and there were only three flights a week. On 1 August 1969 the international airport was completed on the narrow isthmus of land joining Nusa Dua to the south of the island. Jets could land and flights became cheaper. The way to mass tourism was clear.

It was enlarged in the 1980s and several times since. Jumbo jet facilities greatly increased tourist numbers in the early 1990s. The airport now occupies nearly 740 acres (300 hectares) of land. The airport currently handles an estimated 150 flights and nearly 20,000 visitors a day and can cope with 6.4 million passengers a year.

Ngurah Rai International Airport, 2009

There are problems on the horizon. There is only one runway of 1.86 miles (3,000 metres) and a jumbo jet to Europe needs 2.5 miles (4,000 metres) to avoid a refuelling stop in Singapore, Bangkok or Kuala Lumpur. Extending the runway on the east may damage the mangrove forests. Reclaiming land on the west may erode Kuta beach. Building a new second runway in the south destroys a religious site and displaces villagers. Constructing a road tunnel under the eastern end of the existing runway is prohibited by religious laws forbidding road tunnels and overpasses.

At the time of writing, there is no solution in sight, although in February 2006 the Regent of Jembrana announced the intention of his local government to complete a feasibility study for a new international airport near Negara in west Bali. There are also plans for an airport in Singaraja, in north Bali. That would help areas where unemployment is high.

Five Year Development Plan, 1969-74

From 1966 foreign loans poured in, frequently from the World Bank. The hippies discovered Kuta Beach and the magic mushrooms growing nearby. Third World cultures were the fashion. The mushrooms were similar to ones growing in northern Australia. They had a blue underside containing hallucinogens, in fact rather a lot of hallucinogens, the highest concentration of psilocin and psilocybin found in any mushroom anywhere. The hippies called them 'blue meanies' and restaurants added 'blue omelettes' to their menus until the government stopped them.

Pop stars arrived on the scene. David Bowie and Mick Jagger came and went. Mick Jagger stayed in Sanur in 1969 after making a film in Australia where he played the starring role of Ned Kelly dressed as a woman. He liked Bali, visited Donald Friend and bought sarongs on the beach from Murni. Jagger became a frequent visitor where he went about unmolested by fans: nobody knew who he was. He married the American model Jerry Hall at the home of a friend in Ubud on 21 November 1990. They told the high priest that they were Hindus and went through a traditional Balinese Hindu ceremony but the marriage was held to be invalid by the English courts when Jerry Hall tried to divorce him in 1999. It was not recognised by the Balinese authorities either and led to new regulations concerning tourist weddings.

A glorious APA Guide to Bali was published in 1970 with beautiful colour photographs on every page. Growing tourism began to concern the government. There seemed to be a conflict between preserving traditional culture and meeting the tourist demands for security and comfort. With the help of the World Bank, a French consultancy firm, who did not consult the Balinese authorities or any other foreign specialists, drafted a plan to meet these concerns. The government was advised to provide a number of first class hotels in Nusa Dua in south Bali in a segregated enclave of 1,050 acres (425 hectares). The first hotel opened in 1978. A hotel management school was opened and students were taught to speak not only English but German and Japanese.

So, the high-end tourists were packaged into Nusa Dua, but Kuta and its beach and sunsets still appealed to hippies, backpackers and women looking for romance. 'Kuta cowboys' emerged from the waves and acted as guides. These new entrepreneurs saw a gap in the market and strove to satisfy the demand. They wore tight jeans, unbuttoned shirts and dark sunglasses. These Balinese boys were cool before it was cool to be cool. 'Don't worry, be happy' was their daily mantra. They played their guitars and the women looking for romance paid their bills.

Women Entrepreneurs

The role of women cannot be underestimated. They were the major entrepreneurs of tourism. Women ran the hotels. Galleries called 'art shops' started to appear in the 1950s and spread rapidly in the 1970s. According to one estimate, enterprising women owned 90% of them. In 'Ethnicity and Tourism Entrepreneurship in Java and Bali', *Current Issues in Tourism* 3:3, 2000 Michael Hitchcock explains how they did it:

> *Made's Warung* in Kuta and *Murni's Warung* in Ubud are both examples of businesses run by women that were started with a modest capital outlay. They devised menus on a trial and error basis without risking too much of their initial investment. Successful formulas are, however, often copied by competitors, forcing the entrepreneurs to carry on innovating.

The Naughty Nineties: Going Gangbusters

During Suharto's New Order régime (1967-1998) Bali's economy was transformed from agriculture to a tourist service economy. Growth rates of 8% to 10% annually in Bali were the highest in Indonesia and resulted in increased immigration from the other islands. Great increase in wealth has the power to corrupt and destroy communities, but the Balinese concentration on religion and culture, which have absorbed much of the tourist income, has helped balance the corrupting influence. In 1983 tourist numbers rose as visa restrictions were dropped for most countries and Garuda, the national airline, opened up new routes. Oil revenues slumped in 1986 and the rupiah was devalued, which made travelling even cheaper. The Governor of Bali, Ida Bagus Mantra, opened up nine additional tourist areas outside Nusa Dua and his successor Ida Bagus Oka added fifteen more in 1988.

In 1990 there were about 1 million visitors. This increased to 1.14 million in 1996. There were 150 travel agencies on the island. The Asian financial crash of 1997 affected Indonesia worse than any of the other countries and led to a collapse of the economy and the resignation of President Suharto in May 1998. Barely controlled development continued apace. The monetary crisis affected Bali less than Java. The national economy contracted by 14% in 1998, but only by 4% in Bali. In 1970 there were fewer than 500 hotel rooms, which increased to about 4,000 in 1980, 20,000 in 1990 and over 30,000 in 1997. By 1999 there were 1,234 hotels, 34,317 hotel rooms, 642 restaurants and seating capacity for 51,660. There were 40,000 hotel rooms in 2000.

Direct Foreign Arrivals
The Bali Tourism Authority figures for total direct foreign tourist arrivals at Bali's airport paint the picture:

Year	Foreign tourist arrivals
2000	1,412,849
2001	1,356,774
2002	1,285,844
2003	993,029
2004	1,458,309
2005	1,386,499
2006	1,260,317
2007	1,664,854
2008	1,968,892
2009	2,259,000

It should be noted that these figures do not include foreign indirect arrivals; that is, people arriving from other Indonesian destinations, or Indonesian tourists, both of which are sizeable, nor how long they stay. Despite uncertainty over the actual numbers of tourists, it is clear that world events have a large effect on travel. Despite it all, tourism is remarkably resilient. Bali, in the last 120 years, has enjoyed only three decades of relatively undisturbed prosperity: 1919 to 1929 and 1970 to the late 1980s.

World Trade Center, 11 September 2001
Islamic suicide terrorist attacks on the New York World Trade Center

and the Pentagon in Washington DC, the financial and political capitals of the USA, on 11 September 2001, killing thousands of people, had a dramatic effect on tourism. There was an immediate decline. Arrivals from the United States and Europe showed the greatest reduction. At the end of 2001 there was a glut of 36,000 hotel rooms and in real terms hotel prices fell 60%.

Kuta, 12 October 2002

Shortly after 11 pm on Saturday, 12 October 2002, one year, one month and one day after '9/11', bomb blasts killed 202 people in a crowded area of Kuta and shocked the Balinese and the world. Nothing like that could have been imagined in their wildest nightmares. Islamic terrorists exploded a car bomb outside the *Sari Club*, where Balinese were refused entry without a white person, and a suicide bomber walked into *Paddy's Bar* across the street and blew to smithereens himself and others. There were victims from twenty-two countries, Australians bearing the lion's share with eighty-eight dead. Indonesia suffered the second largest loss of life with thirty-five dead, mainly Balinese.

A mass prayer for peace took place on 21 October and a huge cleansing ritual, Tawur Agung Pamarisuddha Paripubhaya, was carried out on Kuta beach to release the souls of the dead and purify the area on 15 November. It was attended by thousands of people and shown live on television. The ceremony was performed by five high priests and seventy-nine animals were sacrificed. It calmed Balinese anger.

The vast majority of ordinary Balinese are dependent on tourism for a living. Fortunately, the police made rapid progress in arresting the radical Islamic perpetrators, but the collapse in tourism caused real suffering among many people for years. Travel warnings from mainly Western governments nearly destroyed the industry and were criticized for being unsubstantiated and playing into the hands of the terrorists. Hotel occupancy dropped to single digits and there were closures and lay-offs. A United Nations survey in mid-2003 revealed that average incomes across Bali dropped by 40%. In 2000 tourism provided 59.9% of Bali's GDP and after the bombs it fell to 47.42%. 30% of workers were affected by job losses.

Three of the Bali bombers, Amrozi, his brother Imam Samudra and Ali Gufron, members of the Southeast Asian militant group Jemaah

Islamiyah, all from Java, were executed on 10 November 2008. From their trials it appears that their motives were not to attack tourists *per se*, but Westerners, and particularly Americans, for their alleged abuses against Muslims. They also saw the behaviour of white people in Kuta as decadent.

SARS, February 2003

Severe Acute Respiratory Syndrome broke upon the world in February 2003 and caused great panic and further worldwide tourist declines. Media reports were sensationalist, alarmist and overblown. Indonesia recorded a 15.6% year-on-year decline in its tourism business in April 2003. SARS was the first global health epidemic since global tourism began in the 1970s and may be the first of many. Avian flu followed. H1N1 swine flu appeared in Mexico in April 2009 and quickly spread throughout the world.

Iraq War, March 2003

The long run-up to the Iraq War and the war itself also deterred travel. Hostilities began on 20 March 2003. Baghdad fell to US-led forces on 9 April 2003 and travelling increased thereafter.

Tsunami, 26 December 2004

Although the massive earthquake and tsunami did not physically affect Bali, tourist arrivals dropped off in January 2004. They fell 33.3% compared with January the previous year. This was a set-back as they had just recovered after the SARS scare and the Bali bombings showing an increase of 33.3% year-on-year in December 2004.

Kuta and Jimbaran, 1 October 2005

At 7.40 pm in the evening of 1 October 2005, just before the Islamic fasting month of Ramadan and the Balinese day of *Galungan*, when the gods and ancestors descend to their temples, three suicide bombers killed twenty people, including themselves, at *Menega's Café* and *Nyoman's Café*, both on Jimbaran Beach, and within minutes at *Raja's Café* a few miles away in Kuta. Tourism figures nosedived and took a couple of years to pick up.

Although total foreign direct arrivals for 2005 declined only 4.92%

from 2004, there was a drop of 39.71% in foreign visitors for the last quarter (October to December) of 2005 compared to the same period the previous year, so the impact of the bombings is clear.

Arrivals, 2007

Foreign tourist arrivals for 2007 were the highest in any one year since records began and an increase of 32.1% on 2006. The figures were undoubtedly helped by the fact that the United Nations Climate Change Conference was held in Nusa Dua between 3 and 14 December 2007. Japan, Australia and Taiwan accounted for the greatest number of arrivals in percentage terms. Budget airlines boosted ASEAN arrivals and visitors from Russia and the People's Republic of China, with their newfound wealth, increased.

Arrivals, 2008

The same trends continued into 2008. There were 924,949 arrivals during the first six months of 2008, an increase of 23.9% over the same period for 2007 when 745,949 foreign tourists came to Bali. July 2008 saw 183,122 foreign tourist arrivals, making it the best July ever, an increase of 11.24% over July 2007 (164,618), which itself was a record breaking performance.

Unknown to those tourists a global economic crisis loomed. The old Wall Street bank Lehman Brothers filed for Chapter 11 bankruptcy protection on 15 September 2008, the largest bankruptcy filing ever in U.S. history. It set off a worldwide wave of panic. The Dow Jones closed down just over 500 points on the day, the largest drop in a single day since the 11 September attacks. This was exceeded by an even larger drop on 29 September 2008. In such circumstances tourist numbers were bound to decline. The target of two million visitors became unachievable, but the year still turned out to be the best ever, with 1,968,892 foreign arrivals, an increase of 18.26% over 2007. Bali's top markets were Japan, Australia, South Korea, Malaysia, Taiwan and China.

Arrivals, 2009

Despite the economic crisis, the first four months of 2009 saw 645,061 foreign tourists come to Bali, an increase of 8.15% when compared to the same period the previous year (596,469). April 2009 was the best April on record and Australians beat the Japanese as the top market.

Stop!

Recognising the oversupply of rooms, the Provincial Government of Bali decided to refuse new permits for hotels, homestays and new commercial villas in all regencies and cities on the island with effect from Wednesday, April 8, 2009.

Chapter 14

Japanese Occupation, National Revolution

The Japanese Occupation, 1942-1945

Japanese troops cycled down Malaya, conquered Singapore, crossed over to Sumatra, moved east a bit and landed on the south coast of Bali on 18 February 1942 at Sanur. The few soldiers of the Dutch colonial army that were in Bali soon capitulated. Most had already fled earlier to Java. Two days before, on 16 February, the Imperial Japanese air force bombed the airport. It was not just Bali. The Japanese were landing on other islands too.

The Battle of the Java Sea at the end of February 1942 ensured Dutch capitulation. The Dutch surrendered on 9 March 1942 and Indonesia became part of Japan's Greater East Asian Co-Prosperity Sphere. Java went on to Tokyo time and the Japanese calendar and Batavia became Jakarta. In a little more than three months Japan was in military control of French Indochina, the British possessions in Malaya, Singapore and Borneo, almost all of Indonesia and Portuguese East Timor. Thailand was independent but had to agree to Japanese troops travelling through her territory. Only Burma and the Philippines remained unbeaten at that time. The Japanese claimed, and still claim, that they were only liberating Asia from colonialism.

The Japanese ruled Bali until the middle of 1945 and promised the Indonesians independence. They gained some acceptability by playing the Independence card. Economic conditions were very harsh. In October 1943 the average price of clothes increased to over 250% of pre-war levels and three months later there were no clothes on the market at all. The Japanese army seized all rice, cloth and other important products. They banned rice for offerings, a particularly painful measure for the Balinese. Malnutrition stalked the land. No new buildings were constructed.

In May 1942 the Japanese navy took over in Bali. They were less brutal than the army, but were still unpopular because of their contemptuous treatment of the Balinese and demands for forced labour. The Balinese were made to construct army facilities, fortifications and airstrips. 100,000 civilians were put into detention camps and 80,000 Allied forces were put into concentration camps, where the death rates were between 10% and 30%. Thousands of Indonesians were sent to build the Thai-Burma railway and thousands died. Indonesia had its own death railway in Sumatra between Pakan Baru and Muaro, where an estimated 25,000 died, although it was never used, being finished on the day after the last day of the war.

Japanese Reforms

They introduced two important reforms. First, they set up schools where all could attend free of charge, with the result that thousands of *sudra* children received an education, denied under the Dutch. Every morning they sang the Indonesian national anthem and the idea of a united Indonesia was reinforced. They also promoted Malay as the national language.

Secondly, they trained young soldiers, an unprecedented experience. The soldiers marched, drilled and saluted the Japanese flag. The training subsequently helped the Balinese in their fight for independence against the Dutch. Resistance to the resumption of Dutch rule was strong in Bali. British and Australian troops accepted the Japanese surrender on 14 August 1945.

National Revolution, 1945-49

Three days later, on 17 August 1945, Sukarno and Mohammad Hatta (1902-1980) proclaimed Independence at Sukarno's house in Jakarta. It was announced that Sukarno was to be President and Hatta Vice-President. The Dutch, however, did not recognise the Republic.

Under the terms of the surrender the Japanese were required to maintain peace and order in the territories they occupied. Republican bodies were to exercise civilian authority. At that time Bali was straining under grinding poverty.

By October 1945 the Republic had been recognised by China, the Soviet Union and the United States. But the Dutch needed the wealth of the East Indies and wanted their empire back. They called upon the British to help them by invoking the Potsdam Declaration of 26 July 1945. British forces invaded Surabaya, the capital of east Java, by air, land and sea in November 1945. They were brutal and the British government apologised during a seminar on the Battle of Surabaya in Jakarta in October 2000.

Dutch Troops Land, 1946

Over 2,000 Dutch troops landed on Sanur beach on 2 March 1946. They were undisciplined in the early months and burned villages and gunned down innocent people. They strafed villages with B-25 and Piper Club aircraft. Balinese Republican forces resisted until late May 1948 and continued the struggle by political means after that.

About a third of the Balinese fought on the Dutch side. The eastern kingdoms of Karangasem, Bangli, Gianyar and Klungkung, where the ruling palaces remained powerful and had been maintained by the Dutch, formed the backbone of anti-republicanism. Republican support came from the weak ruling families of Buleleng, Badung, Tabanan and for a time Jembrana. Bali was divided and the divisions remained for some time following independence.

The most significant battle in Bali was on 20 November 1946 when ninety-six nationalists, led by Lieutenant Colonel I Gusti Ngurah Rai, were surrounded and totally wiped out by the Dutch near the village of Marga in the hills of Tabanan. It is often glorified as another *puputan* and called the *Puputan Margarana*. Ngurah Rai is the only Balinese to be officially designated as a hero of the Indonesian Revolution. The airport is named after him. In November 2005 his portrait was placed on a new 50,000 rupiah bank note, the only Balinese to be honoured in this way.

By late 1949 about 2,000 Balinese had died (about 1,300 on the Republican side and 700 on the Dutch side). Nobody knows the total number of Indonesians who died during the Revolution—it could be between 45,000 and 100,000. Indonesians were also fighting Indonesians. The total number of Dutch and British killed was 700, the majority being British. More Japanese than that died. There was a great social cost too with food and clothing shortages and a chaotic monetary situation with new Republican money, Dutch and Japanese notes all in circulation.

The United Nations expressed its disapproval of the Dutch desire to re-conquer Indonesia and the United States pressured the Netherlands to grant independence. At the Round Table Conference in The Hague, which lasted from 23 August to 2 November 1949, the form and conditions for the transfer of sovereignty to the government of the Republic of Indonesia were negotiated. The United States insisted that Indonesia accept Dutch debts of US$1,723 million plus interest, a figure that many countries could not remotely handle. Instead of the Dutch compensating Indonesia for years of colonial rule, the new country had to pay Holland. The United States' purpose was to reduce the burden of rebuilding Europe after the Second World War. Indonesia paid off the debt within a few years, but the good times did not last when the price of rubber fell in 1953.

Chapter 15

Independence

Beginnings

On 27 December 1949 the Dutch recognised Indonesia as an independent state and transferred sovereignty to the Republic of the United States of Indonesia. On 17 August 1950, which was the fifth anniversary of the declaration of Independence, the country was proclaimed the Republic of Indonesia. President Sukarno became the first President of Indonesia. Mohammad Hatta, a highly efficient Minangkabau economist from Sumatra, became prime minister. The régime is known as the Old Order.

Indonesia has always claimed that the date of independence was 17 August 1945 but the Dutch insisted that the date was 27 December 1949. In August 2005 the Dutch accepted the 1945 date.

Pancasila, the Five Principles

The Indonesian constitution is founded on the *Pancasila* principles, which have the status of holy writ. They are taught in schools. Myth has it that President Sukarno dug up *Pancasila* in a field behind his house in Pegangsaan Timur in Jakarta and first made them public in a speech in mid-1945. The five principles are:

- Belief in one Almighty God
- Humanitarianism
- National unity of Indonesia
- Democracy
- Social justice for all Indonesians

The first principle was promulgated as an alternative to the creation of an Islamic state. The Five Principles are symbolised by a star, a chain, a buffalo head, a banyan tree and twin sprays of rice and cotton. The other symbols of state are the National Anthem 'Indonesia the Great' and the Red and White flag.

Sukarno, 1950-1967

Sukarno was born on 6 June 1901. His mother was a Balinese *brahmana* and his father was a Javanese teacher, who taught in north Bali in the 1880s. Sukarno had a radiant personality and was a brilliant orator. A handsome, charismatic leader, he was an engineer and art lover, who spoke Dutch, English, French, German, Japanese, Javanese, Balinese, and Sundanese. He learned Arabic in order to study the Koran.

He protested against Dutch rule and spent thirteen years in jail or in exile from Java. When the Japanese invaded, he welcomed them and became a special adviser. After the war, he resumed the fight against the Dutch. He married six times and wed his last wife, Dewi, who is Japanese, when he was 57 and she was 19.

As far as Bali was concerned, it was a period of chronic violence and volatility, tremendous poverty, spiralling inflation and hunger. In the early 1960s there were rat and mouse plagues, insect infestations and crop failures. Sukarno did, however, extend health care, which had been initiated by the Dutch. This finally resulted in the eradication of smallpox in 1972.

Business is Business

Before Independence aristocrats were not in business. They had to turn their hands to business as their fortunes declined, and they drew on their old ties and relationships. They employed large numbers of staff and treated them in a paternalistic way. Hotels run by the royal family in Ubud, for example, are still run in a half-modern, half-traditional way.

It is regarded as acceptable for the owners to receive the lion's share of the profits but businesses are expected to be dedicated to the welfare of all. The Balinese have adapted their traditional organisational methods to business, which are in sharp contrast to the small individualist, tightly run, family concerns of the Javanese or Chinese.

Mount Agung Eruption, 1963

In the year that Sukarno declared himself President for Life, Mount Agung erupted. It was on 17 March 1963, just behind Pura Besakih, the Mother Temple. The first major eruption coincided with a huge ceremony, *Eka Dasa Rudra*, which takes place only once every Balinese century. The suffering and distress caused by the enormous eruption, killing more than 2,000 people and taking 153,208 acres (62,000 hectares) out of production was felt throughout the island. The eruption lasted six months.

Famine followed, which resulted in severe malnutrition for more than 10,000 people and an exodus of 75,000 people to neighbouring principalities. The most seriously affected areas were in the east: Karangasem, Klungkung, Bangli and Gianyar. Refugees crowded into Denpasar and Singaraja. In 1963 the unemployment rate was about 30% (in 1956 it was about 14%). Inflation reached 500% and the price of rice rose 900%. People had to eat cassava instead.

The economy was so bad that by 1964 central government contributions constituted nearly 90% of Bali's total revenues. By mid-1965 prices were doubling every week. Many Balinese saw the eruption as a sign of cosmic imbalance and spiritual impurity and a portent of further disaster. It came in the guise of a communist coup.

Failed Communist Coup, 30 September 1965

Every Independence Day Sukarno gave a speech with a title. On Independence Day, 17 August 1964 Sukarno's speech was entitled 'The Year of *Vivere Pericoloso*'—the Year of Living Dangerously—a phrase taken from a speech by Mussolini. He was dead right: a nightmare worse than Mount Agung was about to be unleashed.

General Untung led an alleged communist coup, which involved the kidnapping and execution of six generals of the Army High Command and the establishment of a Revolutionary Council. The national radio station was seized and the Presidential Palace was surrounded by a small force, led by junior military officers with communist sympathies. That much is known. It was claimed by the military that it was a communist coup and a treacherous plot against the nation. The truth of this is not known.

By the early 1960s the Indonesian Communist Party was the third largest communist organisation in the world. President Sukarno adeptly balanced the opposing powers of the communists and the military. Major General Suharto, later President Suharto, head of the Strategic Reserve, mobilised the army, crushed the alleged coup within a few days and became the *de facto* commander of the armed forces. The Communist Party was banned.

The aftermath led to a massacre in Java and Bali. In less than a year between 100,000 and a million people were killed. The precise figures are not known. Some say a realistic figure is between 300,000 and 400,000 people. The worst areas were Bali, central and east Java, where supporters of the Indonesian Communist Party were massacred. Old scores were settled. Creditors, farmers and rivals were disposed of. Clan grievances were avenged.

The trauma lasted about six months. It started late in Bali, in December 1965. Most families in Bali were affected in one way or another and still are. Murni's step-father disappeared forever. It is estimated that 5% of the Balinese population (fewer than 2 million at that time) were killed, that is to say, 80,000 people, but nobody knows for sure. Over a six month period that averages about 440 assassinations a day. Whole families disappeared; whole villages vanished. Some sources say that 100,000 perished or 8% of the population. Later, when the bloodshed had stopped, the Balinese carried out purification ceremonies and cremations all over the island to purge the land of evil.

The CIA described the aftermath as one of the worst mass murders of the century. It is believed, however, that the CIA were implicated and provided death-lists of communists for the military. The US government was sympathetic to the abolition of communism. In percentage terms the figures are comparable to the loss of life in Cambodia under Pol Pot over a longer period (4 years).

Suharto and the New Order Régime, 1965-1998

Sukarno technically remained President until Suharto formally became the next President of Indonesia in 1968 and inaugurated the New Order. Sukarno was effectively under house arrest until he died a broken man in 1970. He was buried in an unmarked grave for the first eight years after his death, and nobody knows for sure if the grave actually contains his body.

President Suharto became the nation's puppet-master and ruled mainly through his close aides in the military. He embraced capital-ism. In the 1990s the economy kept growing at an annual rate of over 7%. There was low inflation and Indonesia was called the 'New Tiger of Asia' but decades of oppression, inequality and arrogance led to Suhar-to's downfall during the Asian financial crisis of 1997. The tag-line for his rule was KKN: collusion, corruption and nepotism. Ironically *harto* means 'wealth' in Javanese. There was, however, a trickle-down effect. A 1999 UNICEF Situation Analysis reported that in Indonesia poverty fell

Sukarno, Indonesia's first President, was placed under house arrest until he died a broken man in 1970.

from 40% to 11% and child mortality was halved during the last twenty years of Suharto's rule.

Education, Education, Education

President Suharto extended education in Bali. Many new village schools were set up in the 1960s, but for secondary education, children went to Surabaya, or if they could afford it, abroad. By the 1970s, however, there were secondary schools and a university.

In 1984 attendance at primary school became compulsory. By 1985 about 85%-90% of Balinese seven to fifteen year olds were attending school. In 1994 compulsory education was extended to junior secondary school. Each generation was better educated than the one before. Although primary education is compulsory, it is not totally free as there are uniforms, lunches and books to pay for. There are other difficulties: of the 27,000 classrooms in Bali, one third needed urgent repair in 2003 and there is a shortage of teachers.

Thoroughly Modern Bali

Bali entered the modern world. Electricity reached the villages: Ubud and Batuan were connected in 1974. During the 1990s streets throughout the island were paved and most families in affluent villages owned cars and telephones. Internet cafés sprouted up everywhere.

Many people gave up working in the rice fields and engaged in servicing tourists. If they were not engaged with them directly, they were earning a living indirectly, through construction, policing, transport and numerous cottage industries. Development became intense. There were placards of President Suharto, wearing a safari suit, proclaiming him as 'the Father of Development'. Many rice fields were sold for commercial projects and buildings multiplied within family compounds.

Two Is Enough

The fertility rate for Balinese women between 1967 and 1970 was 5.8%. In the early 1970s a team of public health workers approached the *banjars* and the *Banjar* Family Planning Project was launched with the goal of two children per couple. President Suharto's two fingers with the words *Dua Anak Cukup* got the message across subtly: 'Two is enough'. Nobody commented that the President had six children. By 1985 the fertility rate dropped to 2.6%. The success drew worldwide attention. It was actually a success for the whole country. In the 1970s it was estimated that if left unchecked the country's population would rise from 110 million at that time to between 250 and 300 million by 2001. In 2000 the population reached the family planning target of 210 million.

Financial Meltdown, 1998

The Asian financial crisis started in Thailand in July 1997 and spread like wildfire to Indonesia. The boom of the 1990s had been built on huge foreign loans. The bubble burst and the country's wealth disappeared overnight. In June 1997 the rupiah was 2,300 to the US dollar. By early 1998 it was 12,500 (having reached 16,000 at one point).

The rupiah fell by almost 80% from July 1997 to early 1998. President Suharto called in the International Monetary Fund, which poured in US$43 billion. Students rioted and there were many deaths. President Suharto resigned on 21 May 1998, aged 76. Only Fidel Castro in Cuba had been in power for longer. Suharto thanked the people of Indonesia and asked their forgiveness for his 'mistakes and shortcomings'. His six-line statement, read from the Presidential Palace in Jakarta, ended the New Order régime. He died in 2008.

Dr Bachruddin Jusuf Habibie, the Vice-President, from Sulawesi, known as PBA (President by Accident), automatically became the third President of Indonesia in 1998.

Under President Suharto, the 'Father of Development', many rice fields were sold for commercial projects.

Fledgling Democracy

Abdurrahman Wahid (1940-2009), popularly known as Gus Dur, a blind East Javanese preacher, who had suffered two serious strokes, became Indonesia's first democratically elected President on 21 October 1999. Megawati Soekarnoputri, President Sukarno's daughter, was elected Vice-President. He apologised to the victims of 1965 and political prisoners and made many enemies. The People's Consultative Assembly dismissed him on 23 July 2001 alleging corruption, incompetence and violating the Constitution. It was a political coup. Megawati replaced him. The Balinese rejoiced as they supported her party, the Indonesian Democratic Party of Struggle, in the election.

Megawati Soekarnoputri, 2001-2004

Megawati, who is one-quarter Balinese and the second child of President Sukarno and his wife Fatmawati, was very popular in Bali because she was partly Balinese, but she turned out to be ineffectual as a leader. She was aloof, gave few interviews and lost the election. Bali voted for her but it was one of the very few provinces which did.

Susilo Bambang Yudhoyono, 2004-

Susilo Bambang Yudhoyono, popularly known as SBY, became the country's sixth President, the first directly elected President, on 20 September 2004. He was a retired general and politically unknown. On 8 July 2009 he became the first Indonesian president ever to be democratically re-elected—a triumph for his cautious, unostentatious style and confirmation of the political stability which has taken root in Indonesia.

Chapter 16

The Earth Moved

Ring of Fire

Bali is firmly on the Ring of Fire, an arc that stretches to New Zealand up to and along the coasts of North and South America. Over 75% of the world's active and dormant volcanoes sit on this 25,000 mile range. There are currently about 1,500 active volcanoes in the world.

There are five active volcanoes in Bali, including Batur, 5,633 feet (1,717 metres), which erupted several times in the 20th century, Batukau, 7,467 feet (2,276 metres) and Abang, 7,060 feet (2,152 metres). Mount Agung, the highest in Bali, at 10,309 feet (3,142 metres) exploded dramatically in 1963 and killed over 2,000 people. The Balinese turn a blind eye to the risk of volcanoes, perhaps blaming themselves for causing the gods to be angry. After an eruption they normally go back and try to continue farming. Life goes on.

Tectonic Plates

Tectonic plates are like giant rafts of the Earth's surface which slide alongside each other, collide and are sometimes forced underneath other plates. There are eight to twelve big plates and twenty or so smaller ones in the world. Around the Ring of Fire, the Pacific Plate is colliding with and sliding underneath other plates. This process is known as subduction and the volcanically active area nearby is known as a subduction zone. Alfred Wegener (1880-1930) published his theory of plate tectonics in 1912, but did not live long enough to see his ideas accepted. That did not take place until 1970. He died in freezing Greenland in 1930.

Earthquakes, Volcanoes and Tsunamis

When the plates move quickly, they can cause earthquakes. If the earth-quake is strong, very high temperatures and energy can melt rock into magma, which rises through weak parts in the surface and forms lava. The vents of the volcanoes, through which the magma reaches the surface, are plugged by solidified magma. This increases the pressure until there is a series of violent explosions.

Some large volcanoes plug themselves so well that huge magma chambers form. When they eventually explode, huge vacant holes, like lakes, are the result. These are called 'calderas' after the Spanish word for 'kettle'. Mount Batur is an example of a double caldera, created by an eruption 30,000 years ago, and one of the biggest in the world. It has been partly filled by Lake Batur, the biggest lake in Bali, and another volcanic cone.

When there is an earthquake under the sea, one side of the ocean floor suddenly drops down, beneath the top edge of the plate. The resulting vertical fault generates a tsunami. The movements of the plates usually give little warning for those at risk in coastal areas. One indication of a tsunami is that there is a rush of water away from the coastline, but the seismic wave may only be minutes away.

The Balinese believe that Bali sits on the back of a turtle, the cosmic turtle, Bedawang Nala, who occasionally stirs and sets off earthquakes.

Bali sits on a Cosmic Turtle

The alternative cosmological theory for the cause of earthquakes is the Balinese belief that Bali sits on the back of a turtle, the cosmic turtle, Bedawang Nala, who occasionally stirs and sets off earthquakes. Bedawang Nala is flanked by two cosmic serpents, Basuki and Anantaboga, one of which is green or blue and the other is red.

Mount Toba, Sumatra, 74,000 Years Ago

Mount Toba in northern Sumatra, far to the west of Bali and Java, suffered a massive explosion. Nobody is quite sure how big it was. It left a huge, beautiful lake: 50 miles (80 kilometres) long and 15 miles (24 kilometres) wide and caldera cliffs rising 800 feet (244 metres) out of the water. There were at least six years of volcanic winter following the eruption, which was felt even in Greenland. It is likely that the effects severely reduced the numbers of humans living on Earth, perhaps to no more than a few thousand. There are still 18 inches (46 centimetres) of volcanic dust on the ocean floor 1,500 miles (2,414 kilometres) away. Because the date of the explosion is known, the dust enables archaeologists and geneticists to date fossils found lying in it precisely.

Tambora, Sumbawa, 5 April 1815

Mount Tambora, on the island of Sumbawa, to the east of Bali, blew its top in 1815, killing more than 92,000 people and wiping out everyone who spoke the Tambora language. It buried the tiny the kingdom of Tambora and vented 11 cubic miles of rock, ash and dust into the atmosphere. The 27 mile high plume dimmed the sun's rays and the world's temperature was lowered by 1 degree celsius. As a result, there was no summer in New England, which is 10,000 miles (16,093 kilometres) away. Rainfall was 50% above average and in England two-thirds of the year's rain fell in the summer months of July, August and September. It was called 'the year without a summer'. The harvest was six weeks late. Wheat prices doubled and real wages fell dramatically. The wine harvest was the latest ever known—in some places extending into November. Crop failures caused riots in England, France and Belgium in 1816 and in most of Europe the following year. Death rates rose and epidemics increased, especially in southern Europe. The effects of the eruption destroyed crops in Bali too.

Krakatoa, Java, 27 August 1883, 10.02 am

Krakatoa, or to use its proper name, Krakatau, is the most famous volcano in the world. It is located between Java and Sumatra (west of Java, not east of Java as the movie title put it). It erupted four times in 1883 and the resulting tsunamis devastated 165 villages, injured thousands and killed more than 36,000 people. It is near the Java Trench, an active subduction zone. The oceanic plate beneath the Indian Ocean moved northward, plunging beneath the continental plate.

Every seismograph in the world recorded the thunderous explosion, which some say was the loudest sound ever produced and heard thousands of miles away. Others say Tambora, which exploded in 1815, holds that honour. People in Saigon, Bangkok, Manila and Perth heard the explosion.

The shock waves reverberated around the world seven times and rocked buildings 500 miles (805 kilometres) distant. The tsunamis affected the water level in the English Channel, which is 11,800 sea miles away, and produced tidal waves up to 121 feet (37 metres) high. A cloud of dust and gas, pumice and fire was hurled 30 miles (48 kilometres) into the air.

It is estimated that over 21,000 cubic metres of debris were ejected. Atmospheric effects lasted for over a year. It lowered the Earth's temperature. The northern two-thirds of the island of Krakatau was blown away. All that was left the day after the eruption was a deep, 820 feet (250 metre) crater and the remnant of an island. The tons of dust thrown into the atmosphere resulted in amazing vermilion sunsets throughout the world for the next two or three years. Turner painted them in England.

Volcano, Mount Batur, Bali, 1905

Mount Batur has erupted more than twenty times since 1800. In 1905 it erupted once again. Miraculously the lava stopped at the main entrance of the temple, Pura Ulun Danu Batur.

Earthquake, Payangan, Bali, 21 January 1917, 6.50 am

There was a very severe earthquake in Bali, which lasted forty-five seconds, in 1917. A source on the Internet placed it at a magnitude of 7, but it is really anybody's guess. Seismologists use a magnitude scale to express the seismic energy released by an earthquake. It was created by the American seismologist, vegetarian and nudist Charles Richter in 1935 and measures how much the ground shakes 60 miles (96 kilometres) from the earthquake's epicentre. A smaller earthquake occurred on 4 February and the tremors lasted for the next two weeks. Temples and houses collapsed all over southern Bali, and it wreaked havoc with irrigation systems. The epicentre was in Payangan, close to Ubud.

One account says 1,372 people died, but another account says 15,000. 1,071 were injured. 64,000 houses, including palaces, 10,000 rice barns and 2,431 temples were destroyed. Besakih was devastated. Ubud was flattened and the whole of Ubud palace was destroyed. No houses were left standing. It was lucky that it took place early in the morning when most people were already up and working in the rice fields. That saved a lot of lives, but it was followed by an epidemic, which killed more than the earthquake.

Rebuilding the damage imposed a great strain on the population, which was much smaller than it is today. Earthquakes are a sign that the gods are angry. In order to restore Pura Besakih a levy was imposed on all married people. The colonial government donated 25,000 florins to the Besakih restoration fund and even Queen Wilhelmina donated 1,000 florins herself. It was necessary to give priority to the temples to regain the protection of the village gods. Without holy water from the temples, ceremonies could not be held.

Volcano, Mount Batur, Bali, 3 August 1926, 1 am

This time the village and temple, Pura Ulun Danu Batur, were buried under a great tide of blood-red lava. The villagers were able to save their possessions and the temple orchestras and ceremonial objects. The village and temple were rebuilt on the rim of the crater in 1935.

Tsunami, Asia, 26 December 2004

On 26 December 2004 the greatest earthquake in forty years happened about 93 miles (150 kilometres) off the west coast of north Sumatra. It generated a huge tsunami that caused destruction in eleven countries bordering the Indian Ocean. The earthquake was felt in Sumatra, the Nicobar and Andaman Islands, Malaysia, Burma, Thailand, Bangladesh and India. There were hundreds of aftershocks. The epicentre was near the junction of three tectonic plates. Fortunately Bali was not physically affected, although tourist numbers were reduced as a result.

The earthquake's magnitude was 9.3 on the Richter scale, the second largest ever recorded. The largest was in China on 22 May 1960 at 9.5. It was the tsunami, however, that caused most of the deaths and destruction. It affected areas that were 1,243 miles (2,000 kilometres) away in the Seychelles and Somalia. The death toll is unknown, but it is certainly in the hundreds of thousands.

Earthquake, Java, 27 May 2006, 5.54 am

An earthquake, whose epicentre in the Indian Ocean was 15.5 miles (25 kilometres) southeast of Yogyakarta in central Java, struck in the early hours of the morning. It measured 6.2 on the Richter scale and affected areas all around Yogyakarta, killing more than 6,000 people. The 9th century Borobudur Temple was not affected but the spectacular 10th century Hindu temples of Prambanan suffered serious damage. Yogyakarta is more than 310 miles (500 kilometres) west of Bali, which was unaffected by the quake.

Earthquake and Tsunami, Java, 17 July 2006, 3.19 pm

Less than two months later, without warning, another earthquake, this time accompanied by a tsunami, hit southwest Java. The 7.7 magnitude earthquake struck 112 miles (180 kilometres) offshore in the Indian Ocean. The depth was shallow at about 6 miles (10 kilometres). These conditions were right for the tsunami, which duly followed an hour later and pummeled 186 miles (300 kilometres) of coastline, destroying houses, restaurants and hotels. Huge black waves, 7 feet (2 metres) high, tossed boats, cars and motorbikes 300 yards (328 metres) inland and killed over 600 people.

Warning System

Under the initiative of UNESCO, an early warning system for tsunamis is being built in the Indian Ocean. The system will use buoys to detect abnormal surface sea movements and send the information to monitoring centres via satellite.

Civilisation

Despite the terrible devastation of erupting volcanoes, Bali can thank them for her civilisation. Tropical soils tend to be poor because heavy rains wash away the nutrients. Bali, however, has been spared this disadvantage. Continuous eruptions throw fertile ash over the island. Volcanic soils are rich in minerals.

Mountains also cause rainfall. Moisture laden air rises, cools and rains. Rain falls on the south of the island. The northern third is in the rain shadow and so is rather arid. So, thanks to her volcanoes and mountains, Bali has fertile soil and good irrigation.

Balinese Orientation

With all this going on, it is not surprising that mountains have acquired a deep religious significance for the Balinese. Mountains are doubly sacred because they are the source of holy water. Bali's centre is mountainous and it is surrounded by sea. Everyday life is orientated by reference to the direction of the mountains, *kaja*, or to the direction of the sea, *kelod*.

The Balinese are aware at all times of their physical position in relation to the mountains and the sea. It is said that a true Balinese knows where Mount Agung is, blindfolded. They give directions using directional terminology and even ask for things to be moved *kaja* or *kelod*. The best place for a rice barn is southwest because animals and crops will prosper. Place it northeast and fatal illnesses will occur. Put it east and there will be family disagreements. In the northwest there will be illnesses and expense. The west will bring wealth but also sickness. The southeast will cause suffering. The north results in good crops and riches but manifold problems. Random location is therefore out of the question.

The Balinese sleep with their heads pointing towards Mount Agung. They believe their mental health depends on it. For the majority of the population this means north. It would be most inappropriate to point one's feet in the face of the gods. Preoccupation with orientation and sleeping in the right direction occurs in Thailand also and can be traced to China and Japan, where cities such as Beijing, Suzhou, Nara and Kyoto are arranged auspiciously. North of the Equator people traditionally sleep with their heads pointing south.

The directions have a moral dimension. The mountains are basically good and the sea basically bad, but the dichotomy is not as great as many books suggest. Such ideas are not uniquely Balinese; they are common among Austronesian peoples. Some books associate Balinese mountains strongly with the divine and the sea with evil, a misinterpretation probably based on Dutch sources.

Mount Agung, the highest mountain, is home to the gods, but also powerful demons. The sea is not a polluting influence as many books suggest. Purification ceremonies regularly take place in the sea. Images of gods, masks, gamelan instruments, shadow puppets and dance headdresses are taken there for purification. Following cremation, a person's ashes are washed in the sea as the final purifying act. The sea is a major source of holy water.

Mountains are symbolically represented in numerous ways in Bali. The shadow play opens with a puppet in the form of a mountain. Offerings are commonly shaped as mountains. *Penjor* look like mountains and Balinese gates are said to represent Mount Meru.

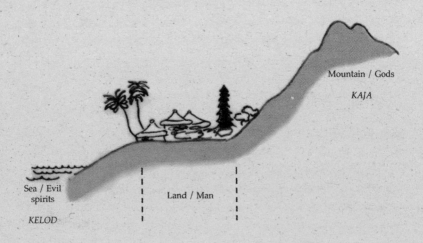

Everyday life is orientated by reference to the direction of the mountains, *kaja*, or to the direction of the sea, *kelod*.

Chapter 17

Balinese Calendars

Would You Like A Date?

We tend to take our calendar for granted and do not give it a second thought. We just use it. If we were asked if there are any alternatives, we might remember that there is a solar and a lunar calendar, but probably we would have no idea how the calendar came about. It may be that we know that a year is equal to the time it takes the Earth to go around the sun, but no idea why there are twelve months and why June has thirty days and July has thirty-one.

Balinese Calendars

There are three calendars in use in Bali:
- Gregorian calendar
- *Pawukon* calendar
- *Saka* calendar

Lunar Calendars

Nearly every ancient culture watched the heavens and worshipped the moon. Many ceremonies are still governed by lunar events. In days gone by the heavens provided measurable certainty and could therefore be used to measure time.

The moon passes through its phases roughly once every 29½ days, from new moon to full moon and back again. A 12-month lunar year is 354 days. However, the Earth goes round the sun every 365 days, in fact every 365¼ days, which creates a problem, because over time, there is a drift and no regular relationship between events in the world and the lunar date.

To solve this problem, the Jews inserted additional months into their lunar calendar; the Greeks and Chinese did the same with theirs, but it was not very satisfactory.

Ancient Egyptians, 4000 BC

The ancient Egyptians were the first to turn to a solar calendar and devised a calendar of 12 months of 30 days each, and added the extra 5 days, and made them the birthdays of various gods. They did that about 6,000 years ago.

The Romans had the same problem with their 12-month lunar calendar. Their priests were responsible for inserting months to align it with the seasons, but sometimes they forgot or manipulated the dates, so that the whole thing was a mess. When Julius Caesar was with Cleopatra in Egypt in 47 BC, he learned about the Egyptian calendar and resolved to adopt it.

Julius Caesar, 1ˢᵗ Century BC

On returning to Rome in 46 BC, Julius Caesar reformed the Roman calendar by adopting the Egyptian model and added leap years to deal with the quarter day. He provided for the months to have alternating 30- and 31- days, except for February. Emperor Augustus subsequently made some more changes, particularly the number of days in certain months. This is the civic calendar that is now used, with some modifications, throughout the world.

Julius Caesar moved the first day of the year from March to January and inaugurated 1 January as New Year's Day. Previously it had been in March around the time of the spring equinox. It is hard to believe but 25 March was still the customary new year in Britain and the American colonies until 1752, when an Act of Parliament brought them into line with the rest of Europe.

Caesar's calendar had a problem: it was also out of sync. It was eleven minutes longer than the actual solar year. This amounts to an entire day every 125 years, and that meant the Christian holy days, like Easter, were being celebrated on the wrong dates, which was of great concern to the early Christians.

Constantine's 7-Day Week, 4ᵗʰ Century

We take the 7-day week for granted, but this was not part of the Julian calendar until 321 AD when Emperor Constantine introduced it. He was not the first—it seems to have originated in Babylon around 700 BC. It did not percolate to Britain until the 5th century.

Most cultures choose weeks of 5 to 10 days. Recent research suggests that certain biorhythms occur on a 7-day cycle, like blood pressure, organ rejection and heartbeats, which may be the reason for the length of the week.

Pope Gregory XIII, 16th Century

The 80 year old lawyer turned pope, Pope Gregory XIII (1502-1585) remedied the problems of the Julian calendar in 1582 by eliminating ten days from 5 to 14 October at a stroke and provided that 1600 and 2000 would be leap years but that 1700, 1800 and 1900 would not be. Most Catholic countries obeyed the Pope's edict, especially after a number of reminders, but Protestants rejected the reforms. That resulted in Catholic and Protestant areas celebrating religious holidays and saints' days on different dates.

The Eastern Orthodox Church rejected the reforms. After 1923, some churches adopted parts of the new Gregorian calendar, but kept the old system for calculating Easter Day, and they still celebrate it on a different day from the West.

Germany introduced most of the new calendar (except Easter Day) in 1770 and fully adopted it in 1775. Britain was one of the last major European countries to accept the new calendar. An Act of Parliament, passed in 1752, went into effect on 2 September and eliminated eleven days, which was the extent of the drift at that time. There were riots in the streets, as people roared, 'Give us back our eleven days'. Bankers in the City of London refused to pay their taxes on the usual date of 25 March 1753 and paid eleven days late, on 5 April, which is still the start of the financial year in Britain.

Eventually other countries followed suit. Japan adopted the calendar in 1873; Greece in 1924. China accepted it in 1912, although it was not really used much until the Communist revolution of 1949.

Now it turns out the Gregorian calendar is wrong—by 25.96768 seconds a year.

Indonesia

The Dutch introduced the Gregorian calendar and the Balinese are totally familiar with it and use it for civil and business affairs. National and commemorative holidays are fixed by the Gregorian calendar, which include:

- **21 April: Kartini Day**

  Kartini Day celebrates Kartini, the Indonesian heroine of women's emancipation, and is a school holiday. She was born in the village of Mayong in the municipality of Jepara in central Java in 1879. Her father, Raden Mas Adipati Arlo Soroningrat, was mayor and had twelve children from several wives.

  She was lucky to receive a Dutch education. This was normally reserved for Dutch and children of royal families. She had to stop at twelve years because of the old Javanese tradition of *pinjit*, which meant she had to stay at home and wait for marriage. During the days at home she wrote to many friends abroad. The letters have been published in *Letters of a Javanese Princess*. She became a feminist and rebelled against the strong tradition of sex discrimination.

  At twenty-four years, however, she obeyed her father and married the mayor of Rembang, Raden Adipati Joyodiningrat, who was fifty and already had three wives and dozens of children. Her hopes of studying abroad were dashed, although she had a scholarship to study in Europe. Instead she established a special school for local girls.

- **2 May: National Education Day**
- **20 May: National Awakening Day**
- **23 July: National Children's Day**
- **17 August: Independence Day**

  On 17 August 1945 President Sukarno proclaimed Independence from the Dutch, but it took another five years of war to achieve it.

- **8 September: National Sports Day**
- **1 October: *Pancasila* Sanctity Day**

  This day commemorates the Indonesian state philosophy, the five basic principles called *Pancasila*.

- **5 October: Armed Forces Day**
- **28 October: Youth Pledge Day**
- **10 November: Heroes' Day**

  Solemn ceremonies are held at national cemeteries around the archipelago. Bali has a national hero. Lieutenant Colonel I Gusti Ngurah Rai and his ninety-six Balinese troops battled against the

Dutch for independence in 1946 and were all wiped out. He was proclaimed a National Hero in 1975. The airport in south Bali, where his statue stands, is named after him.
*   **22 December: Women's Day**
    This is observed in remembrance of the first Indonesian Women's Congress on 22 December 1928.

Pawukon Calendar

The *Pawukon* calendar, whose origin is in east Java, came with the Majapahits in the 14th century, and is the most important of the three calendars. It consists of thirty 7-day weeks. The days and weeks are not numbered, but each has a name, and a date is specified by the name of the day and the week, which combination comes around every Balinese year of 210 days. There are six months of 35 days. It is not a calendar in the Western sense to measure time and cannot easily be related to the Gregorian calendar. Its purpose is to pinpoint certain days, especially coincidence days. It has no correlation with nature or the seasons.

Roelof Goris, a philologist, who lived in Bali for many years, in *Holidays and Holy Days* (1960) lists thirty-two holy days in every Balinese year, which means a holiday on average every seven days. It is not really a holiday. Holy days are a lot of work, and that is not counting days of preparation, and other family ceremonies, like baby ceremonies, weddings and cremations, and family temple festivals. It is difficult for employers, as staff are frequently absent attending to ceremonial duties.

Coincidence Days

The Balinese are not alone in using coincidence days for special days. The Aztecs and Mayans did and the Chinese do.

Take two cycles and run them together. Think of Friday 13th, which is the coincidence of a particular day falling on a particular date.

The Balinese have a 3-day week and a 5-day week. An important coincidence day is when the third day of the 3-day week, *Kajeng*, falls on the same day as the fifth day of the 5-day week, *Kliwon*. This day is called *Kajeng-Kliwon* and occurs every fifteen days: (3x5 = 15). The low spirits are especially active and are given more elaborate offerings on that day.

It gets more complicated. The Balinese actually have ten weeks, ranging from the 1-day week to the 10-day week, and they run concurrently throughout the 210 day cycle. *Galungan* is a very special day, which occurs once every 210 days, falling on the coincidence day of the 5-day, 6-day and 7-day weeks: (5x6x7 = 210).

Significant days fall on the coincidence of the 5-day and 7-day weeks, which is once every thirty-five days. Others fall on the coincidence of the 6-day and 7-day weeks, once every forty-two days, and on the 5-day and 6-day weeks, once every thirty days.

10 Different Weeks

Different weeks are used for different purposes. The 3-day week determines the markets in Bali. The market shifts from one village to another on a 3-day cycle, so that there is a market in every village once every three days. Ubud forms part of a rotation with the markets at Payangan and Tegallalang.

Markets date back a long way in Bali. The first reference to markets and market weeks is in the 9th century. Some of these old inscriptions refer to markets that are still on schedule today. Markets start very early in the morning and are staffed almost entirely by women. They are usually situated outside the royal palace or a noble's house.

The 8-day week provides a clue to a person's past life. Birth on the first day of the 8-day week makes it likely that the baby is the reincarnation of a woman on the mother's side.

The *Tumpeks*

The *Tumpeks* are special coincidence days and always fall on a Saturday. They occur when the sixth day of the 7-day week falls on the fifth day of the 5-day week. There are therefore six of them in each Balinese year of 210 days: (6x35 = 210). The common characteristic of *Tumpek* ceremonies is that they show respect for objects.

The Indonesian *kris* is a ceremonial dagger. UNESCO recognized it as a great achievement of tangible cultural heritage for world humanity on 25 November 2005.

The first reference to markets and market weeks is in the 9th century. Markets start very early in the morning and are staffed almost entirely by women.

Tumpek Landep

This is a special day for metal and items made of iron and steel, like guns, *krises* and computers. The Indonesian *kris* is a ceremonial dagger. UNESCO recognized it as a great achievement of tangible cultural heritage for world humanity on 25 November 2005. Vehicles are washed and blessed. Elaborate palm leaf offerings are tied to their front grills and sides. The purpose is to activate them for the good of man. People born on this day are stubborn and steely. A ceremony is available to tone down the adverse effects.

Tumpek Wariga

Tumpek Wariga is a special day for important trees, such as coconut trees, which are covered in Balinese textiles for the day and requested to be fruitful.

Tumpek Kuningan

This coincides with *Kajeng-Kliwon*, so there is a triple coincidence.

Kuningan marks the end of the 10-day period, starting with *Galungan*, during which the deified ancestors descend and are entertained. Special offerings of yellow rice are made. It also commemorates the spirits of the heroes who were killed during the mythic battle against Sang Mayadenawa. Just to be safe, it is also a catch-all day: the day to bless the spirituality of any items omitted in the normal cycle of *Tumpek* days.

Tumpek Krulut

This is a special day for musical instruments, dance costumes and masks.

Tumpek Andang

Tumpek Andang is special for animals, who are given a bath, a special piece of cloth and offerings, perhaps a biscuit. People born on this day are rude. A ceremony is available to cure the situation.

Tumpek Wayang

This is also *Kajeng-Kliwon*, special for shadow puppets, which the puppeteer takes out and gives offerings to them. It is very unlucky to be born during the week called *Wayang* and especially on this day. The demon Kala's father, Siwa, told him that he could eat children born during this week. It is possible, however, to have the problem cured by a ceremony.

Tika

Every Balinese household has a complicated wall calendar, which indicates the main coincidence days, new and full moons, civic and religious holidays. Most Balinese know the Balinese day and week they were born, their Balinese birthday. They may not know their birthday on the Gregorian calendar, especially older people.

If the Balinese need to check a particular day for a ceremony, they go to a priest or *balian* for advice. *Tikas* are traditional aids for the *Pawukon* calendar, made of wood or cloth, but many people cannot read them.

There are seven horizontal rows, which represent the days, and thirty vertical columns, which represent the weeks. Each week has a name, which is written at the top in the appropriate column. To read the days, you read down the columns from left to right. Every day in the year has a unique combination of day name and week name.

The third day of the 3-day week, Kajeng, is shown by its own symbol every three days on the *tika*. The fifth day, *Kliwon*, is shown by its symbol every five days. When these coincide the day is *Kajeng-Kliwon*.

The *Saka* Calendar

The *Saka* calendar arrived in Bali with the Majapahits in the 14th century. It was developed in north India in 78 AD by the Kushan king, Kanishka and is still used in parts of India. There are twelve lunar months; each has a name in Sanskrit.

Every month has thirty lunar days and ends on the day of the new moon, called *tilem*. The next month begins the following day. Full moon, *purnama*, occurs in the middle of the month. Offerings are always made on the new and full moons.

A number of temples use the *Saka* calendar to fix their temple ceremonies, but most use the *Pawukon* calendar. Every three or four years an intercalary month is inserted to bring the lunar year into line with the solar year. The Ministry of Religion decides the month.

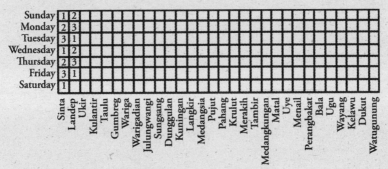

Tika showing a 3-day week superimposed on it. *Tikas* are traditional aids for the *Pawukon* calendar, made of wood or cloth.

New Year's Day

New Year's Day, *Nyepi*, is the only event celebrated all over the island and one of the few ceremonies timed according to the *Saka* rather than the *Pawukon* calendar. It takes place in March or early April. New Year's Eve is the day of the new moon, which falls on the ninth month (*tilem kasanga*).

The Scythian Connection

The Scythians were a nomadic tribe, who flourished from the 8th to the 4th century BC. They spoke an Indo-Iranian language, and were related to the *Saka*, another nomadic tribe that roamed the steppes of central Asia about the same time.

Saka years are numbered from the date that a *Saka* tribe came to power in India, which was 78 AD. The Balinese keep to that date, so the *Saka* year is seventy-eight years behind the Gregorian year. Gregorian year 2005 is *Saka* year 1927.

Anno Domini

The now forgotten Dionysius Exiguus (c500-560 AD) was an abbot in Rome, described as a Scythian. He made a huge contribution to the Western calendar, because he introduced the *Anno Domini* (AD) system of dating, which many people now call the Common Era (CE). Where he got the date for Christ's birth is unclear. It is still a matter of great controversy as the Gospels suggest dates from 5 BC to 7 AD.

He made year 1 the base year for Christ's birth. Year zero was impossible as the symbol for zero had not yet been introduced to Europe. It seems that the first use of the symbol zero appeared in India in the 7th century and was introduced to Baghdad, the capital of the magnificent Abbasid dynasty, by Indian scholars in the 8th century. It eventually appeared in Europe in the 11th century.

Chapter 18

Balinese Hinduism

Religion is Everywhere

Bali's wonderful volcanoes, rice terraces and temples, dramatic ceremonies, cremations and dances, processions, offerings, carvings, paintings, masks, puppets and gamelan music are spectacular and colourful but pretty much devoid of meaning without an appreciation of Balinese religion. The vital thing to appreciate is that there is hardly any division between the religious and the secular. Religion is everywhere and in all things.

A Very Unusual Religion

Balinese Hinduism is unlike the main world religions. There is no founder, such as Jesus, Buddha or Mohammed; no single holy book, such as the Bible or Koran; no schools, colleges or seminaries to train priests; no single religious leader, such as the Pope or the Archbishop of Canterbury. There are certain beliefs, though, that make up Balinese Hinduism or *Agama Hindu Bali*, as it is properly called.

First: Animism

Although it is called Balinese Hinduism, it is not helpful to think only in terms of Indian Hinduism, as the Balinese had a religion before Hinduism arrived on their shores, and many aspects of that old, animist religion are still practised today. Animism is a belief that everything possesses a spirit or spirits, even animals, rocks and trees, and we can communicate with them.

In *Murni's Warung* in Ubud there hangs a painting of the 1970s in which a young girl presents offerings to a large stone across the road from the *Warung*. Such actions may well date back to megalithic times. Stones are not only imperishable, but they often also have fantastic shapes, which lead to exceptional powers being ascribed to them.

The spirits are active and need to be kept happy. This is a belief shared throughout the Pacific and suggests an origin dating back to their common Austronesian ancestry, which is thousands of years older than Hinduism.

Animists worship many nature gods and ancestors. Their temples are open rectangular spaces with shrines, which the gods and ancestors are invited to visit during ceremonies. Fruit offerings are presented to them. These are all very much part of Balinese religion, and probably a more important element than the Hindu side of the religion.

Animism is a belief that everything possesses a spirit or spirits, even animals, rocks and trees, and we can communicate with them.

Then: Animism Plus Hinduism

Hinduism is an Indian religion. Trade with India probably began around 350 AD. Indian ceramics of that period have been found in Bali, but it is thought that the Indians were interested just in trade and not conversions, migration or conquest.

At some point Indian religions, both Buddhism and Hinduism, were introduced to Java and Sumatra. Rock inscriptions in west Java dating from the 5th or 6th century tell of Taruma, an extensive Javanese kingdom near present day Jakarta. The people of Taruma observed Hindu religious rites. Srivijaya in Sumatra was earlier Buddhist but became Hindu by the 7th century. It is likely that the local rulers were impressed by stories of the Indian rajas, and their divinity, and, wanting to strengthen their control over their people, asked the Indian *brahmana* priests for advice. The rulers promoted the Indian religions.

The rituals of these powerful priests could supernaturally legitimise the ruler's power. It is clear that the rulers tried to associate themselves with Indian culture as much as possible and created family trees with roots in India. They claimed to be temporary incarnations of the Hindu gods and they brought these ideas to Bali when in 1343 the Javanese kingdom of Majapahit invaded Bali.

Balinese Hinduism versus Indian Hinduism

The main differences between Balinese Hinduism and Indian Hinduism are that Bali has no untouchables, cow worship or dietary prohibitions (except that priests do not eat beef and nobody eats it before going to the temple). Men and women treat each other as equals (well, most of the time), women can divorce and widows remarry. The so-called Balinese caste system is much less rigid than in India. More differences are set out below.

Polytheism or Monotheism?

Brahma, Wisnu and Siwa are the Hindu Trinity: Brahma, the Creator, Wisnu, the Preserver, and Siwa, the Destroyer and god of rebirth. Siwa is regarded as the most important. There are many more gods and goddesses in the Hindu pantheon. The Balinese did not adopt all Hindu gods, and there are Balinese gods and goddesses that are not Indian at all, such as Rangda. Dewi Sri, the rice goddess, is a very popular figure and her image is seen everywhere. There is a public holiday called Saraswati day, Saraswati being the goddess of learning. Some say all the gods are manifestations of the one God, called Sanghyang Widi Wasa, a name chosen by the Dutch for God in their Indonesian translations of the Bible.

There are few statues of 'Him'. 'He' is defined as the essence common to all the gods. *Sang* and *hyang* indicate 'the divine', while *widi* from the Sanskrit word *widhi* means 'order.' He is neither male nor female.

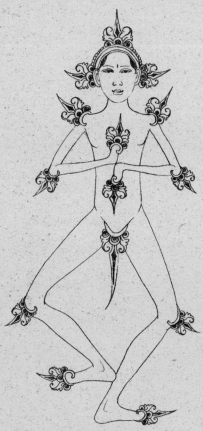

No temples are dedicated to Him, no special day is reserved for Him and no offerings are made to Him.

Sanghyang Widi Wasa does not figure much in grass roots Balinese thinking, but He is useful politically, because the first of the five state *Pancasila* principles is belief in one all-powerful god. Balinese Hinduism was at risk in the 1950s of being classified as a non-religion and thus being prevented access to government funds. If the Balinese believed in Sanghyang Widi Wasa, it solved the problem.

Roman Catholics believe that saints exist and pray to them to intervene in the world and perform miracles. Balinese prayers to the rice goddess for a good crop may not be vastly different. It has been said that the Balinese gods are like the rainbow colours of a beam of white light.

Sanghyang Widi Wasa is the essence common to all the gods.

The Ministry of Religion

Indonesia has a Ministry of Religion, which was set up in 1950. It has a staff of more than 200,000 and the third largest budget behind Education and Culture, and Domestic Affairs. After Indonesian independence, there was a debate over whether Indonesia should become an Islamic or secular state. The debate has been settled for the time being: Indonesia is a secular state.

There are five officially sanctioned religions in Indonesia and all Indonesians have to profess one of them. They are Islam, Hinduism, Buddhism and what the Ministry class as two Christian religions, Catholicism and Protestantism. Thanks to the help of President Sukarno, Balinese Hinduism was accepted as monotheistic and has been represented in the Ministry since 1958 in a separate Bali-Hindu section.

Lively Clashes

The Hindu religion's central secular body is *Parisada Hindu Dharma*, which was formed on 23 February 1959. It runs a teachers' college and a theological school to train religious education school teachers and university lecturers. Its purpose is to ensure a certain minimum uniformity of belief and practice.

There are currently two opposing camps struggling over the fundamental teachings of Balinese Hinduism. The first camp comprises the traditional religious leaders, mostly the high priests and traditional political figures from the *satria* caste. Prominent members of this camp are the nobility of Ubud palace. The other, the modern camp, comprises a loose coalition of various clan-based organisations and progressive Hindu scholars. They are heavily influenced by Indian Hinduism, especially *Hare Krishna* and Gandhian philosophy.

In September 2001 the modern camp, for the first time, succeeded in taking over the executive of the *Parisada Hindu Dharma Indonesia* (renamed in 1986) and appointed a layman as chairman, rather than a *pedanda* high priest, at the national congress. A recommendation was made that the caste system should be abolished. It also recommended an end to animal sacrifices in purification ceremonies. The Balinese branch objected to this. It is the traditional camp and concerned that sacred fundamental teachings should not be destroyed. The Balinese branch held its own meeting in November the same year in Campuan and demanded that a *pedanda* high priest should be head of the *Parisada*. Soon after the central *Parisada* disowned the *Parisada*

Campuan and held its own regional congress in March 2002 at Besakih and ratified the decisions of the national congress and declared itself the only official Balinese branch of the *Parisada*. So, there are two Balinese *Parisada* claiming to be the legitimate representatives of the Balinese Hindu population. *Parisada Campuan* is not only more traditional but more in line with majority thinking.

Balinese Hinduism outside Bali

The Balinese are not interested in converting people, but there is a revival of interest among Indonesian Hindus living outside Bali, for example, in Java, Sumatra and Kalimantan. There are numerous contacts between them and Bali.

Pura Mandara Giri Semeru Agung, a new Balinese Hindu temple honouring Mount Semeru in Java, was built in 1992 at the foot of the mountain with much help from the royal family and people of Ubud. There have been recent moves to establish major temples in other old Hindu sites. These include north Sulawesi in 1993 (Pura Agung Kayangan Jagat Uttara Segara) and central Kalimantan in 1994 (Pura Pitamaha). Again, the people of Ubud have been foremost in advice and assistance.

Indian Hinduism

Indian Hinduism and Balinese Hinduism have evolved separately for many centuries and are practised in very different ways.

For example:

- Balinese temples are architecturally different, open with no roofs, so that the gods can descend and visit
- Balinese offerings are extremely varied and elaborate
- Balinese reincarnation takes place quickly, usually within living memory
- The Balinese emphasise deification of ancestors
- The Balinese have four 'castes' but it is debatable if there really is a caste system at all; in India there are 7,000 recognised castes and sub-castes
- The Balinese have no untouchables
- Employment is not restricted to particular castes with a few exceptions, for example, high priests must be *brahmana* and

blacksmiths used to be members of the *Pande* title group
- Balinese *brahmana* cannot be rulers
- There are usually no statues of gods in the temples
- Balinese gods are present in the temples only during ceremonies
- The Balinese eat beef, except for priests, who do not
- Balinese dead do not have to be cremated immediately, except priests, *brahmana* and members of a royal family
- Ceremonies are different

In India there are many, many Hindu sects, which practise Hinduism, but that does not mean that Balinese Hinduism is a Hindu sect. It is really a separate religion in its own right. There has been very little contact with India for more than a thousand years.

Chapter 19

Core Beliefs

Core Beliefs in Balinese Hinduism

The core beliefs are:

- The need for balance
- *Karma*
- Reincarnation

The Need for Balance

The Balinese believe that the world is divided into opposites: good and bad, day and night, mountain and sea, earth and sky, right and left, young and old, male and female, sun and moon, the seen and the unseen, and so on.

The cardinal Balinese belief is that the world lies between two opposing and antagonistic poles. Left to itself everything would fall into disorder. It takes an outside influence, namely Man, by proper ritual behaviour, to bring order into the world and counteract the natural tendency towards disorder. Balinese myths say that Brahma, Wisnu and Iswara taught human beings to carry out rituals which will prevent the world from being destroyed.

The aim is to achieve a state where the two forces of good and evil are in balance. This is the purpose of the ceremonies, prayers and offerings: to achieve equilibrium, not only for the person, but also for the village, Bali and the world. The equilibrium, however, can only be temporary. The ceremonies must be constantly repeated.

There may be other limited purposes. Certain ceremonies are performed to bring about happiness or prosperity, a good harvest or to satisfy the ancestors. The ceremonies also have a social significance. Even the smallest ceremony requires manpower and help, obtained from members of the family, other villagers or the ruler, and in the case of the grandest ceremonies, all of them work together.

Karma

One's actions, *karma*, determine whether one will be rewarded or punished upon death, and possibly even before. Good works, offerings, performing sacred dances and playing music all create good *karma*. The belief in *karma* is reflected in the Balinese oath, 'If I speak falsely, may a curse fall upon my family for seven generations'. If the matter is sufficiently serious, such as an accusation of theft, a person may be asked to swear the oath in a temple.

Body and Soul

Man's body is a receptacle for his soul. Birth and death are merely the creation and destruction of the perishable body. Reincarnation occurs when the soul is reborn in a different body and to achieve it the old body must be completely destroyed. This can only be achieved through cremation.

After death a person's soul hovers around his body and is capable of bothering his family from the grave, so the family will be concerned to treat it right. Ceremonies are required to detach it from the body. These comprise pre-cremation ceremonies, the cremation, and the second cremation by which the released soul is returned to God.

Life before Birth and Reincarnation

Cremation does not necessarily take place immediately on death. It is quite common for there to be several years in the grave. According to one view, before reincarnation, there are periods in heaven and hell, the lengths of which depend on the person's *karma*.

On rebirth a person may return as a higher or lower caste person or as an animal or even as a one-celled creature. It all depends on the person's *karma*, but the hope and expectation is to return to the same family. Snakes and Ladders is an old Hindu game based on reincarnation.

After numerous reincarnations, when the soul is eventually freed from all desire, it reaches *moksa*. The individual soul merges with the all-loving, all-forgiving universal soul of the Creator. Having so fused, it loses its identity and has reached *nirvana*, the highest state of enlightenment.

Even animals participate in reincarnation, until they eventually reach *nirvana*. As everything has a soul, it follows that there should be respect for all things. Well, that is the theory. Dogs do not seem to get very much respect.

The Greeks believed in Reincarnation too

Reincarnation is seen today as essentially Indian. It comprises a major part of Hinduism and Buddhism, but it is also found in the Western tradition. Pythagoras, who flourished around 532 BC, founded a religion, whose main tenet was the transmigration of souls. His followers, including Plato (427-347 BC), believed in reincarnation. Pythagoras believed that after death souls could even be reincarnated as plants or animals. He himself had 'already been once a boy and a girl, a bush and a bird and a leaping, journeying fish'.

Plato believed that animals evolved from humans. Animals were humans in a previous life who could not reason well. Plants also had souls, but they could not reason, only feel. Aristotle (384-322 BC), who was Plato's star pupil at the Academy, thought that the soul was part of the biological body and died with the body. He did not believe in reincarnation, yet he still believed that plants and flowers had souls, but not consciousness.

Health Warning

It is a dangerous business applying Western terms and values to Balinese beliefs. Often the tourist guides and guide books give meanings, which are totally unrecognisable by the Balinese. Even the language we use contains traps. Bronislaw Malinowski (1884-1942), the Polish anthropologist, pointed out that words only become meaningful in their cultural context.

In English, we typically describe Balinese spirits as good spirits or bad spirits, gods or demons, and thereby imply that they are either consistently benevolent or consistently malevolent, but this falsifies Balinese belief. Every Balinese spirit, god and demon is capable of being helpful and/or harmful. They are just opposite ends of the same stick.

The Seen and the Unseen

The Balinese live in a universe inhabited by the seen and the unseen and they are equally important. Spirits and gods belong to the unseen. The unseen is known to other religions. The Christian Creed, agreed at the Council of Nicea in 325 AD, begins 'We believe in one God, the Father Almighty, maker of Heaven and Earth, of all things visible and invisible...'

High Spirits

The high spirits live high up in mountain tops and in high shrines and receive their offerings high up too. They comprise the gods and goddesses of the Hindu religion as well as the ancestors of the Balinese people. They tend to be good, but are potentially harmful.

Ancestors

Who are the ancestors? When a family member dies, he is usually buried (unless he is a priest or a *brahmana* or member of a royal family), and his spirit resides in *Pura Dalem*, the temple associated with death. It can, of course, move from there if it wishes, perhaps to its own family temple.

It is not until cremation, properly carried out, that the spirit leaves the body and is capable of being reincarnated. It is the most important duty of the deceased's children to ensure that the cremation rites are properly carried out for their parents.

The spirit is rewarded or punished according to its *karma*. Following cremation, reincarnation can take place and usually the spirit returns to the same family in the fourth generation. A female can come back as a male and *vice versa*. There are no constraints. Two people may even be reincarnated in one person. The reverse is true. Murni's father has so far been reincarnated in two people, first as a girl and then as a boy, both of whom are living and displaying his old characteristics. I have even heard that someone's lower body is the reincarnation of one person and his upper body is the reincarnation of another.

The Balinese make offerings in the family temple to all their ancestors generally, and not to specific ancestors. The deified family ancestors can help the family if they are accorded respect. The reverse is also true: they can cause trouble to the family if they are not treated properly. The Balinese therefore take care to invite them to ceremonies, make regular offerings to them and maintain their shrines. Ceremonies are conducted in the best and most pleasing ways possible so as to entertain them.

Ancestors more than four generations back begin to lose their identities and their names are probably forgotten. They may already have been reincarnated. Clifford Geertz, the American anthropologist, calls this 'genealogical amnesia'.

Low Spirits

Low spirits live on the ground and receive their offerings there. They are called *butas* and *kalas*, an expression often translated as 'demons', but they really represent the powers and energies of the earth. *Butas* and *kalas* cannot turn corners, so there are short walls in front of gates, whose purpose is to keep them away from the family compound. They are chthonic powers and so receive their offerings on the ground or close to it. Although they are potentially dangerous and disruptive forces, given the right offerings of blood and raw meat they can be transformed into positive and protective spirits. At a temple festival the priest presents the *caru* offerings on the day before it starts or at midday on the first day in order to purify the area before the gods descend and occupy it. Offerings are also placed in the four directions at crossroads by the priest, who calls on them from the four directions and invites them to eat. The congregation dances around the offerings, yelling and shouting, in an anti-clockwise direction, breaking, throwing and destroying them.

The *butas* and *kalas* were created out of rage. Siwa cursed his beautiful wife Uma in heaven and she descended to earth in anger in the form of Durga. At the crossroads she divided into five—the four directions and the centre. The five Durgas plotted to destroy the world. Regretting what he had done, Siwa cursed himself and became the monster Kala Rudra. He went in search and found her at the crossroads. The five Durgas requested that he touch them. He did and numerous *butas* and *kalas* were created and spread in all directions. Brahma, Wisnu and Iswara were worried and descended to find Kala Rudra and Durga and staged a shadow puppet play for them. Kala Rudra and Durga were ashamed and transformed themselves to their benign forms of Siwa and Uma and the *butas* and *kalas* were changed to nymphs after eating their offerings. The myth explains the origin of the *caru* offerings, the role of temple entertainment and the transformative effect on the audience.

Is there really a God of Thieves?

Yes; one of the more curious and shadowy Balinese gods is the God of Thieves, Pelinggih Sang Hyang Maling. Two temples are dedicated to him: Besikalung Temple near the Hoo River and Petali Temple in Jatiluwih village. There are few visitors to the temples and no priests.

Nobody knows how the god fits into the Balinese Hindu religion or the reason the temples were built. According to Nengah Bawa Atmaja, a local scholar, the Balinese, along with many other societies, have the concept of a 'social bandit', a Robin Hood character, and the God of Thieves represents this ideal.

Harmful People

Leyak are witches, usually but not exclusively married women, who study black magic. They come out at night and most Balinese are scared of them. They do not like to talk or even think about them. The leyak are initiated by a sorcerer, and get their powers through secret rituals in the graveyard. They cause illnesses, death and chaos.

They have the ability to change shape and appear as a wide range of things, such as pigs, goats, snails, monkeys, balls of fire and recently as Honda motorbikes. Sometimes leyak have a burning desire to eat foetuses, newborn babies and small children. Miscarriages and stillbirths are routinely blamed on them.

Likely candidates are women who cannot produce a male heir. Other candidates are abused or jealous women seeking power and revenge over their husbands and those whose mothers or grandmothers have been witches.

Bali is not the only place to have witches. The Salem witchcraft trials of 1692 in Massachusetts resulted in twenty-five hangings and prison for over a hundred women and a few men. There were frequent accusations of witchcraft in Europe from 400 AD until the late 17th century, a surprisingly long time.

On a lesser scale, a person, whom the Balinese will say is a weak person, can go to a sorcerer and explain that he wishes to be able to steal money and become an apprentice. If the sorcerer agrees, he will be trained and asked to use his magic to kill an animal. The spirit of the dead animal, called a Blerong, is captured in a magical amulet and can be called upon to travel at night to steal money. The killing of the animal also brings about the illness or death of a member of the apprentice's family, so an unexpected death can cause suspicion that someone in the family has studied witchcraft. Every shop in Bali has magical defences against these spirits. Bad magic only succeeds against the inadequately protected.

Traditional and Rationalised Religions

Max Weber (1864-1920), the German sociologist, distinguished traditional religions and rationalised religions and said that the rationalised religions evolved from traditional ones, folk cults and folk mythologies. Balinese Hinduism is a good example of a traditional religion.

Traditional religions are close to the gods, more concerned with ritual and less concerned with philosophy. The gods infuse everyday life and are present everywhere: rocks, trees, graveyards, road crossings and so on. Problems of life are dealt with in a piecemeal fashion and typically a ceremony puts things right.

Rationalised religions, like the large world religions, are distant and compartmentalised. They deal with abstract matters in a more or less logical way. There is a concept of the divine, who is a distant character; such as Yahweh in Judaism. To get close to the divine, Weber identified two methods: the first is obeying commands from holy books and the prophets and the second is mysticism.

A Very Social Religion

Most people belong to half a dozen temples, maybe more, and attend them when there is a ceremony. These are social events, attended by friends and relatives. They pay homage to the gods of that temple and enjoy an opportunity to eat, drink, gossip, wear nice clothes, listen to music and watch dances. There are no sermons—only prayers and a blessing. People come and go as they wish.

There is a concentration on image, spectacle and ritual. This is not surprising in a society, which, until very recently, was illiterate. The form of religion takes precedence over its content. Feeling the sense of sacred texts is more important than reading them. The same was true of early Catholicism, which still retains many theatrical features.

Processions

Religious processions have been a regular and important part of devotion in many parts of the world throughout history. Today, even in London, there are occasionally religious processions.

In Bali, however, they are daily occurrences, whether to the sea, rivers, temples, mountains, or graveyards, and they are accompanied by gamelan music. Gods are treated like royalty. They are carried on sedan chairs and sheltered by parasols. Banners surround them. Men carrying spears and daggers protect them. People dress in their best clothes in their presence. Gods visit each other and link temples and draw communities together.

Temple ceremonies typically start by taking the gods, their spirits residing in wooden images called *pratima*, to a holy river or the sea for a symbolic cleaning and purification. Processions may comprise the whole village.

Reality Check

Where does Balinese Hinduism stand amongst the world's religions? There are about 3 million Balinese Hindus. According to the *Annuario Pontificio*, the Vatican Yearbook 2009, the world's total Catholic population rose from 1.131 billion to 1.147 billion between 2006 and 2007, the last year for which accurate figures are available. For the first time there were more Muslims in the world: Catholics accounted for 17.4% of the world population—a stable percentage—while Muslims were growing and accounted for 19.2%. The figures in 2000 were 1.9 billion Christians, 1.2 billion Muslims, 811 million Hindus, 360 million Buddhists, 23 million Sikhs and 14 million Jews.

The Secret of Survival

Bali is a small island in the largest Muslim country in the world. How did it keep its religion and culture untouched by Islam? The answer probably is that Bali was isolated, both commercially and geographically, for most of its history. It did not contribute to the spice trade of the 16th and 17th centuries. The best harbours faced south towards the Indian Ocean, but the merchants, traders and other visitors used the Java Sea to the north where Bali's harbours are poor.

What Happens in the Temple?

Mostly it is:
- Prayers
- Entertainment

Prayers, Balinese Style

Prayers form part of every ceremony. Men sit cross-legged on the ground; women kneel, sitting on their heels, facing the gods and the offerings.

The ladies usually bring their offerings early in the day and place them in front of the gods.

Everyone has a small tray of flowers and a stick of burning incense stuck in the ground in front of them. At large ceremonies someone may announce on a loudspeaker which god is being prayed to. People usually pray five times by holding their palms together, thumbs pointing at or touching their forehead and fingers straight up.

A different coloured flower, held between the fingers, is used for the third, fourth and fifth prayers. At the end of each prayer the flower is flicked forward to carry the prayer. The incense carries the prayer to God, or at least, that is the theoretical explanation. The Balinese do not analyse it; they just do it.

At the end of prayers an attendant or priest sprinkles holy water three times on the hands of those who have prayed. It is sipped. The fourth pouring of holy water is rubbed on the face and hair. Then a few grains of sticky rice are handed to the people. A couple of grains are eaten and the rest are pressed to the forehead, temples and chest at the *chakra* points. The rice serves as a magical protection.

The wife then collects her offerings, leaves the inner temple, where prayers are usually said, and goes home to eat the offerings or she may stay, socialise and take in the entertainment. The essence has already been taken from the offerings and enjoyed by the gods.

Entertainment

The gods have not come all this way not to be entertained. Music, dance and shadow puppet performances are usually on the programme, normally, but not necessarily, in the evening. The holiest dances, purely for the gods, take place in the inner courtyard, whereas performances for two audiences, the gods and humans, are performed in the middle section. Entertainment purely for people is in the outer temple.

Unclean: Keep Out

Like the ancient Greeks, the Balinese do not draw a sharp distinction between the physical and the spiritual. The inner life of a person is reflected by his outward physical appearance.

A deformed person is ritually unclean. During important ceremonies, and this was especially so in the old days, badly handicapped people, like the blind, lame or hare-lipped, were not allowed into the temple. Menstruating women are never allowed in and there are signs outside to that effect.

Chapter 20

Holy Water! Holy Smoke! Holy Moly!

Water, Water, Everywhere

Balinese Hinduism is called the 'Holy Water Religion', *Agama Tirta*, which indicates the centrality of holy water in the religion. It is used in every ceremony, in every ritual, and poured over every offering, every sacrifice, every building, every rice field and every person. This sacred substance cleanses, blesses and purifies. It gets rid of evil and protects. At the end of prayers, the priest pours holy water over the person's head. There are many varieties.

I've Got the Power

Each temple creates its own holy water. It signifies that temple, its god and congregation. It is sacred and the more upstream it comes from, the more potent it is. The most sacred variety is so imbued with the essence of the god that it can be a symbol of the god at other temples. Water from the spring is presented with offerings to the particular god, who is asked to sanctify it. It is treated with the same reverence as the deity.

Priest Makes Holy Water

Both categories of priest, local temple priest, the *pemangku*, and high priest, the *pedanda*, make holy water, using different rituals and mantras. The holy water may be all-purpose, or ritual specific. The most important ritual specific holy water is made by high priests for use at cremations.

Pedanda make holy water every day. When they do this, they are infused with and become Siwa. They make three types of holy water: the first is to purify the body, the second is to purify the mind, and the third is to keep bad thoughts away.

Pemangku, the lay temple priests, make holy water for use in their own temples and purposes associated with the god of that temple. If someone wants the benefits of the powers of that god, he gets holy water from that temple. The holy water the *pemangku* makes is not as powerful as the water made by the *pedanda*.

Dalang, the shadow puppeteers, make holy water too. They make it before performances and dip their puppets into it. The *dalang* is also a priest and the holy water is used in ceremonies carried out by him.

Lay People Make Holy Water

Lay people can make a kind of holy water for restricted purposes. Water is taken from the family well, thrown on to the kitchen roof, and caught in a basket above the person's head. The water runs on to the person's head through the basket. It is imbued with Brahma, the god of fire and kitchens, and purifies a person who has been in contact with a dead person. It is necessary to do this before entering the family compound.

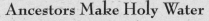

Ancestors Make Holy Water

By placing a bowl of water in a shrine in the family temple and saying a prayer, family members can request the immediate ancestors to make holy water. A bit more ceremony is needed if the ancestors are more distant. The Balinese go to family origin temples to get holy water blessed by the founders of the clan, which will be used in rites of passage ceremonies, such as a birth or wedding.

Holy water container. Balinese Hinduism is called the 'Holy Water Religion', *Agama Tirta*. Holy water is used in every ceremony.

Holy Places, Holy Water

Different kinds of holy water have different powers. For large ceremonies the source is very important. Holy water taken from the wells of special temples is considered to be particularly holy. Some ceremonies require water from certain temples or more than one temple. The huge *Eka Dasa Rudra* ceremony, which takes place only once every hundred Balinese years, requires water from

Mount Semeru in Java, Mount Rinjani in Lombok and the Ganges River in India.

Holy Water Par Excellence

The best holy water is from the Tirta Amreta spring at the north of Besakih. It is the bathing place of all the gods. The water is used in connection with the most important ceremonies throughout Bali. The higher the spring, the better the holy water. Holy water, obtained just by leaving a vessel of clear spring water on the *padmasana* in Besakih, is also regarded as excellent.

Blended Varieties

Like wine, holy water from different sources can be blended and mixed. Blending holy waters symbolically ties communities together. For example, a water temple downstream may have its holy water augmented by holy water from a more important, upstream water temple. Or there may be a mingling of holy water between a local water temple and a village temple.

There is a hierarchy. Holy water is collected from upstream temples and brought to downstream temples, never the other way round—never does an upstream temple collect water from a downstream source. The further upstream the source, the more sacred the water. Major rituals may have their local holy water augmented by distant upstream holy water.

Holy Water Plus Water Equals Holy Water

A large amount of holy water can be made by putting a small amount of holy water into a large container of ordinary pure water. Holy water in the Roman Catholic Church is water blessed by a priest or bishop. The Church has considered the same question and come to the slightly different conclusion that, in their case, once consecrated, more ordinary water can be added to the supply of holy water, and the entire quantity of water remains consecrated, provided that the amount added is less than the amount of water that was originally there.

Carrying Holy Water

If not handled properly, holy water loses its power. It must be treated with the utmost respect and kept in a clean, preferably new, container. Any bottle will do, even an old whiskey bottle, if clean.

It should be held high and only in the right hand, and if possible, handed to another person using the right hand whilst holding the right elbow with the left hand. Women frequently carry containers of holy water on their heads. Put it on the floor, walk over it, treat it badly, and it loses its power.

Holy Smoke

Incense carries prayers to God, or at least, that is the theory.

Sanskrit, Holy Talk

Sanskrit is the language of the gods, very powerful, and never translated. It is only studied by high priests, is the language of literary works and prayer, and spoken by very few people. The same is true in India. Quite a few words of Sanskrit origin are found in the languages of those parts of Indonesia which had contact with Indian civilisation.

William Jones (1746-1794) was a judge serving in Calcutta in India in the late 18th century. He was a brilliant linguist and poet and published poems in Greek at the age of fifteen. Studying twenty-eight languages he had a thorough knowledge of thirteen of them. After arriving in Calcutta in 1785 he studied Sanskrit and uncovered great similarities between Sanskrit, which was an ancient Indian language, and the classical tongues of Greek and Latin. He thought that they were so similar that they must have come from a common source. He reported this flash of insight to an astonished Asiatic Society of Bengal in February 1786 and it transformed language studies. Linguistics thereupon became a scientific discipline. He said,

> The Sanskrit language, whatever be its antiquity, is of a wonderful structure, more perfect than the Greek, more copious than the Latin, and more exquisitely refined than either, yet bearing to both of them a stronger affinity, both in the roots of verbs, and in the forms of grammar, than could probably have been produced by accident; so strong, indeed, that no philologer could examine them all three, without believing them to have sprung from some common source, which, perhaps, no longer exists.

Subsequent research has shown that most European languages are related to one other (except Basque, Finnish, Hungarian and Estonian) and even to some Indian and Persian languages. There was a mother tongue called 'Proto-Indo-European' which was spoken 6,000 years ago by Central Asian people who domesticated the horse, got on them and migrated to north Pakistan around 1600 BC, moved on and thereby provided the base for most Eurasian languages.

Kawi, the Old Language

Kawi is Old Javanese, the language of the Hindu kingdoms of Java from the 8th to the 14th centuries. It became the language of the courts of Bali, but has not been spoken since the 16th century. Nearly half the vocabulary is derived from Sanskrit.

Kawi is used for the epic stories, shadow puppet performances and poetry. It is not understood by most Balinese, who rely on the clowns and servants to translate it into Balinese at the dance dramas.

Chapter 21

Christians and Muslims

Other Religions
The only religions of any size, apart from the Balinese Hindus, are:
- The Christians
- The Muslims

First Christian Commits Murder
In 1867 a Dutch Reformed Church missionary, Jacob de Vroom and his associate, Reverend Van Eck, appeared in Bali. Their mission was not a great success. In 1875 Van Eck got ill and left and on 8 June 1881 de Vroom was murdered. Over the fourteen year period they succeeded in converting only one person, Van Eck's servant, Gusti Wayan Karangasen. The first Christian convert murdered de Vroom. Not a great start.

How did it happen? Rather surprisingly Gusti Wayan was accepted in his village despite his conversion to Christianity. This is unusual as converts normally become outcasts. However, he had problems at work and his wife was implicated in a financial scandal. Thinking he would find comfort from that nice missionary, de Vroom, he went to Singaraja in north Bali.

De Vroom lived in very luxurious quarters. Instead of providing comfort, he gave Gusti Wayan a lecture on the Ten Commandments, followed by one on the Lord's Prayer. Gusti Wayan was deeply disillusioned. Then, after two of de Vroom's Muslim servants angered him still further, he murdered de Vroom and was later hanged.

Not surprisingly, the Dutch authorities decided to exclude missionaries from Bali and did so successfully for the next seventy years.

Tsang Ho Tan, Chinese Christian
In 1929 the Dutch Governor General in Java allowed Tsang Ho Tan, a

Chinese representative of the Christian and Missionary Alliance, to stay in Bali to look after Chinese Christians, many of whom had married Balinese wives. He was told that he was not allowed to proselytise and, if he did, he would be expelled.

At first, he seemed to have taken note, but then he started preaching and attracting followers. In June 1931 he was joined by a Christian missionary, Dr J.A. Jaffray, an itinerant minister with the Christian and Missionary Alliance. They started baptising in secret, first Chinese and then half-Balinese people, and finally full-blooded Balinese. By the end of 1931 they had forty-seven converts and more Balinese were getting interested.

Dr Jaffray started denouncing Balinese Hinduism as pagan and Tsang Ho insisted that Christians reject it. They were getting bold and started baptising in public. In 1932 a public baptism took place and it caused a sensation. Many Balinese were very annoyed. The Dutch Resident Officer insisted that they must stop carrying on aggressive missionary work but the warning went unheeded and they baptised another seventy-five. They had 266 converts. Tsang Ho was ordered to leave Bali in 1933.

The cost of conversion was high. By rejecting their culture the Balinese converts were ostracised by their villages. They were denied burial places and their water supply was cut off. They could not rent land and their crops were destroyed. The Balinese Hindus believed that the gods were angry at the infiltration of the new religion.

In 1934 the Dutch Reformed Church in east Java sent Dr Hendrik Kraemer to Bali to assess matters and the following year they took care of Christians, who had been rejected by their families. In 1935 they sent two Javanese ministers and the Balinese Church remained under the pastoral care of east Java until 1942.

Christian Groups

There were two Protestant groups in Bali: one group which remained loyal to the Christian and Missionary Alliance, whose headquarters was in Makassar, south Sulawesi, and the other group centred on the two Javanese ministers. The two Protestant groups united in 1938 and became the Union of Balinese Christians. There was also a group of Roman Catholics, who were influenced by a Catholic priest, who had permission to work among Dutch Catholic soldiers and civil servants in Bali.

Numbers

The Protestant community established itself in Blimbingsari in west Bali in 1939. The first Balinese minister, Made Rungu, was ordained in 1942. In that year there were 200 Protestants, in 1950 there were 500 and in 1960 there were 2,000. The numbers steadily rose until in 1965 there were 6,500. In 2005, about 2% of the population was Christian, pretty evenly split between Protestants and Catholics.

Contextualisation

In 1972 an important milestone was reached. The Protestant authorities resolved to rid themselves of the anti-cultural legacy of Tsang Ho and, as they put it, contextualise Balinese culture. What they meant was that the Church should use Balinese architecture in its buildings, so that churches would have an outer court and an inner court and be entered through a traditional Balinese split gate, and face the mountains where the Balinese gods reside. Services would be enhanced by gamelan music, Balinese dances, and shadow puppet performances. Paintings and woodcarvings would decorate the place. There would even be offerings. The copying and proselytising nature of Christianity caused and still causes tensions.

Roman Catholics

Catholicism has existed in Indonesia since the arrival of the Portuguese in the 16th century, but it did not make headway in Bali until the 1930s. The first missionaries arrived in Bali on Easter Day 1936 and shortly after converted a number of people in Tuka, a village which is about 6 miles (10 kilometres) north of Denpasar. Now there is a seminary in Tuka and over 1,400 Catholics live there.

In 1937, seventy-two people from Tuka and another thirty from Gumbrih, a village in Jembrana, west Bali, were baptised at the Tuka Catholic Church. The head of the Tuka Catholic Church, Father Simon Buis, requested a plot of land for his congregation from the Dutch administration and Bali's Board of Kings and was granted a piece in the lush forest of Pangkung Sente in Jembrana.

In September 1940 Father Buis and his followers moved to the forest and settled in a village, now known as Palasari. At that time nutmeg plants called *pala* surrounded it. The rest of the word *sari* means 'essence'. It is 75 miles (120 kilometres) from Denpasar and in 1940 that would have been a month's journey by foot, but now it is three hours by car.

The congregation grew rapidly. Father Buis requested and received another 494 acres (200 hectares). First they built schools and a health clinic and then a permanent church, the Sacred Heart (*Hati Kudus*) Catholic Church. It was started in 1954 and finished on 13 December 1958. On 36,000 square metres it is a blend of Gothic arches and Balinese styles, designed by Father Ignatius A.M. de Vriese, who was assisted by two Balinese architects, Ida Bagus Tugur from Denpasar and I Gusti Nyoman Rai from Dalung, Kuta.

Palasari village has eleven *banjars*, three of which are Catholic, seven Hindu and one Muslim. At present there are about 1,500 Catholics in Palasari, the largest Catholic community in Bali. The figure would be even greater if a large number had not gone to Lampung province in southern Sumatra and Umaha in Sulawesi as part of the government's transmigration policy. The programme moved people from densely populated areas to less populous ones, mainly from Java, but also to a lesser extent from Bali and Madura. It swamped tribal peoples with those more loyal to the centre and had a major impact on the demographics of some regions; for example, 60% of the three million people of the province of Lampung in 1981 were transmigrants.

As with the Protestants, the Catholics use Hindu paraphernalia, which causes some resentment among the Balinese Hindus. They even use the tall offering poles, *penjor*, and temple decorations and Balinese formal dress during Christian festivals and masses.

The first missionaries arrived in Bali on Easter Day 1936 and shortly after converted a number of people in Tuka.

Muslims

Islam was a late arrival in Indonesia. One of the earliest surviving indications is a tombstone in east Java, carved about 1082, but they have made up for lost time. Indonesia is now the largest Muslim country in the world, but for the most part it is a rather laid back version, influenced by pre-existing animism.

It is believed traders to Bali from Gujarat in western India and the Middle East brought their religion with them between the 15th and 16th centuries. There may have been a special Islamic mission to Bali to spread the word, but it does not seem to have made much headway. There is, however, a memory of them. Many temples, especially on the coast, have shrines dedicated to Muslim ancestors and they receive offerings and dances during temple celebrations in the same way as for Balinese ancestors, except that the offerings are pork-free.

Invitations

It is also possible that some Balinese kings invited Muslim communities to Bali. A.A.W. Wirawan, the author of *The History of Islam in Bali* states that King Dalem Ketut Ngulesir (1380-1460), the king in Gelgel, visited the Majapahit kingdom in Java, which was Hindu, and brought back forty Muslims, who established a Muslim village called Kampung Gelgel. There is a record that the Islamic kingdom of Demak in central Java sent an envoy to the Balinese King Dalem Baturenggong (1460-1550) to teach Islam, but the king and his subjects refused to convert.

Nirartha, who was the court priest of Dalem Baturenggong during the heyday of the Gelgel dynasty in the 16th century, travelled all over Bali accompanied by a faithful Muslim servant. The servant is worshipped in several temples as the ancestor from Mecca. In contrast, although the Dutch were in Bali too, there is no shrine to the ancestor from Holland.

Refugees

Muslim Bugis soldiers and traders from Makassar in south Sulawesi fled to Bali after having been defeated by the Dutch in the 17th century. They landed in Kepoan on Serangan Island in Badung regency, where there is still a small Bugis community, and in Loloan in Jembrana in west Bali. There is also a group in Klungkung who may have the same origin.

Mercenaries

There are communities in Pagayaman in Buleleng regency in north Bali, which has about 5,000 people, and Nyuling and Kecicang in Karangasem in east Bali. Balinese rulers often hired them as mercenaries as in the case of Pagayaman. In the 18th century King Ki Gusti Anglurah Panji Sakti hired and gave the Muslim community a plot of land and even initiated the construction of a grand mosque in Kajanan village in Singaraja. In Karangasem the nobility provided financial assistance to Muslims wanting to perform the Haj pilgrimage to Mecca.

Muslims also came to Bali from Lombok, part of which came under Balinese control in the reign of King Dalem Baturenggong in the 16th century. There was a gap of a century and Balinese rule resumed at the end of the 17th century. Princely families took Muslims from Lombok as servants and their descendants are in Karangasem. There is also a small Sasak Lombok community in Kramas, Gianyar.

Under the Dutch Madurese fishermen and dry-field farmers from east Java settled in the northern and southern coastal areas of west Bali. As Singaraja and Denpasar grew, traders and workers travelled to these cities and mosques were built.

Economic Migrants

As tourism increased from the 1970s Muslims particularly from Java, Lombok and Sumatra came to find work. They cook and sell food like *saté* on the pavements and walk the streets pushing carts of noodle soup. When they are successful, their family joins them. They work for lower wages than the Balinese and during the boom in Kuta and Nusa Dua in the 1980s many were employed on road and construction projects. The numbers are not really known as many are unregistered and there are conflicting figures. One official figure is that in 2000, 330,000 people or 11% of the population of Bali were migrants, including 6.8% from Java. According to the Ministry of Religion, Muslim places of religion rose from 359 in 1983 to 584 in 2002.

Bali Bombings

There was concern that there would be revenge after the Bali bombings in 2002 and 2005, but there was not. Quite the reverse. There was a great outpouring of solidarity from the Balinese. Many of the victims were themselves Muslims from Denpasar. The first aid workers who arrived were Muslim and Muslim leaders condemned the atrocities. Life, however, was made harder for migrants. The rules on migrant identity cards (KIPP) were changed by the municipal government of Denpasar, so that a migrant had to procure letters from his home village as well as his employer and landlord in Bali. The official cost of the card was also increased. Rightly or wrongly migrants are seen as a threat by many Balinese.

Chapter 22

Rice Glorious Rice

World's Most Important Crop

Rice is the world's most important crop and the staple food of half the world's population. Most of Bali's hills are like giant green staircases covered in terraces segregated into rice fields. Rice cultivation in Bali goes back at least 1,500 years and the current method of irrigation is at least 1,000 years old. Sir Stamford Raffles was impressed by Balinese rice cultivation when, as the British Lieutenant Governor, he visited the ruler of Buleleng in north Bali in 1815. In the well irrigated south part of Bali, wet rice is grown, while in the dryer areas to the north, dry rice is grown.

Origins

It is usually claimed that China discovered rice about 8,000 years ago and rice growing spread southwards from China. Recent discoveries suggest that it may have existed earlier than that in mainland Southeast Asia. Neolithic rice growing seems to have occurred in the Sakai Cave area in the Malay Peninsula 8,000 to 10,000 years ago.

There are no carvings of rice on the 9th century temple of Borobudur in Java, but there is an example of millet. Irrigated rice was established in Java shortly before the ascendancy of the Majapahit empire in the 13th century and may have come from India rather than the north. In Bali an inscription dated 1027 AD refers to rice terraces and mentions the construction of a dam. Rice finally reached Australia and California in the early part of the 20th century.

The Balinese have their own account of the origin of rice. There are four sacred directions, each of which has a sacred colour, being red, black, white and yellow. Siwa, the leading Balinese Hindu god, intended to give rice of all these colours to the Balinese, but there was a problem.

He sent a bird to bring the rice but the bird was disobedient and ate the yellow rice—except for a little bit which it hid under the eaves of its house. That is why yellow rice does not grow in Bali and can only be made by mixing turmeric with white rice. The purpose of the story is clear. For ritual purposes there must be four colours of rice, one for each direction, but there are only three: white, red and black. The myth permits the belief that there was also originally yellow rice.

Eating Rice

Rice is the staple diet of the Balinese. Cooked rice, usually steamed, is the central component of any meal. It is never eaten alone but rather with various condiments and side dishes. A rice grain is about 82% carbohydrate, 10% water, 7% protein and 1% fibre, fat and minerals. Much of the protein and fat is lost through milling, which is carried out to make it white. The husks are removed and polishing powder is added to remove the last of them. Before cooking rice is washed to get rid of the powder.

Nasi, the word for 'rice', also means 'meal'. The Balinese cannot conceive of a meal without rice and the number of words for rice indicates its importance:

• *Padi*: rice growing in the field or rice that has been cut but not threshed, or cut and threshed but not husked (the husk and bran are removed at the mill, or in the old days by pounding with a mortar and pestle); the English word 'paddy' comes from *padi*

Balinese rice farmer. Rice is the staple diet of the Balinese. Cooked rice, usually steamed, is the central component of any meal.

• *Gabah*: unmilled rice that has been separated from the stems
• *Beras*: milled, uncooked rice
• *Nasi*: cooked rice

Rice steamers were traditionally made from bamboo but electric ones are now usual. The Balinese like steamed rice, which keeps what is left of the vitamins and proteins after milling and polishing. Once steamed, it can be eaten.

Types of Rice
There are four different types of rice:
- *Barak*: red rice
- *Injin*: black rice, which is a dark, blackberry purple
- *Ketan*: white sticky, glutinous rice
- *Beras*: ordinary white rice

White rice is the most widely planted. Red rice is a dry field variety, grown high up the mountain slopes above the irrigated areas. Black rice is usually planted a few rows deep at the edges of white rice fields.

It's a Miracle
During the 1950s Indonesia was forced to import nearly a million tons of rice every year. After 1965, President Suharto made self-sufficiency a major goal. *Padi Bali*, traditional Balinese rice, grown from time immemorial, takes 210 days to grow, the length of a Balinese year. Planting is staggered but some rice is always growing somewhere. That started when there was famine in Bali and the king promised the gods that if the rain came he would sacrifice his only son when the harvest ended. The rains came and there was a great crop. The king was crafty and saved his son by ordering his people to plant small areas of rice continually so that harvesting never finished.

The International Rice Research Institute in the Philippines developed a high-yield, disease and insect-resistant strain of dwarf rice in the 1960s, which could produce many more tons of rice per hectare (2.47 acres) than *Padi Bali*. It takes about ninety days to grow. Bali was one of the first places in the world to test 'new' or 'miracle' rice and the Green Revolution.

New rice was planted from 1970 to 1979 to feed Indonesia's increasing population and there was a 43% increase in production. There could be three crops of new rice a year, but in practice only two are grown in order to allow the fields to rest in between. If a farm of about 1 hectare produces an average yield, it could feed a family of six. New rice has now largely replaced *Padi Bali* except for ceremonial purposes. In the 1980s

Indonesia even exported a few hundred thousand tons of rice.

The disadvantage with the Green Revolution has been that the wholesale adoption of miracle rice in Southeast Asia has led to a rice monoculture, making crops more vulnerable to pests and disease and more dependent on pesticides. The new varieties taste bland and have lower nutrient content. It has also increased unemployment. New rice is harvested with large sickles, rather than a small knife, so fewer people are required. Further, in Bali fertiliser containing high levels of phosphate and nitrogen has travelled down the rivers and destroyed coral reefs on the coast.

New rice has also resulted in a decline of income for the temples. Villagers donate their labour to the temple, which used to hire out large communities at harvesting time. With fewer people required to harvest new rice an important source of revenue has been lost to the temples.

World Market

Indonesia does not figure in the leading world rice exporters. Thailand is the number one exporter. Indonesia imports a small amount.

Rice Cycle

After harvesting, rice fields are flooded to deprive pests of a home. They look like reflecting mirrors before being ploughed by cows. Balinese cows are handsome and light tanned, more like deer. They do not graze but are kept in small open thatched huts and fed grass every day by their owners. Much of the grass, grown on the supporting walls of rice terraces, is cut by hand-sickle. This gives Bali's landscape its striking manicured appearance. Tractors are used in some parts of Bali.

The rice fields are artificial ponds which are fertilised and planted by hand with seedlings over several days. This is carried out in a prescribed order. The first nine seedlings are planted in a square starting at the centre and then spiralling out in a clockwise direction. The pattern represents the Balinese mandala, *nawa-sanga*.

The fields must be kept flooded while the plants are growing. Yellow-green shoots sprout up in the silvery water. When the rice is ripening, birds are not welcome. Scarecrows, wind chimes, bamboo bird-scarers and pulleys of cloth are erected to frighten the birds. People keep watch and yell.

Two months later the rice will have grown taller and green. When the tops droop, the plants are mature and ready to harvest. In the old days people would go into the fields quietly with a small knife called an *ani ani* hidden in their hands so as not to frighten the rice. These days sickles are used. Harvesting involves gangs of men and women and keeps community living and working relevant. In England, 60 or 70 years ago, a whole village would turn out for hay-making or harvesting, but now a single tractor can do the work of fifty men, women and children. Farming in England has become a solitary occupation and village life has changed forever. After harvesting, the stubble in the Balinese rice fields is flooded, so that the old rice stalks slowly decompose under the water. Alternatively the stubble is burnt.

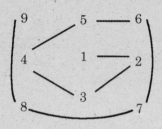

Order of planting rice. The first nine seedlings are planted in a square starting at the centre and then spiralling out in a clockwise direction. The pattern represents the Balinese mandala, *nawa-sanga*.

Water Buffalo Races

At planting time water buffalo races are held in west Bali. This helps prepare the rice fields and is fun at the same time. The water buffalo wear gilded leather ornaments, silk banners on their yokes, bells on their necks. Young men ride them and bets are placed. At a signal they're off and running, wallowing as quick as possible across a muddy rice field, which is usefully churned up. A referee judges the winner, which is not the fastest, but the most elegant.

Dewi Sri, the Rice Goddess

Almost all cereal growing societies believe in a female grain goddess. There was the Graeco-Roman Ceres and the Anglo-Saxon Corn Mother. Dewi Sri, the rice goddess, is the favourite manifestation of God among the Balinese. She is male and female, as indeed are all the gods, people and things in the cosmos. At important times in the rice cycle, images of Dewi Sri, made of rice stalks, are set up in the rice fields, in the shape of two triangles with a pinched waist. This is called a *Cili*.

There is a nice story of Dewi Sri's origin. Anta, a deformed junior

Dewi Sri, the rice goddess, is the favourite manifestation of God among the Balinese.

god was depressed by his failure to find any gift for Batara Guru's new temple. Batara Guru is a manifestation of Siwa. Anta wept three tears, which turned into eggs. An eagle swept down and forced him to break the eggs. He smashed two of them but the third then hatched and released a beautiful baby girl. She was given to Batara Guru's wife, Uma, to be breast fed and was named Samyam Sri. Sri grew up to be very beautiful and Batara Guru lusted after her. This was forbidden, of course, as she was technically his daughter.

He tried several times to rape her. This angered the other gods so much that, to rescue her, they killed her and buried her body. Plants grew from various parts of it. Sticky rice grew from her breasts and ordinary rice from her eyes. In remorse Batara Guru gave these to man as food. Sri became a goddess called Dewi Sri and the spirit of fertility, protectress of the rice fields and guardian of rice barns.

Dewi Sri, as befits her importance, is a symbol of Bali and appears in many guises. She is also very popular in Sunda and Java. She is the spouse of Rambut Sedana, who is regarded as an aspect of Wisnu.

Ceremonies

The Balinese respect the rice plant as a living female spirit. Rites of passage are conducted as befits a divine being. When the seeds are developing the rice is said to be pregnant. When they appear, a birth ceremony is performed which includes 'singing to the baby'. Each stage in the rice cycle is carried out on an auspicious day and accompanied by appropriate offerings.

The rice farmers carry out rituals at water opening, field preparations, transplanting, during growth, at panicle appearance, flowering and harvesting. Some are performed at small temporary shrines in the upstream corner of the rice fields. Others are performed at the water temples.

The upstream corner of the rice field is sacred. Offerings are made at this spot to Dewi Sri. At harvest time a sacred image of Dewi Sri is made from the rice that grows closest to this place. It is not eaten and is carried to the rice barn and given offerings.

There is a Balinese saying: 'As the rice bows its head when it is heavy and ready for harvesting, so a wise man bends his head and is silent.'

Subak

Every rice farmer belongs to a *subak*. The members of the *subak* go to the water temple priests, who set the cropping patterns and irrigation schedules. They attempt to optimise water sharing and reduce pests through co-ordinated fallow periods. The trade-off is between water sharing and pest control.

Water Temples

Karl Marx (1818-1883) had proposed that Asian kings derived their powers from their control over irrigation and gave Bali as an example, but he was wrong. It was not possible in Bali. No single kingdom controlled an entire river.

The Dutch and their successors, the Indonesian government, did not understand the power of the water temples. The Dutch were more concerned about collecting tax. As temples and priests posed no threat, they were not of interest. The Indonesian government did not even know that the water temples existed.

When new rice was introduced in the 1970s, on the advice of consultants from the Asian Development Bank, the Indonesian government passed laws demanding constant cropping. Farmers were forced to abandon traditional cropping patterns. Soon there was chaos in water scheduling and terrible outbreaks of pests. Harvests failed and there was hunger. The Bank now acknowledges that the results were catastrophic. It was only when the farmers returned to their traditional methods that harvests recovered.

It was not until well into the 1980s that the role of the water temples in setting cropping patterns and controlling irrigation was appreciated, thanks largely to anthropologist Stephen Lansing, who describes the situation in his book *Priests and Programmers*.

Offerings

Rice is an indispensable part of nearly every offering. Pure rice is used without the everyday additions of sweet potato. New rice is just as acceptable as *Padi Bali*, except for using with the *penjor*.

And What's More

Rice fields do not just produce rice. They are a rich source of protein; there are dragonflies, frogs, eels and fish in the fields. Balinese children love to hunt dragonflies with long,

In the evening, the duck farmer collects his ducks from the rice paddies. They follow him home, keeping a beady eye on his fluttering piece of cloth tied to a big stick.

sticky rods, pull off their wings, pierce them alive on a stick and roast them. Tasty!

Rice fields also provide a living for ducks. Balinese ducks cannot fly and can be safely left alone in a wet rice field. After the harvest, the duck farmer brings in his flock, which spends all day clearing up old pieces of grain and disposing of insects, like brown planthoppers, that would otherwise destroy the next rice crop. In the evening, the farmer collects his ducks, which follow him home, keeping a beady eye on his fluttering piece of cloth tied to a big stick.

Alcohol can be made from rice. *Brem*, pronounced 'brum', is rice wine made from glutinous rice. It is used in almost all ceremonies. The rice is cooked for hours and yeast is added. It then ferments for a few days and is drained into a pan and ready to serve.

In the old days the Balinese used rice paste as a cosmetic. It was also a useful protection against the sun.

Genetic Code of Rice

In April 2002 the genetic code of rice was published and it was discovered that rice has 15,000 more genes than humans. Perhaps rice is more complicated than a human being.

Chapter 23

Balinese Eating Habits

The Family Meal
It is very hard for the tourist to get Balinese food in Bali, which is partly explained by Balinese eating habits. A Balinese family rarely sits down to eat together. The concept of the family meal is almost unknown. They rarely (if ever) give dinner parties. Snacking is popular, and then, but only then, do they eat together.

Two major meals are usually eaten shortly after the household's rice has finished cooking and has cooled somewhat. This occurs between 10 am and 12 noon. A second meal is eaten right before or right after dusk around 5 pm to 6.30 pm. There is no attempt to co-ordinate household members' activities so that a joint meal can be taken.

Rice Rules
Most meals revolve around rice as the prime focus. Rice is 'breakfast, lunch and tea'. Indeed the Balinese word *ngajeng* (in Middle Balinese) means both 'to eat' and 'to eat rice', which gives an idea of the central importance of rice. The Indonesian word *nasi* means both 'food' and 'rice'.

A Bit on the Side
The Balinese add a small amount of whatever happens to be available that day to a plate of rice: perhaps steamed green vegetables, a bit of fish, some rice field eels, a little *tempé* , maybe tofu and the like. *Tempé* is a very healthy fermented soya bean cake from Eastern Indonesia. It is full of protein and fibre. Insofar as is possible, all items should be kept distinct on the plate. Intentional mixing or stirring of components, especially where white rice is involved, is considered to be the behaviour of young children who 'do not yet understand'.

Almost always there is a hot chilli *sambel*. *Sambel* are small dishes served on the side, consisting of red chillies, sweet purple shallots, small garlic cloves and shrimp paste. Food is served at room temperature.

Formal Gatherings

Even at formal gatherings, such as weddings, there is no set meal. Guests arrive at the family compound at different times. It is quite possible to be invited to a friend's house in Bali and find your hosts have already eaten and you are on your own! The food is ready and waiting buffet style. People help themselves.

The Balinese believe that food contains *amerta*, the life force, which is brought alive by cooking, and talking can disturb it. People usually eat quietly, sitting alone. Social interaction is kept to a minimum. While several compound members may eat at the same time, they do not really eat 'together' in the same sense as in the West. There is practically no sharing or exchange of food. Food, once on the plate, is almost never eaten by any other person except in the case of infants eating with parents.

It is a cardinal rule of Balinese etiquette that one should never eat the leftovers of a social equal or inferior. All food, whether or not the meal is finished, becomes a leftover in this context as soon as a person begins to eat from his plate. The idea, much less the actual act, of eating such leftovers evokes a strong physical sensation of disgust. A quite different situation occurs when a social inferior consumes the leftovers of a social superior, for example, a servant in a *brahmana* priest's house or eating an offering after a temple ceremony. In these cases eating the leftovers is welcomed and affirms the patron-client relationship.

When family members do eat together, they rarely sit facing one another or even close. If they do sit close to one another, they usually put their bodies in postures which indicate non-interaction. The conversation, if any, is normally rather subdued, involving emotionally neutral or pleasant topics. One should never discuss unpleasant or sad topics like illnesses or accidents.

If a conversation does take place, the act of eating should not be interrupted. It is called 'leaving one's rice'. If a friend enters, he is politely invited to join, but the newcomer nearly always refuses and moves on immediately to talk with other people who are not eating. It is a gross breach of etiquette to interrupt another's meal. This even extends to breaking a person's concentration by joking with them.

Food Placement

The Balinese mandala, called *nawa-sanga*, which is a map of the cosmic order, is relevant to the placing of food. The mandala is a star with eight arms, pointing to the eight compass points, plus the centre. Each point is associated with a Hindu god and that god's consort, a colour, and many other things.

A special Balinese feast, *Ebat*, for family and friends at big occasions, like a tooth-filing, has dishes placed in the direction of the colour of the food, so green dishes are in Wisnu's north direction, red, bloody *lawar* in Brahma's south direction, yellow turmeric in Mahadewa's west direction and white coconut in Iswara's east direction. In the centre is Siwa with a mixture of white, red, yellow and black dishes.

Finger Food

Finger bowls of water are passed around, one per person. The Balinese prefer to eat with their hands and never use knives. At most, they may use a fork and spoon, believing that food tastes better by hand, untouched by metal. Like many Asians they only use their right hands. The left hand is used for washing the body and is unclean. In fact it is quite difficult to use the left hand as it supports the plate.

They usually take a bit of meat or vegetable and set it on the rice and then add *sambel* and/or salt, if these are desired. A portion is then taken up using all four extended fingertips and thumb of the right hand and placed in the mouth while the head is tilted slightly back. Meanwhile, the plate is raised to just below the mouth. Sometimes the rice, especially sticky rice, is pressed slightly a few times just before it is taken up in the fingers. This is done to ensure that it will not fall apart on the way to the mouth. It also improves the taste. Each handful of food is chewed thoroughly, often with the mouth open, and swallowed before the next handful is taken in.

It is bad form to consume everything on one's plate before adding more. A portion should remain on the plate if more is to be taken. A small portion of rice should be left when one is finished for the invisible spirits and the spiritual siblings. The siblings are called the *Kanda Empat* and are conceived and born at the same time as the individual. After finishing the meal, the plate is rinsed off and returned to the shelf or if it is a banana leaf simply thrown into the rubbish bin and left to bio-degrade.

The Balinese prefer to eat with their hands and never use knives. At most, they may use a fork and spoon, believing that food tastes better by hand.

Dessert

There is no concept of three courses—or dessert for that matter (except possibly fresh fruit in season). Guests visiting a Balinese family are almost always immediately presented with a selection of sweet cakes and a beverage before they partake of the main (savoury) course.

Beverages

Woody Allen observed, 'Why does Man kill? He kills for food; and not just for food: frequently there must be a beverage.' Alcohol is hardly ever served in Bali. Normally, it is sweet tea or water. If alcohol is served, it will probably be *tuak*, *arak* or *brem*, although Balinese yuppies go for Hatten Wines.

Tuak

Tuak is made by cutting the undeveloped flower of either the coconut or sugar palm tree. The sugary liquid that exudes is collected in a bamboo container and fermented. It is the 'toddy' of the English colonialists and has about the same alcoholic content as beer.

Arak

Arak is distilled *tuak*. It has a much higher alcoholic content than *tuak* and is colourless with a very sharp, biting taste. As the taste is unpleasant, the Balinese mix it with spices. It can also be added to coffee or mixed with *brem*. Having no sugar content, *arak* keeps for a long time.

Brem

Brem, pronounced 'brum', is rice wine. Like *arak*, it is used in almost all ceremonies. It is a pleasant, sweet drink, made from glutinous rice or sticky rice (as it is also called), and can be drunk neat, over ice or mixed with *arak*. The rice is cooked for hours and yeast is added. It is then allowed to ferment for a few days, whereupon the *brem* is drained into a pan and ready to serve.

Hatten Wines

Hatten Wines started production in Sanur in 1994 with Alphonse Lavelle grapes. Wine buffs derided them, but they were wrong. The winery was awarded a Bronze Medal at the London International Wine and Spirit Competition for its Alexandria White Wine in 2003. Hatten Rosé is a pleasant, medium-dry, fruity wine, which is a good accompaniment to many Balinese dishes.

Going Home

After eating, guests go home quickly. As they jokingly say *Sudah makan, pulang*! 'Eaten now, going home!'

Hot Dogs

The Balinese classify foods into cool, neutral and hot. Pork and freshwater prawns are cool, while the fruit of a pineapple and chicken are hot. Durian is hot and so is alcohol, so they should not be taken together.

Mangosteen fruit is cool and is a good balance to durian. Dog is very hot, hence the popularity of 'hot dogs'.

The distinctions are used primarily in traditional healing and are not important in terms of everyday eating. The purpose is to maintain or re-establish a balanced body temperature. Remedies are designed for the individual and his or her illness and usually comprise a number of substances mixed with others, such as egg white, honey or salt. All parts of the plant or tree are used, roots, bark, flesh, leaves, fruit and sap, but the knowledge is dying out. Sometimes the traditional healers make up the prescriptions, but sometimes they instruct the patient's family what to do. A trip to the pharmacy is a lot easier.

Angela Hobart has researched traditional healing methods and produced the following classification table of plant substances according to their properties as cool, neutral and hot:

Plant	Roots	Bark	Flesh	Leaves	Fruit
Dadap	Cool	Neutral		Cool	
Betel	Cool	Neutral		Cool	Hot
Frangipani		Neutral	Hot		
Hibiscus	Cool		Cool	Cool	
Jackfruit	Neutral			Neutral	
Kasiligwi	Cool		Cool	Cool	
Mangosteen	Hot	Hot		Hot	
Onion(white)			Neutral	Cool	
Pineapple	Cool		Neutral	Cool	
Papaya	Cool		Neutral	Cool	
Pule	Cool			Cool	
Sembung	Neutral		Cool	Neutral	

Chapter 24

Balinese Recipes

Murni's Warung, Ubud

Murni's Warung was the first real restaurant in Ubud and was founded by the eponymous owner, Ni Murni Murni, in 1974.

Murni's Warung was the first real restaurant in Ubud and was founded by the eponymous owner, Ni Wayan Murni, in 1974. The following are some of her family recipes, passed down from mother to daughter. If the recipe calls for grinding with a blender, the Balinese prefer a mortar and pestle. The taste is noticeably better. When things go wrong in the kitchen, remember the old Balinese proverb, *Nasi sudah menjadi bubur*: literally 'The rice has already become porridge' or 'There's no use crying over spilt milk'. *Selamat makan*! 'Happy eating!'

SATÉ LILIT
Balinese Style Chicken Saté
Saté lilit differs from the usual Indonesian *saté*, which is usually chicken pieces threaded on a skewer. This *saté* is a combination of spices and

minced chicken meat, moulded on to a skewer, or better still, a thick stem of lemongrass.

900g minced chicken
8 shallots
4 large garlic cloves
10 red chillies (more if you like it hot!)
4 candlenuts
1 tsp coriander seeds
1 tsp cumin powder
4 cloves
1 tsp ground nutmeg
1 tsp turmeric powder
1 tsp lesser galangal
1/2 tsp shrimp paste
2 tsp vegetable oil
1 tsp lime juice
2 tsp chicken powder or 2 crumbled chicken stock cubes
5 tsp coconut milk
5 tsp brown sugar (palm sugar is better, if available)
1 tsp salt
Fried shallots, handful

Saté Lilit, Balinese Style Chicken *Saté.*

Method

1. Place all ingredients (except minced chicken) in a blender and pulse until reduced to a smooth paste or, for even better taste, grind with a mortar and pestle. Add a little water if necessary.
2. Combine with minced chicken in a bowl. Mix thoroughly.
3. Using your hand, divide into small balls about the size of a golf ball or a little smaller.
4. Take a bamboo skewer (approximately 8 inches (20 cm) long and 1 inch (2 cm) wide), mould the chicken mixture on to the end of the stick, tapering the mixture slightly, so that the end is slightly thicker. It should look like a drum-stick.
5. Cook over glowing charcoal or a low fire. Alternatively grill under a pre-heated griller. Rotate the sticks to make them evenly brown.
6. Garnish with fried shallots and serve.

Serves 4-6.

ARES
Balinese Banana-Trunk Soup

Banana trunks are admittedly hard to find, but it is worth enquiring at speciality Asian stores. The flavour of banana trunk is similar to celery.

2,000g banana trunk, finely sliced
10 shallots
2 garlic cloves
10 red chillies
5 hot chillies
4 candlenuts
1 tsp coriander seed
1 tsp cumin seed
4 cloves
1/2 tsp grated nutmeg
1/2 tsp lesser galangal
1/2 tsp white pepper
4 cm lemongrass leaf
1 tsp shrimp paste
1 tsp black pepper
3 tsp vegetable oil
2 litres chicken stock
2 tsp chicken powder or 2 crumbled chicken stock cubes
1 tsp salt

Method

1. Keep aside the finely sliced banana trunk, vegetable oil, and chicken stock.
2. Place remaining ingredients into a blender and pulse until reduced to a smooth paste or, for even better taste, grind with a mortar and pestle. Add a little water if necessary.
3. Using vegetable oil, fry the paste for a few minutes, taking care not to scorch. Add the sliced banana trunk and continue to sauté until the banana wilts.
4. Add the chicken stock and gently simmer until the banana trunk is tender.
5. Serve.

Serves 4-6.

GADO-GADO
Steamed Vegetables in Peanut Sauce

Gado-gado, or *jukut mesantok* as it is called in Balinese, is not exclusively a Balinese dish. In fact, it can be found all over Indonesia and in many different versions. *Tempé* is a very healthy fermented soya bean cake from Eastern Indonesia. It is full of protein and fibre and usually available in Western health food stores. The peanut sauce is the constant. *Gado-gado* in Indonesian means 'mixed', so feel free to experiment with different combinations. It is normally served barely warm and sometimes cold.

250g cabbage, sliced

250g carrots, sliced

250g green beans, halved

250g Chinese cabbage, sliced

250g bean sprouts

250g water spinach or spinach

5 boiled eggs, sliced or quartered

30 bite sized pieces of tofu (bean curd), fried

30 bite sized pieces of *tempé*

20 slices cucumber

Krupuk (shrimp crackers)

Fried shallots, handful

Sliced tomatoes, to garnish

Method
1. Steam the cabbage, carrots, green beans, Chinese cabbage and water spinach or spinach and set aside.
2. Fry the tofu (bean curd) in a little oil.
3. On a serving plate, layer the steamed vegetables with the tofu (bean curd), bean sprouts, *tempé* and cucumber.
4. Decorate the eggs, sliced tomatoes and pour peanut sauce over part.
5. Sprinkle fried shallots on top and place shrimp crackers on the side.
6. Serve.

Serves 4-6.

BUMBU KACANG
Peanut Sauce

Peanut sauce is one of Bali's favourite condiments and accompanies *gado-gado*. The secret is to use the best quality peanuts.

400g raw, unsalted peanuts
50g tomatoes, chopped
4 garlic cloves
2 tsp taucho sauce
2 tsp fried shallots
Lime or lemon juice – a squeeze (lime juice is better)
1 tsp salt (sea salt is best)
1 tsp black pepper
1 tsp *kecap* asin (normal soy sauce)
1 tsp *kecap* manis (sweet soy sauce)

Method

1. Fry the peanuts, a handful at a time, until brown.
2. Place all the ingredients in a blender and pulse until smooth or, for even better taste, grind with a mortar and pestle. The quantities of salt, pepper and the two *kecaps* can be varied to suit individual taste. Serves 4-6.

AYAM BETUTU
Smoked Chicken

Smoked chicken and smoked duck are Bali's most famous dishes. Cooked for many hours, the tender, spiced meat falls off the bone and melts in the mouth. The chicken or duck can be roasted in the oven (as described here) or barbecued, instead of smoked.

2 small chickens, washed and dried
10 shallots
8 garlic cloves
10 small red chillies
1 tsp coriander seed
1 tsp cumin powder
4 candlenuts
4 cloves
1/2 tsp nutmeg

1 tsp turmeric
1 tsp lesser galangal
1 tsp galangal
1 tsp white pepper
4 cm lemongrass
1 tsp salt
3 tsp vegetable oil
2 tsp chicken powder or 2 crumbled chicken stock cubes

Method
1. Wash and pat the chickens dry and set aside.
2. Combine all the other ingredients and spices in a blender and pulse until reduced to a smooth paste or, for even better taste, grind with a mortar and pestle. Add a little water if necessary. Divide into two portions, one for each bird.
3. Place the mixture into each bird's cavity and rub a little on to the outside skin.
4. Place in greased baking pan and cover with aluminium foil. If time permits, let stand for 2-3 hours to allow the flavours to penetrate, preferably in the fridge.
5. Place in a pre-heated oven at 150C and cook for approximately 3 hours or until very tender.
6. Remove foil after 2 hours to allow the birds to brown.
7. Baste occasionally with the pan juices.
8. Serve with steamed white rice and *sambels* of your choice.
Serves 4-6.

BABI KECAP—BALI STYLE
Pork in Sweet Chilli Sauce

Pork features heavily in the Balinese diet. Nearly all ceremonial dishes include pork. The most famous is *Be Guling* (literally 'turned meat')—a pit-roasted suckling pig. As this is a little difficult to re-create in the average Western kitchen, this recipe for *Babi Kecap*, Bali style, captures the flavour of Bali, whilst being much easier to cook. It is always eaten during the great Balinese festivals of *Nyepi* and *Galungan*. This dish can be prepared ahead and refrigerated; the flavour improves and can easily be re-heated.

1 kg pork fillet, cut into bite size pieces

200g shallots (substitute brown onion, but shallots are better)
150g garlic cloves
100g lesser galangal
50g galangal
50g turmeric
10g ginger root, peeled
10g candlenuts
1 tsp coriander seeds
1 tsp cumin seeds
1 tsp shrimp paste
2 red peppers (capsicums), roughly chopped
2 crumbled chicken stock cubes
30 ml vegetable oil
5 tbs sweet soya sauce
5 tbs tomato sauce (try to find an Indonesian brand, as they are less sweet than commercial Western brands)
1 litre chicken stock
Salt to taste
Black pepper to taste

Method
1. Place all ingredients (except the pork and chicken stock) into a blender and pulse until reduced to a smooth paste.
2. Using just a little vegetable oil, quickly brown the pork on all sides—best done in small batches and in a heavy-based pan. Take care not to burn and do not over cook.
3. Bring the chicken stock to a simmer and add the spice paste. Add salt and black pepper to taste.
4. Mix and add the browned pork.
5. Gently simmer until the meat is tender.
6. Serve with steamed white rice and a selection of *sambels*.
Serves 4-6.

AYAM KAMPUNG BALI
Bali Style Village Chicken
Chickens in Bali are totally free range and taste very different from the commercially produced chickens in the West. While they may not be as

meaty as their Western cousins, they make up for it in flavour. In fact, they taste like chicken! This recipe uses the typical *basé genep*: literally, 'complete spice'.

30 chicken pieces (breast, thigh or leg), washed and dried
100g shallots
200g garlic cloves
100g lesser galangal
50g turmeric
10g ginger root
10g candlenuts
5g coriander seeds
4 tsp chicken powder or 4 crumbled chicken stock cubes
1 tsp shrimp paste
1 tsp salt
1 tsp black pepper
30 ml vegetable oil
1 litre chicken stock

Method

1. Place all the ingredients (except chicken pieces, vegetable oil and chicken stock) in a blender and pulse until reduced to a thick paste.
2. Using the vegetable oil, fry the paste for a few minutes, taking care not to scorch.
3. Stir in the chicken stock, mixing well, and add the chicken pieces. Gently simmer (do not boil) until the chicken is tender.
4. Serve with steamed white rice and *sambels* of your choice.

Serves 6-8.

VEGETARIAN *LAWAR*

Apart from rice, *lawar* is the most important food and is prominent in all ceremonies. Always prepared for ceremonial meals, even when other foods may not be, it is a complex mixture of raw vegetables, coarse grated coconut, numerous spices and sometimes raw blood. It comes in several varieties. Chicken pieces can be added.

1 kg long green beans

200g grated coconut
15 shallots
5 cloves of garlic
5 red chillies
5 hot chillies (small green ones)
1 lime (the Balinese actually use a bitter fruit called a *lemo*, but it may not be available in the West)
Salt to taste
Pepper to taste
300 ml vegetable oil

Method
1. Cut the green beans into short lengths and boil or steam until done. Allow to cool.
2. Finely chop all remaining ingredients and mix together. Quickly fry for a few minutes in the vegetable oil. Do not scorch. Cool.
3. Mix the beans with spice mixture (see below). Add salt and pepper to taste.
4. Serve.

Serves 4-6.

BASÉ GENEP
Balinese Spice Mixture

Basé genep translates as 'complete spice' and every grandmother in Bali has her own secret recipe passed down from generation to generation. It is the mainstay of many Balinese dishes and is easy to make and store in the fridge for up to a week.

200g shallots
200g garlic
100g lesser galangal
50g turmeric (fresh, not the powder)
50g galangal
10g fresh ginger
10g candlenuts
5g coriander seeds
5g black peppercorns
5g grated nutmeg

1 tsp shrimp paste
5g fresh lemongrass
Salt to taste

Method

1. Place all the ingredients into a blender. Pulse blend until a smooth paste forms. Add a little water if too dry.
2. Fry a little vegetable oil for a few minutes. Do not scorch.

Serves 4-6.

PISANG GORENG
Banana Fritters

Usually served as a dessert in the West, *pisang goreng*, served with a cup of Bali coffee, is a typical breakfast in Bali.

6 large ripe bananas – *pisang raja*, king bananas, are best
1 cup plain flour
1 egg
1/2 cup milk
1 tsp vanilla essence
Vegetable oil for deep-frying

Method

1. In a bowl, mix the flour, egg, milk and vanilla essence to a smooth batter. Allow to stand for one hour.
2. Heat oil gently in a frying pan until almost smoking.
3. Cut each banana in three, or according to size.
4. Dip in the batter and carefully drop into the hot oil. Fry until golden brown.
5. If desired, roll the cooked fritter in a mixture of sugar and cinnamon.

Serves 4-6.

Pisang goreng, banana fritters.

Chapter 25

Three Balinese Stories

The Kebo Iwa Story

Kebo Iwa, sometimes called Kebo Truna, was a *sudra*, who was born in Blahbatuh. Before he was born, his parents were childless and went around the temples praying for a child. Their wish was granted. He was immensely strong as soon as he was born, and ate enormously.

On the day of his birth, he ate six large packages of rice and grew into a giant. He ate more and more and his parents could not earn enough to feed him, so they decided to kill him, but their schemes failed. They sent him away and he had to fend for himself. He travelled all around Bali building temples. Arriving at a village now known as Batuan he started building a temple (Pura Desa Batuan.).

His appetite was so huge that they could not feed him and started putting rocks in the rice to make it look larger. Kebo Iwa was furious and cursed them and gave the village a new name—Batuan. *Batu* means 'rock.'

Kebo Iwa went to other villages and annoyed them, but nobody could succeed in killing him. Eventually a king sent him to the king of Majapahit in Java with a note to kill him. The king failed several times, until Kebo Iwa let slip that the only way to kill him was to bury him in white lime, but he would come back as a person with white eyes.

He did. Kebo Iwa returned in the form of a Dutchman, with white eyes and white hair.

The Kala Rau Story

The gods churned the sea, using Mount Meru as a paddle, and made ambrosia, called *amerta* in Old Javanese. This gave immortality to anyone who drank it. Wisnu was about to give it to the gods, when the sun god, Surya, and the moon god, Candra, noticed that a demon, Kala Rau, with the body of a god, had slipped in.

They warned Wisnu just as the demon had started to swallow the liquid. Wisnu immediately cut his head off, but he had already swallowed a drop. The demon's body dropped dead to the ground, but his head stayed alive, because it had already come into contact with the *amerta*. Kala Rau took revenge on the sun and the moon by swallowing them regularly. It still happens during an eclipse.

Kala Rau, a demon, with the body of a god.

The Boma Story

Wisnu and Brahma were arguing over who was the stronger. Siwa decided to test them and turned himself into a jewel. When Wisnu tried to pick it up, it grew into a tall tree. He could not pick it up. Both gods tried to climb the tree but could not reach the end of it. Brahma turned himself into a bird and flew up. Wisnu turned himself into a boar and dug down. Neither of them could reach the end of the tree, and they were both angry. Wisnu, when he was down in the earth, met the goddess Pertiwi and tried to make love to her. She refused because he looked like a boar, so he raped her, and Boma was born.

Wisnu represents water and Pertiwi the earth and from the mixture plants grow. Boma, who has a bulging head and popping eyes, also has plants coming out of his mouth. Usually shown with a full set of upper teeth and long fingernails, he frequently appears over temple gates and protects the courtyard.

Chapter 26

Names, Titles and Castes

What's your Name?

Hildred and Clifford Geertz in *Kinship in Bali* (1975) studied Balinese kinship by reference to the whole culture. In Bali you can describe a person in at least five ways:

- Personal names
- Birth order name
- Kinship
- Teknonym
- Status or caste name

Personal Names

All Balinese have personal names but they do not pay much importance to them. Personal names are given to children on the first anniversary of their birth, sometimes before. The name, which does not change during a person's life, is often a totally made-up name, like 'motorbike' or 'Sony', not taken from a standard stock of names. The name would not be used by anyone else in the same village.

Birth Order Names

A person's birth order name is taken automatically at birth. Even a stillborn child is given a birth order name, so everyone's position in the family is immediately apparent.

- 1st born: Wayan, Gede or Putu
- 2nd born: Made, Nengah or Kadek
- 3rd born: Nyoman or Komang
- 4th born: Ketut

Then the names are repeated, so the fifth and ninth children are called Wayan, etc. Usually only the last syllable is used in speaking to the person. It makes no difference if it is a boy or girl. The system resembles the endless cycle of birth and rebirth, the repetitive days of the week and the music of the gamelan.

To find Wayan in Bali is like trying to find Paddy in Dublin or David in Wales. There are so many Wayans, another identifier is needed, like Wayan Restoran (Restoran may mean she owns or works in a restaurant), Made Tabanan (Tabanan is a large town in west Bali) or Ketut Klungkung (Klungkung is a large town in east Bali).

Once a child is born, Mary for example, the parent's birth order name ceases to be used, and the teknonym makes an appearance, which means the parent will henceforth be called 'Mother of Mary' or 'Father of Mary'. *Pan* means 'father' and *Men* means 'mother' as in the famous story about Pan Brayut and Men Brayut. To a certain extent, therefore, birth order names are reserved in the Balinese mind for children. This subliminally reinforces the point that having children is the adult thing to do. A man without children does not carry much weight in village affairs.

Family or Surnames

Surnames do not exist in Bali. Even Western surnames are a relatively recent phenomenon. It was only in the 16th century that Francis I of France and Henry VIII of England required every person to take or be given a surname. This was necessary because of an increase in the population and also because of increased mobility of the population.

Many famous people of the time are still known by their first names: Rafael, Leonardo, Michelangelo, Dante. If confusion is likely, a place name is added: Rafael da Urbino, Leonardo da Vinci.

Kinship

Kinship in Bali has two aspects:
- Private kinship
- Public kinship

Private Kinship

Balinese kinship within the family compound is quite a simple system. Anthropologists call it the 'Hawaiian' or 'Generational' system. People are classed according to their generation—one layer, your own layer, comprises siblings, half-siblings and cousins; above you, mothers, fathers, uncles and aunts; below you, children of brothers, sisters and cousins; two layers above you, grandparents; two below you, grandchildren.

The Balinese refer to a person of the third generation above and third generation below by the same name. The great-grandparent and great-grandchild are both called *kumpi*. They are culturally identified. If you are *kumpi*, the eldest in your family of four generations, you have reached the ideal. It is like living for three score years and ten.

The identity of generations reveals itself in praying to the dead. Prayers are offered to gods and seniors only. Three generations below the deceased pray to him in the graveyard, but the fourth generation, the great-grand-children, the *kumpi*, do not. They are culturally identified and regarded as the same generation. They are not junior to the deceased. Likewise, the deceased's contemporaries do not pray to him either.

The next generation, the great-great-grandchild is senior to the deceased and so he also does not pray to him. Like so many Balinese systems, it is circular.

Four generations. If you are *kumpi*, the eldest in your family of four generations, you have reached the ideal.

Public Kinship

Balinese public kinship is an unusual, perhaps unique, system. The basic unit is called a *dadia*, that is to say a unit composed of all those individuals who have a common ancestor. A *dadia* is a kin group. It can be of any size. Each *dadia* is a self-contained entity, which, by definition, cannot break into segments. According to tradition, in the case of the gentry, the *triwangsa*, an illustrious Majapahit immigrant would be the common ancestor.

Dadia compete for power and a number of characteristic practices operate to enhance that power. One practice is the preferred marriage partner. *Dadia* groups are not exogamous. By preference they are endogamous (that is, they marry within their own circle of close kin).

The ideal partner is a patriparallel cousin, which, for a male, is his father's brother's daughter, that is, his first cousin on his father's side. This ensures that the resources of the bride stay within the *dadia* and enhance it. It prevents fragmentation of land and other property. The bride does not have to leave her family. Her children belong to the same descent group.

Keeping it in the Family

Marriage within the family is not uncommon in Asia, Africa and the Middle East. In parts of Saudi Arabia 39% of marriages are between first cousins. Buddha married his cousin. In ancient Egypt, 3,500 years ago, Rameses II married his eldest daughter when his wife Nefertari died and promoted her to principal wife. Later he married another daughter. Ten of the fifteen Ptolemy rulers married their sisters.

In many parts of Europe, men and women married within their extended families until the Christian church banned marriages between cousins in the 4th century. The Roman Catholic Church still bans it, but gives dispensation to couples considered worthy. There is no Biblical support for the prohibition. Jacob married two of his first cousins, Rachel and Leah.

Charles Darwin married his cousin Emma and had ten children, including four brilliant scientists. Albert Einstein's second wife Elsa was his first cousin. Queen Victoria married her cousin Albert.

The *Journal of Genetic Counselling* 2002 published research indicating that marriage between first and second cousins is not as dangerous as previously believed. Unrelated couples have a 3% to 4% risk of having a child with a birth defect, significant mental retardation or serious genetic disease. For close cousins the risk jumps only by 1.7% to 2.8%.

Kinship *Dadias* and Sinking Status

Geertz explains the sinking status pattern that applies within royal and gentry *dadia*. It determines relative status. The head of the *dadia* is the eldest son of the eldest son, stretching back to the common ancestor, which, in the case of the gentry, would be to a Majapahit founder of the family.

The other sons of the head of the family found their own families, which are continued by the same primogenitural succession rules. The status of the *sub-dadia* diminishes as time goes by and as they become more distant from the current head of the family, who is in the direct line.

Each royal or noble house has its own authority, which is ranked according to the sinking status pattern, but all houses within the same *dadia* are related to one another and are an inseparable whole. *Dadia* are, in effect, power blocks. They can be viewed as a set of concentric circles radiating out from the central head of the family.

Teknonyms

This is how the Balinese, or at least the *sudra*, commonly refer to each other most of the time. As soon as a person's first child is born (even if the child dies) they are called 'Mother of Mary' or 'Father of Mary', as the case may be. This name continues until their first grandchild is born, when the name changes and they are called 'Grandmother of Tommy' or 'Grandfather of Tommy'. When their first great-grandchild is born, all the names shift again and they become 'Great-Grandmother of Billy' or 'Great-Grandfather of Billy'. The names do not change as more children of the same generation come into existence.

Eventually the family forgets individual identities and only a few contemporaries remember the person's original name. Anthropologists call the practice of being named through one's descendants 'teknonymy'. It immediately indicates one's position in the family.

This is in sharp contrast with Western societies where a wife loses her name to her husband's. The Balinese system defines a person by reference to descendants and not husband or wife or ancestors.

Title System

Every person inherits a status title. It does not depend on any other group the person may belong to or his or her job. It places the person on a particular rung of the social ladder and requires appropriate politeness.

Common titles are *Ida Bagus*, *Gusti*, *Pasek*, and *Dauh*. There are numerous titles, passed down through the paternal line. No census has ever been done as to exactly how many titles there are or how many people belong to them.

One's standing comes from one's ancestors and governs daily behaviour. An appropriate code of etiquette regulates one's speech, posture, dress, eating, marriage, burial ground, mode of cremation and even house construction.

As all titles come from the gods, the system has a religious basis. Some titles are closer to the gods than others. The code of etiquette respects the religious origin, not necessarily the person himself. A person may have no moral worth, but his title deserves respect.

Caste

The word 'caste' comes from the Portuguese *casta* which itself comes from the Latin *castus* meaning 'pure'. The Dutch thought that the Balinese title system derived from the Indian caste system and imposed the caste system on the title system and the whole thing became rigid. The Balinese themselves now refer to caste, but it is based on a misconception.

The Dutch liked the concept because it was tidy and controllable. The Dutch set up a system to register the caste of every Balinese person. It did not take long for the Balinese to realise that registering yourself as a high caste excused you from compulsory labour. The successful falsification of family genealogies caused bitterness on the part of those registered as *sudra*.

The gentry or nobles are called the *triwangsa* or 'three peoples'. The commoners are called *sudra* or *jaba*, which means 'outsider'. About 93% of Bali's population are *sudra*. The gentry are also referred to as *wong jero*, which means 'insiders' because they lived in or near the royal palace, and the *sudra* as *wong jaba* or 'outsiders' because they lived outside it.

The fine nuances of social titles matter considerably. Members of the gentry are referred to and called by their titles, such as *Dewa*, *Anak Agung*, *Ida Bagus*, *Cokorda*, *Gusti* and so on. The *sudra* have no title.

The gentry, in descending order, are:
- *Brahmana*
- *Satria*
- *Wesia*

According to Balinese accounts, the *triwangsa* and members of the *Pasek* clan have their ancestors in Java, whereas the *sudra* are the descendants of the original indigenous population.

Where Do You Sit?

In the old days when a *sudra* met a nobleman, he bowed his head. Pavilions in palaces and houses are still tiered to allow people to sit in accordance with their status. High castes sit high. That is why they are called 'high caste'. It is not polite to ask directly which caste a person belongs to. A round about way is to ask, 'Where do you sit?' When Balinese meet Balinese strangers they are always anxious until this matter is sorted out.

At meals, the highest ranking person eats first and in formal settings nobody leaves until he declares the meal over. The Balinese language has levels relating to status. When Balinese people meet they tend to speak in Middle Balinese. As soon as it becomes apparent that a person is a *brahmana*, he is spoken to in High Balinese, no matter what his job may be, and a lower posture on the part of the non-*brahmana* is adopted. If one is talking about a high caste person High Balinese is used. To speak Low Balinese when High Balinese should be used is an insult.

Flexibility

The Balinese title system is flexible. Kapakisan, who ruled Bali in 1350 AD, under Majapahit suzerainty, was born a *brahmana* and changed his status to a *satria* in order to rule. *Brahmana* are debarred from ruling. The king could raise a person's status, for example, award him the title of *Gusti*.

Marriage Partners

Mixed marriages are permitted in certain circumstances and result in a change of status. A high status man may marry a lower status wife, although if this continues for three generations, the high status may be lost. The children automatically receive their father's status. His wife remains a *sudra*, but she enjoys a higher position and changes her name and receives the title *Jero*. A high status wife, however, should not marry a lower status man. The Dutch tried to forbid any change of caste through marriage, which caused bitterness.

Caste Discrimination and Abolition

The Dutch forbade discrimination on account of caste. This was adopted by the Republic of Indonesia, which holds that everyone is equal.

Caste is controversial in some quarters. Pujung, a woodcarving village near Ubud, abolished caste in the 1970s, so that everyone in the village was to be of equal status. Anyone who disagreed with the ruling of the village council was free to leave, and go into exile, but nearly everybody decided to stay and give up their titles. Pujung, however, is unique in Bali in that it has long been accepted that holy water from its village temple can be used for all rituals, including the worship of gods as well as rites of passage. There is no need to get it from other places such as caste origin temples. According to the Balinese if two families use the same holy water for rites of passage they are of equal caste status. On this basis it seems that Pujung is the only community that can choose to abolish caste.

Indian Caste System

In India caste is an outcome of one's actions in previous incarnations. The *Rig-Veda*, the oldest religious text in the world, probably composed between 1500 and 900 BC, tells the story of Prajapati, a primaeval man, who existed even before the Universe. How he came into being is not clear. The gods appear to be his children.

He was sacrificed and cut up to make all things in the Universe. The 'Hymn of the Primaeval Man' tells us how the *brahman* came out of his mouth, the *satria* out of his arms, the *wesias* or *vaisya* out of his thighs and the *sudra* out of his feet:

> When they divided the Man
> Into how many parts did they divide him?
> What was his mouth, what were his arms?
> What were his thighs and his feet called?
>
> The Brahman was his mouth,
> Of his arms was made the warrior,
> His thighs became the Vaisya,
> Of his feet the Sudra was born.
>
> The moon arose from his mind,
> From his eye was born the sun,

From his mouth Indra and Agni,
From his breath the wind was born.

From his navel came the air,
From his head there came the sky,
From his feet the earth, the four quarters from his ear,
Thus they fashioned the world.

With Sacrifice the gods sacrificed to Sacrifice
These were the first of the sacred laws.

These mighty beings reached the sky,
Where are the eternal spirits, the gods.

This indicates an early classification of people and the particular parts of the body would appear to be significant. The caste system in India was not closed at that time and there was mobility between castes.

In India the caste of a person depended on his job. *Brahmans* were the priests; *satria* the rulers, *wesia* the merchants and the *sudra* were there to help the others. At the bottom of the ladder were the untouchables or outcastes, people without caste, who were identified with the pre-Aryan native Indian tribes or those who had done something so awful that they could not be admitted to society and had no status whatsoever.

Over time it became more rigid and by 200 BC it had evolved into a hereditary system, which was not dependent on a person's job, but on birth. Marriage between castes was forbidden.

Clans

In Bali, people are also divided into *warga* or 'clans', which is a separate category from title. There are about twenty-two clans and they relate to ancestors. They claim to be direct descendants of influential religious or political figures, for example, the *Bujangga Waisnawa* clan claim descent from Rsi Markandeya.

Some cut across status boundaries. The biggest and most important is the *Pasek* clan, to which about 60% of the population belongs. Within the *sudra*, the *Pasek*, *Pande*, *Bandesa* and others enjoy higher status than ordinary commoners.

Pasek

The *Pasek* trace their origins to a *brahmana* sage called Empu Genijaya, who was one of four *brahmana* invited by a Majapahit ruler to come from Java to sort out various disputes with the *Bali Aga*. His seven children, all sages, are the founders of the *Pasek* clan. The *Pasek* have many responsibilities, the most important of which is to maintain four sacred and important temples in Besakih, Gelgel, Padang Bai and Amlapura.

Pande

Early iron came from meteorites falling from the sky on the ground, a gift from the gods, and not from rocks. Many people in the world regard meteorites as sacred and respect ironsmiths who forge from them.

The respected *Pande* clan started as blacksmiths and specialise in forging metals. They consider themselves set apart from the caste system and command respect because of the importance of their job. In the old days, even *brahmana* spoke to them in High Balinese. They are permitted to have eleven tiers on their cremation towers, an honour only permitted to persons of very high caste. They have their own priests.

The respected *Pande* clan started as blacksmiths and specialise in forging metals.

Bandesa

The *Bandesa* trace their origins back to a holy Javanese Empu.

Divine Titles

Gods and goddesses have titles too. Gods are referred to as *Dewa* and goddesses as *Dewi*. The higher ranking males are called *Batara* and females *Batari*. In some cases they are given a further name, like Batara Guru or Dewi Sri.

They do not have distinctive personalities, like Greek or Roman gods. They have jobs and regulate certain important matters, such as fertility, power, knowledge, death and so on.

Gentry Titles

Titles are almost never omitted, even in casual conversation:
- *Brahmana*: *Ida Bagus* for men, *Ida Ayu* or *Dayu* for women
- *Satria*: *Cokorda, Anak Agung, Dewa Agung, Dewa Gede, I Dewa, I Gusti*
- *Wesia*: *Gusti*

Titles indicate important nuances in status within a particular group.

Gender Markers

Ni is used for women and *I* for men. These are prefixed to personal names and are only used in correspondence.

House Titles

Even houses have titles. *Brahmana* live in compounds called *geria*. Royal or noble people live in either a *puri* or *jero* according to their rank. The central palace is usually called the *puri gede* which means the 'great puri'. *Puri* meaning 'palace' and *pura* meaning 'temple' derive from the same Sanskrit word for fortified town.

Change of Name

If you are having a run of bad luck, one remedy is to change your name. Consult an expert to check the calendars and your reincarnations. Sometimes the new name is kept secret. There is a similar belief in Java. President Sukarno is an example. He was called Kusno Susro, which names were dropped in childhood, because he was a sickly child and his father renamed him Karno to bring him better health.

Chapter 27

Everything Comes in 3s and Balinese Etiquette

A Special Number

The Balinese conceive of everything as having a tripartite structure. It infuses their philosophy of life. They are not alone in attributing three as a special number. Christianity does: the Father, the Son and the Holy Ghost. The ancient Egyptians were also very interested in the number three.

The Balinese divide everything into:

- A high or sacred part
- A middle or everyday part
- A low or unclean part

The Outer and Inner Worlds

Things belong to:

- The outer world; or
- The inner world

They are connected. Something amiss in the outer world causes problems in the inner world. This is a fundamental Balinese belief and corresponds to a similar belief in Tantric thought.

Outer World Tripartite Divisions

Examples are:

- **The Universe**
  - Heaven
  - Middle world of human beings
  - Underworld
- **Bali**
  - *Kaja*, towards the mountains, where the gods reside
  - *Tengah*, in the middle ground where men live

- *Kelod*, towards the sea, away from the gods
- **Village Temples**
  - *Pura Puseh*, associated with the deified ancestors
  - *Pura Desa*, associated with humans
  - *Pura Dalem*, associated with the cemetery
- **Temple Architecture**
  - *Jeroan*, where the holy relics are kept
  - *Jaba Tengah*, where the storerooms and kitchen are
  - *Jaba*, where blood sacrifices are made and cockfights held and where people eat, chat and play cards
- **Religious Imagery on Structures**
  - Top, symbols of the gods and the upper world
  - Middle, scenes from the human world
  - Base, turtle and serpents from the underworld

Inner World Tripartite Divisions

Examples are:
- **Family Compound Architecture**
  - Family temple, in *kaja* direction
  - Living areas
  - Kitchen, rubbish and pigs, in the *kelod* direction
- **Buildings**
  - Roof
  - Walls
  - Foundation
- **Tall Offerings**
  - Top, symbolic image of the gods
  - Middle, where the fruits and flowers are
  - Base
- **Balinese Language**
  - High, for priests and referring to holy matters
  - Middle, for normal speech
  - Low, coarse speech

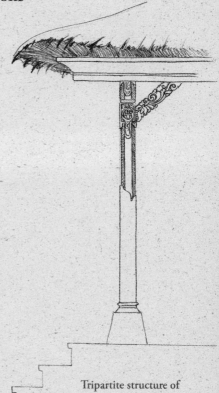

Tripartite structure of a pavillion and pillar.

- **Human Body**
  - Head, where the soul is
  - Middle, where the organs are
  - Feet, which touch the profane ground
- **Life**
  - Birth
  - Life
  - Death

Rituals and Understanding

Rituals are carried out on three basic levels, according to their complexity and elaboration:

- Elaborate
- Average
- Simple

There are also three levels of understanding: the highest is that of the high priests and scholars, who know the *lontar* texts and understand the significance of the rituals, the middle level is that of the village priests and local leaders, who can lead the preparations for a ceremony and the lowest level is that of the ordinary people, who know how to make offerings and carry out manual work.

Etiquette

Much of Balinese etiquette and manners are explicable in terms of the Balinese attitude to elevation and orientation.

Examples are:

- Take off your shoes before entering a dwelling
- Do not pat anyone on the head
- Apologise if you have to touch someone's head
- Do not let a baby touch the ground for the first three months
- Do not point with your foot
- Do not eat or hand somebody something with your unclean left hand
- Do not put clothes on a temple wall
- Do not walk under a clothes line, which may contain underwear, which would then be above your head

- Do not take sacred objects under an aqueduct
- Put underwear on the lowest rung of a clothes line
- Do not hang laundry higher than a man's head
- Sit lower than sacred objects, such as *Barong* and Rangda masks in a temple
- Sit lower than higher castes and priests
- Speak High Balinese to high priests and speak softly, as to speak loudly is considered coarse and unrefined
- Do not walk in front of someone, but if you cannot avoid it, adopt a submissive posture and ask forgiveness
- Carry offerings and holy water on your head
- Do not step over an offering or a sacred object, such as a shadow puppet, mask or gamelan
- Do not sit on a pillow
- Sleep so that your head points in the *kaja* direction

Most Balinese will not point out a breach of etiquette. That itself is rude. Yet, breaches of etiquette can have unforeseen consequences. It is a grave offence for a commoner to insult a nobleman in public. It pollutes him and a special ceremony called *pamariscita* has to be carried out to cleanse his mind and body.

Chapter 28

Balinese Offerings

If there is an important ceremony, such as a temple ceremony, enormous towers of flowers, fruit, cakes, meats and eggs are made at home and carried to the temple by women on their heads, often for long distances.

Words, Words, Words

Offerings are called *banten* in Balinese, a word that may come from the Sanskrit word *bali*, which means 'tribute', 'obligation' or 'gift'. This may even be the origin of the name of the island. It has also been suggested that *banten* may be derived from the word *enten*, which means 'to wake up' or 'be conscious', so that offerings represent a consciousness on the part of the gods.

What Are They?

An offering is something that is offered for a religious purpose. It can be anything. Dances, music, cockfights and readings from the scriptures in the temple are all offerings. Usually they are accompanied by prayers. More common, however, are offerings made of natural, perishable materials, like food, fruit and flowers.

Why Are They?

The guides say that the offerings are gifts: a means of giving something back to the gods and ancestors. Perhaps; but it is unlikely that the Balinese analyse it. It is more likely that they make them because that is just what they do. It is what their mothers did and their grandmothers did before them. Offerings are usually made by women, although some kinds are reserved for men.

The guides say that the gifts create obligations on the part of the gods and ancestors who receive them, so a system of mutual obligations or favours is set up between humans, gods and ancestors. It is most unlikely that the Balinese see it in such stark terms. They do it because they do it, in other words it is a ritual, and the purpose is to protect the family, the village, Bali and ultimately the world. Making them is also good for a person's *karma*.

Classification

There are two kinds:

- Ritual Offerings

These are necessary for the ritual to take place. For large ceremonies, there are lists of how many of a particular kind of offering are needed. Certain rituals require a particular bird or animal to be sacrificed, such as a duck, chicken, pig or dog. A duck is considered purer than a pig or chicken. Dogs are offered to the low spirits. One particular exorcism ceremony, the *resi gana*, requires a dog of a special reddish skin colour. There are requirements as to how the meat is prepared.

- Family Offerings

These depend on the persons using them, who exercise their own discretion. An example would be the offerings brought to a temple ceremony by members of a family.

Who Makes Them?

Most women can make about fifty different styles of offerings, but there are thousands. They learn as young girls. Some Balinese women spend most of their lives making offerings. They are very important and a large amount of money is spent on them. Large offerings may cost several days' wages. During important ceremonies, there are often shortages of materials and prices rise. If, for some reason, a woman is unable to make and/or present the offering, men step in and do it. Ready-made offerings are for sale in the markets.

There are women, who make a profession of it, and sell their services. They just need to know the type of ceremony and whether it is large, medium or small scale. High caste women in the family of a high priest make offerings for special ceremonies.

Men prepare offerings made of flesh and meat, such as pig skin, fat and entrails, and if ceremonies require it, kill, clean and roast the animal.

Some ceremonies need grilled or roasted chickens and ducks. Men also cook the *saté* and chop hundreds of bamboo *saté* sticks, and prepare the *lawar*. Work takes place on the morning of a ritual or ceremonial event, usually beginning around daybreak (5 am) or earlier. Depending on the scale, it may continue from three to seven or eight hours. They try to finish before noon.

A large amount of grated coconut meat is used in ceremonial food. Coconut grating is seen as the easiest task and involves up to a dozen or more men and boys gathered around a woven mat chatting and joking as they grate.

Side Benefit

Offerings come in all shapes and sizes. Some are very small and can be made in a couple of seconds. Others are enormous or numerous and take weeks and require a lot of help from friends and neighbours. An important side benefit is that the act of making them brings people together. They are also an outlet for a person's creative and aesthetic skills.

What Are They Made Of?

Every village has its own unique forms, and they are usually made of natural things, like food, flowers and drinks. Once finished, they are kept in a container. They are made by hand with a small, simple, sharp knife.

Bananas form part of many offerings, and tall offerings have a soft banana tree trunk in the centre to serve as a core for inserting bamboo skewers to which the fruits, cakes and other things are attached.

Every offering has at least three ingredients: red areca nut, green betel leaf and white lime. The colours, red, green and white are the colours associated with the three gods, Brahma, Wisnu and Siwa. These ingredients allow the gods to be present and witness ceremonies. Rice is also a common component.

Offerings vary considerably in complexity. Some are very simple and may be tiny; others can be several metres high. If there is an important ceremony, such as a temple ceremony, enormous towers of flowers, fruit, cakes, meats and eggs are made at home and carried to the temple by women on their heads, often for long distances. Incense sticks are usually stuck into or placed on or beside them. Before they are used in a ceremony, offerings are normally covered with a woven or metal cover.

Sacred Cows

There are ceremonial and non-ceremonial foods. The distinction depends on their degree of ritual purity or cleanliness.

Edible mammals (except for cows), reptiles and avian species, all of which are slaughtered, are generally appropriate ceremonial food and can be used for offerings. There is a hierarchy: duck, chicken, pig and dog, duck being the most pure.

It seems that animals which live or forage in rice fields are considered purer than those which live in other environments. Hence, ducks, eels, and other animals from the rice fields are thought to be purer than pigs and chickens which live in the family compound. Ducks which live only in the family compound and do not forage in the rice fields are inappropriate for *brahmana* high priests.

Another test is their sociability. Pigs and chickens are highly individualistic in their behaviour and rank behind ducks, which are more social characters and are always careful about what they eat.

Banned Foods

Non-slaughtered food is not appropriate for offerings, for example, insects, crustaceans, gastropods, amphibians, fresh-water and sea-water fish. It seems that most of the foods introduced during the colonial period are not used in ceremonial food, for example, bean curd, peanuts and soybeans. In fact, it looks like no new ceremonial preparations have been introduced since 1900, except for the new varieties of rice and white sugar.

Care For Offerings

After an offering has been made, it is treated with respect, and kept in a high place. They are carried on the head, the head being associated with purity. Offerings for the low spirits are not treated with the same reverence.

When Are They Used?

They are part and parcel of every ceremony, whether in the public village temples or in private family temples. There are daily offerings for shrines, wherever they may be, and for the low spirits, on the ground. When there are special coincidence days, such as *Kajeng-Kliwon*, every fifteen days, or the *Tumpeks*, which are special days devoted to objects, offerings are presented.

Before a Balinese goes on a long trip, he visits certain temples and gives offerings for a safe trip. Dangerous places, like crossroads, normally have plentiful offerings. During a temple ceremony offerings are made to many different gods. They may be to the god of the temple or to the god of the main temple to which the temple itself belongs or to the gods of the nearby village temples or to the god of the origin temple to which the village temple belongs and/or to a nature god, perhaps the Earth, Mother or Sea God. When offerings are given to the higher spirits during a ceremony, they are also given to the lower spirits, either just before or just after. Both rituals are required and are complementary.

Presentation

Every Balinese family presents daily offerings to its shrines. They are usually presented in the morning, normally after the first meal has been prepared, but before it has been eaten. Usually a female member of the family, dressed in Balinese costume, presents the offerings. The offerings are carried on her head in a tray with a stick of burning incense. At each place the offerings are put out, a few drops of holy water are poured on the offerings and she wafts the essence of the offering towards the shrine with her right hand.

Offerings at a temple ceremony are dealt with in three ways. A local *pemangku* priest sits cross-legged to carry out a ritual. Within easy reach in front of him are a pile of offerings, which he takes and recites mantras over. Other offerings are placed in front of him and not touched. A third set may be in front of the shrine, which is the focus of the ritual in question.

Kepeng: Chinese Coins

Chinese coins, *kepeng* in Indonesian and *pis bolong* in Balinese, made of bronze with a hole in them, are an essential part of many offerings and temple decorations. One side of the coin has four Chinese characters. They are sold in bundles of 200, but supplied in loops which are slightly less than that, as 200 is an unlucky number.

In the 17th century, Indonesia was so great a drain on the currency

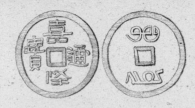

Chinese coins, *kepeng* in Indonesian and *pis bolong* in Balinese, made of bronze with a hole in them, are an essential part of many offerings and temple decorations. One side of the coin has four Chinese characters.

that the Chinese government tried to stop the export of coins, but they failed. During the Dutch colonial period, it was difficult to find the raw materials and tin was used. Hoarding was a risky business, as the Dutch imposed a prison sentence on anyone found collecting them. One of the first European entrepreneurs in Bali, Danish Mads Lange imported a huge amount of the coins from China between 1839 and 1856. He bartered Balinese rice for them and became very rich.

They are used in cremation ceremonies and placed in the foundations when a building is constructed. Offerings in the temple usually have some of these coins in them. They are left by the ladies when they take their offerings home, as the coins are intended for the priest.

Temple decoration made of Chinese coins.

There was no local state currency in Bali or indeed the rest of Indonesia until the 20th century. Chinese *kepeng* were the currency in Bali but, in practice, most people bartered in the markets.

Sarad: Tall Offering

One or more tall offerings called *sarad* may be made to celebrate a very special occasion, like a wedding or a tooth-filing. They take almost a week to make and are fashioned out of figurines of coloured fried rice dough, attached to a huge bamboo frame, several metres high, which symbolically represents the Universe, with ascending levels. There is usually a gate, shaped like a temple gate, symbolising the gateway to heaven. There are representations of flowers, fruits, leaves and other floral elements. Boma, the son of Pertiwi and Wisnu, looks down from the top above the gateway, with his large round face and bulging eyes, a symbol of fertility and the middle world.

The Cili, symbol of the rice goddess and fertility, always has a place in the huge figurine. The base is usually Bedawang Nala, the cosmic turtle, on which the world rests, flanked by the two cosmic serpents. A *sarad* lasts about a week and is never eaten.

One or more tall offerings called *sarad* may be made to celebrate a very special occasion. They take almost a week to make and are fashioned out of figurines of coloured fried rice dough, attached to a huge bamboo frame, several metres high, which symbolically represents the Universe, with ascending levels.

People hang a *lamak* from the top of the main shrines in their family temples to the ground and in front of their houses during the *Galungan* festival. They are runners, made usually of palm leaf, but they can also be made of cloth.

High on the Hog

Beside a *sarad* stands a tall meat offering, three or four metres high, consisting of a tree of pig meat, intestines and fat. The base is a banana tree trunk into which are stuck various kinds of *saté* and pig skin-fat combinations which represent the Balinese mandala through representations of the weapons of the gods of the nine directions.

Large ceremonies have a boiled pig's head, ornamented with various types of *saté* and pork fat, including tusks. These two offerings are usually prepared by old men as it takes a lot of experience.

Lamak

People hang a *lamak* from the top of the main shrines in their family temples to the ground and in front of their houses during the *Galungan* festival. They are runners, made usually of palm leaf, but they can also be made of cloth, whose main function is to decorate an altar or shrine. They also serve as a base for offerings. Fairly narrow, they vary in length from about 12 inches (30 centimetres) to more than 33 feet (10 metres).

The short ones have geometric patterns only, but the longer ones also have representational shapes, often of a Cili, the rice goddess. The tree of life, sometimes on a little mountain, is a common motif, symbolising the unity of all forms of life on Earth. The patterns are made by pinning contrasting dark green or dyed red leaves.

Penjor

Penjor are tall, decorated bamboo poles, whose curved upper ends have attached elaborate offerings, perhaps in the form of a Cili, dangling graciously over the middle of the road. The point may be that the gods on Mount Agung and visiting ancestors can see them clearly.

They are erected outside temples and family compounds during certain ceremonies, and always at *Galungan*, beside a temporary altar

Penjor are tall, decorated bamboo poles, whose curved upper ends have attached elaborate offerings, perhaps in the form of a Cili, dangling graciously over the middle of the road.

dressed with a *lamak*. They honour Pura Besakih. In Gianyar, if there has been a wedding, two *penjor* are set up, a large one representing the man with a white cloth and a smaller one representing the woman with a yellow cloth. If *Galungan* falls on the same day as a full moon, additional decorations and strings of shells are attached, which emit a beautiful tinkling sound in the wind.

There are many theories about the symbolism of *penjor*. One is that the *penjor* represents and honours the cosmic serpent Anantaboga, whose name means 'food without end'. The bottom is his head. The decorations on his arching back are his scales and the wind chime is the tip of his tail.

Lawar

Apart from rice, *lawar* is the most important food and is prominent in all ceremonies. Always prepared for ceremonial meals, even when other foods may not be, it is a complex mixture of animal parts, raw vegetables, coarse grated coconut, numerous spices and sometimes raw blood. It comes in several varieties.

The actual making of *lawar* takes place during the last stages, because it tends to spoil in a short time. It is made by men. The finely chopped ingredients are mixed and stirred with the right hand. Spectators are usually given some to taste. It is received in the outstretched right palm and usually shifted to the left palm and immediately popped into the mouth, chewed and discussed. Food is popped into the mouth rather than being eaten from the hand as is the usual practice. Strangely, popping food into the mouth would, in other contexts, be considered rude.

Saté

Saté is made from pounded meat, grated coconut, spices and blood, moulded carefully on to a bamboo stick. *Saté* sticks are always notched at the lower end. The notching is done so that the *saté* maker can identify the high end of the stick. The high/low distinction is based on the vertical orientation of the tree trunk from which the stick was taken. The stick should always be held in the same direction as the living tree from which it came.

The sticks are laid on both sides of a long charcoal grill filled with coconut husks. Men sit on opposite sides roasting them, all the time waving leaves over the hot coals. The *saté* is lightly browned and never fully roasted, producing almost raw meat and coconut, occasionally burned black on one side.

Mountain Symbolism

Mountains are represented in the shapes of offerings in many different ways. Rice is frequently moulded like a cone. The big offerings themselves are mountain shaped. Mountains often appear on *lamak*. *Penjor* look like mountains, and may represent Mount Agung, the highest and most sacred mountain in Bali.

Colours and Directions

The compass points, colours, numbers and other symbolic attributes have direct relevance to the assembly of offerings. Different gods are associated with different directions and colours. Rice and other components follow the colour and directional scheme.

Size Matters

The size of the ceremony is relevant. A small offering for the low spirits need be only one multi-coloured chicken. A bigger offering would be five chickens in the colours of the cardinal directions. A very big offering would need, in addition to chickens, other animals placed in the directions appropriate for their skin colour.

Very large ceremonies may have as many as 500 sacrificed animals, ranging from pigs, goats, ducks, chickens, puppies, water buffaloes and others. It is not regarded as cruelty to the animals as it is their *karma* and assists them in being reincarnated in forms that are more favourable. Priests chant mantras consigning the souls of the animals to heaven and acceptable reincarnations.

Cock and Drake

Offerings appear in other religions, but Balinese offerings are unique and mostly unrelated to Indian Hinduism. They are often hard to understand, but there is one ritual, where the secrets are revealed in the manuals for priests dealing with purification ceremonies and concern the cock and drake. A woman assistant carries the cock and drake and the priest recites a mantra requesting the cock and drake, which are brought live to the ceremony, to peck and fly off with the impurities and sins of the person who is to be purified. They are wafted at that person. The cock and drake are dedicated to the gods of the four directions and are identified with Garuda, Wisnu's vehicle. The ritual is sometimes seen at marriage ceremonies. The birds are not killed or eaten and are buried when they die.

After Use

An offering is never reused. After a ceremony, an offering to the gods may be taken away and eaten. Following a private ceremony the offerings are carefully packed and delivered to those who have helped. In the case of saté the total number of saté sticks in a bundle is indicative of the social rank of the person or household receiving it.

They range from five to eleven, only odd numbers being used. Five sticks are appropriate for a sudra. Seven sticks indicate an elevated sudra, such as a Pasek. Nine sticks usually indicate a non-ruling gentry household. In some villages, the temple priests, pemangku, and banjar heads receive nine. Eleven sticks are appropriate for aristocratic households which bear the titles Anak Agung or Cokorda.

Offerings for low spirits are just left, thrown away or eaten by the dogs. They are never eaten by humans.

Chapter 29

Balinese Cockfights

Banned!

The British banned cockfighting in England in 1840 and the Dutch banned cockfighting in Indonesia. The Indonesian government also banned it in 1981 because of the Muslim anti-gambling movement, except in Bali where three sets are allowed for ritual purposes. Once started, though, three bouts can go a long way.

Temples Tax Cockfights

Taxing cockfights was an important source of revenue for temples. The Dutch law banning fights made it impossible for temples to tax cockfights openly. It is hard to know if the law was observed in practice, as it is difficult to enforce, even today. In 1928 the rulers responsible for Pura Besakih held a special cockfight to raise funds to pay the temple's debts and to raise money for future expenditure. The event lasted twelve days and raised huge sums of money.

History

Ancient texts indicate that the ritual has existed for centuries. It is mentioned in the Batur Bang inscriptions, written in the *Saka* year 933, which is 1011 AD. The edict of a Balinese king in the Pura Desa Batuan, written in the *Saka* year 944, which is 1022 AD, refers to the taxing of cockfights.

Purifications

Cockfights are required for purification ceremonies. Nobody knows when they started. The essential point is that blood is spilt on the ground three times for the evil spirits.

A Very Male Affair

Only men participate. Women do not even watch. It is much more than a religious ritual. According to Raffles in his *History of Java* (1817):

> Their predominant passions are gaming and cockfighting. In these amusements, when at peace with the neighbouring states, all the vehemence and energy of their character and spirit is called forth and exhausted.

Men in villages tend their roosters lovingly. They identify with them and much conversation turns on them. The vast majority of men own at least one rooster. They are symbolic expressions of their owners. The sound of roosters crowing to each other early in the morning is the standard Balinese wake-up call.

Tender Loving Care

Roosters are kept in bamboo baskets placed outside their owners' houses daily. It is important that they get used to the commotion of everyday life and are trained not to be distracted by unusual sounds. Their life is a preparation for the fight. The birds are at their peak at about three years old. They eat a special diet of maize, and red pepper is pushed down their beaks to give them spirit.

Sacred Rules

Cockfighting is a sacred matter. The rules are written down in ancient *lontar* palm books, which are village heirlooms. The umpire's word is final. In the case of cocks dying at virtually the same time, he decides. Before a cockfight begins, a local priest presents offerings to the evil spirits and the gods. Then the serious business begins.

Time and Place

In pre-colonial times cockfights were normally held on market days, which take place every three days. The ring is usually near the market in the meeting hall in the centre of the village. They are also held in the outer courtyard of a temple. Anyone can attend. It is a noisy, busy affair. There are normally about nine or ten matches. They usually start in the late afternoon and last three or four hours until sunset.

The Fight

The men sit in a circle with their roosters, while the women sell chicken and pork *saté*, grilled meats, snacks, *lawar* and brightly coloured drinks. As soon as one fight ends, the men look around for a suitable match for the next. The aim is to match roosters of equal ability for a good fight. It is no good if the fight is predictable. If a good match cannot be found, the spur on the stronger bird is adjusted slightly to give him a handicap.

The sharp steel spurs are single blades, about 4-5 inches (10-12 centimetres) long, tied around one leg with string. They are sharpened only at eclipses and during a dark moon and the process should not be seen by a woman.

Once the spur expert has affixed the spurs, the cocks are placed on the ground in the middle of the ring. In the right hand corner of the ring the timekeeper sits at a desk. He keeps time by piercing a coconut with a small hole and puts it in a bucket of water. It takes about twenty-one seconds to sink. There are two rounds. At the start and end of each fight he beats a slit bamboo drum.

As soon as one is injured, the cock that lands the blow is picked up, so that both birds are not injured. The one that lands the blow is put back down again to walk around for twenty-one seconds, the time it takes a coconut to sink. He is then picked up and the coconut is sunk two more times. The injured bird is tended during this time and then the fight starts again. The second round is the final one. Usually the bird that lands the first blow lands the fatal blow. The loser is the one that dies first.

If the cocks do not fight during the first twenty-one seconds, their owners pick them up and encourage them. The process is repeated. If they still refuse to fight, they are both put into a wicker cage and they always fight then, to the death. It is not a satisfying end.

The Birds

The rules of the fight, the colours and the shape of the birds have been laid down for centuries. In the past only local birds were allowed. Now, cocks from Lombok, Java and even as far afield as the Philippines, Japan and the United States make their way to Bali. They must be healthy and there are regulations against specific marks, such as black freckles on their legs, which are unlucky. Cocks with red splotches on their muscles, tongues or skins are also forbidden.

Gambling

Nearly everyone gambles. There are two sorts of bet:
- Between the principals
- Between members of the audience

Between the Principals

This bet is usually large and made between the owners of the two birds, although they may have backing from friends and relatives. The bet is even money. The umpire holds the money and oversees the bet, which is the formal one. The winner takes his bet and gets to keep the body of the beaten bird, which ends up as dinner. Out of the takings about 10% is paid to the umpire and the sponsors of the fight. If there is no winner, a draw is declared.

Between Members of the Audience

After the main bet has been concluded, side betting takes place and it is a noisy process. The bets are usually small and between individuals, who yell and gesture to each other from their positions in the audience. The bets are always odd. The odds are 10-9, 9-8, 8-7, 7-6, 6-5, 5-4, 4-3, 3-2, and 2-1.

There is a favourite picked by a hard-core group of experts. The gambler wanting to back the underdog shouts the short-side number of the odds he wants to be given by someone else. So, if he wants four to three, he shouts three, which means he puts up three. On the other hand, a person wanting to back the favourite yells the colour of the bird, brown, speckled, or whatever.

They search for a suitable partner in the audience. The man backing the underdog indicates how large a bet he wishes to make with the relevant number of fingers in front of his face. If his partner does the same, the contract is concluded and the bet is made. The number of fingers is the multiple of the underdog's bid, so, for example, two fingers in a 6-5 bid means 2x5, that is 10,000 rupiah is bet against 12,000. All bets are settled immediately after the fight.

The Psychology

Clifford Geertz analysed the psychology of cockfights in an essay called *Deep Play–Notes on the Balinese Cockfight* (1972). He concluded that the male participants identify with their cocks so much that the bets are a laying of their public self, their masculinity, on the line.

What is at stake is personal triumph or humility. The big even bets should not affect the gamblers financially in the long run. The small bets can affect one's pocket and family fortunes are frequently lost.

Cockfighting is a sacred matter. The rules are written down in ancient *lontar* palm books, which are village heirlooms.

Chapter 30

Balinese Symbolism

What is a Symbol?
A symbol is something that represents something else. Balinese culture is very rich in symbolism.

Balinese Swastikas
Visitors to Bali look askance at swastikas which sometimes adorn walls and temples and probably do not realise that they have been a Hindu symbol for over 3,000 years. They are also associated with Buddhism. The word 'swastika' is derived from the Sanskrit word for 'well-being' and is partly uttered in the Balinese greeting *Om Swasti Astu*, which means 'May God grant that you are well'. There are hotels and restaurants called 'Swastika'. The typical village crossroads is designed as a swastika.

The sun wheel represents life, death and reincarnation. It also has nine positions and symbolises the Balinese mandala, which illustrates the four cardinal directions, intermediate directions and centre. The swastika is not a symbol of evil and may have been inspired by the constellation of the Big Dipper around the North Star.

In China 卐 is a general superlative and a sign for the magnificent number 10,000. There is some confusion as to whether the clockwise swastika 卐 or the counter-clockwise 卍 is the sign with the more positive meaning. Both types have appeared in many different contexts. Where the sign is

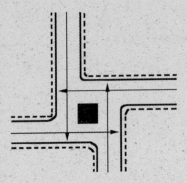

The typical village crossroads is designed as a swastika.

an official or national symbol, 卐 is always preferred. The instances of 卐 are more numerous than those of 卍.

OM

OM represents the Balinese Trinity and is the most important sound in Bali. It starts every mantra and prayer. Brahma, the Creator, is symbolised by the letter A, Wisnu, the Preserver, is symbolised by the letter U and Siwa, the Destroyer, is symbolised by the letter M. This spells AUM or OM.

Writing

Writing is as sacred as the message it conveys. Powerful symbolic writings hang above Balinese doorways on pieces of white cloth. Written symbols are written on the teeth during a tooth-filing ceremony, on offerings and on the shroud of a deceased person.

Weapons

Gods are symbolised by their weapons. Wisnu's weapon is the *Cakra*, a magical discus with eight spokes. Mahadewa's weapon is *Naga*, the snake.

Mountains

Mountains symbolise the dwelling places of the gods.

Temples

Temples symbolise the underworld, the Earth and the Heavens.

Geese

The goose is the only animal in Bali that can live in the sea, on land and in the air. It represents the three levels of the Universe.

Garuda

The eagle-like bird, Garuda, is Wisnu's carrier and symbolises him.

Bull

Siwa rides a bull, called Nandi, which symbolises him.

Rice
Rice symbolises life.

Betel
Betel chewing is an old Asian habit consisting of three ingredients, the green betel leaf, the red areca nut and white lime. The colours of the components symbolise the Trinity. The green leaf is Wisnu's colour, red saliva caused by chewing betel is Brahma's colour and white lime is Siwa's colour. Nearly all offerings have these three ingredients tucked away somewhere. The god sits on his own colour while he enjoys the offering.

Green
Rama has a green mask in the dance dramas and shadow puppet plays, because he is an avatar of Wisnu, whose colour is green (or black).

Red
A red or black mask indicates a coarse or rough person.

White
A white mask symbolises a refined person.

Water
Water cleans and purifies. Rainfall is a manifestation of a king's power and purity.

Penjor
The arched peak of the tall bamboo pole represents Mount Agung, the body symbolises the Earth and the dangling head represents man's earthly needs.

Chapter 31

A Passion For Classification

It Takes Two

Ancient Balinese classification started out analysing the world in terms of linked pairs. The same idea appears in Indian Hindu thought, so when it arrived in Bali it did not contradict the Balinese worldview.

The world is divided into opposites: good and bad, day and night, mountain and sea, earth and sky, right and left, young and old, sun and moon, the seen and the unseen, and so on. The Indian Hindu idea related the male and female principles of existence and the Balinese may have been influenced by this concept too.

Three Part Classification

Three part classification is widespread throughout Balinese religion and culture. It sometimes seems as if everything comes in threes. The most important threesomes are: left, centre and right; black, white and red; and Brahma, Wisnu and Siwa.

Five Part Classification

The next logical step is the four cardinal compass points around the centre. Siwa resides in the centre, Wisnu in the north, Brahma in the south, Iswara in the east and Mahadewa in the west.

Linked to the cardinal points and the gods are a wide range of other things, such as colour, elements, syllables, numbers, weapons and days. The Balinese already had a five part classification system before Indian thought reached them, based on directions towards geographical features, such as towards the mountains and the sea: *kaja, kelod, kangin, kauh* and the centre. The structure of offerings and rituals is based on these principles.

There have been unresolved difficulties reconciling the Indian and Balinese systems. Some people follow the Indian system and some the Balinese system. It is particularly apparent in rituals where five animals have to be sacrificed, such as five chickens, each with different coloured feathers. White are placed in the east, red in the south, yellow in the west, black in the north and mixed colours in the centre. Followers of the Indian system place them according to the cardinal points whereas followers of the Balinese system place them according to the position of Mount Agung.

Nine Part Classification: The Balinese Mandala

The Balinese mandala, called *nawa-sanga*, is a map of the cosmic order. Drawn as a star, it has eight arms, pointing to the eight compass points, plus the centre. Each of the directions is associated with a Hindu god and that god's consort, a colour, a day in the week, a number, a sound, a written symbol, an organ of the body, a weapon and so on. There are two more points: up and down.

The gods' consorts are regarded as their husbands' spiritual power or *sakti*. Parvati is Iswara's consort, Saraswati is Brahma's consort, Lakshmi is Wisnu's consort and Durga is Siwa's consort. At the centre all the gods merge into Siwa, who constitutes a higher unity, and so he combines all the colours.

The days are from the Balinese 5-day week. East is linked with the day *Umanis* and the number 5; south with *Paing* and the number 9; west with *Pon* and the number 7; north with *Wage* and the number 4; and the centre with *Kliwon* and the number 8.

The location of offerings reflects the mandala. The enormous ceremony, *Eka Dasa Rudra*, held only once every Balinese century, required many animals to be sacrificed. The animals were assigned to directions, based on the mandala.

White cow, goose and duck are sacrificed in the east, goat in the southeast, cow in the south, dog in the southwest, buffalo in the west, deer in the northwest, black monkey in the north, and horse in the northeast.

Animals of the central group are further sub-divided into an eleven-fold structure. Birds other than fowl are placed in the northeast, footed reptiles in the west, fishes in the north, creatures that crawl (like a centipede and snake) in the nadir, beetles in the zenith and flies and hornets in the centre.

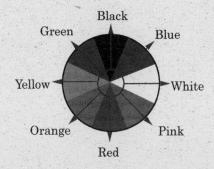

Direction	God	Syllable	Body Organ	Weapon	Colour
East	Iswara	Sang	Heart	Thunderbolt	White
Southeast	Mahasora	Nang	Lungs	Incense	Pink
South	Brahma	Bang	Liver	Club	Red
Southwest	Rudra	Mang	Intestines	Sword	Orange
West	Mahadewa	Tang	Kidneys	Snake-arrow	Yellow
Northwest	Sangkara	Sing	Spleen	Banner	Green
North	Wisnu	Ang	Bile	Club	Black
Northeast	Sambu	Wang	Diaphragm	Trident	Blue
Centre	Siwa	Ing	Tip of the liver	Lotus	Multi-coloured

The Balinese mandala, called *nawa-sanga*, is a map of the cosmic order. Each of the directions is associated with a Hindu god, a symbol, a body organ, a weapon, a colour and other things.

Chapter 32

Balinese Temples

What is a Temple?

A Balinese temple is a place to entertain the gods when they visit human beings. This is where they are worshipped, fed and entertained. They are the most important buildings for the Balinese. Pilgrimages to special temples or a series of temples are very popular.

How Many are There?

It is said that there are more temples to the square mile in Bali than anywhere else in the world and this could well be true. There are hundreds of thousands of them, many more than the 20,000 that is often cited. This underestimate came from Swellengrebel, who was a Christian missionary in the 1930s, 1940s and 1950s in his book *Bali: Studies in Life, Thought and Ritual* (1960). There may be half a million shrines.

There are village temples, family temples, royal temples, clan temples, rice temples, mountain temples, river temples, water temples, market temples, temples to particular gods, temples to particular goddesses, and so on and so on.

Each temple has a congregation, which is a defined social unit. Its members build and maintain the temple and, in effect, 'own' it. They usually live close by and carry its gods on their heads to the sea or to other temples or wherever they want or need to go.

Work on the temple is always communal. There are no stars, no heroes, no Michelangelos. Nothing is signed, although the congregation knows who has done what and when. Villagers do what they can. Outsiders may be hired to carry out specialist work like architecture and carving.

Even though many Balinese families have comfortable homes and televisions, social life is still strongly focused in the temples. People belong to several. This is the place to have a good time, gossip and find a marriage partner. Marriage to a fellow villager, met in the temple, is the norm.

Cleanse Yourself

Temples must be maintained as places of purity. Every person should bathe, brush his teeth, dress in clean clothes and wear a sash before entering. Those who have recently had contact with the dead are ritually impure and cannot enter, nor can women who are menstruating or have just given birth. Violation, even by a tourist, endangers the whole community and requires expensive purification ceremonies.

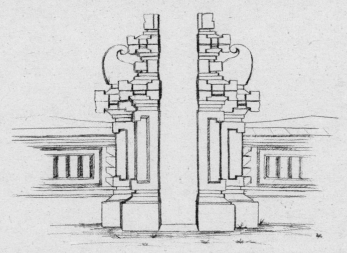

Balinese split gate, called a *candi bentar*, which some believe symbolises Mount Meru, the mythical world mountain. It is oversized and looks like the two sides of a mountain, which were once together, cut in half and pulled apart.

Layout

Experts think that the form of the Balinese temple dates back to the first settlers. They look nothing like a Hindu temple in India. Temples are a series of open rectangular courtyards, surrounded by a series of walls. Public temples are normally divided into three sections, sometimes two, accessed by gates, and divided by walls. As you progress towards the interior, the floor level rises.

The first thing you notice is the famous Balinese split gate, called a *candi bentar*, which some believe symbolises Mount Meru, the mythical world mountain. It is oversized and looks like the two sides of a mountain, which were once together, cut in half and pulled apart. That makes it a reminder of the story that Siwa thereby created Mount Agung and Mount Batur. It also represents the separation of Java and Bali after the end of the Ice Age. A wall, usually partly carved,

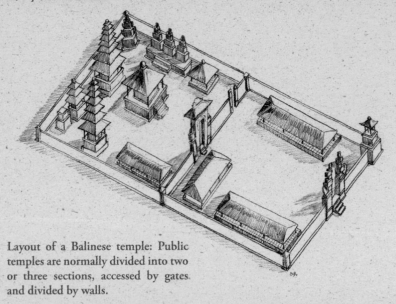

Layout of a Balinese temple: Public
temples are normally divided into two
or three sections, accessed by gates
and divided by walls.

surrounds the whole temple. According to Willem Stutterheim,
the Dutch archaeologist, the purpose of the wall is to set apart the
consecrated area of the village.

Through the split gate lies a large middle courtyard with trees and
pavilions and stone statues. During a ceremony, the courtyard is used
to stage dances. The pavilions are for gamelan orchestras and the statues
dress in coloured skirts.

At the far end of the courtyard is another gate, with a door, called
the *kori agung*, on top of which is an arch or lintel, often with an
elaborately carved Boma, who has popping eyes and a bulbous head.
He protects the inner sanctum. The *kori agung* may be a representation
of Mount Meru, or a head topped by a huge headdress, with earrings,
or a passageway to the world of the gods, or all three.

Several feet in front of a gate is sometimes a free standing wall
called an *aling-aling*, which prevents evil spirits from entering. Evil
spirits are only able to walk and run in straight lines. The *aling-aling*
breaks the line of vision into the courtyard. Belief in evil spirts only
being able to travel in straight lines exists in other places. It explains
the curvy roads in China. Pascal Khoo Thwe mentions the same belief
among the Padaung tribe in the Shan States of Burma in *From the Land
of Green Ghosts, A Burmese Odyssey* (2002).

Many Balinese temples, especially the large ones, have one door for the gods and priests and another one for humans. The smaller one is for humans. Surrounding walls protect the temple from disruptive forces and contain dangerous powers that emanate from the gods when they are in the temple.

Three Sections, Three Functions

Temples are usually laid out in three sections:

- The inner section, the *jeroan*, higher than the rest, at the far *kaja* end, where the holy relics are kept
- The middle section, the *jaba tengah*, the transitional section, with the storerooms and kitchen and pavilions for storing offerings before they are taken into the inner sanctum
- The outer part, the *jaba*, the most secular part, where blood sacrifices to the low spirits take place, cockfights are held and people eat, chat and play cards

The three sections are said to symbolise the head, trunk and feet. More esoteric versions correlate them to the lower part of the female body: womb, thighs and feet.

Altars

Altars, small seats or houses, made of wood or stone, on the top of pedestals, are the most important parts of the temple. They are on the north and east sides, which is in the direction of the mountains, the purest part of the temple.

Priests invite the gods to come down, stay in the altars and attend ceremonies. They receive prayers and requests from their worshippers, partake of offerings, watch the entertainment, talk to their friends and gods visiting from other villages. They are all supposed to have a good time.

Membership

The *banjar* decides who may and who may not be members of the temple congregation. Household membership comprises two people, one male and the other female. They are usually married, but not necessarily. Core members contribute fully, while peripheral members contribute partially and usually only attend for prayers.

Rules

Members' duties are set out in a document called an *awig-awig*. Everyone must take part. Every household gives a specified amount of money, labour and materials at every temple anniversary.

Sanctions for infringements are usually fines, but serious cases can result in expulsion from the *banjar*, which is very grave. This effectively excludes a person from ceremonies. The most worrying punishment is prohibition from using the graveyard, burial rites and therefore any hope of reincarnation.

Financing

The greatest source of funds for temples was hiring out the congregation's donations of labour for harvesting rice. In the 1970s new rice was introduced and removed an important source of income in a stroke. New rice is harvested with large sickles, unlike the small knife needed for old rice, so fewer people are required.

Another important source of revenue for temples was taxing cockfights, but the Indonesian government banned them, except for three sets of cockfights for ritual purposes. The law made it impossible for temples to tax cockfights openly. From the 1980s temples have been relying on donations from rich donors and as an encouragement names and amounts are listed prominently in the temple.

Great Gods, Great Temples

Temples are dedicated to different gods. The rice goddess, Dewi Sri, receives homage and offerings in the rice temples, the market gods in the market temples, the village gods in the village temples and so on. Great gods are worshipped in great temples. The Sea God, for example, has relevance for more than one community and so is not worshipped in a mere local temple.

The temple has a shrine to the principal deity of that temple and smaller shrines to other deities connected in some way to that temple. So, for example, the principal deity in a market temple is Maya Sih, but there are also smaller shrines to Dewi Sri, the rice goddess, as rice is sold in markets.

The Balinese only visit temples that have relevance for them. There are some temples, however, that have relevance for everyone, for example, Pura Besakih.

Temple Anniversaries

Every temple, private or public, has an *odalan* or 'anniversary', usually every Balinese year, which is every 210 days, with music and dancing. Most *odalan* last three days. A few temples fix their *odalan* by reference to the lunar calendar and then they take place either on full or new moon.

Structures within Temples

The temples are open air, with no roofs, containing a number of structures and stone statues.

- *Kulkul*: **Drums**

Every temple has a *kulkul*. The less affluent have them attached to a tree. Rich public temples have tall, square towers, heavily carved, with a roof of black sugar palm fibre, in the outer courtyard, and in them hang two hollow logs, slit drums, the size of a man, of high and low pitches.

Next to the drums is a hammer to call the villagers to the temple to prepare for ceremonies, to the ceremonies themselves or to warn the community of fires, disasters, emergencies or the discovery of a thief. Like Morse code, the double sounding of the *kulkul* followed by rapid striking indicates that there has been a robbery in the area.

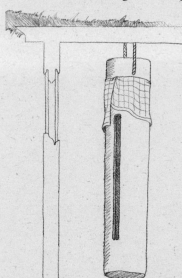

The drums are given daily offerings and dressed in sarongs. During ceremonies they are beaten rhythmically in time with the gamelan to produce a ladder of sound connecting men with the gods.

- *Padmasana*: **Empty Seats**

Public and private temples usually have a *padmasana*, which is an empty stone seat. They were introduced in

Kulkul is a slit drum, the size of a man, of high and low pitches beaten to call people to prepare for ceremonies, to the ceremonies themselves or to warn the community of fires, disasters, emergencies or the discovery of a thief.

the 17th or 18th centuries by the *brahmana*, and are found in almost every family home. In broad terms, *padmasana* represent Mount Meru and through it the Universe. They are located in the most auspicious, northeast corner of temples, the back orientated towards Mount Agung, drawing legitimation from the large one at Pura Besakih.

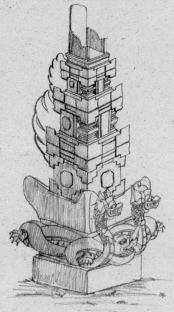

It is Siwa's throne, in the form of a lotus seat. *Padma* means 'lotus' and *asana* means 'seat'. Siwa sits in the centre of the lotus. Wisnu, Iswara, Mahadewa and Brahma are normally represented high on the shrine and in the middle are carvings of the world of man and his daily activities. The base is Bedawang Nala, the cosmic turtle that supports the world, with two serpents beside him, their firm coils preventing the world from moving.

Public and private temples usually have a *padmasana*, which is an empty stone seat. It is Siwa's throne, in the form of a lotus seat.

• *Lingga*: Phallus

Unlike in India, *lingga* are not common. They are oblong rocks, rounded at the top, which represent Siwa's phallus and his creative power. There are some *lingga* at Besakih and other important temples. They are an abstract symbol of the god himself. Combined with the *yoni*, its pedestal and female counterpart, they stand for duality, which dissolves into the supreme unity or totality of all existence.

Lingga are oblong rocks, rounded at the top, which represent Siwa's phallus and his creative power.

• *Meru*: Pagodas

Expensive to build, and very spectacular, *meru* are symbolic of the mythical mountain, Mount Meru, at the centre of the world, which is the home of the gods. *Meru* are likewise the homes of gods when they visit during temple ceremonies. They descend down the open central shaft to the temple.

Meru have an uneven number of tiers, one to eleven, which get smaller the higher they get, resembling a pagoda, thatched with black sugar palm fibre. The higher the *meru*, the higher the status of the god within the *meru* and to whom it is dedicated: eleven roofs for Siwa and nine for Brahma and Wisnu. There are eleven-storied *merus* at Besakih and Mount Batur Temples, the two most important temples in Bali.

The height of the *meru* in family temples indicates the family's caste. The commoners, *sudra*, have one to three roofs, high caste aristocrats five to nine, consecrated kings, with their divine ancestry, eleven.

- ### Stone Statues

Statues of the great Hindu gods are rare. Statues are usually guardian figures and the disembodied heads of Boma and Kala.

Meru on Lake Bratan. *Meru* are the homes of gods when they visit during temple ceremonies.

Chapter 33

Types of Temples

Hierarchy

Temples have a hierarchy and through the hierarchy and interlocking relations no village and no person is isolated. Ritual ties ensure that every person has an identity.

Temples based on locality:

- Village temples
- Regional temples, which draw on a number of village temples, and are often associated with regional courts
- Island-wide state temples

Temples based on irrigation:

- *Subak* temples
- Temples for groups of *subak*
- Island-wide temples, which are the same as the ones based on locality

Temples based on descent:

- Family temples
- Temples for *sub-dadia*
- Temples for *dadia*
- Temples for *sub-warga*
- Temples for *warga*

Village Temples: The Three Sanctuaries

The *adat* village is defined by three, sometimes two, communal temples, in which every member of the village has an interest. They are called the *tiga kahyangan*. *Tiga* is 'three' and *kahyangan* is an elevated word for 'temple' meaning 'sanctuary' or 'place of the gods'. *Pura* is the ordinary word for 'temple'. Individual temples are called Pura so and so. The three temples are *Pura Puseh*, *Pura Desa* and *Pura Dalem*.

According to tradition, Empu Kuturan, the legendary Javanese court priest of the early 11th century and perhaps the greatest of Bali's cultural heroes, established them. Every Balinese person belongs to one and only one *tiga kahyangan* and everyone in the congregation belongs to the same *desa adat*.

- *Pura Puseh*

  Pura Puseh, the Origin or Navel Temple, is built in the mountainward *kaja* direction of the village and is the sanctuary of Brahma, the Creator. The main shrine is devoted to the deified founders of the village. There is usually a pagoda-like *meru*, dedicated to Ratu Gede Puseh, and shrines dedicated to other deities, and often a high stone seat in honour of the god of Mount Agung. There are normally shrines to Dewi Sri, the popular rice goddess, and Rambut Sedana, god of wealth and money.

- *Pura Desa*

  Pura Desa is in the centre of the village, at the main crossroads, and is the sanctuary of Wisnu, the Preserver, and devoted to the affairs of the villagers, the living community. A *wantilan* or meeting hall for cockfights is usually very near and a huge sacred banyan tree often shades the area.

- *Pura Dalem*

  Pura Dalem is in the seaward *kelod* direction of the village, and is the sanctuary of Siwa, the Destroyer, and his wife, Durga, and devoted to the souls of the uncremated. Every village has a *Pura Dalem*.

  Although the temples are formally linked to the three great Hindu gods, they are usually thought of as temples for the local deities and their powers restricted to the village. All members of the village, regardless of status, visit the village temples.

Regional Temples

The main characteristic of a regional temple is that it draws attendance from several communities to its major festivals. The relationship may be formed when a village breaks away from its core village and returns to its core village temples for major ceremonies.

Island-Wide State Temples: The Six Sanctuaries

There is some confusion over the six state temples, as hardly any two texts list the same six. *Sad* means 'six', but it may be that the alternative meaning of the Sanskrit word *sad*, namely 'essential' is a better translation.

The important thing is that they are all ancient historical sites, in which every Balinese has an interest. They protect the entire island and the Balinese people as a whole, and reinforce the notion that despite the so-called caste system the Balinese are one people. Most commentators describe them as:

- **Pura Besakih, the Mother Temple**
  This is the most important temple in Bali and is the spiritual and religious centre of the Universe, where Brahma, Wisnu and Siwa are worshipped, as well as many kings and princes of the past, who have become divine ancestors.

- **Pura Uluwatu**
  This one sits on a cliff in the most southern tip of Bali.

- **Pura Goa Lawah**
  Known as the 'Bat Cave Temple', it is near Kusamba on the east coast.

- **Pura Lempuyang Luhur**
  It is in the Karangasem district of east Bali.

- **Pura Batukaru**
  This temple is on the slope of Batukaru Mountain in the Tabanan district, and some say that it, rather than Besakih, is the oldest temple in Bali, because Siwa sent seven of his children from Mount Semeru in Java to the sacred places in Bali and they arrived at Batukaru first.

- **Pura Pulaki**
  This is the second largest temple in the Singaraja district of north Bali.

Temples Based on Descent

A *dadia* is a group which acknowledges descent from a common ancestor. On marriage a couple immediately supports the *dadia*. There is a head man, the *klian dadia*, in charge of *dadia* affairs, and he may or may not have a secretary or treasurer. He keeps a record of members and their financial contributions. Ritual matters are carried out by the *dadia's* own priest.

Each level of descent is marked by a temple, and the higher up the family tree you go, the more members of that branch there are. It is another example in Bali of a social network extending beyond the borders of an individual's village.

Memory rarely extends beyond the great-grandfather level and records are rare, unless they are gentry, and even then, ancestry may be assumed rather than proven. Descent groups, especially among the *sudra*, are often not known at all. Some families may belong to no group, other than itself. There is, however, a great desire to find out, and *balian*, trance mediums, are the answer. Some people try several before deciding on the correct answer to their prayers. *Warga* is a descent group comprising a number of separate *dadia*. Once found, a new relationship with a *dadia* or *warga*, and their temples, is formed. Nobody applying for membership would be turned away lightly for fear of annoying the ancestors.

It is inappropriate to worship at a *dadia* temple belonging to a different caste. There is a curious rule that if a person of a high caste happens to make a mistake and enters and worships at a *dadia* temple belonging to a lower caste, no one may tell him until afterwards, when it is too late.

Functional Temples
The irrigation societies, *subak*, have temples, the farmers have temples, the merchants have temples, the fishermen have temples and so on.

Family Temples
Every Balinese Hindu belongs to a family temple. Family temples vary, but some shrines are obligatory. The temple is always surrounded by a wall and built in the sacred *kaja-kangin* direction of the family compound.

In this compound there are a number of shrines, on carved plinths about ten feet (a metre and a half) high; the total height of the shrine may be twice that figure. Most of the shrines are dedicated to deified ancestors. Daily offerings are placed on the shrines. Invariably there is a roofed shrine temple with three compartments devoted to Brahma (on the right), Wisnu (on the left) and Siwa (in the centre). It is the central place of worship.

There is always a roofed shrine called *taksu* in the *kaja* direction devoted to the god of one's profession. A performer presents offerings at this shrine for as long as the performance lasts.

There is normally a *padmasana*, the empty stone seat, in the auspicious northeast corner orientated towards Mount Agung. If a family member cannot attend a temple ceremony, he prays at this shrine instead.

There is always a roofed single compartment shrine in the family compound, but not in the family temple, whose spirit protects the property. It usually stands in the middle of the compound. Kitchens and wells always have small shrines, often high up out of the way, devoted to Brahma, god of fire, and Wisnu, god of water.

Chapter 34

Holy Men and Women

The Personnel

Religions can do without popes, prophets, messiahs and archbishops, but they cannot do without holy men and priests. They are the ones who communicate with the spirits.

Bali has many kinds of holy men and they are treated with great respect. They are all involved in rituals of one kind or another.

- *Pemangku*: local priests
- *Pedanda*: high priests
- *Dalang*: puppeteers
- *Balian*: mediums

Pemangku, the local priests, are the most visible. They walk the streets and ride bicycles and motorbikes. Their main job is to tend their own temples. *Pedanda*, the high priests, are very splendid characters, who officiate at the most important ceremonies. *Dalang*, the puppeteers, have a limited priestly role. They give performances during temple ceremonies. *Balian* also have a limited priestly role. They are mediums and faith healers and not normally encountered by visitors, but are consulted by the Balinese when the occasion arises.

The *pemangku*, local priests, are usually from the *sudra* caste and are affiliated to and in charge of a temple. They look after its affairs and maintenance. They dress in white.

Pemangku: Local Priest

The *pemangku* are usually, but not necessarily, from the *sudra* caste and are affiliated to and in charge of a temple.

They look after its affairs and maintenance. Easily recognisable, they dress in white from head to toe, at least when they are on duty, which is most of the time. We do know one, however, who wears a red baseball cap the wrong way round and blue jeans, when not working.

They are mainly men, often poor, but allowed to have small businesses on the side. There are women priests too. As with most occupations, the vocation tends to run in families. Sometimes the congregation appoints them or, as in the case with our friend and his wife, a god informed them of their vocation by means of a person in trance.

They are trained by other priests and study the books. Their duties include saying prayers, inviting the deities to attend ceremonies, sprinkling holy water over offerings and the faithful during prayer. They normally only converse with local gods. Priests may marry. On death they are not buried but cremated as soon as convenient.

Pedanda: High Priest

The *pedanda* come from the *brahmana* caste. All *pedanda* are *brahmana* but not all *brahmana* are *pedanda*. When Islam conquered the Majapahit empire in Java in the 16th century, the *pedanda*, carrying their sacred books, censers, chalices, rosaries, oil lamps and bells, came to Bali.

There are two kinds; the majority are *pedanda Siwa* and the minority are *pedanda Buddha*. They are both Hindus, despite the name, but their paraphernalia, rituals, mantras and dress differ. All important ceremonies require both of them. The *pedanda Buddha* deal with rituals involving the low spirits, the *butas* and *kalas*. They are in a minority because their families are in decline and it is difficult to get the candidates.

The *pedanda*, high priests, are well educated and deeply versed in the holy books. They carry out the most important ceremonies. *Pedanda* pray to the higher Indic gods, such as Brahma, Wisnu and Siwa.

The *pedanda Siwa* are further subdivided into descent lines, who trace their ancestry back to different wives of their founder Nirartha, who was the court priest of Dalem Baturenggong during the heyday of the Gelgel dynasty in the 16th century. Nirartha was an earthly descendant of Brahma. To non-*brahmana*, they all have the same status and there is no distinction in level of seating.

They study for a long time, so most of them are not young. They must know theology, the Balinese calendars, the epics, the rituals and temple ceremonies. Part of the consecration ceremony of becoming a *pedanda* involves his symbolic death, whereby he is wrapped in a shroud, and then he symbolically comes back to life, fully purified. The ceremony is always carried out by another *pedanda*. That is why *pedanda* are called 'twice-born'.

In pre-colonial times, before the Dutch arrived, there was a close symbiotic relationship with the royal families. No priest could be consecrated without the king's permission and no king could be legitimately installed without a priest. It was a convenient arrangement and there was some doubt and dispute as to which caste was the highest in the land. In addition to their other duties, such as advising and praying for royal families and strengthening the ruler spiritually, the *pedanda* presided over the royal courts and acted as judges. In return, they were exempted from paying taxes.

They are well educated and deeply versed in the holy books. They hold the secrets and carry out the most important ceremonies. *Pedanda* pray to the higher Indic gods, such as Brahma, Wisnu and Siwa, and are believed to be descended from them. They are able to carry out ceremonies for any descent group or community.

People speak to *pedanda* in High Balinese, the form of Balinese which is filled with honorific terms. *Pedanda* reply, if they are speaking to a commoner, in Low Balinese. This old-fashioned mode of conversation is changing among some today.

Bells and Smells

As befits their status, *pedanda* dress in splendid black and white, wear rosaries and mitres and tie up their long hair in a knot, into which fresh flowers are stuck. They chant holy mantras, ring bells, waft incense and make elaborate hand gestures called *mudras*, which energise all the senses.

Pedanda suffer a number of restrictions. They are not allowed to carry out manual labour, even if they want to, and are the only group in Bali subject to dietary rules. Beef and chicken are forbidden, but rice field duck is allowed. They must eat off new plates or fresh banana leaves. There are no restrictions on whom they can marry. There are a few female *pedanda*, but they can only marry another priest. *Pedanda* should not display any emotions if members of their families are hurt or die. They renounce all human feelings.

On death, a *pedanda* is not buried. As he has been one with Siwa, he could not be buried and become the servant of the deity of the temple of the dead. The corpse is put on a bier in the shape of a lotus and carried to pure ground, which has never been used for such a purpose. He will not be reborn.

Priests chant holy mantras, ring bells, waft incense and make elaborate hand gestures called *mudras*, which energise all the senses.

Holy Water and the Pedanda

Early every morning, the *pedanda* washes, puts on white clothes, goes to his pavilion, sits down cross-legged and prays. He murmurs passages from the Vedas and recites mantras accompanied by the appropriate *mudras*. This may last from twenty minutes to three hours. His soul is lifted up from his abdomen, leaves his body and Siwa enters him through the fontanelle, which is the soft area between the bones of the cranium. The priest and god become one. Through this means, he becomes a god and makes holy water.

Certain holy springs and lakes produce holy water, but only that made by *pedanda* has sufficient power for certain, especially royal, ceremonies. Strictly, their income is restricted to the consecration and sale of holy water, but they are allowed to accept gifts, and it would be unthinkable not to offer them something.

Mantras and *Mudras*: the Secret Language of the Pedanda

The language of hands is probably the oldest in the world. *Mudras* are symbolic hand gestures, found in India, Tibet, China, Japan and Bali.

They are a means of expression, which has become highly developed in Bali. The mind conceives the thought, the mouth enunciates the mantra or magic formula, and the hands represent it physically through a *mudra*. The whole human personality is brought into force at the same time: spirit (mind), soul (sound), and body (hand gesture).

The *mudra* is a visible expression of the mantra. Mantras include extracts from the Vedas, the most ancient Hindu scriptures, names of gods and goddesses, and many meaningless syllables, which vibrate in the body and mind and produce states of consciousness. The mantras are magical and each mantra has an accompanying *mudra*, which seals the magic. *Mudra* in Sanskrit means 'seal'. The very shape of the letters exerts a mystical influence on the viewer, which cannot be obtained in translation.

Steven Mithen in *The Singing Neanderthals* (2005) describes research carried out into Indian mantras, which are the origin of Balinese mantras. The mantras are lengthy and sound like language, but often the words lack meaning and grammatical structure. Yet some mantras do have meanings as set out and translated by Angela Hobart in *Healing Performances in Bali* (2003). She gives examples of mantras recited by healers and priests with whom she has worked. Correct pronunciation, rhythm, melody and posture are required. It seems that for the most part mantras have the characteristics of language and music, but are neither.

Human language is not that ancient: between 40,000 and 100,000 years old. Ritual is much older than that—the Neanderthals used ritual. It seems likely that mantras are older than language and language derives from them. They have little or no meaning and are repeated endlessly. It explains why the same forms appear in India, Bali, China, Korea and Japan: they are not translatable into local languages. There is an intriguing structural similarity between mantras and birdsong—the same refrains and repetitions appear. This is entirely different from ordinary language.

Many *mudras* are performed with a flower between the *pedanda's* fingers. A member of his family will have picked them a little earlier, probably from his own garden. The most sacred is the white or yellow cempaka. After each *mudra* the *pedanda* flicks the flower towards the four points of the compass. During ceremonies at night and in *Pura Dalem*, the temple associated with death, night flowers are used.

Frits Staal, Professor Emeritus of Philosophy and South and Southeast Asian Studies at the University of California, Berkeley, says that rituals have no meanings, goals or aims. They exist for their own sake and are pure activity. Rituals have to be faultlessly executed in accordance with their own rules. In this respect they are similar to games, which are equally unproductive, or to music, or to dance, of which Isadora Duncan said, 'If I could tell you what it meant there would be no point in dancing it'. I feel, however, that the *mudras* and mantras of Balinese priests must once have had meanings, even if it was only when they were devised and carried out for the first time, meanings which have now been long forgotten.

Dalang: A Puppeteer Gets Ready for Work

The *dalang*, the shadow puppeteer, and his puppets are treated with great respect. The first encounter most people have with a *dalang* is at the beginning of a shadow puppet performance. He is a kind of priest.

Before every performance, he says prayers to bring the puppets to life. He can make holy water. The consecration of a *dalang* is similar to the consecration of a priest. It is performed by a priest and takes place in the priest's or the *dalang's* family temple. If he is a *sudra*, he is henceforth called *jero* and if high caste he becomes a *pemangku dalang*. They are nearly always male.

As he sets off for a performance, which may take place in a family temple or public temple or just in a field, the *dalang* stops at his gate and feels his hair knot. If it pulsates to the right, he puts his right foot forward. If it pulsates to the left, he puts his left foot forward. If it pulsates in the middle, he jumps. He is now all set.

Before entering the stage he tests his breath to see which god will communicate through him. If the breath exhaled from his right nostril is stronger, Brahma will perform. If the breath exhaled from his left nostril is stronger, then Wisnu will perform. If they are of equal strength, then it is Iswara.

He then prays for protection and for the gods to descend and enter him and the puppets, and for the audience to enjoy the performance. Next he sprinkles holy water, which he has made, and makes offerings to ensure that the stage is pure.

He requests Brahma to give the puppets life, so that they dance well. When the puppets are in the large wooden chest, not being used, they are thought to be sleeping. He knocks the chest three times, takes out and prepares the puppets. They are placed on the lid on the *dalang's* right, in the correct order, so that he may pick them up easily. The performance can begin.

Tumpek Wayang

Every 210 days is a day called *Tumpek Wayang*. It is also *Kajeng-Kliwon*, and a special day for shadow puppets, which are taken out and given offerings by the *dalang*. It also happens to be very unlucky to be born during that week. Such a child is prone to illness and injury from Kala, the demon god.

To cure the baby an elaborate ceremony called *sudamala* is carried out by a *dalang* after a day or night shadow puppet performance. It shows the priestly nature of the *dalang*. He makes holy water for the exorcistic ceremony. Only a *dalang* can make this holy water. He narrates the story of how Kala, a manifestation of Siwa, threatened to eat a pair of twin brothers born during the *Tumpek Wayang* week. The *dalang* uses particular puppets for the purpose.

This elaborate ceremony is also performed when someone suffers an unnatural death, for example, a fatal accident. It may also be performed during a cremation, and is used to ensure a person's health.

Balian: Mediums

There are about 2,500 different types of *balian*, who are mostly consulted at times of illness. They are a bridge between the seen and the unseen worlds. Normally they are of the *sudra* caste and are highly esteemed and called by their honorific title *jero balian*. They do not charge a fee but are given donations. Whereas Western trained doctors cure illnesses from natural causes, *balian* cure illnesses from supernatural causes. They communicate with the spirits of the unseen world through trances which normally last between fifteen seconds and twenty minutes. *Balian* get their knowledge from palm leaf manuscripts, messages from the gods, ancestors or spirits, always imparted while in trance, or through pieces of cloth, jewels or *krises*.

They are consulted on the causes of family problems, why fires have broken out, livestock died, crops failed or why there have been family conflicts, motor accidents, premature deaths or suicides. The Balinese believe that such matters have specific causes and the *balian* can ascertain them. The cause is usually a person's fault: it could be a dead person in the family, and often it is because a certain ceremony has not been carried out or has not been carried out properly and the ancestors are annoyed. The *balian* speaks in vague terms and leaves the listener to interpret the answers. There seems to be no objection to recording the proceedings on a tape recorder.

The *balian* advises how to rectify the problem, which is usually that the ceremony in question must be done or redone. In big cases, where a whole temple brings a case, the remedy may be a major temple festival added on to a regular *odalan* anniversary festival. It seems that the spirits are prepared to negotiate and the currency is offerings and ceremonies. A *balian* builds up his or her reputation through satisfied customers.

What's Up, Doc?

There is no conflict between the work of a folk healer, a *balian*, and a scientifically trained doctor. If the patient suspects his illness has been caused by the unseen world, he goes to a *balian* and if he suspects it comes from the seen world, he goes to a doctor. Angela Hobart in *Healing Performances of Bali* (2003) provides a useful table:

Illnesses from the unseen world (*niskala*)	Illnesses from the seen world (*sekala*)
Punishment by the gods and ancestors.	Self-evident causes, eg old age, symptoms such as failing eyesight.
Neglect of the demonic spirits, *butal kala*.	Some infections. These come either from other humans or because the body is unfit.
Neglect of the four spirit siblings, *kanda empat*.	Not having eaten correctly. This may lead to aches and pains or a cold.
Sorcery/witchcraft, including the use of magical tools.	
Due to *karma*, the laws of cause and effect.	

Explanatory model of illnesses.

As the Balinese become more aware of medical science, illnesses move from the unseen to the seen category. X-rays have reduced the *balian's* workload. There is no rivalry: a doctor may refer a patient to a *balian* and *vice versa*.

The *balian* chants mantras and prescribes herbal medicines, provides amulets for the patient to wear and hands out protective drawings with sacred syllables on them. The patient cannot look at the drawings, which are wrapped up in a parcel. They will be buried when he gets home or hidden in the roofspace of his house or even worn. Sometimes the *balian* inscribes drawings on the patient's body. Balinese, especially men, like to wear magic rings. They may request the *balian* to give the rings special powers to calm and purify the mind, give them physical strength or make them handsome.

Balian do have successes. Patients believe in them and that goes a long way. They can shift a patient's consciousness and change his attitudes, so that he engages more fully with his family, enemies and community. After a session the patient or victim of bad luck sees things differently.

Even in the West placebos work in mysterious ways in curing various illnesses. A person's beliefs and hopes about a treatment can have a significant biochemical effect. It seems to be a case of mind over molecules. Changed behaviour and attitudes, how one feels, and how one acts, can even affect one's body chemistry.

Ancestors

Tracing ancestors is important to the Balinese of all levels. Some *balian* specialise in ascertaining ancestral identity. Several days after the birth of a baby, the father or grandfather visits a distant *balian*, secretly and in silence. He does not tell the *balian* the purpose of his visit, and waits silently for an audience, with his offerings. *Balian* are acutely sensitive to moods and the nature of the offerings.

The *balian* goes into a trance, contacts the ancestors and, if he has been successful, informs the father or grandfather of the identity of the soul which has been reincarnated in the baby. Normally it is a member of the family, four generations back. The father or grandfather returns home and reports the news.

A *balian* is also consulted after a death. When a person dies, a member of his family goes to a *balian* to ask what the deceased person would like done during his funeral or cremation. It may be that the deceased wants to be cremated with his favourite sarong.

Specialisation

They tend to specialise, for example in massage, midwifery, or abortion (now illegal), or in contacting ancestors, preparing corpses, starting or stopping rain, handing out charms, casting harmful spells, or explaining misfortunes, and often the reason you have been having bad luck is that some other *balian* has been casting spells on you. People of both sexes, male and female, can become a *balian*. Those who practise black magic are usually old and ugly. It is commonly believed that their powers have declined in the last 150 years or so, but in the old days, they could fly to the moon.

Chapter 35

Balinese Architecture

The Professional Team

Traditional Balinese houses, temples, rice barns and other structures are built according to traditional Balinese rules, called *Asta Kosala Kosali*, written in *lontar* palm books and interpreted by traditional architects called *undagi*. Balinese architects do not design buildings; they merely interpret the traditional rules. Construction work is carried out by men, except for labouring and plastering walls, which are carried out by women, carrying huge weights on their heads and damaging their spines.

Rules is Rules

Traditional methods of construction and rules of proportion date back to the 15th century. Buildings and courtyards are scaled to the size of the head of the family. The *undagi* measures the owner and transfers the measurements to his bamboo measuring stick.

A basic wall measurement is the length of the middle finger to the elbow plus the distance between the middle fingers when each arm is fully extended to the side. A little extra, the *urip*, is added to make the building live. The *urip* is the width of the fist with the thumb extended. The floor to the horizontal beams supporting the roof should be the distance from tiptoe to the highest one can reach. Measurements like these govern the dimensions of the walls, gates, buildings, roofs, shrines and temples.

The client's wealth, status and location are also factors to take into account in configuring the buildings. There are three levels of cost: expensive, moderate and cheap. The *Asta Kosala Kosali* forbid the building of a house that is greater than is appropriate for one's status. Sickness and even death can result.

The *lontar* also specify what kind of wood is needed for various structures. Pillars of a shrine or temple must be cut from trees growing locally and be erected so that the root is nearest the ground, the way they were when they were living. If they get mixed up, the position can be sorted out by weighing them. The root end is heavier.

Buildings and courtyards are scaled to the size of the head of the family. The architect measures the owner and transfers the measurements to his bamboo measuring stick.

Palladian Villas

There is a parallel with Western theories of ideal proportions. In the 6th century BC, Pythagoras, the Greek mathematician, believed that the basis of everything that we find beautiful is mathematical. Using Pythagoras' ratios, Andrea Palladio (1508-1580), perhaps the most influential architect ever, proposed ideal proportions for every kind of building in *The Four Books of Architecture*, which was published in Venice in 1570. He set down principles for the sizes of rooms, the heights of ceilings, and the best measurements for staircases, windows and doors.

The perfect column height should be nine times its diameter. The height of the capital at the top of a column should be equal to the diameter of the column. The perfect capital is therefore one-ninth the height of the column. The distance between columns should be twice the diameter of each column and they should taper in the upper two-thirds. The lower part should be perpendicular. The architrave or frieze on top of the columns should be one fifth their height.

North and South

The Balinese have a highly refined sense of place. Buildings are laid out according to their function in certain positions, which are related to cardinal points and geographical features. *Kaja*, 'towards the mountains', where the gods reside, is the place for sacred buildings, and *kelod*, 'towards the sea', away from the gods, is the place for impure buildings. In central Bali, *kaja* is the equivalent of north and *kelod* south.

East and West

There is a second axis relating to sunrise in the east and sunset in the west. It therefore runs at right angles to the mountain-sea axis. As the sun rises, it brings day and life, which are uranian forces associated with the mountains. As it sets, in the west, towards the sea, it enters a chthonian sphere and sinks into the underworld. The lines of these two axes provide a system of co-ordinates and varying force fields, which determine ritual behaviour and the position of buildings.

Initial Building Ceremony

Before construction begins, ceremonies have to be performed. For sacred buildings, five metals, gold, silver, bronze, iron and copper, are buried in the foundations, along with a coconut, which is wrapped with five differently coloured threads. For secular buildings, a brick wrapped in a white cloth is buried. The day of the ceremony must be auspicious, as must the day that building starts.

Courtyards

The first impression is of a series of courtyards, whether the building is a temple, a palace or a house compound. Balinese structures are defined according to function. Open spaces are necessary as large ceremonies involving hundreds of people may take place outside.

Horizontals

All structures, whether they are buildings, gateways or altars, are built up in horizontal layers. The effect gives stability. Symmetry gives solemnity and dependability.

Buildings

Most buildings follow the same model: pavilions of varying sizes. The walls are concrete, timber or brick. The roof is tiled or thatched. The structure may be closed or open at the sides. There are frequently exposed columns, varying from four to sixteen, which have distinct carved bases, which provide spiritual strength to the structure. Buildings are usually reached by a minimum of three steps. They are assembled with very few nails. Tools are simple hammers, chisels, saws, axes and a plane. Posts and beams carry the load of the roof.

Pura: Temples
The layout of a Balinese temple derives from walled temple compounds of south China and India.

Puri: Palaces
In classical 19th century Bali, the king was quasi-divine and during state ceremonies the palace was seen as a temple. There are nine *puri agung*, which are the palaces of the old rajas of Bali, and about 5,000 mini-palaces, which belong to minor royalty. The palace was considered a replica of the cosmos, a sacred symbol. It derives from the Javanese Majapahit style, always square or rectangular, walled, and containing courts within courts.

Typically there are a number of functional areas:
- Family temple and sacred areas which the gods are invited to visit during ceremonies
- Public areas for the public
- Royal chambers where the king would have met his nobles in the old days
- Living quarters for the king, his father, brothers and male cousins
- Bedrooms for his *sudra* wives
- An impure area for menstruating women, animals, bathrooms and rubbish

As with houses and temples, the parts that are most sacred are to the north and east, towards the mountains, and profane or unclean parts towards the sea. Prestigious and private areas are in the inner parts of the palace and less prestigious and public areas are in the outer parts.

Family Compounds
Like temples and palaces private family compounds are made up of separate structures. As the magic circle in the Ramayana story protects Sita, so walls protect the Balinese household from evil forces. The chink in the armour is the main gateway. To protect the place and make it as safe as houses, an *aling-aling* screen in front of the gateway prevents

demons seeing inside and entering. The inner courtyard contains individual, specialised buildings. These comprise the main sleeping area, which has an open veranda, a guest pavilion, a raised barn for storing rice, a kitchen and a bathing area. There is a family temple and there may be an area for keeping pigs.

The buildings face inwards and each building is in a designated geographical position. Energy flows from the central courtyard outwards. The heir of the household and his family sleep in the northern pavilion. Family heirlooms are kept there. The family temple is in the northeast. The entrance is in the southwest. The kitchen and rice barn are placed in the southerly or westerly directions, away from the family temple, in the impure area. If there are several families living in the compound, they normally each have their own kitchen.

The *bale dangin*, the pavilion used to stage important rites of passage, like weddings, tooth-filings and lyings-in-state, is in the east, close to the family temple. It usually has six wooden pillars, a thatched or tiled roof, and a raised wooden pallet, which serves as a bed and an altar on which to place offerings and where the priest sits. The back area is walled in on two sides and the other two sides are open.

Lumbung: Rice Barn

Every family compound, if they can afford it, has a rice barn, typically located to the south. They have steep sloping thatched roofs and are always built high off the ground on stilts to prevent rodents from getting in and eating the rice stored there. The piles are topped with large wooden discs just below the main part of the granary, another measure to prevent rats entering. The rice is stored in the room at the top, reached by a long bamboo ladder. It has been suggested that the roof shape derives from the upturned boats that were the first shelters of people who migrated across the oceans. Nowadays rice barns are made as, or converted into, tourist accommodation incorporating as many mod-cons as possible.

Houses on stilts are rarely mentioned in the books on Southeast Asian culture, or if they are, it is only a passing reference. They are old: wooden piles have been discovered in south China dating back to 5000 BC. Houses on stilts are depicted on the bas-reliefs of the 9th century Borobudur Temple in Java. There are two co-existing architectural systems in Southeast Asia. One system is of stone buildings, which are land based, and associated with royal and religious functions. The other is of raised wooden buildings, which are linked to water people and their way of life and are characteristic of practical buildings. Rice barns are the only Balinese buildings on stilts, which is curious.

A rice-barn is typically located to the south of the family compound. They have steep sloping thatched roofs and are always built high off the ground on stilts to prevent rodents from getting in and eating the rice stored there.

Sumet Jumsai in *Naga, Cultural Origins in Siam and the West Pacific* (1988) says that houses on stilts were probably the first of all man-made buildings. They are found in an arc of more than 3,730 miles (26,000 kilometres) across the Equator from Melanesia and Indonesia to Japan. These structures give protection from floods and animals, good ventilation, and a useful space underneath to store items and work or rest. They are seen in Malaysia, Thailand, Indo-China, Nepal, the Naga Hills in northeast India and south China. The whole of Southeast Asia has them, with the exception of Bali, parts of Java, Lombok and Buru, where houses sit firmly on the ground. Further research is needed to explain why.

Town and Village Layout

Typically, the royal palace stands in the centre of the town or village, on the highest ground. It is surrounded by high-walled noble compounds and the market is normally across the street from the palace. The smaller commoner family compounds are at the foot of the hill. High-born on the high ground and low-born on the low ground. Temples are scattered about.

Gates

Old Balinese gates have a ramp leading up to them. Newer ones have steps. Gates mark the change from one state of mind to another. There are many styles of gates. Temple gates typically have two styles. The first is the famous Balinese split gate, *candi bentar*, which symbolises Mount Meru, the mythical world mountain. It is large and resembles two sides of a mountain, which were once together, then cut in half and pulled apart.

The second style has a door, the *kori agung*, on top of which is a lintel, often with an elaborately carved Boma face, which has popping eyes and a bulbous head. He protects the inner sanctum of the temple. This kind of gate is called a *candi kurung*, which means 'closed gate'.

House compounds often have thatched gates, which have niches on either side for offerings. Normally, several feet in front of a gate is a free standing wall, called an *aling-aling*, to prevent evil spirits from entering. Evil spirits are only able to move in straight lines. South China has similar screens.

Balinese doors are twin-leafed and elaborately carved. Brass ring handles on each leaf are held in place by lotus-shaped plates and locked together.

Doors

Balinese doors are twin-leafed and elaborately carved. They are similar to doors in south India. Brass ring handles on each leaf are held in place by lotus-shaped plates and locked together. A slab of wood at the base keeps out small animals and trips unwary Westerners.

Windows

Traditionally Balinese windows are two-leaf wooden shutters, which let air and a bit of light in. Most activities take place outside in the compound or on verandahs, so the requirement for light is not important. Glass windows were introduced by the Dutch but were not successful in the tropical heat. With the advent of air conditioning, they are in again.

Roofs

The classic internal roof is a series of bamboo poles, tied together with bamboo string, resting on highly carved beams, stretching up to a point. Roofs are often crowned by a terracotta finial ornament.

It used to be the case that roofs were mostly made of elephant grass, called *alang-alang*, thatch, which could be expected to last a generation or more. They are now expensive and the quality has declined. Tiles are becoming the norm. In poorer areas, such as in the mountains, corrugated iron is used. Shrines use very hard wearing fibre from the sugar palm called *ijuk*.

Walls

Walls are generally not load bearing and are made of brick, tuff or other masonry. They used to be mud. Light weight screens are made of sheets of woven bamboo called *bedeg*.

Wood

The most common wood is the tall coconut palm, which is strong and suitable for beams, rafters and columns. Teak, camphor and jackfruit are also used.

Architects called *undagi* interpret traditional Balinese rules, called *Asta Kosala Kosali*, written in *lontar* palm books. Balinese architects do not design buildings; they merely interpret.

Bamboo
Bamboo is a hollow grass, and very useful in a wide range of contexts. It is amazingly strong, and can be used as scaffolding. It is cheap and grows fast. Thatched roofs have bamboo rafters.

Stone
North and east Bali use local lava rocks from nearby volcanic eruptions. White limestone and slate are popular in central and south Bali. Volcanic tuff, called *paras*, is used for shrines, walls, columns, decorations and stone statues. It is cut from river banks in south and central Bali and has a soft pinkish or yellowish tinge. It has the disadvantage of being fragile and in constant need of renovation.

Brick
Old Majapahit temples and walls throughout the island are made of deep red Roman baked clay bricks. Brick is still used everywhere, frequently ornamented with ornately carved *paras* decorations.

Terracotta
Terracotta roof and floor tiles are popular. Roof tiles are often painted blue and green. They are moulded from clay, baked in the sun and then fired.

Cement
Cement is used skilfully in columns, decorative finishes and floors and not so skilfully in some utilitarian contexts, including small shrines.

Melaspas: Bringing Buildings to Life
All buildings must be brought to life and purified before they can be occupied in a ceremony called *melaspas*. The wood, stone and thatch, cut down and killed for the construction, are, as it were, reincarnated. All parts are symbolically unified; posts and beams are 'married'.

Many offerings are required and there are animal sacrifices. If a ceremony is not carried out the house lacks luminosity. Evil forces can enter and cause sickness. The ceremony is nearly identical to the ritual required to bring a sacred wooden mask to life.

In *A House in Bali* (1947) Colin McPhee recounts his conversation with the priest prior to his own house ceremony:

You need the great ritual, he began, the highest one, and it will take many offerings, and a month to prepare. For this you will slaughter one young bull, one goose, one goat, one dog with a three-coloured hide, one duck with similar markings, one young male pig, one chicken with feathers growing the wrong way, five hens of different colours, and twenty-five ducks. You will also need six hundred duck eggs, six hundred bananas, and five thousand Chinese cash. The offerings prepared in advance will include two roast pigs, ten roast chickens, ten roast ducks, five baskets of rice, flowers and cakes, and five skeins of thread in five colours.

It is also usual to have a gamelan orchestra and Balinese dances and a cockfight. Food and drinks are on the house.

Prayers form part of every ceremony. Men sit cross-legged on the ground; women kneel, sitting on their heels, facing the gods and the offerings.

Chapter 36

A Ceremony A Day

Theatre

Ever since visitors arrived on Bali's shores, they have remarked on the outstanding beauty, complexity and spectacle of Balinese ceremonies. The anthropologist, Clifford Geertz, has called it 'The Theatre State'. There are numerous ceremonies, some private, some public, and not a day goes past without a ceremony taking place somewhere. For the Balinese they constitute real 'work' and important events are recalled in relation to them.

Classification

There are five categories, the *panca yadnya*. *Panca* means 'five' and *yadnya* means 'ritual'. There are rituals for:

- The gods
  An example is a temple anniversary, *odalan*.
- The higher spirits
  This includes the ancestors before they have been deified. An example is cremation.
- The consecration of priests
- Humans
  Rites of passage ceremonies take place from conception to just before death. Examples are pre-natal rites, birth ceremonies, the 12 day, 42 day and three months' old baby ceremonies, tooth-filing and marriage.
- Evil spirits
  Demons are personifications of forces derived from the five elements, which bring misfortune to human beings. The purpose of these ceremonies is to placate the demons and bring harmony to the world. An example is a purification sacrifice, *taur kasanga*, which takes place on the last day of the lunar year at Besakih and elsewhere on the island.

A ceremony is classified because of its primary purpose, but it always has other components, such as rituals for the gods and lower spirits.

Level of Ceremony

Ceremonies are carried out in one of three levels:
- *Utama* or elaborate
- *Madia* or average
- *Nista* or simple

These are sometimes sub-divided. The level rises by the addition of extra offerings and rituals. The basic set is present at every level. When a level increases, everything increases: if the number of offerings is raised, the number of mantras is also raised and eventually the level of priest is also raised from a *pemangku* to a *pedanda*. The cost escalates too.

Wealthy people are expected to carry out ceremonies at an elaborate level and poor people at a simple level. The point is just that people are expected to devote as much as they can afford. The ceremony is equally valid and effective.

One factor to take into account is the importance of the gods involved in the ceremony. There should be great ceremonies for great gods and the gods are great if they protect the village and it is prosperous. Recurring ceremonies, like a temple anniversary, often alternate between elaborate and simple.

Decoration, Celebration, Jubilation

There is never any doubt when a Balinese ceremony is in progress. People, buildings and trees are dressed up and decorated for the occasion. Friezes called *ider-ider* are pinned to the eaves of buildings. Columns and statues are wrapped with colourful sashes. Palm leaf offerings, like giant earrings, dangle from the edges of pavilions. Stretches of long thin woven palm and banana leaf offerings, called *lamak*, hang from shrines.

Rows of tall decorated bamboo poles, *penjor*, arch over roads outside people's houses, and brightly coloured banners called *umbul-umbul* flap in the breeze. *Umbul-umbul* are normally plain but sometimes they are decorated with *naga*, the Asian serpent-dragon, its tail at the top of the pole and its head pointing to the earth. The temple, where the ceremony is taking place, is filled and surrounded by a cast of thousands, a riot of colour and full to the gunnels with offerings.

In keeping with the multi-media nature of a ceremony, there are gamelan orchestras, *a cappella* choirs, that is singing without musical accompaniment, shadow puppets, play readings, dances, cockfights, gambling and food stalls. Everyone has a part to play in the process and that part is an act of worship.

Who Pays the Bill?

There are three elements to a public temple ceremony: preparation, performance and funding. The cost is governed by the level of ceremony. The major costs are the animals required for sacrifice and the materials for making offerings. Funding is either payment in kind or money. Those who prepare and take part in the performance do not necessarily fund it, but those who fund it usually take part in the performance.

Funding can come from the temple's own property holdings, contributions from the *banjar* and voluntary donations from individuals. Lists are displayed in a prominent position specifying everyone's donations. Government contributes to the largest ceremonies, usually at Besakih.

Small tray of flowers and incense.

Chapter 37

Rites Of Passage

From the Cradle to the Grave

The life of a Balinese is crammed with ceremonies from the womb to the tomb, from conception to the grave, and beyond. The main purpose is to remove impurities caused by the sins of previous lives and birth. The passage through the mother's body sullies an infant. If the child were born from her head, perhaps ceremonies would be unnecessary, but passage through her lower regions makes purification necessary.

Four Invisible Brothers or Sisters

Everyone is born with a set of invisible brothers and sisters. The Balinese do not talk about these spiritual beings much, but they are real and feature in all private ceremonies. Ceremonies are carried out for the four siblings at the same time as they are carried out for the person. If not, harm could result. Males may have female spirit siblings and females may have male spirit siblings. They are called the *Kanda Empat* and are conceived and born at the same time as the individual and take up positions inside the baby's body. The siblings can take various forms, change their forms and inhabit various places. They are not known to Indian Hinduism.

Their material manifestations at birth are the amniotic fluid, the uterine blood, the *vernix caseosa* (the yellowish waxy substance covering a baby) and the placenta. The placenta is the most important. Later they live in the heart, the liver, the kidneys and the bile and are associated with the gods Mahadewa, Iswara, Wisnu and Brahma and the four cardinal directions.

It is interesting that European sailors often took along some dried placenta and a piece of umbilical cord with them as protection when they went to sea. This practice lasted up to the 19th century.

The four siblings stay throughout life, protect the person and accompany his or her spirit to heaven and testify to his or her good (or bad) *karma*. *Pemangku*, the local village priests, and *dalang*, the shadow puppeteers, regularly ask their own siblings to assist in rituals. The important point is that they cannot be taken for granted. Their help is conditional on their being treated with respect.

They are remembered at mealtimes: when a mother feeds her baby, a few drops of milk are spilt on the placenta for the four spirit children. In adulthood, a few grains of rice are left on the plate for them.

Pregnancy

A small ceremony is performed to ensure the welfare of mother and child and to anchor the embryo firmly in the womb.

Immediately after Birth

The baby's father collects the placenta, which is the most important element of the child's four invisible brothers or sisters, takes it home, washes it and places it in a coconut with flowers and money. He then wraps it in a white cloth and buries it outside the door of his home.

As you look out, girls' placentas are buried on the left and boys' placentas on the right. The symbolic grave is covered with a black stone and spiky pandanus leaves to protect it. Finally, a symbolic cremation fire is lit on the grave. If the family moves house, the remains are dug up and reburied in the new family compound.

12 Days

At this point the baby may be given a name. In some parts of Bali, a grandparent visits a *balian tenung*, a clairvoyant priest to communicate with the ancestors to identify whom the baby is a reincarnation of.

42 Days

Mother and child are ritually impure for forty-two days after the birth. She cannot enter sacred places, like temples. At the end of forty-two days, the mother and child cease to be impure and a small purification ceremony is held.

105 Days or 3 Months

This is the baby's first big ceremony and takes place in the family compound. It is the day that the baby attains normal human status and may enter temples. Up to this point the baby is a divine creature and very vulnerable to witches and sorcerers.

It is the day when the baby first touches the ground—described as a return to the earth. Before this time the baby will always be carried. The ceremony takes place in the morning. In some parts of Bali the baby is put in a cage, like those used for roosters, after touching the ground, and in some villages the priest gives the child its real name.

The *Kanda Empat* have 108 helpers and an exorcism is held for them, so that they do not harm the child. There is often a shadow puppet performance.

210 Days or First *Oton*

This is the baby's first Balinese birthday, which takes place one Balinese year after birth. The baby has its first haircut, a symbolic release of energies. The hair is cut from the five cardinal directions, which symbolically removes impurities. The hair is either buried or thrown in the river. There is a further exorcism ceremony to expel the 108 helpers.

Menstruation

A small ceremony is carried out at a girl's first menstruation. From this age young people come under the influence of Semara and Ratih, the gods of love.

Tooth-Filing

Tooth shape distinguishes gods and humans from animals, birds and ogres. The former have flat teeth and the latter have pointed ones. The purpose of tooth-filing is to remove impurity by eliminating or reducing the *Sad Ripu*, the Balinese six deadly sins of lust, greed, anger, intoxication (through drink or passion), confusion and jealousy.

The *Sad Ripu* are eliminated symbolically by flattening the two upper teeth that most resemble an animal's teeth, the canines, and the four incisors. The lower teeth are left alone, as desire and passion should not be killed completely. The Balinese believe in balance.

It is impossible to fulfil one's *karma* with these teeth present, so every

The purpose of tooth-filing is to remove impurity by eliminating or reducing the *Sad Ripu*, the Balinese six deadly sins of lust, greed, anger, intoxication (through drink or passion), confusion and jealousy.

Balinese will have his teeth filed, usually at around sixteen to eighteen years, but it can be at any age, and if the person dies first, the ceremony will be carried out on the corpse. Beauty is another consideration. It often takes place at the same time as marriage since the offerings are similar and that saves money.

It is an important ceremony and expensive. The ancestors are invited, the family compound is decorated lavishly, guests are accommodated and fed, musicians and gamelan orchestras are hired, new clothes and jewellery are worn and beautiful textiles used. A high caste *brahmana* priest, a *pedanda*, and his attendants may perform the ceremony, but this is not necessary.

Giving Your Eye-Teeth

The tooth-filing ceremony takes place on an auspicious day. It is usually carried out on a number of people in the same family in the *bale dangin*, the ceremonial pavilion in the family compound. The platform acts as a bed and is covered with a mattress, protective ritual cloths, big pillows, and a woven bamboo mat on which is drawn the images of the gods, Semara and Ratih, male and female figures, the sun and the moon, the sky and the land. Usually two people lie down for the teeth-filing at a time. The eldest goes first. The family crowds around and the gamelan plays throughout.

The *pedanda* 'kills' the teeth by hitting them with a metal rod and draws symbolic letters on them. The person who does the filing chants some mantras and pours holy water over the participants, who lie down on the bed and work begins. A small cylinder of sugar cane is put into their mouths and the six upper teeth are filed. The extent of the filing depends on the wishes of the person. Only a few symbolic strokes are required.

The participants spit the filings into a silver bowl and transfer them to a yellow coconut, which is buried in the family temple behind a shrine. As the filing continues the filees check progress with a mirror and when it is over the person doing the filing brings the teeth back to life with a mantra. Then there are prayers in the family temple and photographs. It is often accompanied by a shadow puppet performance. Sometimes there are village-wide tooth-filing ceremonies.

Marriage
This is the last rite of passage until death.

Chapter 38

Getting Married

I'm Pregnant

Premarital pregnancy is common and probably the norm, but unmarried mothers are not acceptable. Balinese culture is very family orientated and marriage is a must, even for gays and lesbians. It is part of the natural order of things. Pregnancy, often intentional, usually precedes and provokes the wedding. Most people marry in their early twenties.

It is very important that the wife can actually produce children, especially sons. Sons continue the male succession. Daughters leave to join their husband's family when they marry, but a son remains with his parents and brings home a wife, and together they will carry out the cremation rites for his parents. Cremation is a prerequisite for reincarnation; children have an important role and duty.

In addition, great-grandparents are normally reincarnated as great-grandchildren in the same family: a wife must enable that process by bearing children. Infertility, even though nobody's fault, is looked down upon. A man who never marries is permanently regarded as a child and should pray with the other children in the temple, which is a trifle demeaning.

Where shall we Live?

After marriage the wife normally moves into her husband's household and performs her religious duties at his family temple. If accommodation is tight, as it is beginning to be, they set up home elsewhere.

When shall we get Married?

It has to be on an auspicious day: the priest will advise. Weddings cannot occur during or immediately after the ten day holiday between *Galungan* and *Kuningan*. There is always a flurry of matrimonial activity just before *Galungan*.

Whom should I Marry?

There is a preference to marry a patrilineal cousin (father's brother's son or daughter). The ideal partner for a male is his father's brother's daughter, that is, his first cousin on his father's side. If this is not possible, it is desirable to marry within the kin group. This ensures that the resources of the bride stay within the *dadia*, which is a group sharing a common ancestor. It prevents fragmentation of land and other property. There is also the advantage that the bride does not have to leave her family and her children belong to the same descent group. Nowadays, however, marriage to an outsider is common.

Forms of Marriage

There are three traditional forms of marriage:

- Kidnapping a Girl
  This is now against the law.
- Pre-arranged 'Kidnapping'
  Everyone goes along with it but pretends not to know about it. It is common and the least expensive way.
- Arranged Marriage
  This is a wedding agreed upon by the families. Until the 1950s arranged marriages were common, but not now. Conservative communities and social élites favoured it.

Wedding Ceremony

The ceremony takes place in the boy's family compound and can be as elaborate as the family wish. The girl leaves her family temple (unless she already is a relation and belongs to the same family temple), joins the boy's family and ancestral group and thereafter prays to his ancestors. There are two separate ceremonies. First she says farewell to her ancestors at her family temple and secondly she joins her husband's family temple.

The wedding ceremony is fun. They look like a prince and princess. The couple wear their best clothes, sarongs with gold thread and headdresses. Both wear make-up. She wears a crown and he has a ceremonial dagger, a *kris*, at the back of his sarong. The symbolism of the *kris* is not lost on the audience. There are shrieks of laughter as the groom takes out his *kris* at a certain point in the ceremony and punctures a small mat which the bride has just been sitting on. She holds it for him as he stabs. A local priest performs the ceremony. There is often a shadow puppet performance and a Western style reception with Chinese food.

Masculine Women, Feminine Men

The bride joins her husband's family temple and leaves her own. If a couple have daughters only, they have a problem. In time they will be left with no women in the household as the daughters get married and join their husbands. Such a situation cannot be allowed to happen, as it would mean that ceremonies could not be carried out properly and there would be no children available for reincarnation. There would be no one to look after the family temple, present the offerings and the cycle of reincarnation would be broken.

To remedy this situation the couple may adopt a male, who can bring in a wife. Another solution is the creation of the honorary male and female. A daughter takes the role of the male heir in her family and her husband becomes an honorary female. He gives up inheritance rights in his own family. Property stays in his wife's line. These marriages can be difficult because, despite the noble act, the husband often becomes the subject of derision in the village.

A Balinese wedding ceremony is fun. They look like a prince and princess. The couple wear their best clothes, sarongs with gold thread and headdresses. Both wear make-up. She wears a crown and he has a ceremonial dagger, a *kris*, at the back of his sarong.

Polygamous Men

It is possible for a man to have more than one wife, but only a few do these days. Polygamy is usually only practised among the higher castes and the wealthy.

Caste

A high status woman should not marry a commoner. The rule is a matter of current controversy. In the old days of the Balinese kings, both parties could be killed. A high status man, however, may marry a lower status wife, although if this continues for three generations, the man's high status may be lost. The children follow their father's status. His wife retains her caste, but she enjoys respect and is given the title *Jero*.

No Kidding

Balinese have a duty to marry and it is important to have children, as only they can perform the rituals for the dead, which are indispensable for reincarnation. Childlessness and impotence are grounds for divorce. Even homosexuals are expected to marry. Further pressure is imposed by the rule that unmarried men cannot join the *banjar* village organisation.

The Terrible Twins

The birth of twins of the opposite sex to a *sudra* family is regarded as a form of incest. The village is spiritually impure for forty-two days after their birth. Statistically there are twins in every hundred births. The idea that twins bring bad luck may date from pre-history. The wife of a hunter-gatherer could not nurse and carry two children.

In the old days, until President Sukarno abolished the custom in 1962, the whole family had to move to a house specially built for them outside the village. The parents had to pay for purification ceremonies for the village. They may have had to go begging.

Three days before the forty-second day the gods of the three main village temples were taken to the river or sea for purification. On the forty-second day the gods were brought back to their temples. The unfortunate couple returned from outside the village to the crossroads and offerings to the gods and evil spirits were presented. There was music and a shadow puppet performance. When it was over, the family could return to their home and live normally.

In pre-colonial times the twins were taken as slaves by the king. Even today twins born to a commoner result in postponement of major festivals and special ceremonies are held. President Sukarno may have abolished the custom in 1962, but a village insisted on applying their old *adat* rules in April 2004 in northern Bali. None of this applies to twins born of a high caste mother. Quite the reverse. It is auspicious. They bring good luck. They are deemed to have been married in another world and can therefore marry in this world.

Traditional Style Divorce

Traditionally divorce was concluded by living apart. A wife, who returned to her family, could bring only her own possessions. Her rights were so limited that most women did not dare to leave their husbands. Since ancestry is traced through the father's side, children were considered to belong to their father rather than their mother and she lost any rights in respect of them. If her birth family took her back, a ceremony would be required for her to rejoin her ancestors.

It was regarded so badly among aristocratic women that if she returned to the family compound, she would be treated like a servant and had to speak High Balinese to her parents, brothers and sisters. It is quite possible that modern legislation requiring a judicial divorce is ignored in remote villages, which still live by traditional customs.

Inheritance

Marriage is largely about inheritance and responsibility for the family temple. Customarily daughters do not inherit and sons take over responsibility and authority. Farmland is normally divided among sons equally. One son, usually the youngest of the first wife, inherits the family compound and is responsible for maintaining the family temple and carrying out the ceremonies associated with it. If there are no sons or the children are all daughters who marry out, then the *banjar* acquires the land. Primogeniture, the system whereby the eldest son inherits, is, however, usual in high caste families.

Chapter 39

The Balinese Way of Dying

Who is Responsible?
Marriage denotes a break in the life cycle. Up to and including marriage, parents are responsible for their children's purification and ritual protection. Once married, the younger generation becomes responsible for their parents' protection, which primarily means carrying out the death rites properly.

Moment of Death
As soon as someone dies the hollow bamboo slit drum, the *kulkul*, is beaten to summon help from the *banjar*, which comprises men from the neighbourhood. They come to the deceased's house and wash the body.

Preparing the Body
The body is prepared for burial or cremation. It is purified with holy water to wash away the pollution of death totally. The deceased's bewildered soul hovers above the body. Wounds are covered with tamarind paste, so that they heal in the afterlife. Ornaments are placed on the corpse. Coloured string is tied around the wrists. Mirrors are put on the eyes to give clear sight and beauty. The corpse is then wrapped in a white shroud inscribed with symbols and letters.

Bodies are normally prepared and buried within hours of death. The corpse is wrapped in a mat and buried with a bamboo tube placed under the head to let out the spirit. If they are not buried the same day, the family stay up all night to guard the body against bad spirits. People play cards to keep awake.

Cremation

It is not known when cremation was introduced to Bali. A Balinese cremation is very different from a Western one. It is the grandest and most important of all Balinese ceremonies. The correct carrying out of the ceremony determines whether or not the deceased will be reincarnated but cremation does not guarantee a good afterlife. It is 'good deeds' that does that.

Unless the family is rich or the deceased is a *brahmana*, royal person or a priest, the corpse is buried first to allow the family time to save up. Cremations are expensive. It is not uncommon for families to share the expense and it is more and more common for village-wide cremations to be held, which reduce the expense considerably.

Temporary Burial

Burial places the soul under the protection of Durga, goddess of death, who reigns over cemeteries. The uncremated dead require frequent offerings placed on their graves. The spirit, unfreed from the corpse, dwells in the graveyard. Offerings are always given at the festival of *Galungan*.

Cremation should not be delayed too long as uncremated spirits are restless and can cause the family and the village trouble. Village-wide cremations take place every four or five years on auspicious days.

Brahmana, Royals and Priests

Brahmana, royals and priests are not allowed to be buried, as they are too elevated to be laid in impure ground. They lie in state until preparations can be made for the cremation. It may mean that the family has to borrow to pay for the ceremony.

Preparations

The ceremony takes place on an auspicious day. A temporary roof of coconut leaves and temporary shrines are erected in the family compound. A large number of ceremonies are involved, culminating in the cremation itself.

For a medium sized cremation two or three dozen women are required to make the offerings. The preparations take several weeks. High caste priests, the *pedanda*, carry out several preliminary ceremonies and officiate at the cremation.

Sarcophagus

Men from the *banjar* make the sarcophagus in the shape of an animal, made of wood, and decorated with velvet and gold. Status used to determine the appropriate animal, but it is now a matter of choice.

Men from the *banjar* make the sarcophagus in the shape of an animal, made of wood, and decorated with velvet and gold. Status used to determine the appropriate animal, but it is now a matter of choice.

A bull was made for priests and high status men; a cow for women. The bull is the mount of Siwa, who is the god of death and destruction. High nobles had a winged lion and lesser nobles a deer. *Sudra* had a mythological animal with the head of an elephant and the tail of a fish, but were permitted to have a bull or cow if a member of the family had carried out a valuable service for a ruler or noble. The animals always have four feet to symbolise the person's four invisible brothers or sisters.

Cremation Tower

Men from the *banjar* also build the cremation tower, the *bade*, which symbolises the Universe. At the base is the cosmic turtle, Bedawang Nala, flanked by the two cosmic serpents, Basuki and Anantaboga; in the middle, the world of man is shown by leafy forests and mountains, where the corpse is placed; and at the top are an uneven number of pagoda-like roofs.

The roofs represent the tier of heaven to which the deceased aspires. Royal families have eleven tiers, nobles seven or nine, lesser gentry three or five and *sudra* one. At the top there may be a sculptured *lingga* for a king and a *padmasana* for a priest. Below the top section is the shelf for the body (if it has not been buried) or an effigy (if it has been buried). If the body has been buried, it is dug up, wrapped in a white cloth and waits in the cemetery. A big Boma face to scare away evil spirits is carved on the back of the tower.

The tower can be 60 or 70 feet (18 to 21 metres) high and a long bamboo ramp is needed to carry the body into it. The height indicates status. Telegraph poles and electric lines may have to be lowered to let the tower pass. Men of lesser rank than the deceased carry the tower to the cemetery.

Procession to the Cemetery

On the main day guests arrive at the family compound and men from the *banjar* place the body in the cremation tower and tie it to the shelf and cover it with a white cloth.

If the deceased is a king, a *naga* or 'dragon' may be placed to the west side. The *naga* is a symbol of life. A high priest shoots arrows at it, which release the deceased's soul from the world. The *naga* is carried in the procession to the cemetery.

The procession sets off around noon. The empty sarcophagus is tied to bamboo poles and carried by men of the village, who career down the road to the cemetery, shouting as they go, turning the sarcophagus round and round roughly to confuse the deceased's spirit, so that it does not return home. It is turned round three times in an anti-clockwise direction at the crossroads. Gamelan players accompany them with loud gongs, cymbals and drums.

A young member of the family rides on the sarcophagus. A very long white cloth is attached to the tower, held by as many people as possible in a long procession to the cemetery. This enables them to have contact with the deceased. It is a charged atmosphere of chaos.

At the Cemetery

At the cemetery the sarcophagus is opened and the body, or the effigy, is taken from the tower, put inside the sarcophagus and covered with offerings and pieces of cloth. The high priest pours lots of holy water on it. Then the sarcophagus is closed and firewood underneath set ablaze. These days gas jets are becoming widespread and speed up the burning time. Grief is not displayed, as mourning would be an impediment to the soul's passage to the next world. There is the risk that the soul may become doubtful about moving on.

Burning takes a few hours. Throughout the process, the high priest rings his bell and recites mantras to help the soul's release. After the body is burnt, the family collect the ashes and bits of bone. They wrap some in a white cloth and put the rest in a yellow coconut.

Procession to the Sea

The family pray and form a procession to the sea or a river that leads to the sea. They throw the ashes in and the body's elements are purified and returned to the Universe.

Human Sacrifice

Suttee, the Indian word for the practice whereby wives of Balinese rajas sacrificed themselves by jumping into the flames, sometimes stabbing themselves at the same time, dates from at least the 1400s and fascinated Europeans. There was a reported case of *suttee* in northern India in the summer of 2002 and two cases in 2006. A senior Dutch merchant, Jan Oosterwijck, while waiting to see the king of Bali in 1633, witnessed the cremation of the queen mother. Twenty-two female slaves were stabbed and burned in the funeral pyre. Oosterwijck was told that at the death of a king no less than 140 women sacrifice themselves of their own accord by jumping into the flames.

Royal cremations were well attended. In 1847 Helms, a Danish assistant of Mads Lange, thought that not less than 40,000 to 50,000 people attended a royal cremation. That was a large section of the island's population at the time. The practice of human sacrifice, *satya* in Balinese, was outlawed by the Dutch in 1895, but apparently took place secretly until well into the 1920s. The modern custom whereby Balinese women sacrifice their hair during their husband's or a close relative's cremation may be a throwback.

Second Cremation

A number of hours, days or weeks after the cremation, a second ceremony is held. It is called *nyekah* and releases the soul, which still has some links to the body, from earth to heaven.

Many of the rituals are similar. There are no bones, but there is an effigy of the spirit of the deceased, offerings, a tower (this time in white and gold), a procession to the sea or river and a disposal of ashes and everything else into the water. The final ritual allows the soul to become a divine ancestor, taking its place and being worshipped in the family temple, protecting its family on Earth.

At this point the cremated dead are no longer individuals. They are hopefully good-natured ancestor gods.

Rats!

The Balinese have an ethical problem when it comes to rat poison. After all they may be humans who in a previous life failed their spiritual tests. So a few rats eating the rice harvest is normally fine. If there are too many, there are certain ceremonies which can be performed to persuade them to leave. But if all fails, there is another option: a rat cremation.

A number of rats are killed and a full cremation ceremony is carried out. This gives their spirits the chance to be reborn as higher animals, even as humans, and the Balinese reckon that the rats which are still alive should be impressed at the generosity of the villagers. The Dutch were aware of rat cremations and described them. They still take place from time to time. In 1991 there was a ritual cremation for 120,312 dead rats in Tabanan.

Chapter 40

A Temple Ceremony

Temple *Odalan*: Anniversaries

One of the most important public and private temple ceremonies is the *odalan*, which is usually held every Balinese year of 210 days. It is the anniversary of the founding and dedication of the temple and is also said to celebrate the marriage of Siwa and Uma.

If a village has the normal number of three main temples, *odalans* and preparations for them may take up one day in every seven. The work is shared, but it is still considerable, especially when other public and private ceremonies are taken into account.

Variation

Even though they may fall into the same classification, no two ceremonies are alike. They vary from place to place, time to time and situation to situation. The Balinese have a dictum for it, *desa*, *kala*, *patra*, which is translated as 'village, time, circumstance'. Indeed they are intended to vary as they are more interesting that way. The level at which they are held is another variable: low, middle or high. Bali is nothing if not flexible.

Preparations: 2 or 3 Days Before

Two or three days before the ceremony husband and wife, or at least male and female members, from each family in the *banjar* go to the temple. The wife goes to the kitchen, which is usually in the middle courtyard, and joins the other women making offerings for the ceremony. The women are divided into groups, each group carrying out a specific job. One section prepares containers to hold the offerings. Another makes rice flour and fries it in oil to make rice cakes. Another makes a different set of offerings. The men are responsible for cleaning the grounds and building large wooden offering stands, and guarding the temple at night.

Preparations: 1 Day Before

The women cook glutinous rice, fashion it into pyramids or cylinders and pack it into woven palm leaves. They wrap columns and friezes with coloured cloth and hang flat, carved, hour-glass figures made of bronze Chinese coins, with a square hole in the middle, on either side of the altars, as decorations, and place *lamak* in front of the altars.

Final Preparations on the Day: D-Day

Early in the morning, the men gather together and slaughter a pig, whose meat will be used as offerings for the demons.

Correct Performance

Balinese Hinduism is highly ritualistic. Rituals consist of repetitive behaviour, gestures and the presentation of symbolic objects. The rituals have rules and the priests are the guardians of the rules. Correct performance is crucial to a successful ceremony. They are sacred performances. There is a prescribed order of events, which David Stuart-Fox has called the 'idiom of ritual'.

Purification

Before a ceremony, a purification ceremony is required. The priest sits cross-legged on the ground or in a pavilion. He starts by purifying himself, his body and mind and then the religious paraphernalia to be used in the ceremony. He purifies the offerings. Then the ritual instruments are empowered and he asks his assistants, or members of the family, to carry them around the temple or compound and waft their essence over shrines and offerings in order to remove impurities.

Order of Events

A public temple *odalan* has six main stages:
- Inviting the gods to attend
- Giving the lower spirits offerings on the ground in the inner section of the temple
- Gathering the spirits together
- Enthroning them in the inner section of the temple
- Presenting them with offerings in the form of music, dance, drama and prayers
- Closing ceremonies and departure of visiting spirits

Inviting the Gods

About a month before the *odalan*, the temple priest holds a ceremony to notify the temple gods of the intention to hold the ceremony. He also invites other gods and spirits by way of a small ritual. He may visit other temples and invite their gods. Each god has a large retinue of spirits, who attend with him.

Procession to the River

On the day before the formal start of the *odalan*, the priest wakes the gods in their abode and invites them to come out and place themselves in small wooden carved statues called *pratima*. Members of the congregation walk around the temple in a clockwise direction with the *pratima* on their heads and place them on high altars and give them offerings. The *pratima* are always a pair, male and female. They are going to be bathed, dressed and perfumed for the celebrations.

On the day before the formal start of a ceremony, the priests and villagers form a procession to carry the gods to the nearby spring or river. The gods are accompanied by women carrying offerings on their heads.

The priests and villagers form a procession to carry the *pratima* to the nearby spring or river. The gods are carried on the heads of their priests, sheltered by colourful umbrellas and banners, and accompanied by gamelan music. If it is a long distance, the gods sit in ornate gold-painted sedan chairs, decorated with yellow cloth and flowers. If there is more than one god, they travel in order of precedence, the lowest in status first and the highest last. Everyone wears traditional Balinese dress. Women carry ritual equipment on their heads.

Following the bathing, everyone returns to the temple. Offerings are presented to the gods before they pass through the temple gate. The gods are placed in their shrines ready for the others to arrive and the ceremony to begin. Visiting deities and friends arrive, accompanied by gamelan music, stop, circle a temporary shrine, acknowledge the offerings, enter the temple and take up their positions. If the ceremony is large, there may be hundreds of guests and arrivals may take hours.

Gods' Seating Arrangements

There are many kinds of altars in which the gods sit during a ceremony. Some are small, some are miniature houses, and some are tiny open pavilions. The most important gods sit in the highest positions. The seating arrangements depend on what the gods are doing at the ceremony. If they are just dropping in and not staying all the time, they will be seated in a particular place. If they are spectators and not taking part, they will have another place.

The Ceremony

A ceremony takes three days if it is a small *odalan* and many times that if it is a major one. A ceremony for the lower spirits can be as grand as a ceremony for the higher spirits. If it is for the lower spirits, there will be a cockfight.

A cast of thousands attends and that is not counting the audience of spirits. The large ceremonies have groups of high priests, *pedanda*, and *pemangku*, the ordinary temple priests, who perform the rituals, ring their bells, waft their incense, chant their mantras and perform *mudras*, elaborate hand gestures.

Presenting the Offerings

The core of the ceremony is the *pedanda* making holy water. He sits in the *jeroan*, the inner courtyard, and goes through rituals, which take about forty minutes. When the holy water is produced he gives a signal to the *angklung* orchestra—an ensemble of a large number of small, portable four note instruments—in the *jeroan* and it starts to play. The *kulkul* split drum is beaten. The gamelan in the outer courtyard begins to play. The masked dancers dance. The *pemangku* and his helpers sprinkle holy water throughout the temple. There is movement and sound everywhere. The *pedanda* presents the offerings to the gods. The congregation pray and receive holy water instilled with the gods' powers and blessings. The priest sprinkles it over their heads and they sip it.

The priest presents the offerings to the gods. The congregation pray and receive holy water instilled with the gods' powers and blessings.

This is called 'counterprestation' (return). Finally the priest apologises for any shortcomings in the ritual. Technically this is called 'prestation' (payment). The ceremony has achieved harmony. For the time being the dangerous forces have been transformed into positive energies and the gods are down amongst humans.

Entertainment

Ritual dances, music and entertainments follow. One or more gamelan orchestras play, perhaps late into the night. Women sing. Men and women read classic texts from books. Shadow puppet performances are staged. Villagers come and go throughout the day and night with huge numbers of offerings and pray.

Outside the Temple

Temporary stalls are set up outside the temple, selling snacks and drinks, and toys and balloons for the children. Games of chance are played on the ground, illuminated by kerosene lamps. Ceremonies are a time for enjoyment.

Departure

The priest invites the deities to leave and return to their own abode. The decorations are taken away and the shrines and temple doors locked. 210 days later the harmonious effect will have gone and the place will be in danger again. The ritual will have to be repeated.

Theatre

During a ceremony, the place of ritual activity is a stage. The believers are actors, the priests are directors, their helpers are assistant directors, and the gods and demons are the invisible, critical audience. Whether or not we are believers, we should honour and respect the work of art, which is a Balinese temple ceremony.

Chapter 41

The Mother of All Temples, The Mother of All Ceremonies

Pura Besakih: The Mother Temple

Pura Besakih is the oldest and most important temple in Bali and stands 3,333 feet (1,000 metres) above sea level on the southwest slopes of Mount Agung, a 10,000 foot (3,048 metres) volcano in the east of the island. It has grown organically and has no mandala-like design. The temple, which is 13.5 miles (22 kilometres) from Klungkung, looks out over the whole of south Bali, west to Mount Batukaru and south to Sanur.

Pura Besakih, the Mother Temple, is the oldest and most important temple in Bali and stands 3,333 feet (1,000 metres) above sea level on the southwest slopes of Mount Agung.

Hindu-Buddhist Cosmological Model

The Hindu-Buddhist cosmological model has a mountain at its centre called Mount Meru, which is invariably identified with the Himalayas. There are a number of concentric circles around this focal point. They represent alternately rings of continents and oceans. The Hindu version has six rings of continents, whereas the Buddhist one has seven. Beyond the last ring of both versions lies the Ocean of Infinity.

The origin of this model may be even older, pre-Hindu, conceived by early sailors, perhaps in the Pacific. The form is constantly revolving. To stop the movement the Buddhist model has four island-continents in each corner, which has the effect of adding cardinal points to the image. This refined model has become an architectural plan for temples and other structures in Southeast Asia.

The model was transplanted to Bali. Mount Meru has become Mount Agung and the four island-continents, stopping Bali from spinning around, have become Mount Batur in the north, Mount Agung in the east, the Bukit peninsula in the south and Mount Batukaru in the west.

It seems likely that the all-pervasive Asian *naga* became associated with water through the circular form of the oceans in the Hindu-Buddhist cosmological model. *Naga* in Sanskrit means serpent and forms of it range from a snake to a dragon.

The Legend of Mount Agung

According to legend, Bali was unstable and rocked like a boat on the ocean. The high god Pasupati, residing on Mount Mahameru, felt sorry about this and asked the gods to uproot parts of the slope of Mount Mahameru and carry them to Bali. He ordered the cosmic turtle Bedawang Nala to support the base of the mountain and the cosmic serpents Basuki and Anantaboga to be the ropes holding the mountain, while it was carried through the air. It was deposited on Bali in the *Saka* year 11 (89 AD).

Mount Agung erupted twenty years later and threw up Putrajaya and his younger sister Danu. Putrajaya, the son of Pasupati, took up residence in and became the god of Mount Agung, and Dewi Danu took up residence in the temple at Mount Batur. Putrajaya's other name is Mahadewa or Siwa.

The legend expresses Mount Agung's paramount importance and

explains the link between Besakih and Batur and the male and female nature of the two temples.

Complex

Besakih is a complex of temples; there are public temples, descent group temples, locality and other temples. There are 198 structures.

The eighteen public temples are supported by all Hindus throughout Indonesia and are maintained by the *Parisada Hindu Dharma*. Little is known of their origins. The most important is Pura Penataran Agung, which is the central sanctuary of the whole complex and covers six terraces. The highest terrace is dedicated to the spirit of the mountain and the most important shrine is on terrace II, which contains the triple lotus seat, the *padmasana*.

It is the most elaborate *padmasana* in Bali and consists of a single base from which arise three separate lotus seats, resting on a carving of the cosmic turtle, Bedawang Nala, around which are entwined the two cosmic serpents, Basuki and Anantaboga. The *padmasana* honours Brahma, Wisnu and Siwa and is the focus of ceremonies.

Panca Wali Krama

Panca Wali Krama is a large purification ceremony, which takes place every Balinese decade, which is when a *Saka* year ends in a zero. Just as every Balinese New Year is a time of potential danger, so is a new decade. The ceremony was held at Pura Besakih in 1960, 1978 and 2009.

Eka Dasa Rudra

Eka Dasa Rudra is the greatest of all Balinese festivals, an enormous purification ceremony, which takes place once every Balinese century, or at times of potential danger, arising from the likes of earthquakes, eruptions, plagues and wars. A century is when a *Saka* year ends in two zeros. The ceremony was held at Pura Besakih in 1963 and 1979.

Eka Dasa Rudra means the 'eleven Rudras'. Rudra is a god associated with wildness and danger, the Vedic antecedent of Siwa, with whom he later became linked. Eleven expresses the idea that he is everywhere in all directions.

The aim is to strengthen the spiritual life of those taking part, to transform negative forces to positive ones, leading to harmony, justice and prosperity. In 1963 the ceremony had not been held in living memory and how to do it had to be determined by reference to the texts. It was not even clear when the ceremony had been held before. It seems that it may have been performed during the reign of Dalem Baturenggong in the middle of the 16th century, when the kingdom of Gelgel was at its height, under the direction of Nirartha, the court priest.

Gregorian year 1963, *Saka* year 1884 did not end in two zeros, but it was felt by some that natural events existed to warrant the ceremony. This was the first ceremony to involve the whole Hindu population of Bali. The whole island had to be purified before it could start.

All Hindu dead on the island were to be cremated, which imposed a heavy financial burden on many people. Simple cremations were allowed, and many collective cremations took place. During the *Eka Dasa Rudra* ceremony the Balinese were asked not to bury their dead but to cremate them immediately or keep them at home and not announce the death publicly. Post-cremation rites that purify the soul of a body already cremated were, however, allowed.

The 1963 ceremony was the most remarkable that has ever taken place in Bali. The festival began on 10 October 1962 and was due to end on 20 April 1963. Holy water from the opening ceremony was distributed to every home throughout the island.

As preparations were being made for the most important part of the ceremony on 19 February 1963, Mount Agung started to rumble. The focal point of the whole ceremony, the great sacrifice, *taur eka dasa rudra*, was due to start on 8 March 1963, the last day of the *Saka* year. The mountain had lain dormant for 120 years. It was an amazing coincidence and many thought that it was a sign that the ceremony should not take place, but the committee, which was running the event, announced in the newspapers, '*Eka Dasa Rudra* To Go On'.

On the due date, 8 March 1963, the main ritual took place, 10,000 people attended, schools closed. In the days that followed 4,000 to 5,000 people attended. Scores of animals including an eagle, an elephant and a tiger were sacrificed as well as thousands of ducks and chickens, more than fifty buffaloes and other animals. Rumours that a child was to be sacrificed were scotched. The offerings were mind-boggling: tens of thousands of bananas, coconuts, eggs and tons of rice.

Mount Agung Eruption, 1963

The first major eruption was on 17 March. There were hundreds of victims. Lava covered the ground to a depth of between 8-12 inches (20-30 centimetres). On 2 April all inhabitants had to evacuate the area around Besakih. The committee decided to proceed with the ceremony with the smallest number of people possible. People could worship from a safe distance. The final ritual took place on 20 April.

The next great eruption took place on 16 May, after which volcanic activity gradually subsided. An earthquake on 18 May destroyed Pura Besakih, a month after the ceremony had ended. More than 2,000 people were killed. Thousands of animals perished, seventeen villages were

Mount Agung Eruption, 1963. More than 2,000 people were killed. Thousands of animals perished, seventeen villages were destroyed, and many suffered damage.

destroyed, and many suffered damage. Much of Bali was covered in ash for months. The suffering and distress were felt throughout the island.

153,208 acres (62,000 hectares) were taken out of production. A famine followed. More than 10,000 people suffered severe malnutrition. The most seriously affected areas were Karangasem, Klungkung, Bangli and Gianyar. 75,000 people left for neighbouring principalities and refugees crowded into Denpasar and Singaraja. In 1963 unemployment rose to 30%. In 1956 it had been about 14%.

Many Balinese saw the eruption as a sign of cosmic imbalance and spiritual impurity and a portent of further disaster. They were right. President Kennedy was assassinated on 22 November 1963. 1965 saw massacres on a massive scale in Java and Bali. A Turkish Airlines DC10 crashed near Paris killing all 345 people on board in 1974. An 8.3 magnitude earthquake in China killed hundreds of thousands in 1976. *Parisada Hindu Dharma*, the religion's central body, decided to hold a *Panca Wali Krama* in 1978 and an *Eka Dasa Rudra* in 1979, both dates being in a *Saka* year ending in two zeros, 1900. There seemed to be no doubt about correct timing this time.

Eka Dasa Rudra, 1979

As in 1963, all dead were cremated. The ceremony opened on 27 February 1979. Holy water was distributed to everyone in Bali. The main day was on 28 March and tens of thousands attended, including the President of Indonesia. The final ceremonies took place on 9 May, the auspicious forty-second day after 28 March. All told millions of hours were put into it and half a million people visited Besakih. The ceremony was covered by the international press, national television and magazines. Everyone remembered the 1963 eruption and was apprehensive but the Mother of all Volcanoes remained calm throughout.

Chapter 42

A Selection of Major Temples

Pura Ulun Danu, Lake Batur

Batur is a profoundly sacred part of Bali. It is about a forty minute drive, 22 miles (35.4 kilometres) north of Ubud, the road rising all the way. The area comprises a live volcano, Mount Batur, 5,633 feet (1,717 metres), which is often smoking and rumbling, Lake Batur, Bali's largest lake, and a lava scarred terrain with many temples.

Mount Batur is one of the biggest double calderas in the world. It is 8.5 miles (13.7 kilometres) wide and has been partly filled by the beautiful Lake Batur, which is 4 miles (6.4 kilometres) north to south, and a volcanic cone. Pura Ulun Danu, the head of the lake temple, is at the northeast shore. It is not to be confused with Pura Ulun Danu Batur, which is on the rim of the caldera.

Holy water is collected from the lake itself in front of the temple. Visitors have to wear a sash and not go near. Bathing is forbidden. The lake is the ultimate source of water for the rivers and springs that irrigate central Bali. It is therefore of the utmost importance.

The temple priests say that the lake is fed by springs located at each of the directions of the wind. Each spring is the origin of water for that region of central Bali. Villagers from north Bali collect their holy water from the northern spring and so on.

Pura Ulun Danu Batur, Temple of the Crater, Batur

Bali's second most important temple after Pura Besakih is the ceremonial throne for Dewi Danu, the goddess of the lake. A dwarf guards the main entrance. There are dramatic, many-tiered, pagoda-like *meru*, often covered in mist from the lake. The goddess is honoured with a tall *meru* of eleven tiers, the highest possible number. The *meru* of her consort, the god of Mount Agung, has only nine. That indicates her importance.

According to legend, the god of Mount Agung and his sister Dewi Danu emerged from an erupting Mount Agung in 89 AD. Together they took control of the lands and waters of Bali. She refused to accept marriage and subordination to her brother and founded her own temple on Mount Batur where she could be independent. They are the complementary male and female gods of the island. There are two other nine-tiered *meru*, dedicated to the god of Mount Batur and the deified King Baturenggong.

One of the most interesting shrines is a pavilion in the inner courtyard on the far left. It is Chinese looking and dedicated to a Chinese princess, who resembles one of the *Barong Landung* characters in the dance play. She is tall, white faced with a jutting chin.

The age of the temple is unknown but there are references to it in the 11th century. It used to be located at the lake. In 1905 Mount Batur erupted and lava stopped at the main entrance. The 1917 eruption, however, damaged it, although lava stopped at the walls. On 3 August 1926 at 1 am it was covered in tons of rubble and the village was buried in many feet of rocks. Some shrines were saved and brought up the cliff to the rim of the crater. The whole temple was moved and built around the shrines.

The present temple is a reconstruction of nine previous temples and stands at the head, physically and symbolically, of the water temple system, and controls all water to central Bali. It is the supreme water temple and receives tribute from several hundred *subak*, the irrigation societies, of the surrounding regions. They pray to the goddess of the lake for rulings on water distribution and the Greater High Priest, her earthly representative, lays down the goddess's rulings. The temple priests do not actively manage irrigation but they settle any disputes referred to them from *subaks* or groups of *subaks* and give permission to the building of new irrigation works. The crater lake has no water outlets itself; the water percolates into the porous volcanic soil and becomes part of the groundwater system.

The Greater High Priest is an interesting character. When a Greater High Priest dies, mediums in trance pick out a young virgin boy from the village of Batur as his successor. He and his family move into a house adjoining the temple and the temple pays his living expenses for the rest of his life. He will be from the commoner descent group called the 'Pasek of the Black Wood'. He wears his hair long, dresses in white, and has complete control over the temple. Called *Jero Gede*, he is neither fully divine, nor fully human and has a job for life. He represents the goddess.

The *Pasek* of the Black Wood believe that they are the oldest of the Balinese descent groups and that they pre-date the kings. Soon after the gods took possession of Bali, following the emergence of the deities of Mount Agung and Mount Batur, the great priest-god Mahameru visited them. He bathed in Lake Batur and then decided to go to Besakih. On the way he saw a statue of black wood, which looked human and he brought it to life. This was the first Balinese human being. The priest-god taught him sacred knowledge, so that there would always be priests in Bali.

The second ranking priest is called the *Lesser Jero Gede*. He comes from another descent group, the *Pasek* Gelgel. They were commoners who became loyal servants of the Gelgel kings. He is identified with the god of Mount Agung, the goddess's brother, and the nine-tiered *meru* and is linked to Besakih and the court of Klungkung. The two main priests therefore derive their powers from different sources. The second-ranking one is definitely subordinate to the first as the god of Mount Agung has no role to play in the temple. He represents the goddess when the Greater High Priest is absent.

The other forty-three gods of the temple speak through trance mediums, all of whom have equal status. Trance mediums are common in Bali and contact a number of ancestors, but in Ulun Danu Batur they contact only the god who selected them. When a priest is replaced, all the mediums meet together in trance and reach a consensus. The most revered mediums are twins of opposite sex. They are considered to have been intimate in the womb and are married from birth and expected to become temple mediums. If a male appears first it is auspicious and the village will be prosperous, but if a female appears first it is dangerous as Durga is restless and purification ceremonies have to be carried out in her temple of death. In both cases the parents' house must be destroyed, and the family live outside the village in another village called Tasu, which was created for such temporary exiles, while purification ceremonies are taking place.

The temple is managed by members of the village of Batur by means of the priests, trance mediums and village elders. It is always open with a permanent staff of twenty-four priests, who are commoners and serve for life. It is the only temple in Bali where the priests are chosen

Mount Batur is a live volcano, 5,633 feet (1,717 metres), often smoking and rumbling, Lake Batur is Bali's largest lake.

by the gods themselves (through the mediums). Once appointed they try to limit the role of the aristocracy. Brahman priests are excluded from most ceremonies.

Batur village is governed by twenty elders, who meet monthly in the village temple. Both they and the priests of Ulun Danu Batur are divided into a west category associated with the female principle and an east category associated with the male principle. The monthly temple rituals are also divided into male and female categories according to the phase of the moon. The east priests perform the rituals and the west priests prepare the offerings for the fifteen day new moon phase. The west priests perform the rituals and the east priests prepare the offerings for the fifteen day full moon phase. The point is to create balanced harmony between male and female.

The same principle applies to the four most senior elders of the village, two of which are eligible to become Beautiful Kings. Those from the eastern group may marry their opposite numbers from the western group, who become their 'wives', in a series of ceremonies lasting forty-five days. It is very expensive as they have to feed the entire village throughout this time. The two kings can issue commands to the other elders and they rival the two high priests of the temple in terms of authority. Because of the expense, no doubt, there have not been any marriages of elders for the past century.

Pura Luhur Uluwatu: Temple above the Stone

Pura Luhur Uluwatu is perched on a cliff overhanging the Indian Ocean 295 feet (90 metres) below on the southwestern part of Bali in an area called the Bukit. It is a very sacred, beautiful temple. The name means

'Temple above the Stone'. The Bukit is a raised seabed of greyish, white coral rock. There is a rule that nobody can carry a red hibiscus flower or wear *poleng*, the black and white chequered cloth, in the temple.

Its history is not well recorded and it is difficult to date the temple. Two famous people are associated with it. The first is Empu (Sage) Kuturan, who came to Bali from Java in the 10th century AD on a deer, arriving at Padang Bai, which is the harbour on the east coast. He was a Saiwite priest, but strongly influenced by Buddhism. Religion was in a state of decline. He renewed religious ceremonies, customs and ethics, and built many *meru* throughout Bali. When he came to Pura Uluwatu, he built the *meru* and added shrines. Perhaps he even built the temple.

The other famous person is Nirartha, also a Saiwite priest who arrived from Java in 1537 AD. He incorporated some Buddhist principles into Balinese Hinduism, and travelled all over Bali building new temples and shrines, including Tanah Lot, and adding *padmasana* to existing temples, including Pura Uluwatu. Nirartha died at Pura Uluwatu and achieved *moksa*, which is *nirvana*, eternal bliss, when the spirit is united with the spirit of God. Cremation is not required for such a pure soul to be released from its body.

The temple has several unique architectural features. It is built of strong coral stone and fairly well preserved, although the sacred monkeys have caused some damage. Set on a spectacular cliff, the tip of Java is 30 miles (48 kilometres) away and visible on a clear day. A troupe of monkeys lives in the temple stealing food and brightly coloured jewellery. Sea turtles come up for air in the crashing waves far below, while wide winged frigate birds soar against the sky on their way to nests in the cliffs.

It is one of a number of sea temples on the south coast, which include Tanah Lot, Pura Sakenan, Pura Rambut Siwi and Pura Petitenget. All pay homage to the guardian spirits of the sea. Pura Uluwatu is sacred to fishermen, who pray to Dewi Laut, the sea goddess, and believe that the temple is a ship turned into stone.

For many years only the Raja of Badung, who owned the Bukit, was allowed to enter. He visited the temple right up to his death in the *puputan* massacre of 1906. Pura Uluwatu now belongs to the Balinese people and is administered by the royal family in Denpasar.

Pura Luhur Uluwatu is perched on a cliff overhanging the Indian Ocean on the southwestern part of Bali in an area called the Bukit. The name means 'Temple above the Stone'.

Tanah Lot: Sea Temple of the Earth

Tanah Lot is one of the most beautiful temples in Bali, as well as one of the most important. It means 'Sea Temple of the Earth' and looks like a small pagoda. It is built on a huge eroded outcrop of rock on black volcanic sand in Berabon village, which is 8 miles (13 kilometres) west of Tabanan. World Monuments Watch lists it as one of the hundred most endangered historical sites in the world.

It is part of a magnificent series of temples along the south coast, all dedicated to the protective sea spirits. Each temple is visible from the next along the entire southern coastline. You can see Pura Uluwatu on a clear day.

It is said that Nirartha built Tanah Lot in the 16th century. Bendesa Beraben, the area's holy leader, became very jealous when his followers joined Nirartha and ordered him to leave. Using his magical powers,

Nirartha left by simply moving the rock upon which Tanah Lot was built into the sea and changed his scarf into the sacred, poisonous snakes that still guard the temple. Bendesa Beraben later converted to Nirartha's teachings.

The snakes live in sandy holes just above the waterline along the beach. When the tide is out, they slide into the temple. Snakes are holy creatures in Bali and should not be disturbed.

Tanah Lot's anniversary *odalan* celebration falls close to the festivals of *Galungan* and *Kuningan*. Four days after *Kuningan*, Hindus from all over Bali come laden with offerings, rice cakes, carved palm leaves, holy water and fruit, to pray to its gods and goddesses. Women carry towers of offerings on their heads, waiting until low tide to walk over the concrete walkway and up rock cut steps to the temple.

Tanah Lot is one of the most beautiful temples in Bali, as well as one of the most important. It means 'Sea Temple of the Earth' and looks like a small pagoda.

Chapter 43

Island-Wide Ceremonies

New Year's Eve

For weeks before Balinese New Year's Eve a great din is made, banging tins and letting off firecrackers to frighten away the evil spirits. On New Year's Eve every Balinese community carries out a ritual called *tawur kasanga*, the aim of which is to transform the destructive energies into positive ones. It is preceded by a procession to the sea with *pratimas*, the small figures representing the gods, *Barong* and Rangda masks, and sacred paraphernalia from all the village temples. They are given offerings on the beach. The process of purification begins. They are then brought back to the village.

At midday the *tawur kasanga* ritual takes place at the village crossroads and at district, regency and provincial levels. It also takes place in other parts of Indonesia where there are Hindu communities, like Kalimantan, Sulawesi, Sumatra and Jakarta. The priest invites the evil spirits to a feast of offerings and then dismisses them with magic formulas. People make small *caru* offerings in their homes and walk round their properties banging metal pots and pans and letting off firecrackers to chase away the low spirits. The aim is to purify the people, the houses, the temples and the community.

In the evening, huge grotesque statues, accompanied by loud gamelan music, are paraded around the villages. They are symbols of demonic spirits, called *ogoh-ogoh*, made from wood and bamboo, covered with *papier-mâché* and Styrofoam, and painted with garish colours. Some reach 10 feet (3 metres) high. The 'tradition' became popular in the 1980s.

Youths raise money to make the *ogoh-ogoh*. They are inventive and frightening. There is always a black, hooded, faceless angel of death. There are usually dragon-like figures and mythical creatures. In the early days the artists were inspired by Balinese folklore but latterly Hollywood

characters have come to the fore, some sporting Mohawk hairstyles. After the parade they are usually burned at the village crossroads, but recently, as they are really works of art, some have been kept for display in community halls, temples and private houses.

Nyepi: New Year's Day

New Year's Day is calculated according to the *Saka* calendar and usually takes place in March or April. Total silence prevails. There are four basic restrictions: no fire, no working, no travelling, and no leisure activity. Nobody is allowed to leave the family compound. It is forbidden to turn on electricity, light fires or cook. Balinese radio and television stop. Many people fast. The ports shut down. In 2000 the international airport was closed for the first time and has closed on *Nyepi* every year since.

In the evening of New Year's Eve, huge grotesque statues, accompanied by loud gamelan music, are paraded around the villages. The *ogoh-ogoh* are symbols of demonic spirits, made from wood and bamboo, covered with *papier-mâché* and Styrofoam, and painted with garish colours.

The idea is that Bali looks deserted. Entrances to villages are barricaded with piles of branches. The *pecalang*, who are the 'traditional' village guards, patrol the streets to ensure compliance and levy fines on transgressors. It is a new beginning. It symbolises the beginning of the world, which started with a void, and the next day everything is back to normal again.

Med-Medan: Kissing Day

On a small green called 'the kissing fields' in South Denpasar, in the afternoon after *Nyepi*, a strange and unique kissing ritual takes place in the village of *Banjar Kaja*. The ritual is named *med-medan*. Young boys assemble on the left and young girls on the right, in traditional dress. They slowly approach each other, break into a run and an exchange of kisses takes place. Every youth in the village takes part, as otherwise something terrible might happen. Before the activities prayers are said in the community temple and during the ritual parents keep buckets of holy water handy to ensure that things do not get out of hand.

Galungan

This is the start of an extended holiday timed according to the 210 day Balinese calendar, when the deified ancestors descend for ten days and are presented with special offerings. It is always on a Wednesday in the eleventh week of the Balinese year. Most businesses and schools close.

Villages are beautifully decorated with *penjor*, tall bamboo poles. Each village has its own style of *penjor*. Special foods are eaten: *tapé*, a mildly alcoholic fermented rice pudding, special cakes, *saté* and *lawar*.

According to an 11th century medical treatise the origin of *Galungan* began in the reign of King Jayakasunu. A smallpox epidemic had broken out and many died. The goddess of death, Durga, advised the king to hold an annual religious festival to appease the evil spirits. The same manuscript mentions the *Barong* and recommends that *penjor* are erected in front of households.

Families visit each other. Relatives go to family graves and leave offerings. There are *Barongs* on the street, accompanied by crashing cymbals and gongs. Owners request them to dance outside their properties to banish and transform the evil spirits into positive ones and absorb them into itself. They give the *Barong* a few coins. Dances also take place in village squares for up to half an hour. *Barong Landung*, two giant masked characters, one male, the other female, also tour the streets singing and flirting with each other.

Girl presenting offerings at a *penjor* at *Galungan*, which is the start of an extended holiday, when the deified ancestors descend for ten days and are presented with special offerings.

The parades through the villages have a curative effect on the community and revitalise energies. Many offerings contain blood and meat for the low spirits in order to transform them into positive energies. The holiday ends on the day called *Kuningan*.

Galungan also commemorates an historic battle, celebrating good over evil. In 8 AD a bad king called Sang Mayadenawa forbade the Balinese people from carrying out religious ceremonies. A fierce battle took place and the king was killed.

Kuningan

The ancestors return to heaven on *Kuningan*, which is the end of the ten day festival beginning with *Galungan*. It is a day of prayers and visiting. Special yellow rice offerings are made. The word for yellow is *kuning*. Decorations called *tamiang* are hung around the house to celebrate the victory of order over disorder. Bali has been purified and energised with positive forces. It also commemorates the spirits of the heroes who were killed during the battle against Sang Mayadenawa.

Saraswati

Saraswati Day takes place on the last day of the 210 day calendar and is devoted to the goddess of learning, Saraswati, who is the wife of Brahma, the god of creation. She lives on the tip of the human tongue and on written letters of poems inscribed on palm leaf manuscripts, the *lontar*, and on the petals of lotus blossoms.

Her day is a public holiday in Bali. Offerings are made to books, which are covered with an ornate piece of cloth. There are no school classes but there are special ceremonies in the schools. Students pray at the shrines in the school. No letters may be crossed out or any writing deleted. Reading is forbidden.

Banyu Pinaruh

Banyu Pinaruh is the day after Saraswati Day when the Balinese clean themselves with holy water. Many people go to the beach in the morning, pray and bathe themselves with sea water. In the evening they eat a smoked duck feast including yellow rice.

Coma Ribek or Somaribek

The following day the Balinese pray to Dewi Sri, the rice goddess, for wealth. No money is supposed to change hands on this day. It is unclear if credit cards are acceptable.

Siwa Ratri

The same evening the Balinese fast, stay awake and meditate for thirty-six hours. On this day Siwa carried out his most important meditation. Those who do the same are blessed.

Pagerwesi

The following day offerings are made to Pramesti Guru for his blessing. This achieves balance in the world.

Saraswati, the wife of Brahma, is the goddess of learning.

Chapter 44

Balinese Organisations

Get Organised

Organisations are at the heart of Balinese social structure and demonstrate the communal nature of Balinese life. The Balinese like to do things together and actually many things are done better if done with others, but, as Margaret Mead observed, more people are often involved than are strictly necessary. The Balinese like bustling activity. They rarely do things on their own. Putting the needs of one's group above one's own is a central Balinese value.

Everything in Bali is inseparable from religion and is infused with religious meaning. Virtually every Balinese institution is deeply involved in religion. The communal organisations intersect and overlap and bind the Balinese people together as a whole.

There are many organisations. Voluntary groups are called *seka*, which means 'to be unified'. The *seka* can have religious, political and economic functions. Some are social groups, maybe comprising ten to twenty people, dedicated to a narrow goal, such as harvesting, reading poetry, making gamelan instruments, roofing houses, transporting goods.

The most important organisations, after kinship groups, are:
• *Banjar*: hamlet groups
• *Subak*: irrigation societies
• *Pemaksan*: temple congregations

Banjar: Hamlet Groups

The *banjar* controls the religious purity of the village and large villages may have several. As a unique institution it is not really possible to translate the concept, but 'hamlet group' comes close. It is unknown when they first came into existence and they vary from village to village.

- **Duty**
  The overriding duty of the *banjar* is to maintain the ritual purity of the village, which is achieved by carrying out a number of activities, some major, some minor. It is, in essence, a civic body.
- **Membership**
  Married couples are the typical members. In many *banjars* the gentry do not belong. The men must be adults, married or at least have a female partner, who can be a sister, mother or daughter. This is necessary, as women are required to deal with the village offerings. In most villages, a man can become a member on marriage or after the birth of his first child (often these events take place in short order).

  Retirement usually occurs when the youngest son marries and becomes a member or on the death of a spouse. Occasionally dire poverty is accepted as a reason for leaving.
- **Activities**
  The activities include most non-governmental issues:
  - Cleaning the public temples
  - Constructing, maintaining and restoring the hamlet meeting house, the *balé banjar*, granaries, cockpits, market places and cemeteries
  - Local security, including night watches, apprehension, and punishment of thieves
  - Settlement of disputes concerning traditional rights and duties
  - Controlling access to village land
  - Legitimising marriage and divorce
  - Lending money from its treasury
  - Organising and requiring participation in communal village work
  - Assisting with rituals, like tooth-filings
  - Ensuring compliance with *adat* rules, such as observing silence on *Nyepi*, the Balinese New Year, and fining offenders
  - Constructing sarcophagi and cremation towers, carrying and accompanying the deceased to the cremation ground, collecting wood for the funeral pyre and setting it alight

Matters concerning wet rice agriculture are excluded. These are the responsibility of the *subak* organisations.

The *pecalang* are the 'traditional' village security, the tradition going back to October 1998, when a man in traditional Balinese costume calmed a heated crowd during a PDI-P political congress. Throughout Bali villages formed their own private groups to protect their territories and *adat*. They have a distinctive uniform: T-shirt with the name of the village and the word *pecalang*, a sleeveless safari jacket, a black and white chequered *poleng* wrap over a sarong, a *kris* blessed in the temple tucked into their belt and a walkie-talkie.

- **Temples**
  Each *banjar* has its own temple.

- **Meetings**
  Traditionally the *banjar* meets once every Balinese month of thirty-five days, but this varies from village to village. Special meetings may be called for special reasons. Attendance is expected and absentees have to pay a fine on top of their normal subscriptions. All members sit at the same level irrespective of their status and speak in High Balinese to each other to indicate equality. At the end of the meeting the headman carries out a small ritual to take away any impurities caused by disagreements.

- **Headman**
  They elect a headman, the *klian banjar*, for a period, which is normally 420 days (the time between two major temple anniversaries). To refuse to serve entails severe punishment. He may be assisted by a secretary and treasurer, or just by a single assistant.

- **Property**
  The *banjar* owns collective property. This includes streets and paths between houses, ditches, and public buildings like the *wantilan* or meeting place. The *banjar* also inherits property where a family dies without heirs. The *banjar* may own a gamelan orchestra.

- **Rules**
  The *banjar* can make rules for village behaviour, *awig-awig*, which are written on *lontar* palms and kept in the temple. The oldest predate the coming of the Dutch. All important decisions are decided consensually and members enjoy equal rights and responsibilities.

  The sanctions for transgressing village custom, *adat*, can be severe. *Adat* covers everything from caste and land tenure to kinship, economics, religion and law. It can vary in each village.

This is because historically there was no strong central government in Bali but a collection of kingdoms. The *banjar* can impose large fines, prohibit members from praying at village temples and even refuse use of the cemetery.

- ***Desa Dinas***

  The Dutch created villages, *desa dinas*, in order to administer the island. Their borders do not always overlap with the old Balinese villages, *desa adat*. They may encompass several *desa adat* and several *banjars*. The head of the village, the *kepala desa*, is responsible for ensuring that national and regional government decrees are implemented.

Water rushes down from the mountains, where the gods reside, from higher level terraced rice fields into the lower level terraced rice fields. Downstream farmers are totally dependent on upstream farmers, who could take all the water away for their own use, but they co-operate. They form *subak* associations to ensure that the water is fairly distributed.

Subak: Irrigation Societies

We do not think about irrigation. We just turn on the tap and have water, but irrigation is fundamental to civilisation. The earliest civilisations in the Fertile Crescent were built on the control of irrigation. Without aqueducts bringing water over long distances to Rome the Roman Empire would not have existed. If the Incas had not mastered irrigation, canals and aqueducts, their greatest achievement, Machu Pichu, would not have been constructed in 1500 AD. It is therefore not fanciful to suggest that without the inventions of Balinese rice farmers concerning water over a thousand years ago, Balinese culture, sustaining every kind of craftsman, would not have reached the heights it did. Irrigation is necessary for civilisation, and so is a central authority to enforce the sharing of water.

Water rushes down from the mountains, where the gods reside, from higher level terraced rice fields into the lower level terraced rice fields. Downstream farmers are totally dependent on upstream farmers, who could take all the water away for their own use, but they do not; they co-operate. They form *subak* associations to ensure that the water is fairly distributed during the long dry season, which stretches normally from April to October. Although always called 'irrigation societies', it would be more accurate to call them 'agriculture societies' as they are concerned with matters other than irrigation.

Subak associations were established over a thousand years ago and pre-date the Majapahits. According to legend, Rsi Markandeya, the great Hindu saint and first person to set foot on Bali, is credited with founding them. Tunnel builders were mentioned in 896 AD and a *subak* was mentioned in 1022 AD. The old Balinese kings offered tax incentives to clear the land and build irrigation systems, but they did not control them. Management was left to the farmers.

The ruggedness of Bali meant that the irrigation systems used in Java and other parts of Southeast Asia were unsuitable. So the Balinese perfected a new kind of intensive microengineering. Employing sophisticated engineering principles, they constructed canals and tunnels, which can be nearly 2 miles (3 kilometres) long and 130 feet (40 metres) deep, and aqueducts to supply water to rice terraces several miles from a water source. On average a continuous flow of at least two litres (0.44 Imperial gallons) of water per hectare (2.47 acres) is needed over an entire growing season.

- **Membership**

  A *subak* area is land watered by a common source. Everyone who owns land within a *subak* area must join and pay a fee. There are about 1,300 *subak* in Bali and each has about 200 members, depending on the size of the plots involved. A head of the *subak* is voted in and everyone must attend the meetings. *Subak* boundaries do not necessarily overlap with village boundaries, so a *subak* usually includes members from several villages. People tend to own small parcels of land, often some distance from their village, and therefore have to join several *subak*.

Clifford Geertz, in *Peddlers and Princes* (1963), makes the point that membership of the *subak* introduces almost every adult male to the workings of a well-organised group devoted to economic ends of a specific sort. It provides a business education. He could have added that it is also a lesson in democratic decision-making.

- **Activities**

Subak members, like *banjar* members, have equal rights, regardless of title or indeed the size of their land. They meet every month, under their elected head, the *klian subak*, and decide all matters concerning rice cultivation: times for planting, harvesting, rotation, offerings, ceremonies, repairing dams, fertilising, using insecticides. *Subak* give or withhold permission for new rice terrace construction. They keep land records. The *klian subak* is responsible for ensuring compliance with government regulations.

There are also monthly meetings of *subak* heads, run on the same basis, which regulate relations between *subaks*. The *Greater Subak* co-ordinates irrigation and cropping patterns on a regional scale.

The Dutch underestimated the *subak* system, as did the Indonesian government until a few years ago. In *Priests and Programmers* (1991) Stephen Lansing describes how the careful co-ordination of rice planting times has a very important role in keeping pests down, a role well understood by the *subak*. The effectiveness of burning or flooding a rice field after the harvest as a means of controlling pests depends on the co-operation of all the farmers in a given area. A sizeable block has to be burned or flooded to kill the pests; otherwise they just move to the neighbouring field.

Stephen Lansing shows in his latest book *Perfect Order* (2006) that that is why upstream farmers co-operate in supplying downstream farmers with water—it is in their own interests to do so. By synchronising the flooding of rice fields, pests are reduced for the benefit of all. The result is higher, and more or less equal, yields. The farmers compare the yields of their neighbours to their own and if they are better imitate them and over a short time the optimum position for the ecosystem is reached.

- **Temples**

There are *subak* temples, which provide the institutional framework for water management. Farmers share information about harvests and pests. They are places to worship the ancestors, whose existence derives from the older Austronesian tradition, not the Indian Hindu gods. After the 9th century most were built beside natural springs and incorporated bathing pools. Pura Ulun Swi, literally 'head of the rice fields temple', is usually located towards the upper end of the fields and is at the spot where the water first enters the fields. It has an annual celebration, like all other temples. Shrines do not. Downstream the canal splits in two and there will be another temple at that point.

Subak also have an interest in the *Pura Desa* temple of the village and send offerings during their *odalan*s. This ties the *banjar* and the *subak* together. There are also small individual shrines near dams and weirs. These are called *dugul* and are places where the gods stop to rest on their journeys. Resting places are common in the Balinese temple system.

Ceremonies are held at each stage in the rice cycle. The water ultimately comes from the mountains, so the *subak* make regular pilgrimages to the temples in the mountain lakes. The priests in the lake temples have considerable influence, especially Pura Ulun Danu Batur, Temple of the Crater, at Batur. It is normally the case in early agricultural societies that chiefs, clan leaders and priests try to ensure that they influence, or even control, the food surplus and redistribution and the settlement of conflicts. As non-producers of food, they are the most vulnerable in the community.

- **Disputes**

Nearly every farmer could grow a bit more rice if he took a little extra water, but this would disrupt everyone else's water supply. There is a sacred aspect to the *subak*, so an infringement of the rules is a violation of the divine order and can result in negative consequences for the whole community, for example, bad harvests. This results in immense peer pressure to act properly.

Disputes concerning boundaries, water rights and so on are

normally settled informally, but in serious cases the *subak* arbitrates and its decisions are binding. The sanctions are fines and penalties and the most severe is expulsion from the *subak* and loss of water supply.

Pemaksan: Temple Congregations

Most Balinese belong to about half a dozen temple congregations. The members share responsibility for maintaining the temple and performing ceremonies. The most frequent ceremony is the *odalan*, which is the temple's anniversary. That is the time that the gods visit the temple. The congregation have to prepare and organise elaborate offerings of food, flowers and cloth, and participate in various rituals. There are also financial obligations and activities to raise money for the temple.

Chapter 45

The Epics

Background

The Ramayana and the Mahabarata, the very famous Indian epics, are well known and well loved throughout Asia and provide the stories for many Balinese dances, paintings, sculptures, carvings, dramas and puppet performances.

The epics were originally written in Sanskrit, and then translated into Kawi, and flourished in the courts of east Java between the 11th and 15th centuries. A palm leaf *lontar* from the 10th century has been found of the text of the first book of the Mahabarata in Old Javanese. The kings liked them because they enshrined, explained and justified the authority of god kings. Both are extremely long.

The stories reflect old Javanese values, where there was an unequal social order and each person had his duty and function, determined by fate, everyone in his pre-ordained place. There are many versions of the stories.

From the cradle onwards Balinese children hear and see the epic stories in shadow puppet performances, dance dramas, operas, carvings and sculptures. They know the gods and demons, the heroes and villains, the kings and queens, their quarrels and struggles, their successes and defeats, and their qualities and lack of them. The Balinese particularly like Arjuna (one of the Pandawa brothers from the Mahabarata) and Sita (the heroine of the Ramayana).

Lontar

Palm leaf *lontar* manuscripts are still made and read in Bali. This is virtually unique in the Malay-Indonesian area. In other countries they are exhibits in a museum. In Bali *lontar* are read by priests, puppeteers, traditional healers, scholars and special reading groups. Many deal with astrology, magic and sorcery. Readers tend to be older men. They are

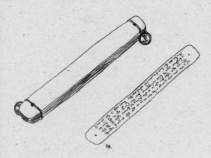

Lontar palms are specially prepared, flattened and dried to make manuscripts. The leaves are all cut to the same size and a hole is drilled in the centre of the margin through which a cord is threaded to hold the leaves together. Thin hardwood covers, the same size as the leaves, protect the manuscript. Sometimes a Chinese *kepeng* coin is tied to the end of the cord to prevent it slipping out.

written in beautiful Balinese script, Sanskrit and Kawi, and some are illustrated. *Lontar* are treated with great respect, even by those who cannot read them, because they contain sacred information and are receptacles of mystical power. Saraswati, the goddess of literature, knowledge and poetry holds a *lontar* in one of her four hands.

The text is written on leaves of the *lontar* palm, which are specially prepared, flattened and dried. The leaves are all cut to the same size, usually between 9 to 18 inches (25 to 50 centimetres) long and 1 to 1.5 inches (2.5 to 4 centimetres) wide; a hole is drilled in the centre of the left margin through which a cord is threaded to hold the leaves together. Thin hardwood covers, the same size as the leaves and usually carved, protect the manuscript. Sometimes a Chinese *kepeng* coin is tied to the end of the cord to prevent it slipping out. When the cord is pulled tight only the edges of the leaves are visible.

Normally there are four lines of text, inscribed by a special steel blade. The surface of the leaf is wiped with oil mixed with burnt candlewood soot. The soot remains in the grooves. The leaves are wiped clean and the black text can then be read. Each leaf is numbered in the left margin. There is usually a blank leaf at the beginning and end. Some give the name of the scribe or owner and the date of completion of the manuscript using the Balinese 210 day calendar.

Until the founding of the Gedong Kirtya Library in Singaraja in north Bali by the Dutch government in 1928, there was no central or public collection of *lontar* texts. Now anyone can go and consult them. There is also a collection of them at Pusat Dokumentasi Budaya Bali in Denpasar. Some were brought to Bali from Java in the 15th century after the fall of the Majapahit. Several have been translated and published in English.

The Mahabarata

Composed around the 10th century BC, the Mahabarata, which is eighteen books, is one of the longest poems ever written, although originally it was oral, with about 90,000 couplets. It is about seven times the length of Homer's Iliad or three times the length of the Old and New Testaments combined. It developed gradually and had a great number of anonymous authors, although the poet Vyasa is often claimed as the author.

It is about the battle between two related families, the Pandawa and the Korawa, for the control of the kingdom of Astina and culminates in a great war, the Bratayuda, in which the five Pandawa brothers confront their first cousins, the ninety-nine Korawa brothers. After eighteen days' fighting and thousands of deaths, the Pandawa win.

The story begins with Abyoso, the common grandfather of the Pandawa and Korawa. He was the king of Astina and ruled the great kingdom in peace, justice and prosperity. His three sons were afflicted. Drestarata, the first, was blind; Pandu, the second, was an albino; and Widura, the third, was lame.

Abyoso abdicated in middle age to devote himself to meditation and nominated Pandu as his successor on the understanding that the throne would revert to Drestarata's line. Pandu had five sons, Yudistira, Bima, Arjuna, Nakula and Sadewa. Pandu died early and many thought Pandu was entitled to name his own successor. This was the origin of the dispute between Drestarata's sons (the Korawa) and Pandu's sons (the Pandawa), which was settled by the last war, but not before many adventures, trickery and battles.

It is essentially a moral epic, portraying rectitude, perseverance and wisdom. It extols integrity and filial devotion, and the *satria* have these qualities. Virtue triumphs over vice. The Balinese tend to concentrate on the personalities and battle scenes.

The Ramayana

The Ramayana has about 24,000 couplets and was written by the sage Valmiki in the 3rd or 4th century BC. There is only one version in Bali based on the Old Javanese one but in India there are many versions. It pervades all aspects of Balinese life. Readings of parts of it take place at ceremonies, such as baby ceremonies, tooth-filings, weddings and cremations.

Kausalya gave birth to two of King Dasarata's sons, Rama and Laksmana. Shortly afterwards Dasarata's second wife, Kaikeyi, gave birth to his third son, Barota. Dasarata decided to abdicate and make Rama his heir to the kingdom of Ayodya in India. Kaikeyi, however, wanted Barota to be his heir and made unfounded allegations against Rama. Rama refused to defend himself and was banished for twelve years. He went into exile in the forest of Dandaka with Sita, his wife, and Laksmana.

While in the forest, Sarpakenaka, sister to the demon king, Rawana, discovers them and is determined to seduce Rama and Laksmana. Although she wears a disguise, Laksmana senses her and cuts off her nose and ears. She is outraged and flees to her brother's palace in Alengka to complain.

Rawana goes to find Rama, Sita and Laksmana. He falls in love with Sita and decides to capture her. He orders the ogre Marica to change himself into a golden deer and entice Sita. The plan works and Sita, wanting the deer as a pet, pleads with Rama to capture it. Rama asks his brother to protect Sita and goes into the forest in search of the deer. He finds it and shoots with his arrow.

Before the deer dies it resumes the demon shape of Marica and imitates Rama's voice calling for help. Sita is distraught and asks Laksmana to go and help. Before he leaves, he draws a magic circle around her for protection.

Rawana disguises himself as a beggar and seizes the chance. He asks Sita for food. When she steps out of the circle, he captures her and carries her off to his palace. Rama and Laksmana return and cannot find her. Jatayu, the giant bird, tries to rescue Sita, but Rawana catches him and cuts off his wings. As he lies dying, he tells Rama of the kidnapping.

Rama summons help from Sugriwa, the monkey, who lends him his monkey army and Hanuman, the outstanding white monkey commander. Meanwhile Sita has been resisting Rawana's advances. Hanuman arrives at the palace, disguised as a fly, and finds Sita. He transforms himself back to normal and explains that he has come at Rama's request. Sita thinks it is a trick and it is Rawana in disguise until Hanuman shows her Rama's ring and she is then convinced. In return she gives Hanuman a letter and a hair clip for Rama.

On his way out Hanuman purposely gets caught, so as to ascertain Rawana's strength. He taunts Rawana, who attacks him and ties him up.

Hanuman grabs a torch and burns the palace and escapes, but carefully ensures that Sita's apartment is safe. He returns to the forest and shows Rama the letter and hair clip.

Rama sends Hangada, the red monkey, to Rawana to persuade him to return Sita and avoid bloodshed, but Rawana tries to kill him, whereupon Rama's army appears and a huge battle ensues. Rama and Rawana direct the battle. There are massive casualties and finally Rama kills Rawana.

Rama and Sita are reunited and return to Ayodya and Rama is enthroned. Sita becomes pregnant, but Rama suspects his wife of adultery in Alengka and puts her to trial by fire. She is proved innocent, but he still banishes her to the forest, where she meets the sage Valmiki, who helps raise her twin sons. Eventually Rama realises his mistake and tries to find Sita, but she has gone. He takes his sons back to Ayodya and gives them the throne.

Modern Times

Modern rulers appeal to the epics. President Sukarno referred to them in a speech in Denpasar in an effort to stop revenge killings in Bali in 1950 after the Revolution. He said,

> You want to be the heroes of the Revolution, but where in your Ramayana or Mahabarata do you find heroes who murder in the dark with their daggers, and when did Krishna and Arjuna take revenge on children and women?

Television

Indian versions of the epics have been shown on television since the early 1990s and have changed Balinese perceptions. The puppet performances are highly stereotyped and symbolic. Events take place in a mythical world and have been the perfect symbolic vehicle for teaching morals. The television soap operas portray real people in real life situations in India. They are not good for education, but they are good entertainment.

Chapter 46

Traditional Balinese Painting

Kamasan

The village of Kamasan in the kingdom of Klungkung in east Bali became the centre for traditional Balinese painting. Originally, the Kamasan artists served the kings of Gelgel from the 16th century. Kamasan is only about 2 miles (3.2 kilometres) from Gelgel, where the court reigned during Bali's golden age.

The village of Kamasan in the kingdom of Klungkung in east Bali became the centre for traditional Balinese painting.

The unique *wayang* style of painting was Bali's only form of pictorial representation until the 20th century when the Western artists arrived in central Bali and influenced the Balinese artists to paint realistic scenes of everyday life. Both styles still exist. The earliest known Kamasan paintings down to the present portray the same techniques, conventions and styles.

Traditional painting takes place in other parts of Bali, but Kamasan is the most well known and has influenced many other areas, such as Kerambitan in the southwest kingdom of Tabanan. Paintings for ceremonial use are done by men. There are women artists involved in commercial paintings.

Palace of Klungkung

The court moved to Klungkung in 1710. It is 26 miles (42 kilometres) east of the present capital, Denpasar. The court became the centre of culture and the painters' art matured. The first raja of Klungkung, Dewa Agung Gusti Sideman, commissioned a large new palace. He appointed painters and sculptors. They became official court painters for generations and received requests from other kings as their reputations spread.

Rivalry between the courts was a major stimulus to the arts, as a court's prestige was measured by its ability to do things in style. The ceremonies had to be grand and the palaces had to impress. Their power depended on it. The highest praise that a Balinese can give a painting is to say that it has *taksu*, spiritual strength.

Use of Paintings

Paintings were used to decorate households and temples. They are offerings to the gods and ancestors during a ceremony. After the ceremony they are sometimes put away and stored in baskets. Originally, paintings were on bark paper. Later, hand woven cotton was used, and later still, machine made cloth. Traditional cloths called *ider-ider* are pinned under the eaves of buildings on special occasions. Paintings on wooden panels decorate the back walls of pavilions, offering platforms and shrines, bed heads, windows, doors, boxes, cradles and bowls. There is usually no monetary payment for works done for the temple.

Rubberised cloths are painted for a gambling game called *kocokan*. There are six large squares with a painted figure in each and three large dice painted with the same motif. Punters place their bets on the squares and the operator rolls the dice. The winners are those who bet on the figure that comes up on the dice. The images vary and include dogs, birds, snakes, fish, turtles, babies, girls and clowns. The game is played during cockfights, shadow puppet performances and public temple ceremonies. Even children bet and at night they are illuminated by atmospheric kerosene lamps. The amounts are small.

Subject-Matter

The subject-matter tends to come from Balinese versions of the Ramayana and Mahabarata epic stories; frequently battle scenes and especially the story of Rama, Sita and Rawana. They are like picture books, which are read and examined closely, and no part of the 'canvas' is left empty. There are gods, demons, birds, flames, giants, monsters, bushes, trees and mythical animals. They are from the unseen world of myth and magic, the world the Balinese call *niskala*, which is very real to them. Originality is not admired as much as talent and craftsmanship.

Sometimes there is Balinese writing on the paintings. It derives from Sanskrit brought from India, about 1,500 years ago, and is phonetic. It briefly describes the characters and the subject. Time is shown by depicting the same characters at different stages in the story. They can be several feet long and one and a half feet (half a metre) wide.

Reading the sequence of events in a painting is not easy as there are no fixed rules. Very often, however, the story begins in one of the lower corners and proceeds along that layer, then up to the next level and along, and up and along, and so on. The most important episode may break the sequence and be placed in the centre of the painting.

The Palette

The 'canvas' is white cotton cloth which is sized with rice paste and polished with a cowrie shell. The rice paste sizing provides a smooth surface for painting. It is of a consistency that allows for rolling up the cloth and not damaging the paint. Pigments are black made from soot or Chinese ink; red from Chinese vermilion; grey-blue and yellow from ground rock; and bright white from burnt bone or antler. They are ground and mixed with water and Chinese fish glue.

The palette was extended later by the addition of bright yellow imported from China, blue made from indigo and laundry bluing and dark red from a berry. Mixing pigments produced other colours, like orange and green.

It was and is not uncommon for several people to work on a painting. The master painter draws the outlines first in black with a sharp pen. He and perhaps others then fill in the colours. There may be overlapping layers of colour. The more gradations, the finer the painting. Finally, the master redraws the outlines, puts the finishing touches and may add gold leaf to very refined works. The cloth is then polished with a cowrie shell.

Artistic Conventions: the Language of Paintings

There is a vocabulary. The rules are the same as for shadow puppets. There is no shading. Once you know the language, you can recognise the characters. Until the 1930s the conventions were strictly applied. The influence of the European painters led to innovations.

Clothes, ornaments and headdresses portray who the characters are and correspond to those of the shadow puppets. Crowns and headdresses of queens and princesses, but not of kings and princes, are shown from the front, even though their faces are in three-quarters profile. Warriors wear lobster-claw hairdos; holy men wear robes and turbans. Certain characters, for example, Bima, wear black and white chequered *poleng* sarongs. Noble and divine characters are placed on the viewer's left of the painting, while coarse and evil ones are on the right.

There is no *kayonan* (tree puppet) or *gunungan* (mountain puppet) as in the shadow puppet theatre, but there are some analogous features. A tree or rock is usually in the middle, unless the picture is a battle scene. A tree-fern separates people in conversation. There is no perspective and no background, except for filler motifs, normally tear-drop designs or winged horseshoe shapes. They symbolise the wind and clouds. Battle scenes sometimes have fillers of flying weapons. There is no horizon to separate land and sky.

Animal heads are usually shown in profile and humans in three-quarters view, except for people who are meditating, who are shown full face. Pamurtian, who are gods in anger, huge, many-armed and multi-headed, are also an exception, painted full frontal. Kumbakarna, Rawana's giant brother, is also shown full face. Normally shoulders and chest face the spectator and legs and feet are pictured from the side, one behind the other as if walking. Noble characters have long thin arms and legs, delicate hands with curved fingers and long fingernails, narrow straight noses and smiling mouths. Coarse characters have large nostrils.

The male eye looks alert whereas the female eye appears demure, modest, shy and very feminine. Demons' eyes and noses are at a three-quarter angle.

Both eyes are visible and eyelashes of the distant eye project beyond the edge of the face. Noble male eyes have the top part of the eye curved and the bottom part a straight line. For females, it is the reverse. The male eye looks alert whereas the female eye appears demure, modest, shy and very feminine. Demons' eyes and noses are at a three-quarter angle but the mouth is in profile. Eyebrows are arched for the refined and touch at the top of the nose. The unrefined have two small lines for wrinkles. Demons' eyebrows end in fangs.

Refined lips are thin and graceful with white, straight teeth. Coarse characters and animals have large mouths and pointed teeth. Demons have fangs. Refined males do not have beards. Moustaches indicate virility and strength. Coarse characters have hair sprouting from their faces. Animals and demons are hairy.

Gestures show emotions. The right hand is active, the unclean left is still. Jewellery indicates rank. The gods and nobles wear bangles and bracelets on their arms and ankles and their costumes are decorated with flowers.

Colour indicates character: the faces of gods and refined *alus* humans are light brown or beige, while rough *kasar* characters are brown and red. Size matters. The most powerful, oldest and highest in rank are also the biggest. They retain their size whenever they appear. Otherwise adult men are all the same size. Women are smaller and children are smaller still. They do not age even if they do in the narrative. Gods appear in a yellow cloud, the outline of which is scalloped concavely.

Early paintings have a red border or none at all and later ones resemble a carved wooden frame.

Dutch Invasion

The Dutch invaded Klungkung on 17 April 1908 and the palace caught fire. There is a rumour that the Balinese started the fire themselves in an act of rebellion against the raja. As was the custom in the face of defeat, the Dewa Agung and his retinue marched on the invading army and died in an act of self-sacrifice.

By 28 April 1908, the Dutch were in control of the last Balinese kingdom. Kerta Gosa, a few other buildings and the gate survived the fire. We do not know if the paintings on the ceiling of Kerta Gosa were damaged or even if they were in place.

Kerta Gosa

Kerta Gosa literally means 'the place where the king meets his ministers to discuss questions of justice'. It is usually called the law courts. The open air pavilion was placed in the most sacred position of the palace of Klungkung, facing Mount Agung.

The king could sit there and have a clear view of his palace and the town and all the neighbouring land. He met the *brahmana* judges and discussed legal matters and breaches of customary law. Most cases involved the aristocracy, unless matters were very serious, in which case he would hear cases involving villagers. The villagers, being *sudra*, would not be permitted to enter the sacred area, or any part of the royal palace.

The Dutch used the pavilion as a Western court of justice from 1909. Before then the Balinese would have sat on the floor, which would not have suited the Dutch. Furniture was brought in. *Sudra* villagers were allowed to attend for the first time and prisoners on trial could be seen from the road. It was used as a court until Independence in 1950 and then became an historical monument.

Restoration of Kerta Gosa

At the beginning of the 20th century under Dutch rule, the courts lost their power, patronage waned and the arts declined.

There was a brief flowering of Kamasan art, however, when the Dutch employed Kamasan artists to restore the palace in the 1920s, following the

1917 earthquake, which damaged the entire region of Klungkung. The arts declined after that. A new patron was required and it was the tourist.

Walter Spies took a photograph of the Kerta Gosa paintings in the 1930s, probably after a restoration in 1930. There was a major restoration in 1960 when the ceiling was replaced, panels enlarged and new paintings added, using no artificial dyes. In 1982, eight panels were replaced.

The Paintings

The paintings are on 267 wooden panels in the ceiling and are traditional *wayang* or puppet style. It is impossible to know when they were painted. The only mention of any painting at all is in 1842, when a palm leaf manuscript records that the paintings in Kerta Gosa are splendid but does not describe them. The story called *Bima Swarga* ('Bima goes to Heaven'), is read clockwise starting with the painting in the northeast corner.

There are some peculiarities: no use of blue and no filling of empty spaces. Other Kamasan paintings and other traditional paintings in most parts of Bali ornament empty spaces to give the overall busy effect called *ramai* beloved by the Balinese in the arts and life.

The Story

The story involves characters from the Mahabarata, but the story is not in the Mahabarata. It is a pure Balinese invention. Kunti, the mother of Bima, the second eldest of the five Pandawa brothers, asks him to go to Hell to rescue the souls of his father, Pandu, and his stepmother Madri. Then he must get them into Heaven. To achieve this he has to steal the elixir of immortality from the gods, which is not easy. He is accompanied throughout by two loyal Balinese servants.

The Importance of Kerta Gosa

It is not just an exquisite building. As Idanna Pucci explains in her book *Bhima Swarga, The Balinese Journey of the Soul* (1992), Kerta Gosa embodies nearly every aspect of Balinese culture: painting, literature, architecture, religion, philosophy, history and law. It is now a tourist attraction and has no function in daily Balinese life.

Chapter 47

Artistic Endeavour

Term of Art

Art is universal in human societies, whether it is found in music, dance, painting, carving, pottery, weaving, metalwork or stonework and Bali has all of them. We think of art as a luxury but even the hunter-gatherers found time to paint. In 1994 sophisticated cave paintings were discovered in Chauvet Cave near Avignon in France dating back 31,000 years. The paintings seem to relate to their way of life and spiritual beliefs. That is also the case in Bali; art in Bali serves social and religious needs.

E.H. Gombrich begins his book *The Story of Art*, first published in 1950, 'There really is no such thing as Art. There are only artists'. The Mexican artist-ethnographer, Miguel Covarrubias, who was in Bali in 1930 and wrote *Island of Bali*, the first major book on Bali, began his chapter 'Art and the Artist' with the sentence, 'Everybody in Bali seems to be an artist'. He also noted that there are no words in the Balinese language for 'art' and 'artist'. That is frequently mentioned but it is not important; the artists of Chauvet Cave probably did not have a word for 'art' either nor did the Native Americans of the New World. That is because every carving, dance or song had a practical purpose and could not be imagined without that purpose. Their meaning was their function. Dance, music and song went hand in hand with religious ritual.

As far back as the 9th century AD there are Balinese royal inscriptions. One provided terms for a refuge for artists and exempted them from taxes. The inscriptions refer to blacksmiths, goldsmiths, musicians, singers, dancers and shadow puppet performers. All these arts had a function. The European idea of art for art's sake, for pleasure only, invented by the Romantics in the 19th century, had no place in Bali at that time. Art was not made to be sold; it was made for a practical, religious purpose. They were skilled craftspeople supplying a commodity. There were no schools for artists until the 1930s. That was the time perceptions changed. Artists would become professionals, a special breed, creators and enjoy prestige.

Provenance

Provenance, so important in the West, is of little concern to the Balinese. Paintings are not usually signed, nor are they dated. Painters traditionally painted for the temple, not for personal renown or reward. In theory art is produced through the artist rather than by him. He is the agent of a higher power called *taksu*. Skill comes not so much from personal qualities but a closeness to divine origins.

It is difficult to date them. Most do not last more than thirty years because of the weather and insects. That fact does not greatly concern the Balinese. Everything is temporary. The highest compliment is to say that a work of art has *jiwa*, that is to say, it is alive, has spirit and is powerful, qualities that are more highly regarded than fine craftsmanship.

Patrons of the Arts

The courts and temples were the main sources of patronage. The arts were required, and still are required, for the frequent temple ceremonies. Artists congregated near the temples. So, in places where there are many temples, there are many artists. Balinese temples and the ceremonies within them are entirely given over to the arts: sculpture, carving, music, painting, offerings, dances, drama, poetry readings, shadow puppet performances and so on.

People sometimes renovate their family temples and decorate the shrines for the ceremony of *Galungan*. This is generally a busy time for artists. Usually the family decides on the themes but they may leave it up to the artist.

Classification

The main genres of Balinese paintings can be classified as:
- Traditional Balinese Painting
- *Pita Maha*, Ubud
- Young Artists of Penestanan
- The Community Artists of Pengosekan
- Batuan
- Western Artists

- Contemporary Artists
- Reverse Paintings on Glass

Traditional Balinese Painting

It is not known how long drawings and paintings have been made in Bali. It is likely that the techniques and styles came to Bali from India during the Hindu-Buddhist expansion throughout Southeast Asia between the 6th and the 9th centuries. There is, however, no evidence for this. None have survived. The earliest non-narrative paintings in existence are of elephants on wooden panels in the temple of Besakih which have dates inscribed on them of *Saka* years equivalent of 1444 AD and 1458 AD.

The earliest narrative paintings probably date from the first half of the 19th century. In all probability they would have been used for religious purposes. The earliest examples are the *wayang* puppet style, which was, and is, carried out in the village of Kamasan in the southeast part of Bali. That was the situation until the Western artists, including Walter Spies, came to Bali in the late 1920s and 1930s. There were Western artists in Bali before him, but they did not influence the Balinese.

W.O.J. Nieuwenkamp, 1874-1950

In 1904 the Dutch artist W.O.J. Nieuwenkamp was the first European artist to visit Bali. He had already visited Java in 1898 and this was his second trip to the colonies. Within minutes of arriving at the northern port of Singaraja, he was drawing a temple split gate. He liked Balinese architecture and it was a constant theme in his work. Overall, he made over 1,000 paintings, drawings, lithographs, woodcuts and etchings of Bali and Indonesia.

Visiting a large number of local painters he thought that Balinese art was perfect and had a purity lost to the West. Balinese society, nature and art were one and not separate entities. Aesthetics embraced every aspect of life. He approved of that and did not agree with later Western commentators that Balinese art was stagnant. Rather than comparing it with European art, he tried to learn from it. This is in contrast to the later visitors in the Thirties who tried to teach the Balinese how to do it.

He brought the first bicycle to Bali but it was difficult to ride on the bad roads. It made a great impact on the Balinese, who had never seen

In 1904 the Dutch artist W.O.J. Nieuwenkamp was the first European artist to visit Bali. On his second trip to Bali in 1906, he was amazed to see himself and the bicycle immortalised in a stone relief in a temple wall at the Meduwekarang in Kubutambahan.

anything like it. On his second trip to Bali in 1906, he was amazed to see himself and the bicycle immortalised in a stone relief in a temple wall at the Meduwekarang in Kubutambahan.

He wrote home to his wife that Bali was 'in short a fantastic place, a small paradise'. A bit later he wrote, 'I have decided to make an illustrated book about Bali, the most wonderful land I have ever known'. The book *Bali en Lombok* was published in three parts, the first part in 1906, the second part in 1909 and the third part in 1910. Its lavish paintings of innocence and beauty established Bali's reputation as a paradise. There were more than 250 original illustrations and the book was very highly praised. Although Bali had been known for centuries, his book was the first to introduce Balinese art to the West.

He returned to Bali in 1906 and witnessed the Dutch invasion of Sanur, which he found deeply shocking. He travelled extensively throughout the island and immersed himself in the culture, at the same time buying for museums and himself. He returned to Holland in 1907 and participated in the first large exhibition of Balinese art in Amsterdam in 1917.

Shortly after the exhibition he returned to Indonesia and arrived in Bali in 1918. The 1917 earthquake had damaged many of the island's buildings, including the stone relief of him riding a bicycle in a temple wall. It was repaired as were many of the buildings, but Nieuwenkamp was unhappy to see cement and corrugated iron being used. He blamed outside influences and returned to Holland the following year.

Nieuwenkamp always paid attention to architecture. During his fourth trip to Bali in 1925 he went to Bedulu to make a drawing of the Elephant Cave, Goa Gajah, not far from Ubud. It was an early rock hermitage for Saiwite priests and had been discovered by a colonial official called Evertsen. Nieuwenkamp was the first person to explore the interior of the cave and determined that the stone carving at the entrance was not an elephant at all but a giant. He was told by an old man about Yeh Pulu and set out to find it. It turned out to be a 30 metre rock wall carved with huge figures.

In 1937 he made his fifth and last trip to Bali, but by this time, the public had lost interest in his style of painting. He had been eclipsed by the younger, modern generation of artists, who lived in Bali. They were now the experts. He died of a heart attack in 1950. By the 1980s Nieuwenkamp, the first European artist in Bali, and his art were almost totally forgotten.

Maurice Sterne, 1877-1957

The first Western artist actually to live in Bali was Maurice Sterne. Brought up in Russia, his family went to America in 1889, when he was twelve. He travelled widely in the Far East and arrived in Bali almost by accident in 1912. He stayed for eighteen months. In an interview in the *New York Times Magazine* in 1915 he said,

> One day in the bazaar I saw the group of strangers, beautifully formed men and women almost nude. I was amazed; they looked like ancient Greeks. I asked the Controlleur who they were. He said, 'They are South Balinese.' I asked, 'Are there any more people like that in South Bali?' He answered, 'Oh, yes! They are all crazy in South Bali; they all go around like that.' So I went to South Bali.

Sterne wanted to paint nudes in nature, not in a studio. Balinese bodies, like velvet, fitted well into the warm, satin landscape. He admired their civilisation. Holland had only just annexed Bali, so it was still pure. He felt more at home than in any other part of Asia and worked furiously, making more than 10,000 studies, but he destroyed most of them before leaving Bali.

Sterne loved the artistic experience he found in the Balinese way of life. He called it 'aesthetic caviar'. He felt he was losing touch with reality and left in 1914, never to return. He always thought of Bali as paradise. Sterne became very famous. The Whitney Museum bought a painting 'Bali Bazaar' and President Eisenhower hung one of his paintings in his office in the White House.

In 1933 there was a retrospective exhibition of his work in the Museum of Modern Art in New York. Lewis Mumford wrote in the *New Yorker* in May 1934:

> The vital part of that exhibition was the Bali paintings. The fact is that these magnificent little paintings and drawings date from his great period in Bali between 1912 and 1914 and they have, apparently, been stored in a trunk all these years. The artist has very modestly called these pictures Bali studies, but the fact is it is these studies that one must crown as the very height of Sterne's work.

It is strange that none of his works are in any museum in Bali and he is not mentioned in most books on Balinese art.

Walter Spies, 1895-1942

Walter Spies came to Ubud in 1927 at the invitation of the royal family in Ubud. He was an artist himself and noticed that the local artists were merely churning out the same old religious and mythological themes and suggested that they should paint scenes of daily life and nature, planting rice, harvesting, temple festivals, dance performances and markets. They did so. The figures were still puppet-like, but, at least, they had been emancipated and given artistic licence.

The Dutch had taken away the power of the courts to be patrons and the temples were not commissioning works of art. Spies was aware of the arrival of tourists and thought that they could finance a revival. The new themes were easier for tourists to understand than the old mythological stories. Spies introduced artists to the frame and they started to paint with frames in mind to fit a tourist's suitcase.

Spies gave painting classes and hundreds of artists went to his house in Campuan for lessons. Miguel Covarrubias also attended and tried to teach them to express personality. Spies' first pupil was also his best: Anak Agung Gede Sobrat (1911-1992).

Rudolf Bonnet, 1895-1978

In the 1920s a young Dutch artist, Rudolf Bonnet, visited Nieuwenkamp, who was then living near Florence. Bonnet was the son of an Amsterdam baker and also lived in Italy. He had heard about Nieuwenkamp's travels and art collection and asked the older man for advice. Nieuwenkamp strongly advised him to go to Bali and he left shortly thereafter.

Bonnet joined Spies in Ubud in 1929. He was more hands-on than Spies and encouraged and taught the local artists. He gave them modern paints, materials and canvases and explained depth and perspective. This increased the verisimilitude of paintings. It took perspective a long time to reach Bali. Linear perspective was invented in the early 15th century in Italy, possibly by Filippo Brunelleschi (1377-1446), built on and improved upon by Leon Battista Alberti (1404-1472) and Piero della Francesca (1410/1420-1492). It gave added realism to paintings and required an understanding of mathematics. Parallel lines never meet in reality but they appear to. They converge at a vanishing point on the horizon. To depict this is to depict the appearance of reality, which makes a painting easier to understand. It increased their popularity. Bonnet's own paintings were also an influence, which is still seen today. He painted portraits in academic poses with an emphasis on realistic anatomy. Most of them are, in my opinion, rather cold and dreary.

After a while, the local painters started to produce sub-standard paintings for the tourist market, which concerned Spies and Bonnet. To maintain standards, they turned to the Bali Museum in Denpasar, which opened in 1932, as an outlet for the artists' work. Spies was able to use his position as the first curator of the museum to buy paintings. Throughout his life Bonnet was active in schemes to improve and preserve Balinese art; his most notable achievements were *Pita Maha* and Museum Puri Lukisan.

Pita Maha, Ubud, 1936-1942

The painters continued in their bad ways, so a new solution was devised to improve standards. Spies and Bonnet got together with the best local artist in Ubud, I Gusti Nyoman Lempad, and two princes of the royal family, Cokorda Gede Agung Sukawati and his brother Cokorda Gede Raka Sukawati, and created an artists' association in 1936, called *Pita Maha*, which means 'great vitality'. It also means 'ancestor', an idea that reverberates in the Balinese mind. The aims were to provide guidance, maintain standards and guarantee the artists' livelihoods.

The membership of about 125 people included painters, sculptors, silver workers and later, weavers. Every week the artists brought their works to Spies and Bonnet and the committee. They discussed them with the artist and if they thought the quality good enough, agreed a price and arranged for them to be sold or exhibited. Until 1937 the Bali Museum was the major purchaser but Bonnet also bought some. He donated many of them years later to the Museum Puri Lukisan in Ubud.

At the meetings, Bonnet, in particular, explained to the artist why any paintings were not being selected. This led to a generation of painters, who copied his style, recognisable from their half-turned torsos and an emphasis on line and form. Painters from villages outside Ubud, such as Kamasan, Batuan and Sukawati, were also members of *Pita Maha*, but were not so influenced by Bonnet and retained their individual styles.

Pita Maha organised exhibitions in Java and outside Indonesia, and for the first time individual artists came to be recognised. They started to sign their paintings. The association experienced some disruption when Spies was arrested in late 1938. He was detained for almost a year. In mid-1940 he was arrested again, this time for being a German national, when Hitler invaded Holland. The ship deporting him to Ceylon was bombed by the Japanese and he died.

The final exhibition was on 3 December 1941, just thirty-six days before the Japanese attacked Pearl Harbour. *Pita Maha* ended when the Japanese invaded Bali in 1942. Bonnet was deported and interned in Sulawesi in 1943. He returned to Ubud in 1947 and tried to revive the painters' association in 1951 around artists like I Gusti Nyoman Lempad and Anak Agung Gede Sobrat, but it was a pale reflection of *Pita Maha*.

Hans and Rolf Neuhaus, Sanur

Two German businessmen, Hans and Rolf Neuhaus, managed a well-known shop in Sanur, which opened in 1935. The local artists of

Sanur used to congregate there and were often inspired by the brothers' aquarium into painting scenes involving fish.

Spies sold paintings to them and souvenir shops that were just starting to appear. Like Spies they were arrested with other German nationals and were deported to an internment camp in Sumatra in 1940. They were luckier than Spies and were shipped to a prison camp in the Himalayas. Their business was closed and most of their pieces went to the Bali Museum.

Lempad, 1862-1978

I Gusti Nyoman Lempad was the most remarkable painter that Bali has ever produced. He was a Renaissance man. His father, also called I Gusti Nyoman Lempad, was an excellent painter, as well as being talented in many other fields, but he offended his patron in Blahbatuh and fled to Peliatan. He received the protection of the court of Ubud in 1875. Lempad was thirteen at that time. From then on the family lived in Ubud. Lempad's first wife could not produce children, so he married her younger sister and that did the trick. He foretold the date of his own death and died in Ubud in 1978 at the remarkable age of 116.

Multi-talented, like his father, he originally painted in the *wayang* puppet style, but moved on to a more expressive, freer style of painting and drawing in black Chinese ink on paper. His paintings are full of energy, yet tremendously elegant. Many bear a remarkable resemblance to the magical drawings of *balian* faith healers. He painted scenes of everyday life as well as religious themes. Lempad departed early from the Kamasan style and was a founder of *Pita Maha*.

He was also an architect and talented wood carver. After the very bad 1917 earthquake Lempad and his father designed the elaborate Ubud royal palace gate. He also designed Spies' house in Campuan. There are collections of his works in the Museum Puri Lukisan and the Neka Art Museum, both in Ubud.

Over the space of a few months, in 1978, three friends who were important in Balinese art passed away: first, Bonnet died in Laren, Holland on 20 April, then Lempad died in Ubud on 25 April and finally Ubud's prince Cokorda Gede Agung Sukawati died on 20 July. Although he never became a Hindu, Bonnet's family posted his ashes to Ubud, where they were thrown into the Campuan river in a Balinese ceremony. On 30

January 1979 his soul was called upon to inhabit a red winged Balinese bull sarcophagus, which was cremated, along with his friend Cokorda Gede Agung Sukawati, in one of the greatest cremations ever.

The Young Artists of Penestanan, 1960s

The Dutch painter, Arie Smit, who was born in 1916, came to live in Campuan in 1956 at the invitation of Rudolf Bonnet. He arrived in Indonesia in 1938 on a military contract and was assigned to the Topographical Service as a lithographer. During the Second World War he was a prisoner of war in labour camps in Singapore, Thailand and Burma. In 1950 he became an Indonesian citizen and taught graphics at the Institut Tecknologi in Bandung, Java, before moving to Bali in 1956. He stayed in Ubud for a month and then other villages including Sanur.

He now lives next to the Neka Art Museum, where many of his Matisse-like paintings hang. In the 1960s he gave six teenage boys in nearby Penestanan paper and paints and showed them how to prepare canvas and make frames but that was all. He did not try to teach them how to paint or suggest subjects to them. They were absolutely free to do their own thing. He even hid his own paintings, so they were not influenced. Smit did not praise their paintings either, so that they would not be encouraged to repeat what they had done to please him.

The results were stunning and the group grew to forty. A new school was born: the Young Artists. Fishes and frogs abounded. Bright colours in naive style filled the canvases: yellow skies, pink oceans, green men. It was vital, it was cheery, it was fun: ducks with hats, frogs riding bikes; there was a sudden freshness in the air. Bonnet organized several exhibitions of their paintings in Holland in 1967.

There has been no better expression of rural, peasant life in Bali. The paintings were mainly bought by foreigners and embassies in Jakarta. The Bali Beach Hotel in Sanur had one in every room. The famous science visionary Buckminster Fuller and anthropologist Margaret Mead, who were both in Bali at various times, were collectors.

The Community Artists of Pengosekan, 1960s

Pengosekan, also adjoining Ubud, saw another group of artists get together in the 1960s. Led by Dewa Nyoman Batuan, the group became known as the Community Artists of Pengosekan.

A generation had broken away from Bonnet's style. It was art for art's sake, just for pleasure, inspired by nature. Birds, leaves and insects, in beautiful matching colours, painted with exquisite refinement, were the order of the day.

Batuan, 1930-1960

Batuan is a large village, 6.2 miles (10 kilometres) from Ubud, rarely visited by tourists until recently. The distance has allowed the Batuan artists to pursue their own style, largely uninfluenced by Westerners and commercial temptations. They were also far from Kamasan, the home of traditional Balinese painting.

Their subject-matter is concerned with controlling the powers of good and evil. The paintings are very detailed; layers upon layers, tiny leaves and plants, butterflies and insects, small people and animals peeping out from among them, with no focal point and a strong emphasis on line.

In the 1930s, Rudolf Bonnet gave them paper and ink and some of them joined *Pita Maha*, but they kept to their old concerns, especially a fascination with the concept of mystical power, called *sakti*. They added simple perspective and scenery and continued to paint in dark hues, which is not typical of painters influenced by Westerners. The reason may just be down to economics. They were poorer than their friends in Ubud and coloured paints are expensive.

Their canvases were covered with many minuscule characters and there was an emphasis on detail. Many depict stories from the Ramayana and Mahabarata epics and there is a disturbing feel of black magic in the air. Life in the village and life in the forest are contrasted; villages represent security and forests represent danger.

The anthropologists Margaret Mead and her husband Gregory Bateson lived in Batuan for nine months in 1937-1938 and asked the painters to record their dreams in paint. They bought hundreds of them and they formed the basis of their book *Balinese Character*. The paintings are not reproduced in that book but there was an exhibition of them in 1994 and a catalogue was printed, *Images of Power* by Hildred Geertz.

In the 1950s, the artists shifted to cloth and tempera paints and more colours were used. Mistakes are more easily corrected on cloth than paper. When Rudolf Bonnet returned to Bali after the War he persuaded some of them to go back to paper.

In the 1960s another Batuan style appeared, with the introduction of *wayang* puppet figures and mythological stories treated in a fantastical manner. The mythological figures then gave way to cars, tourists, helicopters and modern Balinese life.

Museum Puri Lukisan, 1956

When Bonnet returned to Ubud after the War, he was still concerned to establish a means to maintain the quality of the arts. He had long been thinking of building an art museum and had been trying to find a location. Cokorda Gede Agung Sukawati donated land in the centre of Ubud. Bonnet collected works, raised funds, planned its construction, designed the gardens, made the inventory and prepared the catalogue. Museum Puri Lukisan opened in 1956.

Many heads of state visited. President Prasad of India visited in 1967. President Tito and Madame Tito of Yugoslavia visited in the same year. In 1968 Ho Chi Minh from Vietnam, dressed in a white Chinese jacket and black pants, came and did not say a word. Later the same year the King of Thailand, King Bhumibol, and Queen Sirikit showed up. The Vice-President of Egypt visited and after him Bobby Kennedy, who was President Kennedy's brother and the Attorney-General of the United States. In 1971, the Queen of Holland paid a visit. Prince Philip dropped in from England, but he just visited Cokorda Gede Agung Sukawati and not the museum. The ex-king and Queen of Belgium visited and so did Rockefeller, the Vice-President of the United States, in 1975.

Western Artists in Bali

Western artists living and painting in Bali have not influenced Balinese art much. Spies, Bonnet and Smit are the big exceptions. There is a debate in art circles as to the extent that Spies and Bonnet influenced local artists. Spies certainly played a pivotal role; he was in Bali for fourteen years. Some say Bonnet was just as influential and he was in Bali for twenty years. Others say their joint influence was not so great and the changes in style would have happened anyway and were already evident in textile and puppet designs.

Western artists in Bali tend to paint very beautiful, sometimes romanticised paintings with Balinese themes. There are many but the most well-known ones are the Swiss painter, Theo Meyer (1908-1982), who lived in Selat, the Austrian Roland Strasser (1895-1974) in Kintamani, the Belgian aristocrat Adrien Jean Le Mayeur de Merprès (1880-1958), whose model-wife was the famous Balinese *legong* dancer Ni Pollok, in Sanur, the Dutch painter Willem Gerard Hofker (1902-1981) in Denpasar and Australian Donald Friend (1915-1989) in Sanur. The Dutch artist Han Snel (1925-1998) and Catalan Antonio Blanco (1926-1999) both lived in Ubud and married Balinese ladies, who survived them.

Their paintings commanded high prices before the Second World War, but after Indonesia ceased to be a Dutch colony, interest waned. These were also difficult economic times in Europe. It was not until the 1980s that prices started to recover, largely due to Suteja Neka, the gallery and museum owner from Ubud, who started buying. He was followed by Agung Rai, who also owned a gallery in neighbouring Peliatan. In the 1990s the Indonesian economy was booming: it was one of the Asian tigers. Rich collectors from Jakarta started buying. Paintings by Walter Spies achieved over a million dollars in Singapore auctions.

Contemporary Artists

There are many. Probably the most famous are Nyoman Gunarsa (1944-) and Made Wianta (1949-). Nyoman Gunarsa is not only an exquisite painter but also the founder of the Gunarsa Museum of Classical and Modern Painting in Klungkung, in which, among many other exhibits, hang 400 of his own paintings. As a young boy he cycled to Ubud and met Rudolf Bonnet, Antonio Blanco and Arie Smit, the leading Western artists of the time. He also liked the paintings of Le Mayeur and was very influenced by them. His own work is a masterly exploration of Balinese themes, concentrating especially on dance.

Reverse Paintings on Glass

In a little-known village in north Bali called Nagasepaha, a handful of painters work on glass. Other painters scattered throughout Bali also use the medium. It has the great advantage of protection from wind and weather but they are fragile, break and get scratched. Paint does not always stick to the glass, which may not be of good quality. There are three sizes: 14 by 20 inches (35 by 50 centimetres), 16 by 24 inches (40 by 60 centimetres), and 28 by 43 inches (70 by 110 centimetres).

Little research has been done into them. Thomas Cooper in *Sacred Painting in Bali* (2005) mentions examples in Badung and Penarukan from about 1910.

The artist traces the outlines of the drawing in black on tracing paper, reverses it right to left, puts the glass on top and traces the picture on the glass with a pen. Alternatively he can draw directly on the glass with an art pen. The artist may use both methods. He paints the pictures on the reverse surface of the glass, which is viewed through the glass. The characters' clothes are painted first, then the small features, like eyes and toes, followed by the rest of the body and finally jewellery and small decorations.

The colours are done with a brush. Darkest colours are painted first. The artist starts with people, then the rest. Gold paint is sometimes applied to depict jewellery and the background is usually blue. They are in *wayang* puppet style and themes are drawn from the epics.

Chapter 48

Carving Wood and Stone

Traditional Style Woodcarving

There are hundreds of species of trees in Bali and at least thirty-nine of them are used in woodcarving. Up to the 1930s, it was highly formulaic and craftsmen tended to copy each other. Carvings consisted mainly of gods, heroes and demons. In the majority of cases they served a religious function, but they also decorated the royal palaces. They were not made for ordinary home decoration.

Traditionally *balés* or 'pavilions' in temples and palaces are carved on a grand scale. The *balé* has a roof, which rests on horizontal wood beams. Pillars support the roof. Very often the intersection between the beams and the pillars is decorated with a garuda or other birds. The garuda is the eagle-like carrier of the god Wisnu. The beams and pillars are carved in stylised forms, very elaborate and very detailed. Sometimes they are gilded.

Guardian stone carving. Stone carvings in temples are not works of art to be admired as in Western art galleries. They are places where gods and spirits meet and interact with humans.

Modern Styles

Modern styles arose to appeal to the tourists, who were beginning to come to Bali in the 1930s. As with painting, encouragement and suggestions came from Walter Spies and Rudolf Bonnet, who saw that tourism could create a source of income. According to a report in the Indonesian language newspaper Kompas, in 2003 Gianyar recorded 14,368 woodcarving units employing a total of 37,150 workers.

Classification
The modern styles can be classified as:
- The elongated style
- The squat style
- The driftwood style
- The wooden fruit style

The Elongated Style
Walter Spies inspired the elongated style. The subject-matter is realistic and still very much alive. The elongated carvings are made of fine hardwood, sanded and finished without paint. They are polished to a fine sheen, very smooth and good to touch. The shapes are extremely fluid.

The first woodcarver to carve in this style was I Tegelan in the village of Belaluan. He had admirers in Mas, a village a little to the north: Ida Bagus Ketut Gelodog and Ida Bagus Nyana. Mas became the centre of the new style. Perhaps the best carver was I Nyoman Cokot of Jati, who died in 1971. He carved Hindu deities and demons.

The elongated carvings are made of fine hardwood, sanded and finished without paint. They are polished to a fine sheen, very smooth and good to touch.

The squat style is the opposite of the elongated style. The wood is highly polished, simple, massive and fully closed.

The Squat Style

The squat style is the opposite of the elongated style, invented by Ida Bagus Nyana. Still popular, the weeping Buddha is a typical example, his head in his hands. The wood is highly polished, simple, massive and fully closed.

The Driftwood Style

I Nyoman Cokot's two sons developed the driftwood style incorporating faces, animals, demons and plants carved out of the twists and turns, often almost hidden, of the branches of *Jepun Bali*, a variety of frangipani, and the dark maroon *gegirang* wood. Only the carved parts are finished.

The Wooden Fruit Style

The wooden fruit style was produced for the mass market. Painted fruit, banana trees, frogs and cute animals of all kinds are carved from softwood; some of quite good quality.

Stone Carvings

Stone carvings in temples are not works of art to be admired as in Western art galleries, open spaces and museums. They are not ends in themselves, as a modern sculpture might be, but places where gods and spirits meet and interact with humans. That is why every day offerings of rice, flowers and fruit are placed in front of them. *Pura Dalem*, the temple of death, is dedicated to Siwa the Destroyer and his consort Durga, who is associated with Rangda, so statues of her abound in that temple. Smaller statues of Rangda are also placed in graveyards.

The only local stone is *paras* or 'tuff', a combination of volcanic dust, sand and clay. It is soft and grey and plentiful and used by carvers to sculpt the numerous statues, large and small, which guard temples, palaces and houses. Many carvings are characters from the Ramayana and Mahabarata epics. The Balinese do not like unadorned spaces. Walls are usually covered with carvings.

Paras is quarried at the riverbank and cut into blocks. First they are made wet, and then ground and fitted against each other without mortar. Once in place, detailed carving starts *in situ*. *Paras* is almost as soft as wood and very fragile. It weathers badly and therefore requires constant renewal. One consequence is that there is constant work providing opportunities for stone carvers to perfect their skills. Moss grows easily and quickly on *paras* and gives that feeling of timelessness that pervades so much of Bali.

Chapter 49

Balinese Masks

Lightning Rods

Balinese masks are of ancient origin and act like a lightning rod in the sense that they attract the spirit of the person to be portrayed. They are the vehicles of the gods and are sacred. The Balinese believe that living masks provide inspiration for the dancer or actor. The plot of the dance or play comes from the mask. In other words, as the Balinese say, the mask 'speaks'.

Masks are treated with great respect. They represent the faces of revered gods and heroes and are put on the head, which is the most sacred part of the body. They should never be put on the ground or stepped over and are usually kept out of sight, wrapped inside a box, which is often covered with a white cloth.

Origins

Masks have been used throughout history, usually for religious purposes. The Chinese used bronze masks during the Zhou dynasty in the 8th and 9th centuries BC. In Ancient Greece masks were worn in connection with the cult of Dionysus. The oldest record of a Balinese masked dance is on a copperplate charter dated 896 AD. The inscription lists the names of the dancers, but not the dances.

Oldest Masks

The oldest masks in Bali are kept in the village of Blahbatuh. They are too sacred to be photographed and are in a temple called Pura Penataran Topeng. There are six full face masks with a mouthpiece, so that the dancer could hold it clenched between his teeth. This kind of mask is no longer seen in Bali. Modern masks are held on with an elastic band.

Topeng

The word for 'mask' is *topeng*. It comes from the root word *tup*, which means 'cover'. The mask covers the face.

Mask Makers

The art is often passed down from generation to generation in particular families, who are frequently *brahmana*. The mask maker is consecrated to his profession in a special ceremony. He must know special prayers and ceremonies connected with masks.

Mask of *Jauk* Dancer. Balinese masks are of ancient origin and act like a lightning rod in the sense that they attract the spirit of the person to be portrayed.

Mask Making

Masks take many forms and are usually carved from a fine-grained, cream-coloured, light wood called *pule* (*alstonia scholaris*), which grows in graveyards. The tree must be 'pregnant', that is to say ready and suitable for carving, evidenced by the bark swelling slightly outwards. The mask maker goes to the tree on an auspicious day, presents his offerings and requests the tree's permission. He then chops a slab of wood with his axe and takes it back and waits for inspiration. The wood is soaked in water for a few days and then put to one side for several seasons to allow it to dry out.

Initially he draws the outline of the mask on a piece of paper. The paper is folded in two to ensure that the mask is perfectly symmetrical. The eyes and mouth are drawn in. Using a dozen or so chisels, gouges and a mallet, holding the slab of wood between his toes, he carves the mask, using the paper outline. The first cut is accompanied by a small ritual.

The back of the mask is carved in the harder heartwood and the facial features are carved in the softer sapwood. This way the circular growth rings correspond to the rounded features of the face. Holes for the eyes, nose and mouth are hollowed out. The finished

The mask maker chops a slab of wood with his chisel, holding the mask in place with his foot.

mask will be about 1¼ inch (3 centimetres) thick. Endless sanding and at least forty coats of paint achieve a striking glossy surface. While the mask surface needs to be smooth, it should not be overworked, muting the details.

White priming paint from ground calcified pig bone, boiled fish and glue is mixed to watercolour consistency and needs fifteen to twenty coats. The mask maker sandpapers the mask every fourth or fifth coat to smooth the surface. Pigments from a variety of shells, insects, fruits, plants and beans, including coffee, are used for base coats. Traditional black is made from the soot of burnt coconut shells. Yellow comes from special stones found on the south coast of Bali. Red and gold leaf are imported from Hong Kong and Singapore. Calcium and ground betel nut leaves are added to the red, black and yellow to make the colours glow.

Contemporary mask painters sometimes use acrylic house paints, which are thinned to a watercolour consistency. Irises, wrinkles and facial accents are added by several washes of grey-black paint. Moustaches, eyebrows and hair, made from goat hair, finish the job.

As the feet are used in mask carving and the feet are considered polluted or unclean, it is necessary upon completion for a priest to purify the mask before it may be worn for a religious ceremonial performance.

Magical Letter

Another ceremony must be performed before a mask can be used in the temple. A magical letter is written on the inside of the mask and it is taken to a sacred place with an offering. The spirits are invited to enter the mask. The mask is then ready to be used in the temple.

Barong Ket

Sacred *Barong Ket* masks get special treatment. Only *brahmana* carvers are allowed to carve them and the work takes place in the temple. Men sleep in the temple at night guarding it and women present daily offerings during the whole process. The mask is the most important part of the *Barong* and it is carved and painted in a special raised pavilion. Once the mask is carved by the *brahmana* woodcarver, commoners from the *sudra* caste polish the surface with sandpaper.

The *brahmana* carver paints the first brush stroke and hands over to specially trained craftsmen, who use traditional paints. The *Barong* may have up to 150 coats of paint. It is gilded in parts and highly polished. The eyes are large and bulbous, ringed in red, black, yellow and white, the colours of the gods Brahma, Wisnu, Mahadewa and Iswara. The *Barong's* penetrating gaze portrays mixed expressions of fury and fun.

The *Barong's* beard is powerful, its black hair donated by a pre-pubescent girl. It can bring people out of trance, purify and cure. His inner mouth, lips and eyes are inscribed with magical signs and protective charms are attached to the back of his neck. A protrusion at the top of his head indicates Siwa's thunderbolt.

As the mask and body are joined three ceremonies take place in the temple to bring the *Barong* to life. A further ceremony takes place in the cemetery around midnight. Only priests, the mask maker, senior craftsmen and principal headmen are allowed to attend the secret rituals. At about 2 am a flaming ball enters the *Barong* and the sky turns a luminescent purple. The ceremony is finished.

Angela Hobart in *Healing Performances of Bali* (2003) summarises the paradoxical nature of the *Barong*,

> While male, he has female features, as evidenced by his beard made from the hair of a pre-menstruating girl. Created by humans, he is a vehicle of the supreme god—especially Siwa.

Tiger, Wild Boar and Elephant *Barongs*

There are other kinds of *Barong*, which are less common than the *Barong Ket*. The tiger *Barong* symbolises the vitality of the forest. His hair, moustache and beard are made from monkey pelts. His body is orange cotton, painted with red stripes. He has a magic white cloth on his shoulders as he dances. His power derives from Brahma, the god of fire,

The tiger *Barong* symbolises the vitality of the forest.

and his purpose is to remove illnesses and demons. The wild boar *Barong* also banishes suffering and gets rid of evil spirits. Unlike the others, which require two men, the elephant *Barong*, can be danced by one person.

By passing through the villages, especially at *Galungan*, the various *Barong*s revitalise energies within communities. They take villagers' minds off daily problems and bring the protective and healing powers of the gods to them.

Barong Landung

Barong Landung is the name given to two giant puppets, one male, the other female, who also parade in the streets at Balinese New Year and *Galungan*. They are elderly and have a special kind of singing and flirt with each other. Together they cure and bring fertility.

The female is called *Jero Luh* (female person). She has a white mask, overhanging forehead, slanting eyes which suggest Chinese origins, an enigmatic smile and protruding chin. She is broad-shouldered and flat-chested. Unlike most Balinese women she does not wear earrings on her distended earlobes. Her hair, made of sugar cane fibre, is tied in a bun at the back. She has big hands, is calm and elegant with the bearing of an English maiden aunt.

The male called *Jero Gede* (big person) has a huge black mask, with large white prominent teeth, very red lips and tusks. He has human hair. His bushy white eyebrows and moustache are made from civet cat's hair. His cheeks bulge and he wears a chequered *poleng* band and a belt. There are secret signs on his temples. Like *Jero Luh*, he has a magic cloth which protects the community.

Sacred Power

Sacred masks have a power called *tenget*. If a mask has *tenget*, it is alive

Barong Landung is the name given to two giant puppets, one male, the other female, who parade in the streets at Balinese New Year and *Galungan*. They are elderly and have a special kind of singing and flirt with each other.

and when a dancer puts it on, he actually becomes the person or god portrayed by the mask. These very powerful masks are brought to life by a ceremony conducted by a high priest.

They are kept in special shrines and receive offerings every full and new moon, on *Kajeng-Kliwon*, which is every fifteen days, and also when they are used. In addition, they get special offerings on a day known as *Tumpek Krulut*, which occurs every 210 days.

Other objects and places can be *tenget*. A typical example is a *kris*, the two-sided ceremonial dagger. These objects are permanently endowed with power and become family heirlooms. *Tenget* increases over time as the object is handed down from generation to generation.

Performances

Traditional Balinese masked theatre has no stage, dressing room or auditorium. Open-air performances are the most common. The direction of the playing area is dictated by the cardinal points, which affect the entrances and exits of important characters. Masked dances in a temple ceremony always use at least one sacred mask or headdress.

Chapter 50

Balinese Dances

Trip the Light Fantastic

You are never too young to learn to dance. From the age of four, young girls learn the *legong* dance. There are about two dozen dance schools in Denpasar, Bali's capital, and there are dance clubs and people giving lessons in most villages. There are also classes on local television.

In the 1960s two schools, SMKI (*Sekolah Menengah Karawitan Indonesia* or 'High School of Performing Arts') and ISI (*Institut Seni Indonesia* or 'Indonesian Arts Institute'), were established in Bali and have a high reputation for teaching, research and creating new works.

Teaching methods are unique. There are no mirrors. The teacher sings the song, imitates the instruments, beats time and announces the steps. She holds the pupil from behind and guides the child's arms and legs and torso into position.

Why, When and Where?

Balinese dances have a religious background. They are offerings to the gods and ancestors and staged to please and entertain them at religious ceremonies to which they are invited by the priests. The best place to see them is in one of the many temples.

The temple is packed with people in splendid Balinese attire. White-clad priests are intoning mantras, ringing bells and muttering prayers. Ladies are carrying offerings of fruit and flowers on their heads and placing them on special pavilions. The moon and the stars illuminate the proceedings. Suddenly there is a frisson and the performance begins.

Dances accompany rites of passage, which mark a turning point in a person's life, such as baby ceremonies, tooth-filings and weddings, and these take place in family temples and compounds.

There are exciting dances at exorcism ceremonies, held to rid the place of disruptive forces, and truly sensational dances are performed at times of crisis, such as epidemics, famines and plagues. At these events dancers, and sometimes even spectators, fall into trance. The spirits responsible for the crisis are called and dismissed.

The Stage

If the rectangular stage is not ritually pure, perhaps because it is outside the inner sanctum of the temple; a priest makes it ritually pure before the performance. He presents offerings to the low spirits, burns incense, chants prayers and pours holy water. The ground is where the low spirits live and the dancers do not wish to offend or step on them.

The stage is carefully aligned according to the important directions, *kaja*, towards the mountains, and *kelod*, towards the sea. The dancers make their entrances and exits appropriately.

Jauk dancer. Balinese dances have a religious background. They are offerings to the gods and ancestors and staged to please and entertain them at religious ceremonies to which they are invited by the priests.

Lost the Plot?

Some dances have a story, often based on the old Indian epics, the Ramayana and the Mahabarata. It is almost impossible for the first time spectator to follow the plot. Boys dance girls' parts; girls dance boys' parts. You cannot tell which are which. Both wear heavy make-up. The same person may dance several roles and scenes change with the barest of announcements. It is best just to sit back and enjoy the extreme beauty of the movements, the expressions and the dazzling costumes.

The Characters

Balinese dances are not about individuals. The story is not the important thing. It is the rhythm, the atmosphere and the feeling for space. The characters exist in their own formal, spiritual world. There are stock characters, who represent respected and not so respected qualities.

The king and queen are nearly always refined or *alus*. The king's ministers may or may not be refined. The witch and the monster are coarse or *kasar*. They all have their own stylised movements, their own dress and speak in Kawi, which few understand. The only individuals are the clowns, who improvise, joke, and explain to the audience in Balinese what is happening on stage.

Eyes move quickly from side to side to stress the rhythms and accents. Fingers quiver. This indicates strength radiating from the dancer's body. The movements, the eyes, the fingers and the dancer are at one with the music.

The Dancers

The dancer's individuality is not important. He or she is admired for technique, not his or her ego. The dance movements are within a narrow frame and the beauty lies in this. Balinese dance is not emotional, but formal and detached, and carefully worked out, almost mathematically. The gestures and movements are traditional, reserved and understated.

Before the dance, the dancers pray to the gods of the place where they are dancing for permission to perform. They also request Panju, the god of dancers and actors, to make the performance a success. Entrances are dramatic. Special melodies are played and the entrance is delayed as much as possible. If there is a curtain, the only hint of the dancer is his voice or the twitching fold of the cloth. When the curtains are finally parted, the dancer is framed in the entrance and advances slowly. If there are servants, they precede their master or mistress.

The Movements

The gestures in Indian dancing tell a story, but not in Bali. Faces are like masks. Emotion is underplayed. Gestures are purely abstract, although a few have dramatic meanings. Shading the eyes with the hand indicates weeping. First and second fingers pointing at the end of a stiffly extended arm is a gesture of anger or denunciation. Both hands together in a prayer position is welcoming.

Eyes move quickly from side to side to stress the rhythms and accents. Fingers quiver. This indicates strength radiating from the dancer's body. The movements, the eyes, the fingers and the dancer are at one with the music. Coloured bamboo fans are extensions of the body, which point at others in anger or menace.

Transformations

Many Balinese stories involve a transformation of character, for example, in the Ramayana, Marica transforms himself into a deer and Rawana takes on the appearance of a beggar to trick Sita. This is shown conventionally by the dancer stopping and assuming a meditating pose. He then leaves the stage and another dancer comes in and adopts the same pose. This indicates that the original character has been transformed.

Make-Up

Many hours are devoted to making-up. They pay great attention to the eyes. A continuous black line surrounds the whole eye and the eyebrows are emphasised. Dancers apply blue eye shadow to the eyelid and red and gold under the eyebrow. A third eye indicates strength and concentration. Three dots on the temple symbolise the three great Hindu gods, Brahma, Wisnu and Siwa. Both men and women use lipstick and rouge.

The Music

Gamelan music drives the dance. In some dances, the dancer follows the music and there is no room for improvisation. In others, such as *Jauk, Topeng, Arja, Baris* and *Barong*, the dancer leads and signals to the drummers and the musicians follow. The clowns always improvise and are skilled in sensing audience reaction. When they want to be heard, they clap once, and the gamelan stops playing. If they feel it is time to leave the stage, they indicate to the gamelan to play the exit song.

The Audience

The audience are the divine and the not so divine. The Balinese do not normally watch dances intently. The story does not trouble them. They know it already and do not mind at which point the story is taken up, nor at which point it ends. The clowns give information about the main characters in a series of witticisms and improvised comments.

The Patrons

As a result of colonial measures the powers and fortunes of the royal families were reduced and their ability to provide patronage to the arts shifted to the temples and the villages. In the 1920s and 1930s there was a general renaissance all over Bali in popular music and drama and performances that used to take place in front of palaces moved to the front of temples. Government dance schools also help the development and preservation of dance.

In the 1930s tourists arrived steadily and have not stopped. Attending a dance on a cultural tourism trip is always on the itinerary. Tourists have become valuable patrons and dances, based on the traditional models, have been specially choreographed for them, for example, the *Kecak* and a one-hour version of the *Barong* and Rangda.

Consecrated masks are not used in tourist performances and the dancers rarely go into trance. The income enables the village to buy new gamelan instruments and dance costumes, which can be used in traditional performances.

Dance Classification

Dances were classified by I Gusti Bagus Sugriwa, a well-known expert on Balinese culture, at a seminar in 1971 as follows:

- *Wali*: the Holiest
  Addressed only to the gods, these take place in the *jeroan*, the inner section of the temple, and are rituals in themselves. They tend to be old group dances, danced in a row or circle, with no plot, like *Pendet, Rejang, Topeng Pajegan, Baris Gede* and *Sang Hyang* Trance Dances. Sometimes the dancers fall into trance. They belong to the native Balinese tradition and are not usually as difficult as other Balinese dances.

- *Bebali*: Dual Purpose
  They take place in the *jaba tengah*, the middle courtyard of the temple, and have two audiences: the gods and humans. These are less holy and are danced in conjunction with a ritual but are not a ritual in themselves, like *Gambuh* and *Wayang Wong*. They tend to be more recent than the *wali* dances and come from the dance dramas of the Majapahit period.

- *Balih-Balihan*: Secular
  Literally 'things to watch', they take place outside the temple or in the courtyard, where the atmosphere is relaxed and crowded. The dances in this category are performed for humans only and do not concern the gods. Examples are *Legong, Arja, Baris Tunggal, Topeng Panca, Kebyar Trompong, Kebyar Duduk, Joged* and *Janger*. The emphasis is on excellence, aesthetics and entertainment. The dancers require lengthy training. The choreography is intricate. New dances tend to fall into this category, for example, the *Kecak* ('monkey dance'), *Oleg Tumulilingan* ('bumblebee dance'), *Genggong* ('frog dance'), *Belibis* ('wild duck dance') and *Cendrawasih* ('birds of paradise dance').

Chapter 51
Dance Review

Skip the Light Fandango

The dancer is the music made visible. Using the dance classification devised by I Gusti Bagus Sugriwa in 1971, we shall review the main dances currently performed in Bali.

Wali: the Holiest

- ### *Pendet*

  This dance is performed by women on the first and last nights of a temple anniversary ceremony. There are no special costumes. They wear normal temple dress and welcome the visiting spirits. It is performed in the holiest inner part of the temple. The movements are simple and improvised. Part of the dance is the presentation of offerings.

- ### *Rejang*

  Rejang is an ancient, processional, group dance performed by pre-pubescent girls, unmarried women or post-menopausal women, who are called the 'heavenly maidens'. It is a very simple, elegant dance in the inner temple, and takes place during the day; usually in the early afternoon. There may be forty to sixty women, who face the main shrines and dance towards them with outstretched arms, holding their fans. When each row of dancers has been presented to the shrines, the dance is over. It is a purification dance.

- ### *Baris Gede*

  The *Baris Gede* is an inner temple dance performed by men, who are dressed as warriors, with triangular helmets covered in pointed mother of pearl shells. It is a simple dance involving between four and as many as sixty men. They carry spears, lances, shields, daggers or sometimes rifles but only one kind of weapon at a time, and go through warlike movements in front of the shrines. *Baris* means 'line'. The *baris* dance has been known since at least the 16th century and its purpose is to protect the visiting spirits.

- *Topeng Pajegan*

  This is a masked dance, which takes place in the inner courtyard of the temple, always on the first day of a ceremony. It is a male dance where one dancer plays all the parts of an entire story, changing masks as the characters change, danced at the same time as a high priest prepares holy water for the ceremony. It is also danced in family compounds at important rituals, such as marriages, tooth-filings and cremations.

  It is extremely difficult; few dancers can do it. The dancer tells a story by acting a succession of characters. He uses *mudras*, hand gestures, similar to those of a high priest. The stories are usually about the famous legendary Balinese kings and their high priests.

  He alternates refined and unrefined characters and leaves the stage to change masks, full face for princely persons and half-faced for servants and clowns. He switches scenes with the clap of a hand. References to the refined characters are in Kawi and the unrefined in Balinese. Only the servants and clowns speak.

  The last dance is always Sidhakarya, who makes his entrance with an offering bowl of rice in his hand. His mask is white with slit eyes, buck teeth and long, wild hair. When he wears this mask, the dancer is performing a priestly function. He flings the rice in the four cardinal directions to ensure wealth and fertility and sprinkles holy water on the audience. He also throws Chinese *kepeng* coins into the audience and there is a mad scramble to pick them up.

Balinese mask and half mask. The Balinese believe that living masks provide inspiration for the dancer or actor. The plot of the dance or play comes from the mask. In other words, as the Balinese say, the mask 'speaks'.

Suddenly he lunges into the crowd, snatches up a young child from the audience and carries him over to the shrine and holds him up to the gods before giving him a small present. He sets the child down and the performance is over.

- **Sang Hyang Trance Dances**
  True trance dances are rare and performed to exorcise illnesses from a village. The famous one, *Sang Hyang Dedari*, involves a couple of young girls. The ritual begins in the inner section of the temple, when women sing special songs to encourage the spirits to enter their young bodies. The men chant and after about twenty minutes the girls collapse and then dance with their eyes closed. They are carried on the shoulders of men and sway to the music.

Another trance dance is the hobby horse dance, *Sanghyang Jaran*, where the dancers ride hobby horses over burning charcoal coals, whilst the community sits around in a circle watching, and men chant *chak-achak-chak*.

Bebali: Dual Purpose

- *Gambuh*
  This narrative dance is at least 400 years old and came from Java with the Majapahit kingdom. It is performed without masks. The story concerns Panji, a prince from east Java, and his adventures with the beautiful Princess Candra, who becomes his bride. Middle Javanese is spoken.

  Gamelan Gambuh uses old-fashioned musical instruments, including metre long flutes that rest on the ground and produce low, haunting notes. They blow the flutes in a difficult circular technique that produces a continuous sound. The dance is the prototype of many later dances, like *Topeng*, *Wayang Wong*, *Arja* and *Legong*.

  Full length, it can take six hours. It almost died out in the early 20th century when the royal families lost most of their power. Fortunately it has revived somewhat and is performed in several villages, especially in the village of Batuan on the first and fifteenth of each month and on the anniversary of *Pura Desa*.

- *Wayang Wong*
  Wayang Wong means 'shadow men' and the movements mimic the

jerky movements of the shadow puppets. It is a sacred masked dance-drama and not performed often.

Its origin is thought to have been a request by the king of Klungkung, Dalem Gede Kusamba (1772-1825), who wanted a new dance form using the royal masks and featuring the Ramayana stories. *Gambuh* influenced the presentation and costumes and *Wayang Kulit* influenced hand gestures and the accompanying music. A small gamelan ensemble plays the music.

Dialogue exists but is much simpler than *Wayang Kulit*. Most of the scenes are battle scenes and the dancers sing their lines in Kawi, which is translated into Balinese by four clowns. The story is usually just an episode of the Ramayana and its choice is governed by the nature of the masks owned by the village.

Balih-Balihan: Secular

* *Legong*

Possibly the *Legong* is Bali's most famous dance, which is known worldwide through films and travelling troupes. This graceful, feminine dance is about 200 years old and was originally intended for pre-pubescent girls. There are various versions, but the most popular is *Legong Lasem*. It is essentially pure dance with minimal story.

One account says that I Dewa Agung Made Karna, the prince of Sukawati, had a vision of heavenly maidens performing a trance dance, like the *Sang Hyang Dedari*, except that they were wearing colourful costumes, rather than white, and golden headdresses, rather than head-cloths. When he woke, he asked his head man to create a dance like that.

Danced by three young girls, in tight gold-leafed costumes, the first to appear is the *condong* or servant. Her costume is slightly different from the other two girls. She dances over the whole stage for about ten minutes with two bamboo fans, which she picks up from the floor in front of her. She also plays the role of the garuda bird later.

Then the two *legongs* appear, dressed identically, their gold leaf headdresses quivering, full of fresh frangipani flowers, like a mirror image. There is a white beauty spot on their powdered faces between their shaved eyebrows, which have been repainted in black. The *condong* presents the girls with a fan each, exits and the girls dance together, perhaps for twenty minutes, in perfect unison. The pair should look as alike as possible, in complexion, beauty and form. They dance with stylised restraint.

In the final section, the gamelan doubles its tempo, and the girls face each other, and dance as if in mirrored reflection, their eyes darting from side to side on the beat and fans in active motion. They never speak or sing.

In pre-colonial Bali, the royal courts were in constant search for talented, young, beautiful girls to dance *Legong*. Many later became royal wives or concubines.

Possibly the *Legong* is Bali's most famous dance, which is known worldwide through films and travelling troupes. This graceful, feminine dance is about 200 years old.

- *Arja*

This is the Balinese version of musical comedy. The cremation of the highest raja of Bali, I Dewa Agung Gede Kusamaba of Klungkung, was its unlikely origin. Kings from other regencies commissioned a special new performance for the occasion, which took place in 1825. The Dewa Agung had reigned for fifty years and his cremation was one of the grandest in Balinese history.

Arja is technically very difficult. The characters are clearly defined: princess and maidservant; false princess and stepmother; prince and minister; usurper and minister; and attendants. Each has his or her own music. Princes and ministers sing in a small voice, high and sweet; other ministers and attendants sing in a middle or deep voice. They sing continually and improvise songs in a set meter, which takes a great deal of skill. Long training is required. They must also be able to dance well. Only men acted in the original form, but since the 1920s women replaced men in the main roles.

There are stock characters, whose personalities are either sweet or crazy. There are usually eight clowns, so it is very funny. The stories are sentimental and romantic. The costumes are sumptuous. It is very popular among the Balinese, who also listen to it on the radio and watch it on television.

- **Baris Tunggal**

Created at the beginning of the 20th century, the *Baris Tunggal* is danced by a young solo dancer, usually a young boy. Physically very demanding, the young

Baris tunggal is danced by a young solo dancer, usually a young boy.

warrior stakes out his territory through a series of rapid movements, all the time keeping his arms lifted high, fingers extended and shoulders touching his neck. His eyes dart back and forth, looking for enemies in all directions. There is no plot.

Movements are improvised and call for close collaboration with the musicians. The colourful costume is comprised of cloth strips cascading down his torso. They swish as he twirls around on one foot at great speed. His hat is a pyramid of small pieces of mother of pearl shells. Although quintessentially male, a few females perform.

- **Topeng Panca: Masked Dance**

Invented at the end of the 19th century by *topeng* dancers in the court of Badung, now Denpasar, this masked dance is played in the outer courtyard by a group of five men. *Panca* means 'five'.

The stories are about the lives of Balinese kings and queens. Many different masks are used, ranging from clowns to prime ministers to kings and even deformed people, and changed throughout the performance. It is faster than *Topeng Pajegan*, as there is always someone on stage, and the characters can banter with each other. It is accompanied by a gamelan orchestra, which is cued by the dancer.

Entrances are full of drama and expectation. The dancer enters through a curtained doorway, emerging from the invisible into the visible world. Refined characters dance in the doorway for a long time; coarse characters open the curtain suddenly. Lower status characters enter first, announce the higher status ones and bow to them. Last to appear is the king.

The king never speaks. His servants speak for him and wear a half mask to make speech possible. They explain the story to the audience and add a lot of references to modern life. A favourite is the white haired old man, who remembers his younger days. There is room for innovation; especially popular are comic characters from modern life, such as tourists, pop and hip-hop dancers.

Dancers are usually men, who undergo a ceremony with a *brahmana* priest before dancing for the first time. They thereby become 'married' to their masks. Before dancing, the dancer makes two offerings, one to Siwa, the god of dance, and the other to the low spirits. He taps the box containing the masks three times to wake them up. Then he takes them out, sprinkles them with holy water, and waits for the priest to indicate the auspicious moment for the dance to begin.

Before he exits the stage, the dancer turns away from the audience, performs a closing sequence, then turns round for a final bow, paying homage to the audience with his hands together as a gesture of respect.

In Java, the early rajas insisted that the masks were held in place by the teeth, so that the dancers could not speak and ridicule them. Perhaps they were wise. During the Dutch and Japanese occupations, there were cases of dancers being imprisoned for satire.

- *Kebyar Trompong*

In 1919, the king of Tabanan ordered one of the new *Kebyar* gamelans from north Bali to play at an important cremation. I

Nyoman Mario, the famous dancer, who was from Tabanan, heard the dazzling new sound and was very impressed. When he danced, Mario chose the players he wanted in the gamelan.

He created a new dance. The trompong instrument had fallen into disfavour and he decided to restore it and sit the dancer behind the gongs. The dancer strikes the gongs in flashy movements and twirls his sticks flamboyantly. It is rather camp and gave him the idea for his next dance, the *Kebyar Duduk*, which is Mario's great contribution to Balinese dance.

- *Kebyar Duduk*
  Mario presented this dance in 1925. It is the most difficult of all Balinese dances and only young men have the strength to perform it. The dancer dances in a sitting position at all times and determines the pace of the music. The orchestra may comprise twenty-five to thirty musicians, who play for about twenty minutes. There is no story, just a series of moods, typical of those that a youth passes through. By turn, he is flirtatious, bashful, melancholy and angry.

- *Joged*
  In pre-colonial times, *Joged* was associated with prostitution run by the royal palaces, which the Dutch made efforts to suppress when they took over. It is a secular dance and now a vehicle for fun at weddings and other parties. The female Joged dancer dances alone, full of smiles and flirtatious movements and taps one of the men in the audience with her fan. He is obliged to dance with her. She wraps a sash around his waist and they dance a duet to the loud appreciation of the audience. When she has finished with him, she approaches another man, who shares the same fate.

- *Janger*
  Janger is a social dance created in the early 20th century, probably in north Bali. It means 'infatuation' and is influenced in several respects by the West, not least in the costumes. The women wear distinctive, fan-like headdresses, which quiver when they move. Some movements are also Western, but the format is Balinese. Twelve men enter first and dance. They sit down, forming two sides of a square. Then twelve women enter, dance, and sit opposite the men. They sing love songs to each other in a question and answer form.

- *Oleg Tumulilingan*: the Bumblebee Dance

  Mario choreographed a new dance for John Coast's dance tour of Europe and America in 1952. The stars were two bumblebees. The lady has long wings, which she stretches out. This was the first time that a woman had raised her arms above her shoulders and it caused a stir. She flits and flirts like a bee from flower to flower. A young male bee appears and they dance around each other and finally lightly embrace. The dance is firmly established in the repertoire and just called *Oleg*.

- *Barong*

  Walter Spies and Beryl de Zoete observed that *Barongs* are '…at once the most familiar and the most obscure…' figures in Balinese tradition. *Barongs* come in many forms, but the most common is like a baroque Chinese lion, the *Barong Ket*, with big eyes and clacking jaws. It is one of the most sacred masks in Bali and probably every village has at least one. *Barongs* parade the streets during full moon. Sometimes a cry goes up, 'He wants to see his girlfriend!' and the *Barong* and its entourage tear down to the next village.

  The *Barong* protects the village from harmful influences. It parades the streets during every *Galungan* festival, dancing in front of shops and houses, warding off evil. There are Tantric associations. The Balinese wait in front of their buildings and bow in reverence when it passes. *Barongs* also parade just before *Nyepi*, at the time of the Balinese New Year.

  The *Barong's* origins are obscure. In the 13th century a Chinese lion dance was seen on the coast in south Bali and this may have provided the inspiration. The Chinese lion dance appeared during the T'ang Dynasty (7th – 10th century AD).

  Two men are inside; one operates the wooden head and lower movable jaw, and the other holds up the back and arched tail. The men have no special qualifications as long as they belong to the same *banjar* as the *Barong*, but they need to be very strong as the whole costume weighs about 187 pounds (85 kilos). The front, especially, is heavy and the dancer will need to be relieved during long processions.

  The beard of human hair from a pre-menstruating girl is the most powerful part. If it is dipped in water, it creates holy water and can cure. The hairy hide, made of palm fibres or the hair of a white horse, is covered with small bells, mirrors and decorations. It takes about three months to make a good quality *Barong*. If the masks of several *Barongs* come from the same tree, they are considered to be brothers and visit each other during ceremonies. They all attend the anniversary festivals of the temple where the tree from which they were carved grew. When a *Barong Ket* is old and in shreds, it

Barongs come in many forms, but the most common is like a baroque Chinese lion, the *Barong Ket*, with big eyes and clacking jaws.

is ceremonially cremated in the *Pura Dalem*, the death temple in the village, and its spirit transferred to a new one.

- **Rangda**

  A British politician, Ann Widdecome, once described her boss, Michael Howard (who later became party leader), as having 'something of the night' about him. Rangda has the same quality. Uniquely Balinese, she is the *Barong's* counterpart, described by Miguel Covarrubias in his book *Island of Bali* (1937) as

Rangda is the formidable Queen of Black Magic, head of witches, who sports a long, flaming tongue, pendulous breasts, long, trembling fingernails and human entrails around her neck, flicking a magic white cloth.

'undoubtedly the most interesting character on the island'. She is the formidable Queen of Black Magic, head of witches, who sports a long, flaming tongue, pendulous breasts, long, trembling fingernails and human entrails around her neck, flicking a magic white cloth as she goes. Rangda is tall and has tusks. Some temples have two Rangda masks, one red and the other white. The red one represents the more dangerous Rangda. The white one stresses her royal birth—some say Rangda is based on the 11th century Princess Mahendradatta.

Men dance Rangda; they do not have to be professional dancers because Rangda does not keep time to the music. She is powerful and threatening but she is not all evil, just as the *Barong* is not all good. Her powers can be turned to protect the village against harm. She wears magical Balinese textiles: the black and white chequered *poleng*, which symbolises the duality of her naure, and a protective *cepuk*. There are no extremes in Bali. Tourist literature, neatly packaging Balinese culture, usually describes her as totally evil and is misleading in this respect. Jane Belo, the anthropologist, likened Rangda to Santa Claus, the Tax Collector, and the Angel of Death all rolled into one.

The purpose of the *Barong*-Rangda dance is to restore balance. There is a battle. The *Barong's* followers try to attack Rangda. Through her magic they turn their *krises*, daggers, against themselves but through the *Barong's* magic, they fall into trance and do not stab themselves to death. The dance-drama often ends at this point, where neither good nor evil triumphs, which is the balance that the Balinese strive for. The controlled anger of the dancers is a cathartic release in a society where displaying such emotions is frowned upon. At one time kris dancers were male and female but in the 1950s women stopped performing this role and as a result they have no such outlet.

The *Barong* is Siwa transformed and Rangda is his wife Uma transformed. The confrontation culminates in Siwa, the male principle, bringing her, the female principle, under control. She has been prevented from destroying the world and becomes a positive and creative force again. There is no question of her being killed. It is not a matter of good over evil. The drama lies in the tension between good and bad. The fact that they are husband and wife adds another dimension. Both are necessary components of the natural order.

Rangda is also the goddess of death. She was so depicted on post office posters in the 1990s. The aim was to stop drug trafficking. The *Barong* represents creation and Rangda destruction.

- *Calonarang*
Calonarang means 'the candidate witch' and is a version of the *Barong*-Rangda story. It is an exorcism rite that starts at the crossroads and ends up in the cemetery, both ritually dangerous places. Originally it was a 12th century Javanese tale, which lost importance with the spread of Islam, and regained popularity in 19th century Bali, especially at the palace of Gianyar. The dance is thought to have originated in Batubulan about 1890.

The primary character is Rangda or *Calonarang*, the Queen of Witches and goddess of death. The dance is often performed at an *odalan*, the anniversary of a temple, which is timed for the full moon. It is also often performed if there has been an outbreak of disease. The purpose is to control Rangda's destructive powers and return them to beneficial uses. In fact she looks like a plague victim, a point made by Barbara Lovic in an essay *Bali: Myth, Magic and Morbidity* in 1987. She is a symbol of pestilence.

Calonarang was a widow, who lived during the reign of King Airlangga in east Java in the 11th century. Nobody would marry her daughter, Ratna Manggali, for fear of her mother and the fact that she had been banished to the forest by her husband for practising black magic. Who wants a witch for a mother-in-law? In revenge Calonarang goes to the graveyard with her apprentices, dances wildly and makes offerings of corpses and appeals to the goddess Durga to be allowed to devastate King Airlangga's kingdom of Daha.

It is played at night in the villages and the dance actually moves to the graveyard and frightens most of the audience. The forces of good and evil are abroad and engaged in a battle through the agency of human dancers. It is a risky time. It is not a story, but

Kecak: Monkey Dance is based on the old exorcism *Sang Hyang* trance dances. About a hundred bare-chested men, wearing *poleng* sarongs, sit in concentric circles around an oil lamp. One of them serves as the leader and chants. There is no orchestra.

real black magic fighting real white magic. It can be dangerous to dance Rangda. Calonarang calls on all the witches to join her. In the final scenes a character called the *dulang* is carried off to lie in a grave until dawn.

Lying there his spirit fights off attacks from invisible witches. The *dulang*, if he is not strong enough, may die. It is dangerous to leave a performance once it has begun. There are *leyaks* about.

Durga is the female incarnation of the destructive aspect of Siwa. Death and rebirth are intertwined in this manifestation. Durga agrees to Calonarang's request and terrible plagues and epidemics break out.

King Airlangga appeals to Siwa, who advises him to enlist the help of the sage Empu Baradah, who practised white magic. Empu Baradah sends his son Bahula to marry Ratna Manggali. Bahula steals Calonarang's book of spells, shows it to Empu Baradah, who memorises them. Knowing them, he can reverse them.

Empu Baradah confronts Calonarang and kills her in a battle. Then he brings her to life again, this time in human form, in order to purify her soul. She is then laid to rest. King Airlangga thanks the Empu Baradah and the kingdom prospers so much that, when he decides to retire and become a hermit, it is large enough for his two sons to succeed him with a kingdom each.

- *Kecak*: Monkey Dance

This is a very exciting dance, frequently photographed, and one of the best-known dances in Bali, always performed outside at night and called the Monkey Dance. It was created by dancers in Bedulu village at the request of and with suggestions from Walter Spies and Katharane Mershon, for Baron von Plessen's film *Island of Demons* in 1931. It was one of the first attempts to capture the romance of Bali and transmit it abroad and was met with instant success.

It is based on the old exorcism *Sang Hyang* trance dances. About a hundred bare-chested men, wearing *poleng* sarongs, sit in concentric circles around an oil lamp. One of them serves as the leader and chants. There is no orchestra. They chatter and sway like monkeys, arms splayed out, chanting *chak-achak-chak*, which is the sound of the male chorus in the *Sang Hyang* dances once a state of trance has been reached. The pitch and rhythm varies.

Inside the circle scenes from the Ramayana are danced, usually the abduction of Sita, followed by a battle and death of Rawana.

In the 1970s a photographer hired a troupe to dance the Kecak on a beach as he thought the light would be better for a postcard he was making. The postcard became famous and now there are Kecak dances every day on the beach near Tanah Lot Temple. In 2008 Gusti Ayu Sukmawati, one of the great beauties of Bali and one of the island's most exciting and electric dancers, led a hundred women in the first ever all female *Kecak* performance in Bali.

- *Genggong*: **Frog Dance**

This was created for children in the 1950s from an old story. The prince of Daha is hunting in the forest, where he urinates into a coconut, which a woman finds and drinks. She then gives birth to a frog.

The frog wants to marry the king's daughter, so his mother goes to the palace to ask for the king's permission, but she is killed. The frog brings her back to life. This happens three times. Finally the frog marries the princess, but he is very unhappy because he is so ugly. He makes a wish to be turned into a handsome prince and Siwa grants his wish. Instruments similar to the Jew's harp are played in the gamelan and sound like frogs. Young children play the frogs.

- *Belibis*: **Wild Ducks**

Created in 1984, the dance portrays a flock of wild ducks in their natural habitat. The choreography stresses their beauty and grace. Five to seven female dancers take part. They wear pink and white costumes with white wings. The king is changed into a duck by his three wives for spying on them.

- *Cendrawasih*: **Birds of Paradise**

This dance concerns two birds of paradise and was choreographed in 1988. Two women dancers play courting birds of paradise, a female bird and a male bird. Their duets portray the beauty and grace of the birds' movements.

Chapter 52

Trance Dances

Why and When?

Trance dances are not performed regularly at temple ceremonies. They are danced to cure or prevent a disaster, such as an epidemic of smallpox. As a result of increasing health care, a village may not perform a trance dance for years. When it takes place, the dance is continued every night until it is felt that the danger has passed.

Who Dances?

The most famous trance dance, *Sang Hyang Dedari*, is danced by two pre-pubescent girls. The whole village attends.

Where Does It Take Place?

The dance starts in the most sacred part of the most important temple in the village, *Pura Puseh*. The villagers sit on the ground facing the main shrine, where the priest and his assistants, a chorus of women and the group of dancers, including the two girls, stand.

Inducing the Trance

The two girls kneel in front of the priest and he invites the gods and goddesses to descend. There is a lot of incense. The women chant songs to establish the mood. After perhaps an hour of this, the girls' eyes close and they fall into trance. They sway back and forwards and from side to side. The priest wipes their faces as they sweat profusely.

When the priest is sure that the deities have descended and entered into the bodies of the girls, he asks them to speak. In strange voices the girls tell the villagers what to do to cure the illness or disaster that has befallen them. The remedy usually involves preparing traditional medicines or rituals.

The women stop singing when the spirits enter the girls. Often the spirits request the men to take over and start a *cak* chorus. Burning charcoal embers are prepared in front of the girls and to test the strength of trance they jump on the red hot coals and walk over them in their bare feet.

Dance

The next stage is the dance. The gamelan orchestra plays in the outer courtyard of the temple. Two men lift the girls up and place them on their shoulders. The girls stand and in total trance, eyes still closed, sway to the music. Their movements are improvised. They sway like trees in the wind, dragonflies on the wing or deer being bitten by flies.

The Procession around the Village

The priest leads them out into the street and the girls are carried to all corners of the village and the crossroads. The girls make warding off gestures to the demons and the priest liberally pours holy water. The purpose is to purify the whole village. After a couple of hours the procession goes back to the temple. While they were away, the gamelan was playing the whole time. The men put the girls down and the priest brings them out of trance using holy water. There are prayers and the women chant again.

What Happens during Trance?

There are other trance dances, which are not so sedate. A famous case is when the *Barong's* supporters turn their *kris* daggers upon themselves stabbing at their chests. Dancers who have been interviewed say that demonic spirits enter them. It is hard to know what is really happening as it is not possible to carry out controlled scientific experiments. It is possibly a form of hypnosis. Suryani and Jenson in *Trance and Possession in Bali* (1993) say that trance may be a way for people to express behaviour and emotions which would otherwise be unacceptable to society.

Dr Denny Thong, a Western trained psychiatrist, was the director of a small mental hospital in Bangli in 1968. He discovered a report of 437 different societies throughout the world where people enter into altered states of consciousness. Dr Thong noticed that the Balinese tend to suppress their emotions in everyday life and the dances and dramas are a means of releasing them. It is a catharsis for the audience too and aids mental health.

Chapter 53

Shadow Puppet Performances

Shadow Puppet performances have three functions: they are instructive, entertaining and religious, and have had a profound effect on Balinese arts. They bring together dance, drama, literature, visual art and music.

The Words

The 1982 film *The Year of Living Dangerously*, based on Christopher Koch's novel, set in Indonesia in 1965 and filmed in the Philippines, opens with a *Wayang Kulit* or 'shadow puppet' performance. These ancient, atmospheric, magical performances symbolise Indonesia. *Wayang* means 'shadow' and *kulit* means 'leather'. The word *wayang* also refers to the puppets, and by extension, the show.

Why, When and Where?

The performances have three functions: they are instructive, entertaining and religious, and have had a profound effect on Balinese arts. They bring together dance, drama, literature, visual art and music. The puppeteer has to be expert in all these arts: it is a one man (or woman) show.

Performances are sacred and form an essential part of many ceremonies in village and family temples. They accompany temple anniversaries and rites of passage, such as baby ceremonies, tooth-filings and weddings, and the consecration of priests. Therefore Balinese children are familiar very quickly with the world of shadow puppets, their personalities and family relationships. Every performance is unique, largely improvised; there are no scripts, no rehearsals and no long runs in the shadow puppet theatre.

Origins

Shadow theatre has existed in the lands between Turkey and China for over 2,000 years. Many think that Indonesian shadow puppet performances originated in India (it was performed there in the 1st century BC) and came to Bali between the 11th and 14th centuries from Java.

It is mentioned in Bali in an inscription dated 896 AD. A Balinese royal inscription of 1053 mentions a performance. The first person to describe a Balinese performance was Chinkah, a Siamese master of a junk, who landed in Bali in 1846. The king of Klungkung gave a performance for him. In the rest of Southeast Asia only the night *wayang* is known. In Bali, there is also a day performance.

Instruction and Propaganda

Muslim preachers employed the *wayang* to spread Islam in the 15th century, and the sultans of Java employed the puppets to narrate the history of their dynasties. During the Independence struggle against the Dutch in the 1940s, *wayang* plays depicted patriotic leaders, independence fighters, civil servants, governors, Dutch colonialists, Japanese soldiers and common people. It was used by the nationalists to inform the people at a time when many were illiterate.

Patrons

Javanese performances are associated with the court, whereas Balinese performances are a folk tradition and belong to the community as a whole. *Wayang Kulit* was Bali's original cinema, but it is primarily a religious drama. It has the seriousness of a classical Greek drama. (The word 'drama' comes from the Greek *dromenon*, meaning 'religious ritual'.)

Wayang Classification

There are two main types:

- *Wayang Peteng*: the Night *Wayang*
  The most common occurrence of the night *wayang* is during a temple anniversary. A grateful person may also sponsor a performance in gratitude for a prayer being answered. They frequently accompany tooth-filing, wedding and baby ceremonies.

- *Wayang Lemah*: the Day *Wayang*
  The day *wayang* is the most revered form and is performed for the gods. Very few people watch. It is usually done in the morning or late afternoon and is regarded as an offering.

Puppeteer

The *dalang* or 'puppeteer' plays all the characters, in different voices, manipulates the puppets and controls the gamelan by tapping his foot on the wooden box of puppets. He must be able to quote long passages from memory as well as improvise jokes and funny songs and know how to hold the audience's attention for many hours. Performances usually end at daybreak. It demands great physical and mental stamina. *Dalang* have always been men, but since 1980 a few women have mastered the art. The highest praise that a Balinese can give a performance is to say that it has *taksu*, spiritual strength.

Stage and Screen

The audience is separated from the cross-legged *dalang* by a large, white, 6 foot (2 metres) long cloth, bordered in black at the top and bottom and red squares at the side. Behind the cloth sits the *dalang* with a flickering, hanging coconut-oil lamp casting fluttering shadows on the sheet, the puppets of flat buffalo or cow hide and his two assistants, who sit on either side of him and hand him the puppets. The shadows of the puppets on the screen are like moths flying across a beam of light. The *dalang's* puppet

The *Kayonan* is the most important puppet, in the shape of the tree of life. It represents the forest and the sea.

box is on his left. The puppets are all taken out and placed in a yellow-green banana log at the base of the screen, ready for action. The filigree patterns of the puppets against the oil lamp show up on the screen. Behind the screen are four (or more depending on the type of performance) gamelan instruments.

Party of the Right, Party of the Left

The *dalang* places the 'good' puppets on his right and the rest on his left. The good are morally superior heroes. The others are enemies and inferior. In a Ramayana performance, Rama, Sita, Laksmana, the bird Jatayu and many members of Rama's monkey army, as well as servants Tualen and Merdah, belong to the party of the right. Their opponents belong to the party of the left and include the demon king Rawana, his son Indrajit, his brothers Kumbakarna and Wibisana, his army of demons and the two servants Dalem and Sangut. The *Kayonan* (tree puppet) and *Gunungan* (mountain puppet) and the Supreme god puppet belong to neither party and are placed in the centre of the screen.

The Stories

Three types of *wayang* stories are popular:

- **Mahabarata**
  Most of the *wayang* stories are from the Mahabarata epic and concentrate on the battles between the Pandawa and the Korawa.
- **Ramayana**
  The Ramayana epic is the second great source of stories, especially

the battle scenes involving Hanuman and the monkey armies in
their struggle against the evil Rawana.

- *Calonarang*

  The story of Rangda the witch is rarely played because the
  puppeteer has to summon dangerous witches to the performance.
  Only a few may come, but this is unpredictable. Many may
  attend. The gamelan for *Calonarang* is larger than normal: there
  are four *gender* or xylophones, three different kinds of gongs, two
  cymbals, two drums and a bamboo flute.

The Performance

The *dalang* always starts with a long poetic introduction, when he
mentions the text from which the story is taken. Action and dialogue
take up the rest of the performance, where neither good nor evil prevails.
There is a constant battle between the two.

The story is finished in one sitting, unlike in Java, where it can last
days. The plot usually starts and ends in the palace and moves to the village and forest. The village represents civilisation, the court, the temple
and home. The forest is the place to meditate, make contact with unseen
forces and wage battles. The *dalang* may create variations on traditional
themes and insert new episodes and topical references into their lives but
he cannot change the characters or their style of speaking or dress.

The Balinese know the outcome before they arrive, so the *dalang*
can cut or extend scenes at will. He can bring the show to an end at any
moment if an unexpected downpour of rain should happen.

The Puppets

A standard collection comprises about a hundred puppets, which are
made of cowhide with a tapering buffalo horn or wooden handle.
They are not strictly leather as the hide is not subjected to a tanning
process. The handle ends in a point and is stuck into the banana stem.
Each puppet is chiselled, coloured and has a conventional headdress,
which provides instant recognition. They are kept in a wooden chest
in a prescribed order: the most important, ritually speaking, on top,
the animals and demons at the bottom. The scenic *Kayonan* is the
uppermost figure. Puppets of a hundred years ago look almost the
same as modern puppets. The style has hardly changed.

They are not naturalistic and may be derived from temple sculptures and reliefs. They have disproportionately long necks, long arms, and toes that are not in the correct position. Stylised hand gestures are similar to the hand gestures of priests. The eyes and headdress are the most important parts of the puppet, because the eyes reveal expression and the headdress indicates status. Spectators normally recognise the characters from their headdresses, but it can be difficult. A *dalang* may use the same puppet for more than one character.

Some attributes are restricted to certain characters. Bayu, the god of wind and his sons, Hanuman and Bima, and Bima's sons, have a large, lethal thumb-nail. Only these characters, and Tualen, wear a black and white chequered *poleng* sarong. All the monkeys in Rama's monkey army are black, except Hanuman, who is white.

As they are objects involved with religious matters, shadow puppets are treated with great respect and reverence. They have an invisible power and life force of their own. They are more than skin and bone.

Tree of Life and the Mountain

The *Kayonan* is the most important puppet, in the shape of the 'tree of life'. It represents the forest and the sea. It is also a palace and more generally, earth, wind, fire, water and air, the five elements that make up the Universe. The *dalang* waves it to indicate the start of the story. It swoops, trembles and flutters and brings the Universe and the parties to life. The *dalang* also uses it to indicate scene changes and the end of the performance.

The *Gunungan* or 'mountain puppet' represents Mount Meru, the Mountain of the Gods and sacred centre of the Universe. Mountains and trees link the three zones of the underworld, earth and heaven. Mountains arise out of the depths, through the earth and into the sky. Trees have their roots in the underworld, grow through the earth and branch into the sky. Mountains represent permanence and trees represent transience.

Human Animals

There is a group of animals which includes monkeys, snakes, tigers, deer and pigs, that have clear characteristics of their species, like stripes, antlers and snouts, but they are not ordinary animals: they also have human attributes. Rama's monkey army, commanded by Hanuman, have human limbs and bodies, and monkey faces. They wear warriors' clothes and ornaments and lobster-claw hairdos. All these animals have tails that end in a jewel.

The monkeys also have god-like qualities. Hanuman is the son of Bayu, the god of wind. He has supernatural strength and powers of enlargement and diminution. Hanuman and the monkeys can fly so quickly that trees are blown down. They do not use man-made weapons. They throw rocks and sticks and sometimes trees and hills. Only Hanuman, Bayu and Garuda can cross the ocean.

Bring on the Clowns

The *dalang* speaks in Kawi, which few understand. For the benefit of the audience, four clowns translate and comment in Balinese. The clowns are the most important and popular characters. In the Mahabarata stories they are Tualen and his son Merdah, servants of the Pandawa, and Dalem and Sangut, servants of the Korawa. They are short, pot-bellied, crude and silly, but with lots of personality.

Body Colour

Noble, *alus*, characters, like royalty, have light bodies, straight noses, flat teeth in slightly open, slightly smiling mouths and slit, almond-shaped eyes. They have no facial or body hair and their legs are close together. Examples are Arjuna of the Pandawa and Karna of the Korawa. They speak in high voices. Noble princesses are small and slim, large breasted, with flowing hair, narrow waists and slender hips.

There is a sliding scale. Less refined males have neat moustaches. Further down the scale, there is more facial and body hair and eyes become round. They speak in louder, deeper voices. Examples are Bima, the second of the Pandawa brothers, and his son Gatotkaca, whose mother Arimbi was a demon. At the bottom of the scale are the coarse, *kasar* characters, like the ogres, who have hairy, muscular, red or brown bodies, thick hands, pointed teeth and bulbous, round eyes.

Body colours represent values in Balinese society. The colours are the basic colours. White represents purity; green for fertility and steadfastness; black for evil; blue for bravery and intelligence and red for fire and strife. The gods, and those associated with them, have their own colours. Rama has a green mask, because he is an avatar of Wisnu, whose colour is green or black. Siwa is white. Brahma is red.

Station in Life

There is another scale which indicates the status of each character. The scales do not necessarily coincide. Kings and princes can be demonic. Demons can be refined, like Wibisana, Rawana's brother. Rank is shown by clothing, ornaments and hairstyles. Gods and kings wear crowns and gold ornaments. Lesser nobles and officials wear lesser ornaments. Commoners and servants dress in simple clothes. All Balinese characters are barefoot in contrast to Javanese shadow puppets, where the gods wear black shoes.

Puppet Making

The art of puppet making is passed down from one generation to the next. Apprenticeship takes between two and five years. Often a *dalang* makes his own puppets, but not necessarily. The puppet maker carries out a ceremony to Wisnu and Siwa before he starts and places a daily offering on a small shrine. He wants to remain in a state of spiritual purity.

The puppets are made of carefully prepared cow or buffalo hide, which is scraped and smoothed. They are about 1 inch (5 mm) thick, stiff but flexible. The outline is traced on to the hide from paper or another puppet. The puppet is then cut out and the puppet maker chisels the edges and holes. The holes add elegance and make the puppet visible and recognisable on the screen.

The head, torso and legs are one piece. The arms are separate and attached to the shoulders. There are joints at the shoulder and elbow. The arms move by means of rods tied to the puppets' hands. Gods and humans are represented with their heads in profile. Their bodies are frontal but turned a little in the same direction as the face. Arms, legs and feet also point in the same direction. Upper bodies of servants are shown in profile. They are all dressed, except for the Supreme god.

Ogres, demons and partially human animals have distinct faces. Noses and mouths are in profile. Fangs protrude from their jaws. Eyes bulge. The upper parts of their heads, including the eyes, eyebrows and foreheads, are shown in three-quarter profile. Both eyes are in view. Many ogres and demons have only one moveable arm. Animals have their whole body in profile with no moving parts. There are also puppet weapons, spears, arrows and discus.

The head is painted first. The puppets are painted using five basic colours: white, red, yellow, black and blue. White is made from animal bones, black from soot and yellow from stones found on Serangan Island in the south coast of Bali. Gold leaf is used for the *Kayonan* and the costumes of the *satria* characters. The colours are predetermined. When the puppets are finished, a high priest consecrates them. A well-made puppet will last for generations.

Wooden Chest

The puppets are kept in a specially made large wooden box. With between 100 and 200 puppets, it takes a couple of men to carry it. After the performance the puppets are put back and covered with a clean cotton cloth. The lid is closed and the box is stored above ground to protect it from insects and damp. As the puppets are sacred, it should be kept high. Before he opens the box, the *dalang* performs a short ceremony and always places the puppets on a clean cloth or mat and never on the ground.

Stage Symbolism

The music, stage and equipment symbolise the macrocosm. The clean white cloth screen symbolises the sky. The cloth separates us from the real world of the gods. The puppets symbolise all that exists. The banana log is the earth. The oil lamp, which gives life and energy, represents the sun and the *dalang* is God. The music symbolises the harmony of the cosmos and the puppets' movements harmonise with the music.

The *dalang* wears headgear, waistcloth and dress, which represent heaven, earth and the underworld. He joins all three together during a performance. The seen and the unseen, the visible and the invisible, the inner world and the outer world are all present during a shadow puppet performance. The dancing shadows represent the illusory and transitory nature of life. To the gods, who are in the real world behind the screen, it is us, the audience, who are the shadows.

The stage details are also symbolic. The stage is orientated to the propitious mountainward, *kaja*, direction, or to the east. The cloth has nine holes at the top, which represents the Balinese mandala. The lamp is lit with three bundles of wicks, representing the Trinity, Brahma, Wisnu and Siwa. There are no stage sets. The audience has to imagine the forest or palace or battlefield.

The Music

There are usually four gamelan instruments, called *Gender Wayang*, which comprise the *gender* or xylophone, the *rebab* or two-stringed lute, the drum and the gong. The *dalang* directs the music and sings songs. Music accompanies the placing of the puppets in the banana log, announces entrances, supports the dialogue, creates a benevolent atmosphere, and adds excitement to dramatic scenes.

Wayang Lemah: the Day Wayang

Lemah means 'daylight'. This version is usually performed during the day and is a religious rite. It is for the gods and normally takes place in the inner holiest part of the temple. As he is already in a ritually pure area, the *dalang* has fewer preparations to carry out, but there are more offerings.

It is a quiet performance, hardly audible to human beings, containing little or no conflict. The gods perceive reality directly, so there is no need for a screen. There are only about five to fifteen puppets, which are stuck close together in the banana log, where they remain motionless, resting against a string of three coloured threads entwined together, white, red and black, the colours of the three main gods.

The string is stretched between two branches of the sacred *dadap* tree about a foot (30 centimetres) above the banana log. The *dadap* tree has supernatural power. Two musicians playing large metallophones provide the music. The music is less rich in tone and colour than the night *wayang*.

The stories are always taken from the Mahabarata and deal with moral and spiritual themes and always relate to the particular ceremony or occasion. If the ceremony is a wedding, the chosen story will be about a wedding. There are no comic interludes.

Wayang Tantri and Electric Wayang

Balinese *Wayang Kulit* is very traditional and conservative, but it admits innovation and new forms. In the 1980s Bali's most famous *dalang*, Wija, created a new version based on tales told by Tantri to a king, who wanted to seduce her, *Wayang Tantri*. Wija made a whole new set of puppets, including many animals, for the purpose. *Wayang Listrik* is a popular new form, launched in 1996. Huge shadows, formed by ten to fifteen puppets and actors, are projected on to a large screen using halogen lamps controlled by dimmers.

Music in Bali

Balinese Gamelan

No place on Earth has as much music as Bali, or as many kinds. There are at least thirty distinct types of gamelan, each with its own traditions, repertoire and functions. The reason for the plethora of musical forms is the limited contact between villages. The great mountain ranges made travelling difficult, especially as roads were poor before the 20th century and the kingdoms were very often at war with each other. Musical styles evolved separately without much interaction.

Javanese Gamelan

Gamelan is mostly Balinese or Javanese. They are different. Balinese gamelan is boisterous and flamboyant, whereas Javanese gamelan is sedate and refined. The Dutch musicologist and colonial civil servant Jaap Kunst (1891-1960), who first visited Ubud in 1921, staying with his wife at Ubud palace, and who introduced the term 'ethnomusicology', described Javanese gamelan in *Music of Java* (1934) thus,

> Gamelan is comparable to only two things; moonlight and
> flowing water. It is pure and mysterious like moonlight and
> always changing like water.

Meaning of Gamelan

Strictly the word 'gamelan' refers to the collection of instruments. The Balinese religion requires music for the success of the thousands of ceremonies performed every year. This is not surprising as music is universally used in religious contexts to serve or glorify the gods. Gamelan music is full of insistent rhythms and elegant patterns. There is hardly any improvisation.

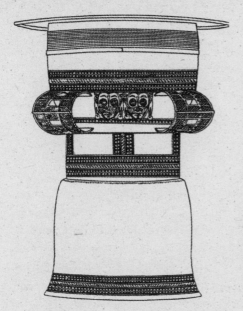

Ancient bronze kettle drums appeared in south China from the 4th century BC and then in Vietnam in a place called Dong Son, from which they get their name. They spread throughout Southeast Asia and the largest one is in Pejeng near Ubud in central Bali.

Dong Son Drums

Ancient bronze kettle drums appeared in south China from the 4th century BC and then in Vietnam in a place called Dong Son, from which they get their name. They spread throughout Southeast Asia and the largest one is in Pejeng near Ubud in central Bali. They are not played in Bali and, although probably they are musical instruments, they are not strictly drums. They are not membranophones but bronze idiophones. An idiophone is an instrument in which the sound producing body comes from the material of the instrument itself. A membranophone is an instrument where the sound comes from a membrane stretched over a resonator or frame.

Origins

Balinese legends say that originally there was only one gamelan and it was created in heaven by Semara, the god of love, and his wife, Ratih. When they heard it, the gods of the four cardinal directions, the gods of the sky and the demons of the underworld, made their own versions. That meant that there were seven gamelans. A very powerful king copied them all.

Java has its own origin story. The Javanese Chronicles say that it was introduced by the nine saints of Islam as they promulgated their religion throughout Indonesia 500 years ago. There are musical instruments on the friezes of Borobudur Temple (9th century) in central Java. Bronze making was a necessary condition for gamelan music in Bali and Java, as most of the instruments are made of bronze.

Gender Benders

Blacksmiths belong to a special clan, called *Pande*, who undergo spiritual training. They pour a molten blend of copper and tin into an earthen mould set in the ground and, when it hardens, place it in the fire and hammer the hot bronze into the desired shape. Then they cool it and repeat the process of heating and beating. This tempers the metal, and once tuned, it maintains its pitch. They make all the bronze gamelan instruments, which include the *gender wayang* for shadow puppet performances known as *gender* for short. Tihingan is the best known village for manufacturing and repairing gamelan instruments. The *Pande* no longer have a monopoly.

The large gongs are the most difficult to make. There is a tradition that they were made in pre-colonial Tihingan, but, if so, the ability was lost in the late 19th and early 20th centuries, and they had to be imported from Java. During the Japanese occupation this was impossible and the Tihingan craftsmen began to make larger gongs.

Tuning

The instruments are tuned when they are made using various techniques of filing and polishing. It takes several weeks. They do not tune up before a performance. There is no universal norm. The tuner decides himself. Each set of instruments has its own characteristic sound and they always stay together.

Most instruments use one of two scales, the *pelog* and the *slendro*. They refer to the intervals between the notes rather than the pitch. The *pelog* has four, five or seven tones. The *slendro* has four or five tones. The five tones have cosmological significance as they are linked to the gods of the five directions, north, east, south, west and centre.

Ding-Dong

Siwa sits in the centre. His sacred syllable is *hing* and the tone for this syllable is *ding*. The Balinese call the five degrees of the scale: *ding, dong, deng, dung* and *dang*. The notation was adopted in the 1960s by KOKAR, the national music conservatory.

Patrons

As with the other arts, the Balinese courts were the main patrons. When the Dutch took control, the courts declined in influence, and ownership of gamelan orchestras increasingly belonged to the *banjars* and the villages. From the 1960s dance and music institutions, especially KOKAR, now known as SMKI, and ASTI, now known as ISI, sponsored research and new compositions. Tourism has also provided a new kind of patronage.

Types of Gamelan

There are different types of gamelan for different purposes. The large ancient *Gamelan Gong Gede* used to be placed on either side of palace gates to protect royalty. The delicate, and now rare, *Gamelan Semar Pegulingan* was played in the king's bedchamber to accompany his lovemaking. The *Gamelan Gambuh* plays for the *Gambuh* dance. The *Gender Wayang* accompanies shadow puppet performances and cremations, and a special exciting set, *Gamelan Balaganjur*, is used for processions.

Kebyar

Until the beginning of the 20th century, gamelan was gentle, sedate and soothing. The Dutch completed their conquest of Bali in 1908 and Singaraja in the north became the capital. In the next couple of decades there was a renaissance of the arts in north Bali and many new gamelan and dance groups were formed. The various groups were very competitive.

In 1915 the *Gamelan Gong Kebyar*, now just called *Gong*, was invented in a village called Jagaraga in north Bali. It is not a coincidence that it was just after the end of the First World War that *Kebyar* took hold. *Kebyar* is loud, dramatic, aggressive and exciting. Literally *kebyar* means 'lightning'. It is all flame and radiance, tense and syncopated. Spreading immediately like wildfire, it is now the most common style throughout the island.

The music is really fast, loud and lively, exciting, with rapid changes of tempo and lots of sudden starts and stops. It is played with great gusto, energy and embellishment. There are usually three contrasting movements; the head of the piece, which is brisk, the main body, which is slow, and the final section, the feet, which is fast and builds up to a climax at the end.

Purpose
The primary purpose is to entertain the gods and ancestors at ceremonies. There is music at temple ceremonies, weddings, cremations, and processions. Sonic spaces are filled with music, just as physical spaces are filled with people. The players rehearse frequently and memorise the music. There are also secular performances, especially for tourists, and competitions between villages.

Classification
As with the other art forms in Bali, gamelan music falls into three categories:

- **Old (pre-Hindu, before the 15th century)**
  These are mostly found in the old Bali Aga villages in north and east Bali. They do not use drums, *rebab* (lutes) or *suling* (flutes) and have a seven tone scale. The music accompanies the holiest dances, which take place in the inner section of the temple. *Gender Wayang* is an example and accompanies shadow puppet performances.

- **Middle (Hindu-Javanese 16th-19th century)**
  This is court gamelan with drums, *rebab* and *suling*. It accompanies the dances, which take place in the middle section of the temple. It developed out of the Majapahit courts and the dances tell stories of Hindu Javanese-Balinese connections.

- **New (20th century -)**
  New compositions developed from the Middle category and feature drums prominently and complex, fast, interlocking patterns. They accompany the secular dances, which take place in the outer section of the temple.

Spiritual Strength
Often the musicians have other jobs during the day and meet in the evening. They play together as one group. There is no individual expression. They aim to play as one musician. The highest praise that a Balinese can give a performance is to say that it has *taksu*, spiritual

strength. There are no rounds of applause, no curtain calls and no cries of 'Encore!'

Communal music making fits in well with the Balinese psyche. People who make music together share an emotional state and mould their minds and bodies to each other. There comes about a loss of identity and a willingness to co-operate. These are all Balinese traits. Music is used in other places for the same purpose: football chants, church choirs, political rallies. Japanese owned factory workers sing the company song before starting work, even in Wales.

Women and Children

Old illustrations show women playing the gamelan, but it had become a strictly male affair by the time the Dutch were in power. In the early 1960s girls at the High School of Performing Arts studied gamelan and a women's group was formed in Denpasar in 1980. Many villages followed suit although men resisted in some communities.

In 1985 a women's gamelan group participated in the annual Bali Arts Festival, and now there are many women's groups playing all over the island. In 2001 for the first time a mixed group of men and women played together in a gamelan competition at the Bali Arts Festival.

The Canadian musicologist, Colin McPhee, created a children's gamelan group in Sayan in 1937. They were not taken seriously by adults but that changed by the 1960s. Energetic children's groups are now in every village and play at temple festivals and competitions.

Learning to Play

Children hear gamelan before they are born and shortly afterwards learn to play. When they get a teacher, he sits opposite and plays backwards on the keys. The student follows the movements.

Sheet Music

There is no sheet music, or at any rate, hardly any, and it is never used in performances. The pieces have to be committed to memory, which entails hours of practice. It is taught by the teacher playing a phrase, which the student learns, then the teacher plays the next phrase and the student learns that and so on until the piece has been completely mastered.

Male and Female Instruments

Gongs and drums are paired. The lower pitched, bigger instrument is female and the higher pitched, smaller one is male. The female drum leads the orchestra but if it is not visible to the players, the lead *gangsa* player, whose instrument, which looks like a xylophone and is high and visible, flourishes his hammer to guide the others. In some cases, the dancer cues the drummer.

The Beat Note

The paired instruments are tuned to the same pitch but one is tuned slightly higher than the other. When they are hit simultaneously, the sound waves emerge at slightly different speeds and produce a third note, called the beat note, which gives a lively, thrilling, shimmering sound. The paired instruments are interdependent and a note struck without its partner is not alive. That is the secret of the pulsating, electric sound of the Balinese gamelan.

Melodic *Gangsa*, *Trompong*, *Suling* and *Rebab*

The *gangsa*, *trompong* (ten inverted bronze gongs), *suling* and *rebab* play the melody or a variation of it, while the large gong and smaller gongs, cymbals and drums keep time and furnish a framework for the melody. The higher pitched instruments play the more complicated music. A composition always ends with a big gong beat.

Punctuating Gongs

The melody is propelled and controlled by the drums and punctuated by the gongs, which delineate circular movements. The large gong, the *gong agung*, is struck on the eighth beat, the smaller gong, the *kemong*, on the fourth beat, and the *kempli*, the very small one, on the second and sixth beats. The medium sized *kempur* alternates with the *gong agung*. The *klenang* is hit on the offbeat.

This contrasts with Western music, which proceeds in a straight line and emphasises the first beat. It has been remarked that the circular musical structure is akin to birth, death and reincarnation.

Crazy Rhythm

Much of the excitement of Balinese rhythms arises out of interlocking pairs of *gangsa, reyong* or drums. Two interlocking musical lines sound as one melody, often played at incredible speed. The composite melody has a faster tempo than any single player could play alone. It is called *kotekan*. The sum of the parts is greater than the whole.

Some people say that the origin of interlocking parts comes from bamboo rice-pounding, whereby women remove husks from the rice. As they pound, they alternate the rhythms into a composite whole.

Street Music

Marching gamelan orchestras accompany processions of deities, *Barongs* and cremations. Instruments that cannot be lifted easily are slung over bamboo poles and are a daily sight on the streets of Bali.

Authoritative Versions

The Balinese do not value authoritative versions. It goes against the grain of variation in all things. Although orchestras may play the same composition, the details of the elaborating parts almost always differ.

Colin McPhee, 1900-1964

Colin McPhee, born in 1900 in Montreal of Canadian and Scottish parents, was probably the most important person to introduce gamelan to the West. He was raised in Toronto, and as a young man went to New York and heard Balinese music on gramophone records played by his friend Eric Clarke in 1929. He borrowed them, played them over and over again and decided that he must go to Bali and discover how music like that could have survived. He probably only heard about twenty-seven minutes of music, but it was enough to change his life. Later he wrote in *A House in Bali* (1947):

> The records had been made in Bali, and the clear, metallic
> sounds of the music were like the stirring of a thousand
> bells, delicate, confused, with a sensuous charm, a mystery
> that was quite overpowering.

Shortly after meeting the rich, budding anthropologist Jane Belo (1904-1968), they married on 6 May 1930, even though she knew he was a homosexual. They were both interested in the exotic. She was the child of rich Texans and had previously been married to the painter George Biddle. The same year they went to Paris and in 1931 met Miguel and

Rose Covarrubias, old friends, who had just returned from their first trip to Bali, both bursting with enthusiasm. Colin and Jane heard Balinese gamelan live at the Colonial Exhibition, and together set sail for Bali in 1931. Miguel and Rose gave them a letter of introduction to Walter Spies. From Marseilles to the East Indies took twenty days. They stayed for six months in Bali until their visas ran out and returned to Paris, but in May 1932 they were back, and Colin was researching, studying and filming gamelan music. He was perfectly attuned to the gamelan with its intricate layers and shifting rhythms and the first person to transcribe it in Western notation. Tape recorders did not exist, so he could not tape the sound. They were not invented until after the Second World War. Sometimes on trips of exploration he brought his gramophone and played records to amazed villagers.

McPhee and Jane Belo lived in Sayan, a village off the beaten track close to Ubud, until 1941. They were members of the expat set of artists and academics, centred on Walter Spies, who was living in nearby Campuan. They rented Spies's house while theirs was being built and he moved into another building on the property. When the house was finished McPhee wrote to an old friend, Carl Van Vechten, 'How I wish you could see [the house]…Twelve servants—all beautiful and naked to the waist.' Margaret Mead and her husband Gregory Bateson were also part of the circle and became firm friends. In 1935 they took a break and went to Mexico where they saw Miguel and Rose Covarrubias almost every day and Colin composed a Western symphonic work, called *Tabu-Tabuhan*, based on Balinese musical ideas. It was conducted by his friend Carlos Chàvez and played by the Mexico Symphony Orchestra. It was a huge success. He was awarded the Pulitzer Prize in Music for it and it is still played. It was the highlight at the London Proms one evening in 2004.

McPhee returned to Bali at the end of 1936 and continued to study the gamelan. He started a gamelan in Sayan devoted to the music of *Semar Pegulingan*, which was a special ensemble dedicated to Semar, the god of love. It had fallen into severe decline after the courts were weakened under Dutch rule. Then he started another group to perform *angklung*, but this time the group comprised village children between the ages of six and eleven. Both revivals were successful. McPhee wrote arrangements for two pianos of some of the gamelan music he heard and he and Walter Spies played them on cruise ships and special events.

Unfortunately his attempted recordings were a failure. There had been none since the 1928 Odeon recordings. McPhee had crisscrossed Bali in his 1931 Chevrolet making detailed notes and the recordings would have complemented them perfectly, but he appears to have been duped in getting the equipment, records and needles. He had left the project to the last minute and ran out of time. Spies commented, 'It is too dreadful—and I think he is a fool—it is so difficult to speak to him about it.'

Jane left Bali in late March 1938 with Margaret Mead and Gregory Bateson. Colin and Jane were divorced in July 1938. They had lived apart for some time. She eventually could not accept his male lovers. News of the Munich crisis reached Bali and the threat of war loomed. Colin was running out of money and the Dutch authorities were, in Margaret Mead's words, 'mounting a witch hunt against homosexuals'. On Christmas Day 1938 he left Bali for America and never returned. Six days later Walter Spies was arrested and thrown into prison for corrupting the youth.

The Swiss painter, Theo Meyer, rented the house, but then it was ransacked by the Japanese. They took the furniture and tore down the beautifully carved rafters. The rest was eaten by white ants and today only the foundations remain. Back in New York Colin McPhee wrote *A House in Bali*, which was published in 1947. It described his life and work in Bali. There was no mention of Jane—hardly fair as she underwrote the trip to Bali, the building of the house and compound, sponsored the musicians and even gave him financial help after their divorce. The next year he wrote a children's book *A Club of Small Men* about the Balinese children's gamelan group. His magnum opus is a 600 page encyclopaedic work with 358 musical examples and 120 photographs all taken by McPhee, called *Music in Bali*, which was finished just before his death and published posthumously in 1966. He led a simple life and was often depressed, fell into alcoholism and died of cirrhosis of the liver in Crescent Bay Convalescent Hospital, Los Angeles, California on 7 January 1964.

Influence on the West

The gamelan has influenced composers like Claude Debussy (1862-1918), Benjamin Britten (1913-1976), Olivier Messiaen (1908-1992),

Lou Harrison (1917-2003), Steve Reich (1936-) and Philip Glass (1937-). It was introduced to the West at the end of the 19th century and by some very successful music and dance tours:

- a gamelan group from Java performed at the Paris International Exhibition in 1889, which was attended by Claude Debussy
- the Odeon company released some recordings of Balinese music in 1931 called *Musik des Orients*. Ninety-eight sides were recorded with the help of Walter Spies and five were made commercially available. They were heard by Colin McPhee in New York, whereupon he immediately determined to go to Bali.
- the Peliatan gamelan group was the first Balinese group to tour abroad: it went to Paris in 1931 to attend the Colonial Exhibition
- the same music and dance group from Peliatan toured London, New York and Las Vegas in 1952, organised by Englishman John Coast, who wrote a book about it called *Dancing Out of Bali*. A digitally remastered CD of the music performed on that tour, entitled *Dancers of Bali, Gamelan of Peliatan, 1952*, was issued by World Arbiter in 2006.

John Cage (1912-1992) was also influenced by the loud, percussive sounds of the gamelan, but not always. His 1952 composition *4'33"* consists of four minutes and thirty-three seconds of pure uninterrupted silence from any instrument or combination of instruments. Its first radio broadcast was on BBC Radio 3 in 2003. Perhaps that piece was influenced by *Nyepi*, Bali's Day of Silence. Please visit Murni's on line shop if you would like to buy a CD of it.

Evan Ziporyn composed a highly acclaimed opera called *A House in Bali* based on McPhee's book, which fuses Western electronic instruments and Balinese gamelan. It had its world première in September 2009, but was performed in Ubud the previous July.

King Crimson, the 1970s progressive rock group, has been influenced by gamelan music and Björk, the Icelander pop star, has used gamelan instruments in a number of her songs, most famously in her 1993 recording of *One Day* and has performed with Balinese gamelan orchestras. Fans of the television series *Battleship Galactica* will have heard gamelan in the show's music.

World Music

Dr Robert Brown (1927-2005), part time resident of Bali, and our neighbour at 'Flower Mountain' in the hills near Ubud, coined the expression 'World Music'. He told me that when he came to Ubud for the first time in the 1950s ducks waddled through Ubud's crossroads every day. In 1971 he helped revive the *Gamelan Semar Pegulingan* group in Teges which Colin McPhee had earlier helped but had ceased to play after he left Bali. Robert Brown also produced recordings of Javanese and Balinese gamelan for the Nonesuch Explorer Series—in the early 1970s—and later worked on the Voyager Golden Record with Carl Sagan. The Voyager Golden Record was launched into space aboard the Voyager space probe in 1977, intended as a record of culture on Earth, preserved for humans and other life forms in the distant future. It included a recording of Javanese court gamelan from Yogyakarta and is expected to survive for 4,500,000,000 years. He was planning a trip to Bali when he suddenly fell ill with cancer and died in California in 2005.

Gamelan in the West

In the 1950s the University of California in Los Angeles received the first gamelan to be exported from Bali. Since that time interest in gamelan has exploded. By 1998 there were over eighty gamelan groups in the United States, Canada, Australia, France, Germany, Japan, the Netherlands, New Zealand and the United Kingdom. At first it was difficult to obtain the instruments but modern technology has made it easy to order them from web sites such as Murni's in Bali (*www.murnis.com*).

Chapter 55

Gamelan Instruments

Mostly Percussion

The bronze instruments are percussive and comprise the gongs, metallophones and gong chimes. In addition, there are drums, flute and lute. A gamelan orchestra comprises a large number of people and instruments, so it is surprising that there is no conductor to lead them. In the West conductors emerged around 1820 at the end of Beethoven's career. Until then ensembles were controlled by the first violinist or the person playing the clavier. At that time orchestras rarely consisted of more than sixty players, although Berlioz formed an orchestra of 150 performers in 1825, and dreamed of an orchestra of 467 and a chorus of 360. He thought—and dreamt—big.

Balinese gamelan instruments are percussive and comprise gongs, metallophones and gong chimes. In addition, there are drums, flute and lute. A gamelan orchestra comprises a large number of people and instruments.

Gongs

Gongs are bronze kettles of various sizes, with a single raised top knot called a boss, which are hit at intervals with a mallet to divide up the composition.

Jaap Kunst eloquently described the sound of gongs in *Music of Java* (1934):

> These gongs possess a sound that grips one through the splendour that emanates from them, spreading an atmosphere of truly lofty restfulness and power. Whoever has been fortunate enough, be it only once, to hear the benefaction of this timeless booming tone, dominating the teeming sounds of the gamelan, and to hear it, as it were, come out of the silence of eternity, will forever carry it with him as a most precious memory.

Colin McPhee played Bach for one of his Balinese teachers on his Steinway concert grand, which he got in Java. The reaction was 'Nice, but where's the gong?' The Balinese find Western music complicated and without order, too many notes, baffling in its emotional climaxes, and leading nowhere. But they like jazz and can feel the rhythm immediately.

- *Gong Agung*
  Large, hanging gong, deep and resonant, hit with a soft, padded mallet, not dampened after it is hit.
- *Kempur*
  Medium, hanging gong, pitched higher, hit with a soft, padded mallet.
- *Kemong*
  Small, hanging gong, high pitched, hit with a hard mallet.
- *Kempli*
  Small, horizontal gong, held on the player's lap or in a wooden stand, hit with a hard mallet, plays the beat evenly throughout, like a metronome.

Metallophones

These are a number of different sized instruments, which look like xylophones, with bronze keys over bamboo resonators. The keys are hit with mallets, causing them to vibrate. After a key has been hit, the left hand immediately dampens it by grasping the key with the thumb and forefinger to stop the sound merging and blurring in the next note. They are housed in elaborately carved jackfruit or teak boxes.

- *Gangsa*
  Ten keys, hit with a hard mallet, these instruments sit at the back and play brilliant, ornamental parts. They give the gamelan a shimmering and luminous sound.
- *Pemade*
  Mid-register.
- *Kantilan*
  Highest register, one octave higher than a pemade.
- *Ugal*
  Fifteen keys, hit with a hard mallet, one octave lower than a pemade.

Gong   *Kantilan*

- *Calung*
  Low, five keys, hit with a soft mallet.
- *Panyacah*
  Low, five keys, hit with a rubber tipped mallet.
- *Jegogan*
  Lowest, five keys, hit with a soft mallet.

Gong Chimes

These are horizontal chimes playing a melody.

- *Reyong*

  The *reyong* is a long framed instrument, holding twelve inverted bronze gongs in a single row, which are hit with two wooden mallets, wrapped with cord at the ends, by four players sitting alongside each other, each player being responsible for his own section of between two and four kettles.

- *Trompong*

  The *trompong* is similar to the *reyong*, with ten inverted bronze gongs in a single row, played by only one person, whose arms need to be long, using a pair of mallets. The *trompong*, along with the *suling* and *rebab*, are the only instruments which improvise. It is placed in front of the ensemble, like the piano in an orchestra, and the player sits on his knees. Sometimes he twirls his mallets.

Trompong

Cymbals

- *Ceng-Ceng*: **Cymbals**

  Ceng-Ceng are small bronze cymbals, fastened on to a carved wooden base facing up, and played with a hand-held one in each hand facing down. They add colour and excitement and play around the *gangsa*.

- *Ceng-Ceng Kopyak*

  Ceng-Ceng Kopyak are a pair of large hand-held crash cymbals.

Kendang: Drums

These are double-ended drums, made of jackfruit with cow skin heads, held across the lap and the most difficult instruments in the gamelan. Two drummers play as one and they sit in the front. The larger, female drum sets the rhythm and tempo and leads the orchestra. Sometimes soft, other times loud, the constantly-changing beat of the drums creates excitement and tension.

Ceng-Ceng: cymbals

Suling: Flute

The *suling* is a high pitched flute, difficult to hear above the noise. It is played using a circular breathing technique to produce a constant tone. The player breathes in through his nose and stores the air in his cheeks while blowing air into the instrument.

Rebab: Lute

The *rebab* is an ancient two-stringed lute which originated in Afghanistan no later than the 8th century, and was spread via Islamic trading routes over much of North Africa, the Middle East and the Far East, arriving in Indonesia in the 16th century. It has a heart-shaped body of wood covered with a membrane from a cow bladder. The bow is made of horsehair and a descendant of the hunting bow. Plucking strings produces a very short sound whereas a bow played over vibrating strings produces a much longer note. The *rebab* is one of the leading instruments in the gamelan and ancestor of the violin.

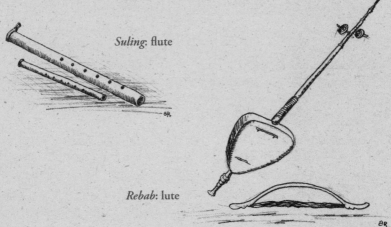

Suling: flute

Rebab: lute

Chapter 56

Balinese Dress

Dress Optional

The ambiguous 'Dress Optional' statement in Western party invitations never applies to Balinese ceremonial dress. Formal dress, called *pakaian adat*, while capable of being a fashion statement, is a symbolic statement and a religious obligation.

Divine Origin

According to the manuscripts, when humans were created they were naked. Siwa's son Kala ate them, which distressed Wisnu, the Preserver. Wisnu and Indra sent some gods and goddesses to Earth to civilise human beings. Ratih, goddess of the moon, taught men how to weave clothes from vegetables.

Humans wore grass to cover their bodies. On rare occasions the aboriginal Bali Aga people of Trunyan on the coast of Lake Batur perform a dance called *Berutuk* when they wear dried banana leaves and look like haystacks on legs. Old Balinese texts say that thread from the leaves of the *bayu* plant was spun and woven into fabric.

Chakras

Chakras are energy centres in our bodies. The Balinese believe that certain emotions and desires are associated with each *chakra* and the purpose of *pakaian adat* is to control them and focus attention on higher purposes. Tantric teachings, from which these beliefs are likely to be derived, also concentrate on the *chakras*.

Formal Dress

The Balinese wear their finest clothes at the temple. These consist of lengths of cloth draped, wrapped or tied tightly around the body. Only flat woven pieces of fabric are worn, never tube sarongs, which are strictly for casual wear.

Men and women wear a *kamben*, usually batik, wrapped tight around the waist. Men wrap it anti-clockwise and tie it into a fold in front of the navel. Women wrap it clockwise and tuck it in at the waist on the right-hand side.

Underskirt

On very important occasions women sometimes wear an underskirt, wrapped so that the left-hand, lower part shows when walking. They also wear a black corset around the body and over it a coloured sash, often adorned with gold leaf or bronze paint.

Women sometimes wear an upper garment, which is wrapped tightly around the upper body leaving the shoulders free, or a larger shawl called a *selendang*, thrown over one shoulder. Until the 1930s Balinese women went to the temple topless, but the Dutch persuaded them to cover up.

Udeng headdress for priest and for an ordinary person.

Formal dress to go to the temple, called *pakaian adat*, while capable of being a fashion statement, is a symbolic statement and a religious obligation.

Kebaya

Slightly less formal is the long-sleeved, lacy blouse called a *kebaya*, which was originally Javanese. The Balinese *kebaya* is different from the Javanese one. The Balinese one has looser sleeves to allow for movement while working in the fields or the market.

Saput

Men also wear a short flat piece of cloth over the kamben called a *saput*, which is often bright yellow or white, but can be other colours, with a decorative border, and a sash is tied over both. If the ceremony is informal, an ordinary shirt is worn, but if it is formal, a white jacket called a safari, is worn with gold buttons.

Udeng

Men also wear a headdress called an *udeng* or *destar*, which is symbolic of the Balinese *Ulu Candra*, which are signs meaning the Hindu Trinity. The front wing-like vertical appendage symbolises Siwa. It is also a symbol for the male *lingga*. The *lingga* is itself symbolic of Siwa. The circular base symbolises Wisnu and the part wrapped around the head, which is like a half-moon or sun, symbolises Brahma. The whole thing may also be a symbolic *yoni* or 'female principle', since Brahma is the creator of life.

Chakras and Formal Dress

Balinese formal dress controls the six *chakras*:

* **The Third Eye**
  The third eye is connected to pure energy and is associated with enlightenment. The purpose of a man's *udeng* is to tie and focus his consciousness to this point of utter purity and remove personal desires, which hold a person down. Women wear a white headband at important ceremonies for the same purpose.

* **The Throat**
  This *chakra* is connected to the ether and is associated with knowledge, wisdom and understanding. This area remains open and flows freely.

* **The Heart**
  The heart is connected to the air and is associated with sharing, love, devotion, selfless service and compassion. It is above the *selendang* and, although it is covered by a shirt or *kebaya*, is open and flows freely.

* **The Navel**
  The navel is connected to fire and is associated with power, authority, immortality, longevity, fame and wealth. These are harnessed by the *selendang*.

- **The Genitals**
  The genitals are connected to water and are associated with family, procreation, sexual urges and fantasy. These are harnessed by the sash and *saput*.

- **The Perineum**
  The perineum is connected to the earth and is associated with security, physical comforts, basic biological needs and shelter. These are harnessed by the *kamben*.

Uniforms

The Balinese are enthusiastic wearers of uniforms. It indicates membership of a group, such as a political party, a gamelan group or a *banjar*. Royal families sometimes dress alike at formal functions.

School uniforms are the same for all government schools: red and white for primary school (the colour of the Indonesian flag), blue and white for junior high school and grey and white for senior high school. A change of clothes has been introduced recently. Balinese children wear formal temple dress to school on special holy days.

The numerous political parties have bright colours to differentiate them at election time. Their supporters dress in the appropriate colours and hand out T-shirts to anyone who will take them. Public servants have a variety of tight-fitting uniforms.

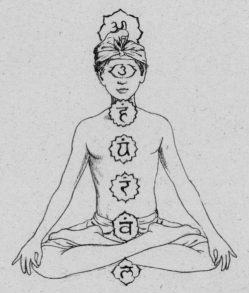

Balinese formal dress
controls the six *chakras*.

Chapter 57

Textile Techniques

Statues Wear Textiles

Textiles are at the heart of Balinese culture. They have ritual as well as economic importance. It is a living tradition and there are constantly new designs and motifs. They are not made for human beings only. Statues, buildings and rocks wear them on special occasions. Gods are given them as offerings and the deceased are covered in textiles prior to cremation. Merchants from abroad may have brought the first materials and it is likely that weaving techniques from South Asia influenced Indonesia.

Early References

Chinese records in the 6th century refer to cotton weaving in Sumatra and to a king in north Sumatra wearing silk. The 7th century Srivijaya empire, based in Palembang in southeast Sumatra, traded in Indian cotton fabrics and sold them to the Chinese. There is a relief of a lady preparing yarn on the walls of Borobudur Temple in central Java in the 9th century.

Silk was being woven by the 11th century in Java, where silk was being produced as well as imported from China. Arabs and other traders used textiles as a medium of exchange. In 1603 there is a report that the price of imported cloth was worth 40 pounds of nutmeg on the island of Banda.

It is difficult to trace their history as Bali's tropical climate means that very few are older than a century. Weaving, particularly the finer textiles, was virtually a monopoly of royal and priestly families in precolonial times. A lot of women lived in the aristocratic houses as a result of polygamy and they had a lot of spare time. Housework was done by servants. It was not appropriate for high caste women to appear in public too often, so weaving was an ideal occupation.

Women and Men

All aspects of textile production are carried out by women: harvesting cotton, dyeing yarn, weaving, selling and controlling the money. Men make the looms and spinning wheels and may also be involved in designing patterns. Daughters learn from their mothers. Good weavers are good wives and much in demand.

Bali

Textiles are a major source of employment, both for weavers and sellers. They work on low overheads and small profit margins. There is constant demand at home as well as from tourists and international buyers.

Cotton

Cotton is used for the majority of Balinese textiles. In the 15th century the Portuguese found a flourishing cotton industry in Indonesia, but that declined, and like most Southeast Asian countries Indonesia now imports most of its cotton yarn from the United States and India. Some cotton grows in Sumatra, Flores, Sumbawa and Lombok. It is often grown in the corner of a rice field or planted between other crops like maize or cassava.

Silk

Silk is light, strong and prized, but expensive. China developed silk production as early as 3000 BC. Hardly any silk is produced in Indonesia. Silk is made from filaments from the cocoons of moths that live on mulberry trees.

Metallic Yarns

Gold and silver yarns are popular in Bali, which is recognised for the quality of its textiles incorporating them. Most of the yarn is imported, though gold and silver used to be obtained by melting down Dutch coins. As the gold and silver threads age, they become brittle and have to be treated with great care.

Synthetic Yarns

Rayon, acrylic and polyester, from Java and Hong Kong, are used extensively, because they are cheaper, lighter and easy to handle. They take dyes well. The colours are varied and do not fade as quickly as natural dyes and they do not crease easily.

Dyes

Natural dyes as well as chemical dyes are used. The procedure is complex for natural dyes, which are mainly obtained from tropical plants. The seeds, petals, fruits, leaves, bark or roots are pounded in a mortar, water is added, and the mixture is left for a week. Impurities are skimmed off and the thread is added and kneaded. A fixing agent like slaked lime is used. Other substances like betel nut juice and tannic acid may be added to strengthen the colour. The yarn is then put in the sun to oxidise the dye. At night it is put back in the dye. This may be repeated as many as thirty times. The recipes are often closely guarded secrets.

Native indigo plants give a dark blue-black colour and have been used for centuries. They are grown all over Indonesia. The root bark of the *morinda* tree is extracted to produce red, purple and brown dyes, used for batik textiles. In Tenganan in east Bali it can take up to six years to make the prized shade of red for *geringsing* textiles. Turmeric is an ingredient for yellows, browns and oranges. The shell of the mangosteen fruit produces a dark purple.

The Germans invented a chemical version of indigo in 1884 and many other colours subsequently.

The light backstrap loom can be set up almost anywhere, allowing the weaver to work indoors, outdoors or on the porch, all the while keeping an eye on other business.

Looms

Textiles are made by intermeshing one group of threads, the weft, at right angles to another group, known as the warp. This is weaving and it is accomplished by a loom, of which there are various kinds.

If you imagine the rectangular shape traditional backstrap loom and the weaver sitting on the floor at one end, the warp threads are the long ones facing her and the weft are the horizontal ones.

Designs and Colours

In colonial and pre-colonial times many designs and colours were reserved for royal families. Some designs were indigenous, others were adopted from textiles imported from abroad, for example, the *patola* patterns of Gujarat in western India, which were traded in Indonesia in the 19th century.

Ritual Use

Textiles have mystical associations, perhaps none more so than the *double-ikat geringsing* from Tenganan, which are thought to ward off evil, and are therefore used in ceremonies involving danger, such as the Balinese tooth-filing ceremony.

Chapter 58

Balinese Textiles

Ikat

The Balinese are known for their high-quality *ikats*. *Ikat* comes from the Indonesian word 'to tie'. The design is dyed on to the threads before they are woven. It could be the warp threads or the weft threads.

In Bali they prefer the weft threads, weft *ikat*. The process by which the pattern is made is very time consuming. Bundles of weft threads are tied together with dye-resistant materials, like palm leaves, grasses and rags, over the areas which are to remain undyed, and then dipped into a dye bath. The pattern is revealed by removing the resist material. The finest designs are obtained by using the smallest number of threads. In some fabrics this may just be three, but it is very laborious.

It is called a resist-dye technique. Repeated tyings and dyeings eventually produce a textile of dazzling multi-hued patterns. Normally light colours are used first, so that extra shades and colours can be obtained by further dyeing. The dye usually penetrates under the edges of the resist material, giving the coloured areas fuzzy outlines, which are typical of these textiles. If the designs are applied to both warp and weft, it is called 'double *ikat*', for which the Balinese in Tenganan are world famous.

Originally only princely families were allowed to weave and wear *ikats*. Now everyone wears them. The earliest pieces, made of cotton, date from the late 19th to early 20th century and came from Buleleng in north Bali. Sometimes silk was used.

The patterns were originally mostly geometric shapes but later representational motifs were used, like animals, flowers, *wayang* puppet figures and stars. Early naturally dyed *ikats* were red, then yellow, then green. In the 1930s weavers outside the courts started making them. New designs and materials like rayon and new colours appeared. Borders disappeared as they came to be sold by the metre, and after Independence production soared. New uses were found for them, like furnishings.

Geringsing

The most spectacular textiles ever produced in Southeast Asia are the *geringsing* made only in the small attractive village of Tenganan in east Bali. There are very few other places in the world where similar textiles are woven: Japan, Guatamala and India. *Geringsing* is mentioned in a literary work of 1365.

The people of Tenganan are Bali Aga people, who believe that the god Indra created them and then taught them the art of double *ikat*. Their rituals have to be carried out by people who are pure in mind and body. That purity is protected by the magical power of the *geringsing* textiles. They protect the village and are only worn during major religious events.

It can take between five and eight years to weave a cloth. They are complicated to dye and difficult to weave. The designs are applied to both warp and weft and they have to be constantly compared and measured to ensure that the pattern is aligned properly on the finished textile.

They are cotton and the most striking feature is the muted colours: red, reddish-brown, dark blue or black violet. The women of Tenganan are not allowed to use indigo and have to go to the neighbouring village of Bug-Bug to dye the yarn blue. Back in Tenganan *morinda* is used to dye the textiles red. It can take many months to get the distinctive red. If the indigo areas are overdyed they become brownish-purple.

The patterns are similar to Indian *patola* textiles from Gujarat in western India. Records show that by at least the 16th century *patolas* were being sent to Southeast Asia. An intriguing piece of research carried out in 1978 by Indonesian and Swiss scientists showed that eighteen of the Tengananese inhabitants had a rare enzyme that is characteristic of Indians. It suggests that there is some genetic connection between the people of Tenganan and Indians.

The designs are built up from little triangles. The central panel's patterns flow horizontally and vertically in some and horizontally, vertically and diagonally in others. Another pattern is the *wayang* puppet style, where semicircular patterns within patterns cover the whole panel. Segments contain stars, emblems, animals and architectural elements. It is interesting that puppet performances are unknown in Tenganan, which possibly suggests that the courts of east Java and Bali commissioned the *wayang* patterns.

They are woven on a continuous warp and are tubular when taken off the loom. They may be offered as clothing for the deities and ancestors in that uncut state, but once they are cut, they can only be worn by humans.

Numerous villages in east Bali use *geringsing* during ceremonies to protect them against danger. They wrap a *geringsing* around the pillow on which the person's head rests during a tooth-filing ceremony. They are also used to cover ceremonial utensils in temples and as a shroud to cover the body before a cremation. The *wayang* style is preferred.

The most spectacular textiles ever produced in Southeast Asia are the *geringsing* made only in the small attractive village of Tenganan in east Bali. (Collection of Ni Wayan Murni)

Batik

This is probably the most internationally famous Indonesian textile and very prevalent in Bali. Batik uses the resist method of dying cotton, or less commonly, silk. Warm wax is applied to the cloth to make the design. The wax will not receive the dye and is removed in warm water after dying. Numerous colours can be introduced. As with *ikat*, light colours are used first to allow for overdying.

Well defined patterns are created by the use of copper stamps called *cap*, which were invented in the 19th century in Java. The stamps themselves are collectors' items. More difficult and time-consuming is the old method of using a brass pipe called a *canting* to create flows of wax. It takes between thirty and fifty days to make a 6 foot (2 metre) length of cloth using a *canting*.

After one side has been completed

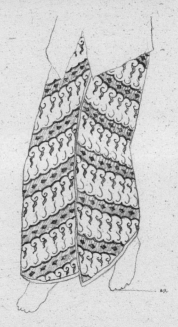

Batik is probably the most internationally famous Indonesian textile and very prevalent in Bali. It uses the resist method of dying cotton.

the patterns are copied on the back. Good batik is reversible. During the process some colour may run along the fine cracks of the wax making a marbled effect that is characteristic of batik.

Songket

Songket is one of Indonesia's foremost textile techniques. Additional patterns are woven into the material by introducing supplementary weft or warp threads which float over the base threads. The earliest ones were silk, followed by gold and silver, originally brought by Indian traders.

Songkets were restricted to the higher castes until the last thirty years or so. They were worn in grand performances and ceremonial displays. There are no restrictions now, but they are expensive. Originally they were made of silk and then cotton and latterly rayon, and silk mixed with artificial silk or viscose in an attempt to keep the cost down.

Sidemen in east Bali developed into a *songket* centre in the 17th century and has remained the leading place ever since. The oldest surviving pieces are unlikely to be more than a hundred years old.

Perada

The Balinese decorate coloured textiles, known as *perada*, with gold patterns of plants and flowers and geometric designs. No weaving is involved. The cotton or silk is adorned with gold leaf or gold dust. The gold is glued to the pattern. Originally it was restricted to the courts and only practised by men. The base fabric consists of simple plain, striped or checked cloth in brilliant colours against which the gold stands out.

Perada materials are stiff and brittle where the gold has been applied and they cannot be washed. People only wear them for special occasions, such as tooth-filings and weddings. *Legong* and *topeng* dancers wear *perada* costumes. To reduce the cost, bronze pigment paint is applied instead, but it is a poor imitation.

Poleng

Poleng is Balinese chequered cloth, wrapped around statues, drums, pavilions, people, stones and trees. It is dazzling and powerful and has a special meaning for the Balinese: it represents duality. The squares are usually black and white or black and red.

The Balinese see the world in terms of opposites, good and bad, day and night, mountain and sea. This duality forms the whole and one cannot exist without the other, so *poleng* is the perfect representation of this worldview.

The squares are perfect black or perfect white. Grey squares contain strands of both, where the weft and warp intersect. White represents goodness, the gods and health; black represents evil, the underworld and disease.

Poleng material is woven or printed on white cloth. The black and white squares may be of different sizes depending on the cloth. When worn, the side of the material with bigger squares is worn on the inside, smaller squares on the outside. *Poleng* is seldom used on shrines, except shrines dedicated to Durga, the goddess of death. It is rarely put in the inner, holiest part of the temple. On those rare occasions it is placed in the *kelod*, impure direction. It is never displayed on the pagoda-like *meru* shrines or the *padmasana*. Sometimes it covers the ground in temple ceremonies. People who walk on it will be free of evil spirits.

Poleng protects human beings. In *Barong*-Rangda dances, Rangda's warriors wear *poleng*. It is associated with the gods of the underworld in the case of inanimate objects. In processions of gods associated with the underworld, one of the accompanying drums is wrapped in *poleng*, sometimes with a red border. If a *poleng* has a red border, it represents the Trinity. It is also worn by the *pecalang*, the men of the village who protect the village and monitor processions.

Poleng is Balinese chequered cloth, wrapped around statues, drums, pavilions, people, stones and trees. It is dazzling and powerful and has a special meaning for the Balinese.

Chapter 59

Mads Lange and Walter Spies

Two Balinese Expats

There are two Balinese expats, one living in the 19th century and the other living in the 20th century, who stand out in their influence on Balinese affairs, one not well-known, Mads Lange, and the other very well-known, Walter Spies.

Mads Johansen Lange, 1807-1856

Mads Johansen Lange, a blue-eyed, blond-haired Dane, known as the White Raja of Bali, is buried in Kuta. He has been forgotten but was very influential in Balinese history. Born on 18 September 1807 in Rudkobing, a port on Langeland Island, he was a merchant, mediator, adventurer and sailor. Lange, three younger brothers and Captain John Burd, a friend and son of Scottish parents raised in Denmark, sailed for Hong Kong in 1833 and established a company called Burd & Co. Lange never returned to Denmark.

From Hong Kong Lange sailed to Bali and Lombok, looking for opportunities. The position of the narrow strait between Bali and Lombok was ideal as it was the main trading route from Singapore, Batavia (now Jakarta) and Surabaya to Australia. He picked Lombok as the base for his trading venture, possibly because rice production was extremely high there and much greater than in Bali. It was high because of fertility from ash deposits from the huge Tambora eruption in 1815. There were two kingdoms, who were rivals, Mataram-Lombok to the north and the more powerful Karangasem-Lombok to the south. Karangasem-Lombok welcomed him and Lange became their trusted adviser and harbour chief and was granted a virtual monopoly of all trading in Lombok. In return they wanted modern weapons and Western luxuries. He built a factory and warehouse and his business grew fast. It did not take long for competition to arrive—in the shape of George Peacock King, born of English parents living in Bengal, who allied himself in 1835 to the raja of Mataram-Lombok. There was enough business for both of them, but a succession of land and sea fights between the two rajas culminated in defeat for Karangasem-Lombok in 1839. Lange escaped to Bali with nothing but his life, a few personal items, his horse and ship.

The Raja Kesiman gave him and his brothers enough land on the beach in Kuta to build a house, factory and warehouses, from which he traded on a large scale and did very well from the start. He was neither Dutch nor English, both of whom they disliked. The Raja had given the Dutch a trading post the previous month next to Lange's land but had imposed so many restrictions that the business failed to take off. After five years the loss making Dutch trading post closed down. In his flamboyant style Lange visited all the rajas personally, arriving on his horse, which was twice the size of the local animals. They were impressed by his respect for local customs.

Lange, the ultimate expat, lived in Bali style, with a well-stocked wine cellar, billiard table, chamber orchestra, two wives, concubines, children, servants and slaves. One wife was Balinese, Nyai Kenyer, who gave him two boys, and one Chinese, Ong Sang Nio, who gave him a daughter. There was also a male Danish dalmation, which liked to mate with the local dogs and probably was responsible for the current breed of Balinese dalmations. The Raja Kesiman often made the three hour journey from his palace to visit for a game of billiards. As a broker in the lucrative slave trade, Lange would have got the slaves at trade price.

Lange performed a useful role mediating between the Dutch and the South Balinese rajas and was instrumental in getting two important, although fudged and misleading, treaties signed with the Raja Kesiman in 1841 and 1842, under which the Raja appeared to recognize Dutch sovereignty and give up Balinese customary rights to take possession of shipwrecked cargo. Mediation became a profitable occupation. As an example, he settled a dispute between the Dutch and the Raja, and in return was appointed *perbekel*, the district official for Kuta and given authority to tax sailing vessels. The taxes were as high as those in European harbours. The Dutch found him so useful that they offered him citizenship of the Dutch East Indies in 1844, which he accepted.

Lange's business grew. He owned or hired (it is not clear which) between nine and twelve ships in the 1840s. His ships gathered rice, coconut oil, animals, cotton, tobacco, coffee and other goods from neighbouring islands, which he sold to visiting traders from his warehouse. Perhaps his most profitable business, however, was importing bronze *kepeng* coins from China and selling them at 100% profit in Bali. He had the monopoly. The coins have a square hole in the centre and Lange employed Balinese women to string them in loops of 200. They were the dominant currency. Goods were often bought by reference to a *kepeng* and even the value of bartered goods was calculated in *kepengs*. The demand was so great that the selling price went up and Lange made a killing. In the 1840s the selling rate in Bali was 700 to the Spanish dollar and by the 1850s it was 1200, but Lange's buying price remained the same. *Kepeng* were and still are used in Balinese ceremonies. He bought silk and opium from China and textiles and weapons from India. Two slaughterhouses owned by him supplied dried beef to the Dutch garrisons in Java.

Lange played a pivotal role as a shuttle diplomat between the Dutch and the Balinese in the wars of Dutch invasion of 1846, 1848 and 1849. The Dutch navy blockaded the island between 1848 and 1849. Lange worked hard and brokered an historic truce, a treaty which was signed by the two sides in his house on 15 July 1849, and gave the Balinese freedom for many years to come. The Dutch were pleased and made him a 'Knight of the Dutch Lion' in December 1849.

The good times were coming to an end. Lange's business was badly hit by the blockade. The rice harvest suffered from the wars, which a plague of rats made worse and exports practically ceased. A smallpox epidemic in 1850 disrupted social life and some of his employees died. Then there was a water shortage. Meanwhile the Dutch were building up Singaraja in the north as the main port. It was also the centre of the opium trade. The Raja of Kesiman, now in his late 60s, retired from public life and spent his time restoring old temples and hunting deer. Lange's protection had gone.

Lange was planning to leave Bali for good and sail to Denmark in 1856 when he was invited to a banquet at Denpasar Palace by the new raja. Upon returning home he was violently sick, coughing up blood and his lips turned blue. He had been poisoned and died two days later on 13 May at home at the age of 48. He was eighteen years in Bali. His forgotten tomb in Kuta, guarded by a dalmation statue, was renovated in 2007, the 200th anniversary of his birth. It lies in a small Chinese grave-yard on a road named after him, Jalan Tuan Langa. Nothing remains of his house.

Christian Peter Lange, his nephew, came to Bali in 1847 to help his uncle. His wife joined him in 1856 and is said to have been the first white woman to come to Bali. Christian inherited the business, but failed to make a profit, sold up and returned to Denmark in 1863. He died in 1869. Kuta declined after Lange's death and did not revive for another hundred years, until the hippies discovered surf and mind-expanding sunsets.

Walter Spies, 1895-1942

Bali's most influential visitor was Russian-born Walter Spies, painter, writer, linguist, musician, dancer, choreographer, curator of the Bali Museum and lover of young men. He was the son of the affluent German consul in Petersburg and lived a Bohemian life in and out of Russia, which ended when he was interned during the Russian Revolution. After he was freed he went to Berlin and inherited a fortune from a friend, which enabled him to live independently.

At the age of 28 Walter Spies decided to leave Europe. He wrote in his journal,

> I then decided to just go somewhere, anywhere, to a faraway
> land. And after going on a challenging and formidable
> journey as a sailor in a cargo vessel I arrived in Java, where
> I decided to jump ship!

He worked first as a pianist in a Chinese cinema in Bandung and then gave piano lessons to Russians living in Java. From there he went to Yogyakarta. In a letter to his family he said that the Sultan of Yogyakarta 'discovered' him when he was playing in a dance-band on the occasion of a visit from the President of the Philippines. He had replaced the usual pianist and was playing in the Kraton, the Sultan's Palace. In the letter he expresses his disgust at having to hammer out Foxtrots on the piano while 'fat white meat-masses wallowed on the dance-floor'.

The Sultan noticed that somebody different was playing and called him in for a chat. The next day he was invited to become the *Kapelmeister* of the Western orchestra as well as the official piano player in the Kraton.

It is perhaps no coincidence that Maria Sitsen-Russer, a conservatory educated classical singer and wife of the Dutch director of the building authority in Yogyakarta had complained that she was aghast at the terrible quality of the Dutch national anthem at the Kraton on official occasions. She claims that she suggested to the Sultan that he employ Spies to train the orchestra.

He stayed in the Sultan's palace for a year, where he directed the European orchestra. The king of Ubud, Cokorda Gede Raka Sukawati, came to the palace on a family visit and met Spies. They became extremely good friends and the King invited him to visit Bali in 1925. In 1927 the King suggested he take up residence in Bali.

Initially he stayed in the royal palace, but then built his own bamboo house, which had a thatched roof and a studio in Campuan on land he rented from the royal family. He brought his baby grand piano, a German bicycle and a butterfly net. A keen collector, he caught butterflies, put them in gold leaf boxes and sent them to museums in Europe. Unfortunately his whole portfolio of detailed paintings of them was lost at sea in 1942 when he perished as well. His house is now in the grounds of the Tjampuhan Hotel, which was opened by Ubud's royal family in 1961.

His contacts, writings, research and encouragement of artistic talent have had the greatest enduring influence on Bali. He was interested in every aspect of Balinese life and culture. In Margaret Mead's words he had 'worked out a most perfect relationship' between himself and Bali. He loved Bali and thought of his life as an eternal birthday party. He wrote,

> I play in life and I believe in the play… This is living a life,
> playing a life, being alive.

Musicologists, anthropologists, novelists and the rich and famous all beat a trail to his door: Clemenceau, Cole Porter, Leopold Stowkowski, Lord Mountbatten, H.G. Wells, Charlie Chaplin on a world-wide tour in 1932 and his brother Sydney stayed three weeks, Noël Coward, the ethno-musicologist, Colin McPhee, his anthropologist wife, Jane Belo, and the novelist, Vicki Baum, to name but a few. In the mid-1930s Bali was the in-place, the jet-set's resort even before jets had been invented. Europe was on edge and not the place to be—Hitler had just come to power.

Margaret Mead, 31 years old, 5 feet 2 inches tall, and her third husband, Gregory Bateson, spent their honeymoon in Bali in 1936. They stayed two years and returned for a brief stay in 1939. Both carried out anthropological research. They measured how long people went into trance, with a stopwatch, took lots of photos (Bateson took 25,000) and collected more than 1,200 paintings and 1,000 carvings.

Margaret Mead set out to research the cultural aspects of schizophrenia. She thought schizophrenia must exist in Bali. This was ultramodern stuff in the 1930s, and sure enough, she came to the conclusion that all Balinese were essentially schizoid. It seems like a fantastic generalisation. At the same time she surprisingly shared and endorsed the descriptions of Bali as a 'dream island', 'last paradise' and 'island of the gods'. Spies seems to have been slightly amused by his friend's theory, but too polite to criticize it.

Even before Bateson and Mead's book *Balinese Character* was published, a leading Dutch psychiatrist Van Wulften Palthe concluded that she was wrong. Gordon Jensen, an American psychiatrist, and Luh Ketut Suryani, a Balinese psychiatrist, also decided that she was wrong in 1992. Bateson and Mead were not equipped at all for psychoanalytical research. They were not trained in psychiatry, nor did they speak Balinese well. Their marriage ended in divorce in 1950.

The most flamboyant of Spies' visitors was the Woolworth's heiress and film star, Barbara Hutton, who fell madly in love with him and may not have realised that he was a homosexual. She dragged him off to Cambodia to look at Angkor Wat. She paid for some paintings and he built her a bungalow and pool next to his but by the time it was finished she had moved to Persia and never saw it. The swimming pool is now a lotus pond.

Spies explained Balinese life to his visitors, including Miguel Covarrubias, the Mexican painter and ethnologist, who wrote the influential book *Island of Bali*, published in 1937. He was also Vicki Baum's main source for her novel *A Tale from Bali*, which contains detailed descriptions of Balinese culture and life. Covarrubias gave him a glowing report,

> In his charming, devil-may-care way, Spies is familiar
> with every phase of Balinese life and has been a constant
> source of disinterested information to every archeologist,
> anthropologist, musician or artist who has come to Bali.

Spies also strongly influenced local painters and woodcarvers. He painted himself in a naïve, Rousseau-like style, and sold his paintings for high prices. One sold for enough to keep him in Bali for a year. He was passionate about insects and marine life and advised on a number of films and choreographed the *Kecak* dance with Katharane Mershon, the American dancer-ethnologist, for a German film.

He took excellent photographs, with an eye for lighting. His photographs appear in a book he co-wrote with American dance critic, Beryl de Zoete, *Dance and Drama in Bali* (1938). His photographic talents are discussed in detail and many previously unpublished photographs were published in Hitchcock and Norris's book *Bali, the Imaginary Museum* (1995).

In the late 1930s the Second World War was looming. The Dutch were becoming alarmed by Germany. In 1938 the government started a widespread crackdown on homosexuals pursuant to a law that had not been previously enforced. In 1938 and 1939, 223 men from all over the Netherlands East Indies were prosecuted for having sex with boys below the age of consent. Europeans, Eurasians, Chinese and Indonesians were charged. The majority who were convicted were Dutch. Spies was German. He was arrested on New Year's Eve, 1938 and charged with turning his house in Ubud into 'a rendezvous for homosexuals' and having sex with a young boy. He was convicted and imprisoned. The Balinese were puzzled and shocked by the arrest. Homosexuality was not a crime to them and they brought his favourite gamelan to play outside the prison window. Jane Belo, Margaret Mead, Gregory Bateson and Katharane Mershon found him a lawyer. The boy's father told the trial judge, 'He's our best friend and it was an honour for my son to be in his company. If both are in agreement, why fuss?' Margaret Mead and other influential people spoke in his defence. She said, 'It's difficult to tell the age of these Balinese boys' and claimed that in Bali homosexuality was simply a pastime for young unmarried men. He was released on 1 September 1939.

When Hitler invaded Holland in May 1940 all German nationals were rounded up. Spies was the last German left in Bali. He was deported in January 1942 and put on board the *Van Imhoff*, a grossly overcrowded ship bound for the internment camps in Ceylon. The day after it set sail, the Japanese bombed the ship off Sumatra, not far from the island of Nias. The Dutch crew abandoned the sinking ship, and did not even bother to unlock the hatches and release the prisoners, who all drowned, including Walter Spies.

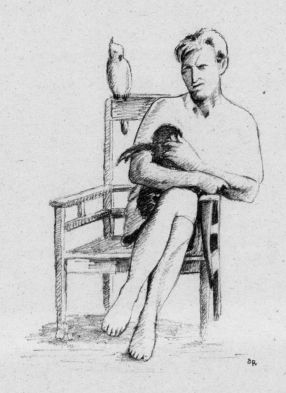

Bali's most influential visitor was Russian-born Walter Spies, painter, writer, linguist, musician, dancer and choreographer.

Chapter 60

Summing Up: Do The Balinese Think Like Westerners?

Exotic

Western tourists and anthropologists have taken a delight in Bali and the Balinese because they are mysterious, exotic and Asian. They are the classic, romantic 'other'. Yet, how different are they? As we have seen, in the scheme of things, *Homo sapiens* is a newcomer to the party of life and Asians have existed for only the last 75,000 years. Could it possibly be that they think differently from Westerners? We usually take it for granted that all human beings perceive and reason in the same way, but the account of Balinese culture in the previous chapters and recent experiments on fellow Asians may suggest otherwise.

West is West and East is East

Western civilisation traces its roots back to ancient Greece of 2,500 years ago. The Greeks had a great sense of individuality. Everyone acted as a sole agent. They debated their individual viewpoints in the marketplace and decided matters by argument rather than being dictated to from above. Democracy began in Greece in the 5th century BC. With this sense of personal agency came the idea of freedom and privacy. Isaiah Berlin (1909-1997), the Russian born Oxford philosopher, pinpointed the start of this thinking to sixteen or so years after the death of Aristotle in 322 BC, when Epicurus and after him Zeno began to teach in Athens. It was a source of pleasure for the Greeks to search for underlying principles to explain the world. Our word 'school' comes from the Greek *schole* meaning 'leisure'.

People became markedly individualistic in the first couple of centuries following the year 1000. The old feudal structure was breaking down and people started to own property. This led to specialisations in work and an increase in trade, markets and money. People saw themselves as independent, not defined by their relationship to the lord of the manor or membership of congregations and guilds. This individuality in Europe manifested itself in many ways, which have continued to this day. There was a rise in self-expression. People wrote autobiographies and diaries and there was an increase in literature written in the first person. Portraits were painted for the first time since the second century AD and Italian artists depicted deep emotional states. In architecture houses had private rooms for study and many people were given nicknames which highlighted personal characteristics. There was an increase in self-confidence which manifested itself strongly in the Renaissance. People became competitive and achievers. They sought fame, the pursuit of which may have started with the chivalry of knights in the Middle Ages. This passion and optimism was apparent in the Age of Exploration.

Very broadly speaking life in the West with this concentration on the individual still follows the same path. What about life in the East? Whereas in the West the focus is on the individual, in the East, as a generalisation, it is more on context and harmony. While a special occasion in London or New York might be a show or a night at the opera, a family get together is more appreciated in Bali or Beijing. A life properly lived is a life lived harmoniously in a network of interlocking obligations. A Balinese person cannot survive alone as a solitary individual; he is part of a large, complex, hierarchical collective, where loners, debate and confrontation are not encouraged.

Social Life
Bali is largely an agricultural society based on rice farming. People in such societies have to get along with each other in a reasonably harmonious way. The Balinese join *banjars* and *subaks* as a matter of course, where decisions are made consensually.

By contrast ancient Greece favoured hunting, fishing and trade. Such occupations require little co-operation of others. There is not the same pressure to create harmonious relations, society can permit debate and there is no need to save the other person's face. Richard Nisbett, the American psychologist, maintains that people in societies which depend on others even have a better memory for faces and social words than independent minded people.

That is not to say that there are no thrusting individuals in Bali and no shrinking violets in the West. There are. Each society has many exceptions but the general picture is reasonably clear, especially in rural Bali.

Nature

The Balinese have a deep appreciation of nature. Spirits dwell in the forests, trees and rocks. Local advertising frequently uses naturalistic settings and paintings and carvings often depict nature. Western style portraiture is not part of the Balinese tradition.

Traditional Medicine

Local healing is holistic, which takes into account the whole body, indeed the whole family and the environment and how they interact. Natural products are the source of many cures. In the West doctors usually treat individual parts. The Western medical tradition tends to be dominated by the views of the French philosopher, mathematician and scientist, René Descartes (1596-1650), the founder of modern philosophy, who proposed the total separation of mind and body, an idea that began with Plato in the 5th century BC.

Work

The Balinese work for the welfare of their entire family, not for themselves alone. Unlike Westerners, they rarely look for individual self-advancement and tend to shun promotion, preferring to avoid a position where they have to give orders to their fellow workers. Ambition is seen as arrogance.

In business the immediate contract is much less important than the continued relationship. More important than immediate profit is feeling good with the other person and typically discussions concern family affairs before business. Pure capitalism is essentially a private, selfish, and individualistic practice.

The Arts

Until recently painters did not sign their works and they still do not sign them if they are made for the temple. The subject-matter of paintings is usually busy, a state which reflects most Balinese activities. The Balinese love crowded scenes, full of bustle and activity. They do not like being alone.

An artist in the West tends to work in isolation, but this is not the case in Bali. Painters frequently work with others even on the same painting. A mask may be carved by several people.

Musical Harmony

Gamelan players play together as one group. There is no individual expression. They aim to play as one musician. The Balinese gamelan reflects the Balinese concern with unity. There are no star performers. There is not even a conductor. Dancers make their entrances and exits from preordained corners of the stage. It is not a personal decision.

Colour Coding

The colours, headdresses, mannerisms, jewellery, clothes and locations of Balinese puppets, dancers and actors follow rules (and the same rules). The scope for individuality is almost zero.

Ceremonial Foods

The desirability of sociability extends to the ranking of animals as suitable offerings. Pigs and chickens, which are highly individualistic in their behaviour, rank behind ducks, which are more social characters.

Balinese Names

One's personal name is barely used and, as Clifford Geertz pointed out, personal identities are forgotten within a few generations.

Self

Bali is a close knit society. Every Balinese inherits a set of obligations at birth according to his status. Obligations exist between ruler and ruled, parent and child, husband and wife, clan member and clan member, villager and villager. The obligations fit into a seamless, harmonious whole, which is reinforced by the divine order.

Personal identity is not important. It is the relationship that matters. Indeed most of the time the Balinese do not call themselves 'I' but refer to themselves in the third person. Children do not move out to live on their own away from the extended family. Even on marriage sons stay in the family compound and their wives join them, although this practice is beginning to change due to cramped conditions in many family compounds.

Face, In Your Face and Being Inscrutable

Asians invented 'face', and having invented it, try to save it. It is extremely unwise to make another person lose face. Westerners teach their children to be clear and unambiguous, so that their utterances can be understood independently of the context. Asians communicate indirectly, expecting listeners to understand the nuances. As a result Westerners find Asians inscrutable and Asians find Westerners too direct and in their face, often to the point of rudeness.

Dinner Parties

The Western style dinner party, where guests engage in lively discussion, does not exist in Bali. It would be a risk to group harmony. Schools teach by rote and debate is uncommon. Democracy is recent and fledgling.

The Middle Way

In Bali, confrontation is avoided. Conflict is managed by striving to find compromise. Face should be saved at all costs. They try to find the Middle Way wherever possible and shun adversarial positions, so typical of Western disputes. Law and lawyers are much less prominent than in the West, particularly the United States.

Architectural Harmony

Village layout throughout Bali is preordained, admitting only small variations to make life interesting. Building proportions are regulated and the position of structures within compounds is prescribed. The substances forming offerings are set down. Even the direction you lay your head in at night is determined. Every person, every building and every thing in its place.

Classifications

Balinese classifications are interdependent: night and day, male and female, good and evil. To understand one, you must understand the other. Indeed one cannot exist without the other. The gods are male and female, and good and evil, at the same time. The world is a unified, harmonious whole, or it ought to be, if kept in balance. There is unity in opposites and a flow from one to the other.

The Balinese do not therefore have any difficulty with the conundrum: how can there be evil in the world if God is good, omnipotent and omnipresent? To them, God is both good and bad.

Balinese Hinduism is tolerant and assimilates other ideas. There is not the concentration on actions being either right or wrong, which is in contrast to the Abrahamic religions. There have been no religious wars in Bali.

Cycles
The Balinese think of time as circular, rather than linear. Birth, death and reincarnation follow each other relentlessly. Gamelans and gongs beat cyclical forms. Birth names repeat themselves endlessly. Temple anniversaries are celebrated in cylindrical patterns. What's round comes around; *karma* sees to that.

Understanding the World
Westerners start by analysing the individual object. The world is in principle simple, knowable and logical. In Bali, and other Asian countries, on the other hand, the world is interdependent, complicated and hard to understand. An appreciation of context is fundamental to any understanding.

Seeing is Believing
It seems that not only do Asians think of the world in holistic terms but they literally see the big picture. Asians physically view objects in relation to their environments, as if through a wide-angle lens, whereas Westerners focus on objects and see fewer of them.

Richard Nisbett describes an experiment with Japanese and American students who were shown pictures of goldfish bowls with several brightly coloured fish, plants, rocks, bubbles and small animals. The students were asked what they had seen. The first answer from the Japanese was likely to refer to the environment: 'It looked like a pond', whereas the Americans were three times more likely to refer to the main fish: 'There was a big fish, maybe a trout, moving off to the left'.

Cause and Effect

Westerners tend to see specific causes, indeed that everything has a cause, while Asians attribute matters to context and appreciate that everything is connected to a multitude of different things.

Summing Up

It is important to appreciate that Westerners and Asians may think differently. There are many domains of life in which misunderstandings could be critical, not least in international affairs. Fools rush in where angels fear to tread.

The goldfish bowl experiment.

Glossary of Balinese Terms and Proper Names

Adat: customary law

Airlangga: 11th century Javanese king

Alang-alang: elephant grass thatch

Aling-aling: small screening wall

Alus: refined, civilised, polite, graceful

Amerta: holy water giving immortality

Anak Agung: title for satria or wesia, literally a 'big person'

Anantaboga: cosmic serpent

Angklung: ancient bamboo percussion instrument, used in orchestra, having only four notes

Arak: strong spirit distilled from the sugar palm

Arja: popular musical drama

Arjuna: the third Pandawa brother of the Mahabarata epic

Awig-awig: basic constitution of a group, usually written on lontar palm leaf manuscripts

Bade: cremation tower

Balé: open air pavilion

Balé Agung: major altar in a temple

Bali Aga: ancient Bali culture pre-dating the Majapahits

Balian: traditional healer

Balih-Balihan: dances done for entertainment

Banjar: village council

Banten: religious offering

Bapak: father

Baris: male warrior dance

Baris Gede: ritual warrior dance by a group of men

Barong: generic term for a masked figure, which is often a mythical animal

Barong Ket: a masked lion-like figure

Barong Landung: tall masked figures, one male, the other female

Batavia: fomer name for Jakarta, the capital of Indonesia

Batu: rock

Bebali: semi-ceremonial dances, partly for gods, partly for humans

Bebek betutu: smoked duck

Bedeg: woven bamboo

Bendesa: traditional leader of a temple

Besakih: the chief mother temple on Mount Agung

Betara: deity

Betel: nut of areca palm, pink inside, chewed with leaf of sireh vine and
    lime paste

Bilibis: dance of wild ducks, a modern creation

Bima: the second Pandawa brother of the Mahabarata epic

Boma: demon with round popping eyes

Brahma: god of creation and fire

Brahmana: the highest of the title system

Brem: sweet white or pink rice wine

Buana Agung: macrocosmos

Buana Alit: microcosmos, the individual

Buta: demon

Buta Yadnya: rituals addressed to low spirits

Cakra: points of energy in the microcosm

Calonarang: tale of the widow Rangda and the Barong-Rangda dance

Canang: offering consisting of betel nut ingredients

Candi: gateway to a temple

Candi Bentar: open gateway to a temple in the form of a split gate

Candi Kurung: closed gateway to a temple

Caru: medium-sized ritual to low spirits on the ground

Caru Agung: major ritual to low spirits

Cendrawasih: birds of paradise dance, a modern creation

Ceng-Ceng: cymbals

Cili: ancient fertility symbol

Cokorda: the title of the king or prince from the satria

Condong: maidservant

Dadap: tree with medicinal qualities

Dadia: preferentially endogamous patrilineal kinship group

Dalang: puppeteer of the shadow puppet theatre

Dalem: literally 'within', often used to refer to a paramount lord or 'king,' his residence, court, or family

Denpasar: the capital of Bali

Desa: village

Desa Adat: a local community defining a sacred space and governed by one set of customary laws

Desa Dinas: civic village organisation

Desa, Kala, Patra: place, time, circumstance

Dewa: God; title for noble of the satria group

Dewa Agung: title of the ruler of Gelgel and later Klungkung

Dewa Yadnya: rituals addressed to the gods

Dewi: goddess

Dewi Sri: the rice goddess

Dugul: small altar, usually of stone, for offerings to the gods

Durga: goddess of death and consort of Siwa

Gado-Gado: mixed salad

Galungan: major holiday every 210 days, lasting for 10 days

Gambuh: traditional musical drama

Gamelan: orchestra

Gamelan Angklung: a small orchestral group, often used in cremations and other ceremonies

Gamelan Balaganjur: processional gamelan of gongs, cymbals and drums

Gamelan Gambuh: gamelan where the melody is played on large vertical flutes

Gamelan Gender Wayang: a quartet of instruments for shadow puppet performances

Gamelan Gong Gede: large ceremonial gamelan

Gamelan Semar Pegulingan: gamelan played in the king's bedchamber

Ganesha: elephant-headed son of Siwa

Gangsa: metallophone, metal keys strung like a xylophone over framed bamboo resonators

Garuda: mythical bird like an eagle

Gecko: lizard

Gede: big, large, great, eg, Puri Gede, Jero Gede

Gelgel: 14th century Balinese kingdom, the primary exemplary state of Bali, founded by Javanese lords and priests, and the kingdom from which other major Balinese kingdoms broke off

Geria: brahmana priest's residence

Geringsing: special handwoven double ikat textile made in Tenganan

Gong: literally means orchestra; eg. Gong Peliatan means the orchestra from Peliatan village; but also gong in the English sense

Gong Gede: full Kebyar orchestra, like a symphony orchestra

Guru: teacher

Gusti: title for noble from wesia group

Hanuman: white monkey of the Ramayana epic

Ida Bagus: title for a noble from the brahmana group

Ider-ider: bunting pinned to pavilion eaves

Ijuk: black palm fibre used for thatching roofs

Indra: god of thunder and rain

Jaba: literally 'outside', used to indicate relatively lower status and greater distance from the centre, so a general term for the sudra

Jaba Tengah: middle courtyard of a temple

Janger: dance between young men and women

Jauk: masked dance portraying a demonic male character

Jero: literally 'inside' used often as a title to indicate a higher status and closeness to the centre and a general term for the three highest title groups; the world of the court and residences and households of lords

Jeroan: the sacred, innermost courtyard of a temple

Jero Gede: residence and household of a major lord; the major lord himself

Joged: flirtatious dance

Kahyangan: great temple

Kahyangan Tiga: the three main village temples: Pura Puseh, Pura Dalem and Pura Desa

Kain: batik cloth, worn by men and women, waist down

Kaja: towards the mountain

Kajeng-Kliwon: a special ritual day every fifteen days

Kamasan: village in east Bali, the centre for painters of the traditional wayang style

Kanda Empat: the four siblings who accompany a person when he or she is born

Kangin: towards the east

Karma: spiritual force generated by a person's actions, cause and effect

Kasar: unrefined, crude, impolite, ungraceful, rough

Kauh: towards the west

Kawi: Old Javanese

Kayonan: tree of life in shadow puppet performance

Kebyar: new genre of gamelan music in 1915

Kebyar Duduk: dance by single male in the sitting position

Kebyar Trompong: dance by single male who plays the trompong

Kecak: Monkey dance

Kelod: towards the sea

Kemong: small hanging gong

Kempli: small non-hanging gong

Kempur: medium sized hanging gong

Kendang: two headed drum

Kepeng: bronze or lead Chinese coin with a hole in the middle used as a currency formerly and for offerings

Keras: coarse

Kidung: ceremonial chant

Klian banjar: head of the banjar

Klungkung: former royal capital of Bali and seat of Dewa Agung, the highest Balinese title

Korawa: cousins and enemies of the Pandawa in the Mahabarata epic

Kori: door

Kotekan: interlocking parts

Kris: double-edged dagger with magical power, symbolic of male strength

Kulit: buffalo hide

Kulkul: hollow wooden drum to summon villagers

Kuningan: important holiday 10 days after Galungan

Lalang: tall fibrous grass used for thatch

Lamak: woven palm and banana leaf offering on shrine

Lawar: Balinese dish of grated, spiced, chopped up raw meats, vegetables

Legong: dance performed by young girls

Leyak: witch or spirit, generally a blood-sucking, flame-dripping female monster

Lingga: phallic image, symbol of Siwa

Lontar: palm leaf manuscript

Lumbung: rice barn house

Madya: middle level between nista and utama

Mahabarata: Indian epic of the battle between the Pandawa and the
    Korawa brothers

Majapahit: East Javanese kingdom (1343-1511) considered by the
    Balinese to be the origin of their civilisation and culture

Mandala: circular symbolic map

Mantra: ritual incantation

Mecaru: religious cleansing ceremony

Melaspas: purification ritual

Melasti: ritual procession of the gods to the sea

Merdeka: freedom

Meru: Holy Hindu mountain, the abode of the gods, also an altar with
    pagoda style roofs

Metatah: tooth-filing

Moksa: ascending to heaven after death without leaving the corpse

Mudra: sacred hand gesture used in rituals

Naga: dragon

Nakula: one of the five Pandawa brothers of the Mahabarata epic

Nawa-Sanga: nine-fold division of the cosmos

Negara: state, realm, capital, court

Nirartha: brahmana priest who came to Bali from Java in the 16th century

Niskala: invisible

Nista: low

Nyepi: day of silence, Balinese New Year

Odalan: anniversary temple ceremony

Oleg Tumulilingan: bumblebee dance

Padi: rice growing in a field

Padmasana: lotus seat, the throne of Siwa

Pandawa: the five sons of Pandu, heroes of the Mahabarata epic

Paras: sandstone, sold in slabs, used in building temples and for stone
    carving

Pasek: upper level commoners of higher status

Patih: minister of the king in dances and dramas

Pedanda: brahmana high priest

Pelog: musical scale

Pemakesan: a temple congregation, responsible for the temple's upkeep,
    and worshipping the gods when they descend

Pemangku: a priest, usually sudra

Pemuda: youth

Pendet: temple dance to welcome the gods

Penjor: a bamboo pole, highly decorated

Pensar: clown servant in dramas and shadow puppets

Perada: gold paint, liquid or leaf

Poleng: chequered cloth

Prabekel: government head of a village

Pratima: figure that serves as a vehicle for a deity

Pule: the alstonia scholaris tree from which masks are made

Punggawa: government head of a region, a lord

Puputan: literally an 'ending', the ritual suicide to mark the end of a
    dynasty

Pura: temple

Pura Balé Agung: great council temple, village temple dedicated to
    fertility of the land and people of a customary law community

Pura Dalem: village temple near the cemetery

Pura Desa: village temple

Pura Penataran: courtyard temple dedicated to enhancing the unity and
    prosperity of the area

Pura Puseh: 'Navel Temple'; village temple dedicated to founding
    ancestors

Pura Ulun Carik: 'Head of the Ricefields Temple'; irrigation society
    temple

Puri: lord's residence, palace, household

Puri Gede: the palace and household of a paramount lord

Pusaka: heirloom

Raja: a Hindu prince

Raksasa: demon, ogre

Ramayana: Indian epic of Rama and Sita

Ramai: lively, busy, crowded

Rangda: widowed queen of the Calonarang play

Rebab: two-stringed lute

Regen: government head of a large region, often a former king

Rejang: a sacred dance by women

Residen: Dutch colonial regional officer

Reyong: set of twelve gongs played by four musicians

Rsi: priest

Sad Kahyangan: the six great temples; all Bali temples dedicated to the prosperity of the island and its people as a whole

Sad Ripu: the six enemies, the uncivilised passions

Sahadewa: one of the five Pandawa brothers of the Mahabarata epic and twin of Nakula

Sakti: mystical power of human, animal or object

Salak: astringent fruit with a snake-like skin

Sanggah: household temple of a sudra

Sang Hyang Dedari: trance dance

Sanghyang Widi Wasa: the Supreme god

Sanskrit: ancient Indian language

Saraswati: goddess of learning, knowledge and the arts

Sari: essence

Sarong: non-batik cloth wrapped around the body, where the ends are sewn and the wearer steps into it

Saté: chunks of grilled meat or fish on a skewer

Satria: the second highest of the four titles, comprising warriors and nobles

Sawah: rice field

Sebel: ritually unclean

Seka: voluntary group

Sekala: the visible world

Seledet: eye movement

Semara: god of love

Seni: art

Sidhakarya: last masked dance in the Topeng Pajegan

Singa: lion

Sirih: leaf chewed with betel nuts and lime

Siwa: one of the three most important of the Hindu gods in Bali identified with the Sun

Subak: irrigation society from a single source of water

Sudra: the lowest of the four Balinese titles, commoner

Suling: bamboo flute

Surya: the sun god identified with Siwa

Taksu: spiritual strength; special shrine

Taur Kasanga: ritual at the end of the ninth Balinese month

Tenget: magically dangerous place

Tingklik: bamboo xylophone

Tirta: holy water

Tirta Amerta: water of immortality
Topeng: mask
Topeng Pajegan: sacred masked dance by one performer
Topeng Panca: masked dance by five performers
Triwangsa: literally the three peoples, the three upper titles considered as
    an aristocratic group against the fourth
Trompong: set of inverted gongs played by one musician
Tuak: palm toddy
Tukang Banten: specialist in making offerings

Ulun Swi: temple on the upper edge of a rice field
Undagi: builder, carpenter, stone carver
Umbul-Umbul: banners
Utama: highest

Vyasa: compiler of the Mahabarata epic

Wali: most sacred dances
Wantilan: large pavilion for dances and cockfights
Wargi: relationship between two kin groups of unequal status established
    by the giving of a wife from the lower status group to the higher
Waringan: sacred banyan tree
Warung: food stall, restaurant
Wayang: puppet
Wayang Kulit: shadow puppet theatre
Wayang Lemah: daytime shadow puppet play with no screen
Wayang Wong: dance in which dancers imitate shadow puppets
Wesia: the third ranking of the four titles
Wisnu: preserver and god of prosperity
Wong: human being

Yadnya: ritual category
Yudistira: one of the five Pandawa brothers of the Mahabarata epic

Note: In 1972, there was a change in the spelling of Indonesian words. The most important differences were c for tj (Campuan rather than Tjampuhan), j for dj (*banjar* rather than bandjar) and y for j (Yogyakarta rather than Jogjakarta).

Bibliography

Anthropology

Boellstorff, Tom; *The Gay Archipelago, Sexuality and Nation in Indonesia*, Princeton University Press, 2005

Covarrubias, Miguel; *Island of Bali*, Knopf, 1937, reprinted Periplus Editions, 1999

Geertz, Clifford; *Negara, The Theatre State in Nineteenth-Century Bali*, Princeton University Press, 1980

——; *Peddlers and Princes*, University of Chicago Press, 1963

——; *The Interpretation of Cultures, Selected Essays*, Fontana Press, 1993

Geertz, Hildred and Clifford; *Kinship in Bali*, University of Chicago Press, 1975

Hobart, Angela, Urs Ramseyer and Albert Leemann; *The Peoples of Bali*, Blackwell Publishers, 1996

Lansing, John Stephen; *Evil in the Morning of the World—Phenomenological Approaches to a Balinese Community*, The University of Michigan Center for South and Southeast Asian Studies, 1974

——; *The Balinese*, Harcourt Brace College Publishers, 1995

Mabbett, Hugh; *The Balinese*, January Books, 1985, reprinted Pepper Publications, 2001

Vickers, Adrian and I Nyoman Darma Putra with Michele Ford (eds); *To Change Bali, Essays in Honour of I Gusti Ngurah Bagus*, Bali Post, Denpasar in association with the Institute of Social Change and Critical Inquiry, University of Woollongong, 2000

Wheatley, Bruce P.; *The Sacred Monkeys of Bali*, Waveland Press, Inc., 1999

Archaeology

Bernet Kempers, A.J.; *Monumental Bali, Introduction to Balinese Archaeology and Guide to the Monuments*, Periplus Editions, 1991

Soegondho, Santoso; *Earthenware Traditions in Indonesia, From Prehistory Until the Present*, Ceramic Society of Indonesia, 1995

Architecture
Budihardjo, Eko; *Architectural Conservation in Bali*, Gadjah Mada University Press, 1986

Davison, Julian and Bruce Granquist; *Introduction to Balinese Architecture*, Periplus Editions, 2003

Dawson, Barry and John Gillow; *The Traditional Architecture of Indonesia*, Thames and Hudson, 1994

Wijaya, Made; *Architecture of Bali: A Source book of Traditional and Modern Forms*, Archipelago Press, 2002

Arts
Fischer, Joseph and Thomas Cooper; *The Folk Art of Bali, The Narrative Tradition*, Oxford University Press, 1998

Helmi, Rio and Barbara Walker; *Bali Style*, Times Editions, 1995

Jessup, Helen Ibbitson; *Court Arts of Indonesia*, The Asia Society Galleries, New York, 1990

Kam, Garrett; *Neka Art Museum in Modern Balinese History, Art and the Passage of Time*, Yayasan Dharma Seni, 2007

——; *Ramayana in the Arts of Asia*, Select Books, 2000

Murni, Ni Wayan; 'The Art of Chewing Betel', *The Times*, Lombok, November - December 2007

Ramseyer, Urs; *The Art and Culture of Bali*, Oxford University Press, 1986

Autobiography
Djelantik, A.A.M.; *The Birthmark: Memoirs of a Balinese Prince*, Periplus Editions, 1997

Hetherington, Paul (ed.); *The Diaries of Donald Friend*, Volume 4, National Library of Australia, 2006

Ingram, William; *A Little Bit One O'clock, Living with a Balinese Family*, Ersania Books, 1998

Koke, Louise G.; *Our Hotel in Bali*, January Books, 1987, reprinted Pepper Publications, 2001

Mathews, Anna; *The Night of Purnama*, Oxford University Press, 1965

Mayerson, Charlotte Leon, (ed.); *Shadow and Light: The Life, Friends and Opinions of Maurice Stern*, Harcourt, Brace & World, Inc., 1965

Sukawati, Tjokorde Gede Agung; *Ubud, 1910-1978, Autobiography as dictated to Rosemary Hilbery*, Mabhakti, Bali, 1983

Thwe, Pascal Khoo; *From the Land of Green Ghosts, A Burmese Odyssey*, Harper Collins, 2002

Birds
Mason, Victor; *Birds of Bali*, Periplus Editions, 1989

Butterflies
Mason, Victor; *Butterflies of Bali*, Saritaksu Editions, 2005

Calendars
Duncan, David Ewing; *The Calendar*, Fourth Estate, 1998

Eiseman, Fred; *Balinese Calendars*, 2000

Ceremonies
Boomkamp, Jacoba Hooykaas-Van Leeuwen; *Ritual Purification of a Balinese Temple*, N.V. Noord-Hollandsche Uitgevers Maatschappij, Amsterdam, 1960

Mershon, Katharane Edson; *Seven Plus Seven: Mysterious Life-Rituals in Bali*, Vantage Press, New York, Washington, Hollywood, 1971

Moerdowo, R.M.; *Ceremonies in Bali*, Bhratara Publishers, Jakarta, 1973

Stuart-Fox, David J.; *Once a Century, Pura Besakih and the Eka Dasa Rudra Festival*, Penerbit Citra Indonesia, 1982

Communities
Warren, Carol; *Adat and Dinas, Balinese Communities in the Indonesian State*, Oxford University Press, 1993

Dance
Bandem, I Made and Fredrik Eugene deBoer; *Balinese Dance in Transition, Kaja and Kelod*, Oxford University Press, 1981, 2nd edition 1995

Coast, John; *Dancing Out of Bali*, Faber and Faber, 1954, reprinted Periplus Classics, 2004

Dibia, I Wayan, Rucina Ballinger and Barbara Anello; *Balinese Dance, Drama and Music*, Periplus Editions, 2005

Murni, Ni Wayan; 'A Dance for Every Day', in Gouyon, Anne (ed.), *The Natural Guide to Bali*, Equinox Publishing, 2005

Racki, Christian; *The Sacred Dances of Bali*, Buratwangi, 1998

Spies, Walter and Beryl de Zoete; *Dance & Drama in Bali*, Faber and Faber, 1938, reprinted Periplus Classics, 2002

Food

Cole, William Stadden; *Balinese Food-Related Behaviour: a Study of the Effects of Ecological, Economic, Social and Cultural Processes on Rates of Change*, unpublished dissertation presented to the Graduate School of Arts and Sciences of Washington University, 1983

Copeland, Jonathan and Ni Wayan Murni; 'Bali-Indonesia', in Williams, Sean (ed.), *The Ethnomusicologists' Cookbook: Complete Meals from Around the World (it's chapati and I'll fry if I want to)*, Routledge, 2006

Owen, Sri; *Classic Asian Cook Book*, Dorling Kindersley, 1998

——; *Indonesian Food and Cookery*, Prospect Books, 1986

——; *Indonesian Regional Food & Cookery*, Doubleday, 1994

——; *Sri Owen's Indonesian Food*, Pavilion Books, 2008

von Holzen, Heinz; *Feast of Flavours from the Balinese Kitchen, A Step-by-Step Culinary Adventure*, Marshall Cavenish Cuisine, 2005

von Holzen, Heinz and Lother Arsana; *The Food of Bali*, Periplus Editions, 1993

Gardens

Eiseman, Fred and Margaret; *Flowers of Bali*, Periplus Editions, 1988

——; *Fruits of Bali*, Periplus Editions, 1988

Warren, William; *Balinese Gardens*, Periplus Editions, 1995

Guide Books

Gouyon, Anne (ed.); *The Natural Guide to Bali*, Equinox Publishing, 2005

Mann, Richard; *Bali, Off the Beaten Track*, Gateway Books, 2005

History

Corn, Charles; *The Scents of Eden, A History of the Spice Trade*, Kodansha International, 1999

Cribb, Robert; *The Indonesian Killings of 1965-1966, Studies from Java and Bali*, Monash Papers on Southeast Asia, no. 21, Clayton Victoria, 1990

Forbes, Cameron; *Under the Volcano, The Story of Bali*, Black Inc., 2007

Hanna, Willard A.; *Bali Profile: People, Events, Circumstances (1001-1976)*, American Universities Field Staff, 1976, reprinted as *Bali Chronicles*, Periplus, 2004

Mabbett, Hugh; *In Praise of Kuta*, January Books, 1987

Milton, Giles; *Nathaniel's Nutmeg*, Sceptre, 1999

Osborne, Milton; *Southeast Asia, An Introductory History*, Allen & Unwin, 8th Edition, 2000

Raffles, Thomas Stamford; *The History of Java*, 1817, reprinted AMS Press, 1983

Scouten, Gustaaf; *Mads Lange, The Bali Trader and Peacemaker*, Bali Purnati, 2007

van der Kraan, Alfons; *Bali at War: A History of the Dutch-Balinese Conflict of 1846-49*, Monash University, 1995

Vickers, Adrian; *A History of Modern Indonesia*, Cambridge University Press, 2005

Watson, Peter; *Ideas, A History from Fire to Freud*, Phoenix, 2006

Winchester, Simon; *Krakatoa, The Day the World Exploded*, Viking, 2003

Interviews

de Neefe, Janet; 'Murni's Warung, Ubud, Bali', *Garuda*, July 2009

Hello Bali; 'Ibu Murni: an Ubud Original', *Hello Bali*, April 2006

Mann, Richard; *Forever Bali*, Gateway Books, 2004

Ramseyer, Urs and I Gusti Raka Panji Tisna (eds); *Bali–Living in Two Worlds*, Museum der Kulturen Basel and Verlag Schwabe & Co AG Basel, 2001

Stephens, Harold; *At Home in Asia*, Wolfenden, 1995

Maps

Suárez, Thomas; *Early Mapping of Southeast Asia*, Periplus Editions, 1999

Masks

Slattum, Judy and Paul Schraub; *Masks of Bali: Spirits of an Ancient Drama*, Chronicle Books, 1992, reprinted Periplus Editions, 2003

Music

Gold, Lisa; *Music in Bali*, Oxford University Press, 2005

McPhee, Colin; *A Club of Small Men: A Children's Tale from Bali*, reprinted Periplus Editions, 1993

———; *A House in Bali*, Victor Gollancz, 1947, reprinted Periplus Classics, 2000

Mithen, Steven; *The Singing Neanderthals, The Origins of Music, Language, Mind and Body*, Phoenix, 2005

Oja, Carol J.; *Colin McPhee: Composer in Two Worlds*, Smithsonian Institute Press, 1990, reprinted University of Illinois Press, 2004

Tenzer, Michael; *Balinese Music*, Periplus Editions, 1991

Novels

Barley, Nigel; *Island of Demons*, Monsoon, 2009

Collins, G.E.P.; *Twin Flower, A Story of Bali*, Oxford University Press, 1934

Cork, Vern; *Bali Behind The Seen, Recent Fiction from Bali*, Darma Printing, 1996

Darling, Diana; *The Painted Alphabet*, Houghton Mufflin Company, 1992, reprinted Tuttle Publishing, 2001

Koch, Christopher J.; *The Year of Living Dangerously*, Michael Joseph, 1978, reprinted Penguin 1983

Mason, Victor; *The Butterflies of Bali*, Periplus Editions, 1992

Toer, Pramoedya Ananta; *The King, the Witch and the Priest, A 12th century Javanese tale*, Equinox Publishing, 2002

Offerings

Brinkgreve, Francine; *Offerings, the Ritual Art of Bali*, Image Network Indonesia, 1992

Eiseman, Fred; *Offerings*, 2005

Painting

Carpenter, Bruce W.; *W.O.J. Nieuwenkamp, First European Artist in Bali*, Periplus Editions, 1997

Cooper, Thomas L.; *Sacred Painting in Bali, Tradition in Transition*, Orchid Press, 2005

Djelantik, A.A.M.; *Balinese Paintings*, Oxford University Press, 1986

Geertz, Hildred; *Images of Power: Balinese Paintings made for Gregory Bateson and Margaret Mead*, University of Hawai'i Press, 1995

Kam, Garrett and Yayasan Dharma Seni; *Perceptions of Paradise, Images of Bali in the Arts*, Museum Neka, 1993

Pucci, Idanna; *Bhima Swarga, The Balinese Journey of the Soul*, Little Brown and Company, 1992

Rhodius, Hans and John Darling; *Walter Spies and Balinese Art*, Tropical Museum, Amsterdam, 1980

Seni, Yayasan Dharma; *Neka Museum, Guide to the Painting Collection*, Museum Neka, 1986

Williams, Adriana and Yu-Chee Chong; *Covarrubias in Bali*, Editions Didier Millet, 2005

Photographs

Hitchcock, Michael and Lucy Norris; *Bali: The Imaginary Museum, The Photographs of Walter Spies and Beryl de Zoete*, Oxford University Press, 1995

Krause, Gregor and Karl With; *Bali, People and Art*, White Lotus Press, 2000

Mabbett, Hugh; *Bali 1912: Photographs and reports by Gregor Krause*, January Books, 1988, reprinted Pepper Publications, 2001

Marais, Gill; *Bali Secret and Sacred*, Saritaksu Editions, 2006

Poetry

Creese, Helen; *Parthayana: The Journeying of Partha: An Eighteenth-Century Balinese Kakawin*, KITLV Press, 1998

O'Brien, Kate (tr.); *Sutasoma – The Ancient Tale of a Buddha-Prince from 14th Century Java*, Orchid Press, 2008

Politics

Kingsbury, Damien; *The Politics of Indonesia*, Oxford University Press, 1998

Loveard, Keith; *Suharto, Indonesia's Last Sultan*, Horizon Books, Singapore, 1999

Maher, Michael; *Indonesia, An Eyewitness Account*, Viking, 2000

Robinson, Geoffrey; *The Dark Side of Paradise, Political Violence in Bali*, Cornell University Press, 1995

Pre-history

Chauvet, Jean-Marie, Eliette Brunel Deschamps and Christian Hilaire; *Chauvet Cave, the Discovery of the World's Oldest Paintings*, Thames & Hudson, 1996

Cook, Michael; *A Brief History of the Human Race*, Granta Books, 2005

Curtis, Garniss, Carl Swisher and Roger Lewin; *Java Man*, Abacus, 2000

Dawkins, Richard; *The Ancestor's Tale, A Pilrimage to the Dawn of Life*, Weidenfeld and Nicolson, 2004

Jumsai, Sumet; *Naga, Cultural Origins in Siam and the West Pacific*, Oxford University Press, 1988

Morwood, Mike and Peny Van Oosterzee; *The Discovery of the Hobbit, the Scientific Breakthrough that Changed the Face of Human History*, Random House Australia, 2007

Morwood, Mike, Thomas Sutikna and Richard Roberts; 'Lost World of the Little People', *National Geographic*, April 2005

Munoz, Paul Michel; *Early Kingdoms of the Indonesian Archipelago and the Malay Peninsula*, Editions Didier Millet, 2006

Nordholt, Henk Schulte; *Bali, An Open Fortress, 1995-2005, Regional Autonomy, Electoral Democracy and Entrenched Identities*, National University of Singapore Press, 2007

Oppenheimer, Stephen; *Eden in the East, The Drowned Continent of Southeast Asia*, Phoenix, 1999

——; *Out of Eden, The Peopling of the World*, Robinson, 2004

Parsons, Paul; *The Big Bang, The Birth of Our Universe*, BBC Worldwide, 2001

Stringer, Chris and Peter Andrews; *The Complete World of Human Evolution*, Thames & Hudson, 2005

Psychology

Nisbett, Richard E.; *The Geography of Thought, How Asians and Westerners Think Differently... And Why*, Nicholas Brealey Publishing, 2003

Suryani, Luh Ketut and Gordon D. Jensen; *The Balinese People: A Reinvestigation of Character*, Oxford University Press, 1992

———; *Trance and Possession in Bali*, Oxford University Press, 1993

Thong, Denny; *A Psychiatrist in Paradise*, White Lotus Press, 1993

Religion

de Kleen, Tyra and A.J.D. Campbell; *Mudras: The Ritual Handposes of the Buddha Priests and the Shiva Priest of Bali*, K. Paul, Trench, Trubner, 1924, reprinted Kessinger (nd)

Eiseman, Fred B.; *Bali: Sekala and Niskala: Essays on Religion, Ritual and Art*, Periplus Editions, 1989

Fossey, Claire; *Rangda, Bali's Queen of the Witches*, White Lotus Press, 2008

Hooykaas, C.; *Religion in Bali*, Brill, 1973

McKenzie, Douglas G. in association with Bishop I. Wayan Mastra; *The Mango Tree Church, The Story of the Protestant Christian Church in Bali*, Boolarong Publications, 1988

Satterthwaite, Terry and Ketut Rusni; *Guidebook for Balinese Prayer*, Wholistic Creations, 1996

Staal, Frits; *Rules without Meaning, Ritual, Mantras and the Human Sciences*, Peter Lang Publishing, Inc., 1989

Stephen, Michele; *Desire, Divine and Demonic, Balinese Mysticism in the Paintings of I Ketut Budiana and I Gusti Nyoman Mirdiana*, University of Hawai'i Press, 2005

Rice

Ammayao, Aurora and Roy W. Hamilton; *The Art of Rice: Spirit and Sustenance in Asia*, University of California Los Angeles, 2003

Owen, Sri; *The Rice Book*, Doubleday, 1993

Piper, Jacqueline M.; *Rice in South-East Asia, Cultures and Landscapes*, Oxford University Press, 1993

Subak Organisations

Lansing, John Stephen; *Priests and Programmers: Technologies of Power in the Engineered Landscape of Bali*, Princeton University Press, 1991

——; *Perfect Order, Recognizing Complexity in Bali*, Princeton University Press, 2006

Temples

Davison, Julian and Bruce Granquist; *Balinese Temples*, Periplus Editions, 1999

Geertz, Hildred; *The Life of a Balinese Temple, Artistry, Imagination and History in a Peasant Village*, University of Hawai'i Press, 2004

Stuart-Fox, David J.; *Pura Besakih, Temple, Religion and Society in Bali*, KITLV Press, 2002

Textiles

Hauser-Schaublin, Brigitta, Marie-Louise Nabholz-Kartaschoff and Urs Ramseyer; *Balinese Textiles*, British Museum Press, 1991, reprinted Tuttle Publishing 1997

Hitchcock, Michael; *Indonesian Textiles*, Periplus Editions, 1991

——; *Indonesian Textile Techniques*, Shire Publications, 1985

Maxwell, Robyn; *Sari to Sarong, Five hundred years of Indian and Indonesian textile exchange*, National Gallery of Australia, 2003

——; *Textiles of Southeast Asia, Tradition, Trade, and Transformation*, Australian National Gallery and Oxford University Press, Australia, 1990, reprinted Periplus Editions, 2003

Murni, Ni Wayan; 'Appreciating Calligraphy Batik', *The Times*, Lombok, August - September 2007

——; 'How to Make Batik', *The Times*, Lombok, September - October 2007

Walker, Carol; 'Buying Textiles in Bali', *Travel Today Arabia*, October 2004

——; 'Weaving A Spell', *Travel Today Arabia*, October 2004

Tourism

Couteau, Jean, et al; *Bali2Day: Modernity*, Kepustakaan Populer Gramedia, 2005

Hitchcock, Michael, Victor T. King and Michael Parnwell (eds); *Tourism in Southeast Asia, Challenges and New Directions*, Nordic Institute of Asian Studies Press, 2009

Picard, Michel; *Bali, Cultural Tourism and Touristic Culture*, Archipelago Press, 1996

Vickers, Adrian; *Bali, A Paradise Created*, Periplus Editions, 1989

Traditional Medicine

Hobart Angela; *Healing Performances of Bali, Between Darkness and Light*, Berghahn Books, 2003

Keeney, Bradford, and I Wayan Budi (eds); *Balians, Traditional Healers of Bali*, Ringing Rocks Press, 2004

Lim, Robin; *Obat Asli: The Healing Herbs of Bali*; Saritaksu Editions, 2005

Travelling

Powell, Hickman; *Bali: The Last Paradise*, Dodd, Mead & Company, 1936, reprinted Oxford in Asia, 1986

Vickers, Adrian; *Travelling to Bali, Four Hundred Years of Journeys*, Oxford University Press, 1994

Ubud

Charles, Andrew; 'Ni Wayan Murni, Balinese Entrepreneur and Traveller', *The Jakarta Post*, 21 July 2006

de Neefe, Janet; 'Back with a song to sing and so many tales to tell', *The Jakarta Post*, 1 August 2009

Goodfellow, Rob; 'Murni, the Ibu of Ubud', *The Jakarta Post*, 11 January 2001

Kruger, Vivienne; 'Art Treasures of Ubud', *Bali & Beyond*, October 2002

Lueras, L., et al; *Ubud is a Mood*, Bali Purnati, 2004

Murni, Ni Wayan; 'Ubud is Just Getting Better and Better, A Look at Ubud's Artistic Centre, Past, Present and Future', *Hello Bali*, January 2005

Warfare and Weapons
Gardner, G. B.; *Keris and Other Malay Weapons*; Orchid Press 2010

Wayang Kulit: Shadow Puppets
Hobart, Angela; *Dancing Shadows of Bali, Theatre and Myth*, KPI, 1987

Moerdowo, R.M.; *Wayang: Its Significance in Indonesian Society*, Balai Pustaka, Jakarta, 1982

Murni, Ni Wayan; 'What to look for in Balinese Shadow Puppets', *The Times*, Lombok, October-November 2007

Woodcarving
Eiseman, Fred and Margaret; *Woodcarvings of Bali*, Periplus Editions, 1988

INDEX